THE WEIR AND THE WONDERFUL

weir's a winner

Photographer Terry Weir is always reluctant to hand over his camera – but not when it means getting his hands of the League Championship trophy!

It's May, 1981, and Terry celebrates Villa's title triumph on the balcony of Birmingham Council House, along with Kenny Swain (left) and Peter Withe.

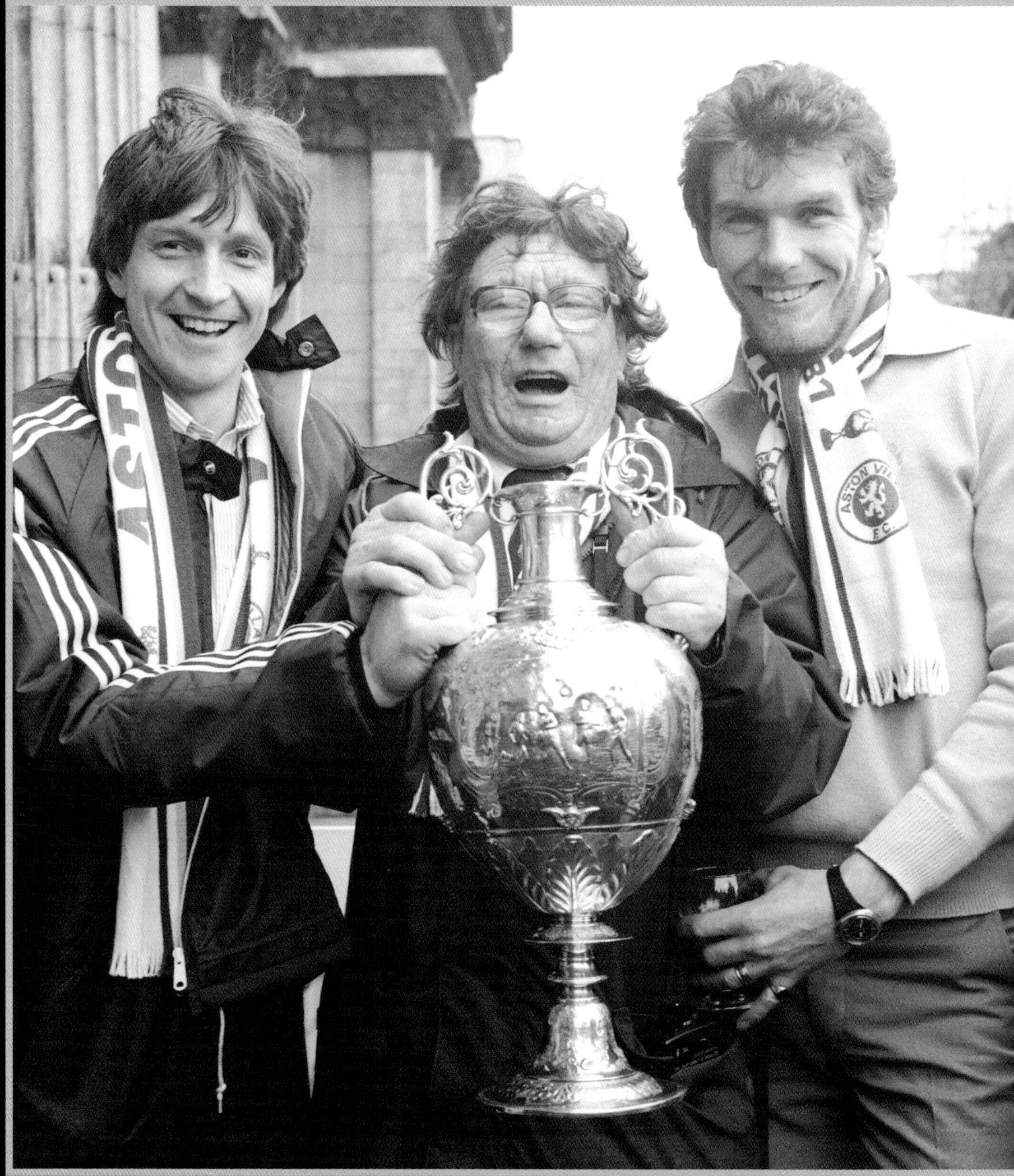

the weir and the wonderful

a classic collection of aston villa images by terry weir

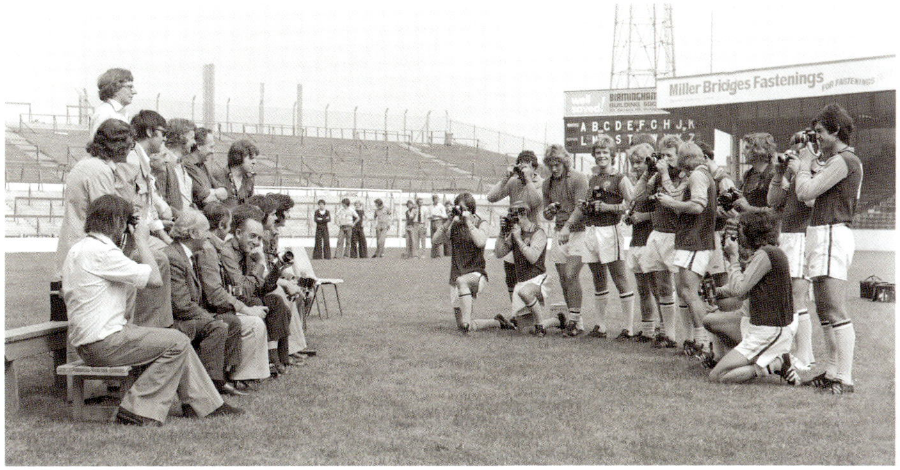

Aston Villa
Football Club

The Weir and The Wonderful

Published by Aston Villa Football Club
Villa Park, Birmingham B6 6HE

ISBN 0 9543120 1 5

Production by Aston Villa Publishing

Editor Bernard Gallagher

Design and layout by Bernard Gallagher
Scans by Nadine Goldingay
Words by Terry Weir, Rob Bishop and Simon Inglis

Special thanks to Steve Stride, Reg Thacker and Jane Thomas

Printed by Polar Print Ltd

contents

foreword by simon inglis

In this digital age of full-colour, instant, interactive recall, in which every pass and tackle is discussed and dissected from sixteen different angles by sixteen different experts, how easy it is to undervalue the power of a simple, single monotone image. The captured moment, like the most memorable of headlines, there before us, in black and white...

Whereas nowadays we can press 'rewind' and 'play' until the batteries on our remotes run dry, or send byte-sized goal clips with the click of a mouse to the other side of the planet, there was a time, a time not so long ago, when the soonest we could relive that wonder goal at the Holte End, or see for the first time that last minute winner at Bolton, would be in photographs printed in the club programme, days or even weeks after the event. And as for glimpses of our heroes behind the scenes, the single lens reflex camera offered our sole eye into the soul of our club.

At the start of the 20th century Aston Villa were fortunate enough to have their affairs captured on camera by a former player, Albert Wilkes, whose son continued in the family's photographic business until the 1960s. But for Villa fans of a certain age – and we know who we are – the eye that counted the most from 1970 until the 1990s was that of Terence Francis Weir.

Throughout those up and down years – from Vic Crowe through to Brian Little – no Villa game was complete without the sight of the impish Weir, cameras flailing, coat flapping, scampering hither and thither across the pitch, interrupting the players' pre-match kickabouts, always with his beseeching grin, often with a breathless mascot in tow.

As a legion of kids and celebrities will testify, he was never knowingly on call without a bag of wine gums. Even after kick-off, after he had settled into his familiar spot behind the goal (only feet away from the pitch-side track where he'd often landed as a schoolboy during the 1940s, handed over heads to save him from the terrace crush), Terry still fussed and jigged about like an excitable supporter allowed up onto the big stage.

There was always the sense with Terry that, having started out as a bricklayer, followed by work at Singer sewing machines, then as a sales rep, he couldn't quite believe his luck in landing the job as official club photographer, and that at any moment a commissionaire might drag him away by his ear and ring his dad. (It was his dad, incidentally, a worker at Lucas, who passed on his love of the Villa to Terry when the family lived in Lozells, a few doors down from Dennis Howell's house and from the Aston Villa Wesleyan Chapel.)

And that, surely, is why so many of Terry Weir's photographs have an immediacy and honesty which engages us still today. Terry looked beyond the action, beyond the stars, and saw instead the community of football, in its moments of quiet pride as well as its Champagne-swilling elation.

However truly we think we can conjure up the recent past in our mind's eye, his photographs remind us all of just how completely our world, our Birmingham, our Villa, have changed in such a short time. Here is an analogue world of chrome bumpers, metal badges and kipper ties; of muddy, logo free kits, of shopkeepers in overalls and girls in mini-skirts. A duffel-coated boy buys his Villa News & Record, a can of fizz stuffed in his pocket. Brian Little looks up coyly from the communal bath. Chico stands proud by his new boutique. Pongo Waring's eyes stare with an intensity that must once have frightened centre-halves.

Look at all the faces on the pitch as thousands celebrated promotion; see the bomber jackets, the knitted sweaters, the man in the trilby, the mother and child. This is how we were when flares first came to town, when the words 'First Division' still held their true meaning.

It is often said that the past is a foreign country. And yet, alien though much of the past may seem so soon after the event, a disarming familiarity leaps up from these pages – page after page. Whether one supports the Villa or not, or even gives a fig for football, these images speak to us all. As Terry himself once remarked, the cry he heard most often from fans, and sometimes even from players, after a Villa goal had been scored was 'Did you get it, Terry? Did you get it?'

On the evidence of these photographs, I think we can agree. Terry got it just fine.

Simon Inglis
July 2002

carriage drive

Even though I was the club photographer, I didn't have a car park pass in those early days, which meant I had to con my way in.

I arrived around mid-day on this occasion and 'bribed' my way in by telling the car park steward I would take his photograph.

After I'd parked the car, I walked back to the entrance to fulfil my half of the bargain, only to find my steward pal had been joined by a commissionaire.

The two of them were chatting away, so I asked the commissionaire to move over so I could take the shot.

As you can see, he didn't get very far, so both of them ended up on the picture.

As promised I gave the car park steward a copy – and sold one to the commissionaire!

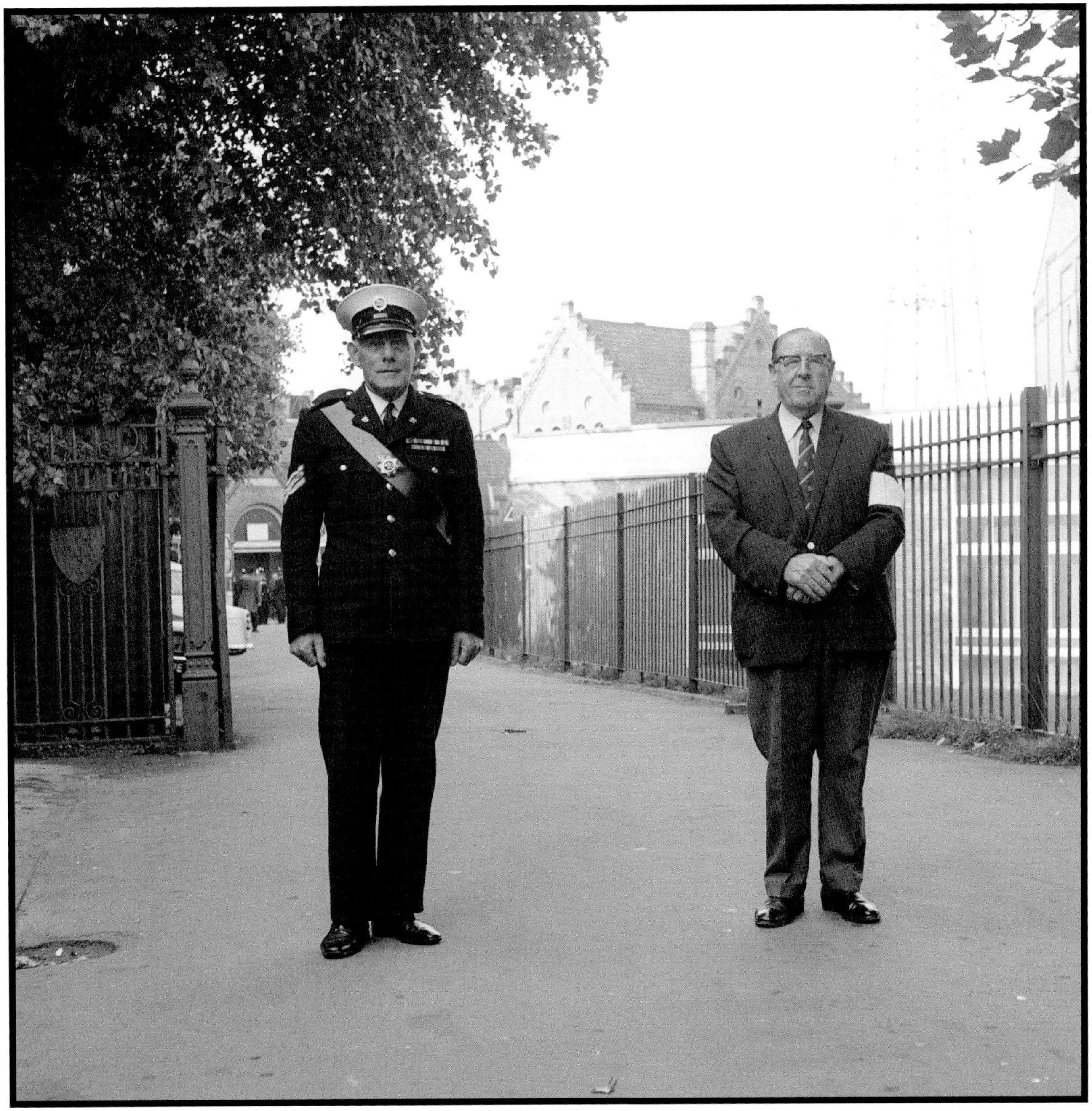

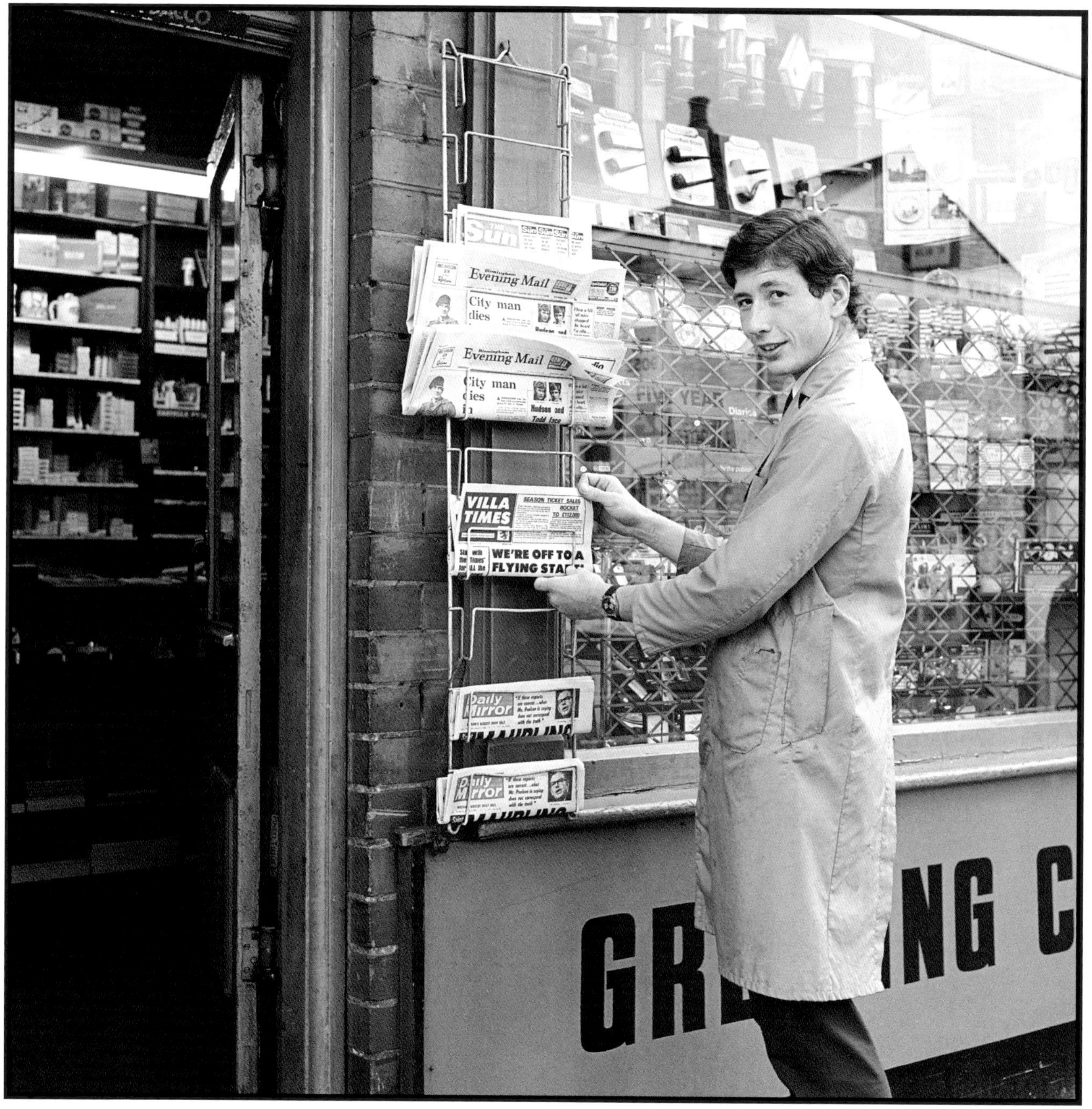
Sun
Evening Mail
City man dies
Hudson and
Evening Mail
City man dies
VILLA TIMES
SEASON TICKET SALES
ROCKET
WE'RE OFF TO A
Daily Mirror
Daily Mirror

sign of the times

No stone was left unturned in our efforts to promote the club's newspaper, Villa Times, in the early 1970s, as these pictures illustrate.

The girl on the stool, studiously reading her copy, is Sue Lerwell, the daughter of a friend of mine and a keen Villa supporter, and I also ventured into the high street to capture the flavour of the new publication.

Pettit's, a newsagents and stationary shop in Wellington Road, Perry Barr, agreed to place copies in their rack outside the store, along with more established journals like The Sun, the Daily Mirror and the Birmingham Evening Mail.

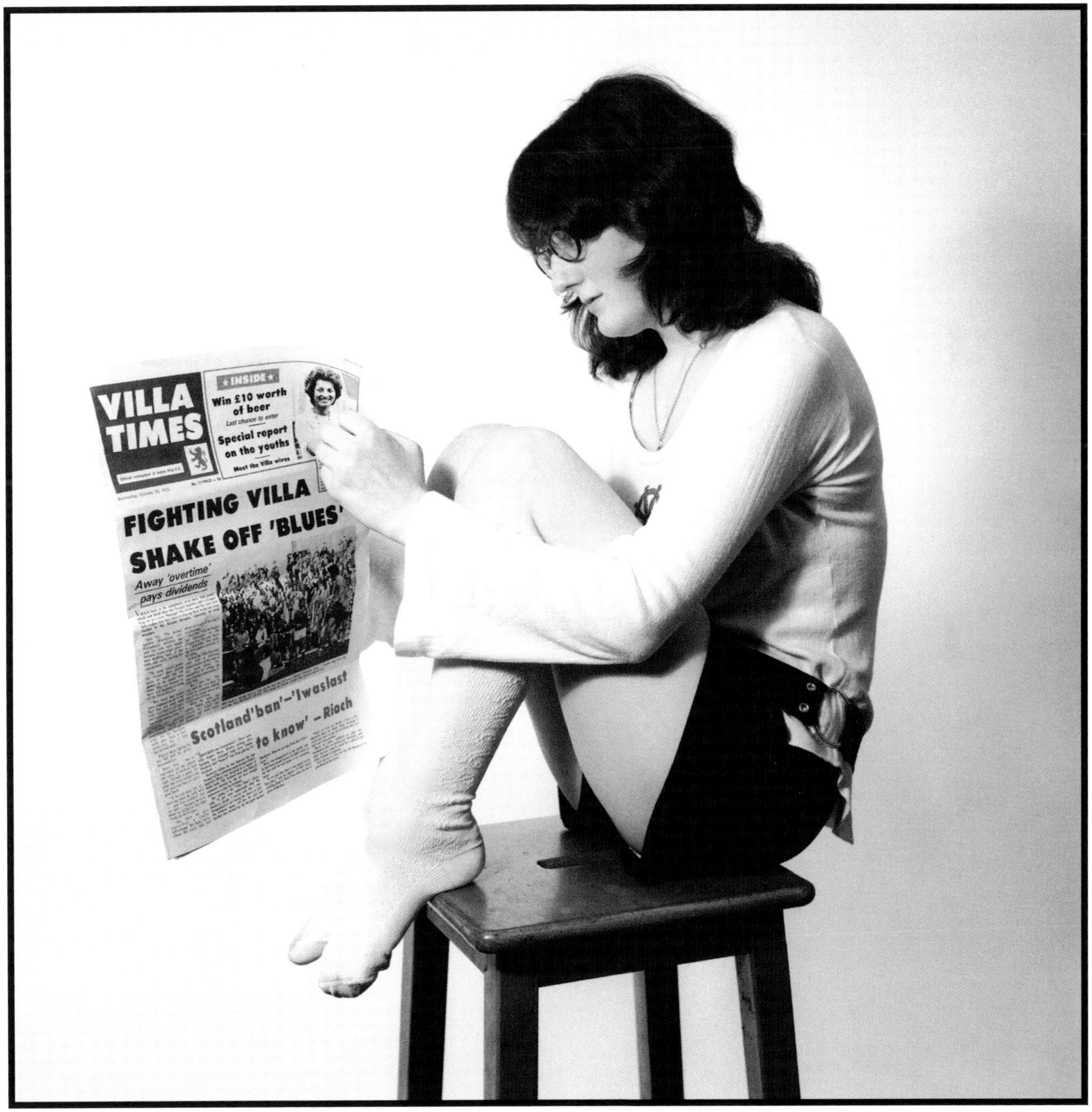

anyone for cricket?

A lot of English footballers enjoy a game of cricket once the summer arrives and the Villa lads of 1972 were no different.

On this occasion, the club entered a team in a triangular six-a-side tournament at Edgbaston, so they had the privilege of playing on a Test ground.

They weren't bad, either, although I can't recall how they fared against their counterparts from Blues and Albion.

Fred Turnbull, reserve team coach Leo Crowther and Chris Nicholl are the players standing, with Neil Rioch, Ray Graydon and manager Vic Crowe kneeling.

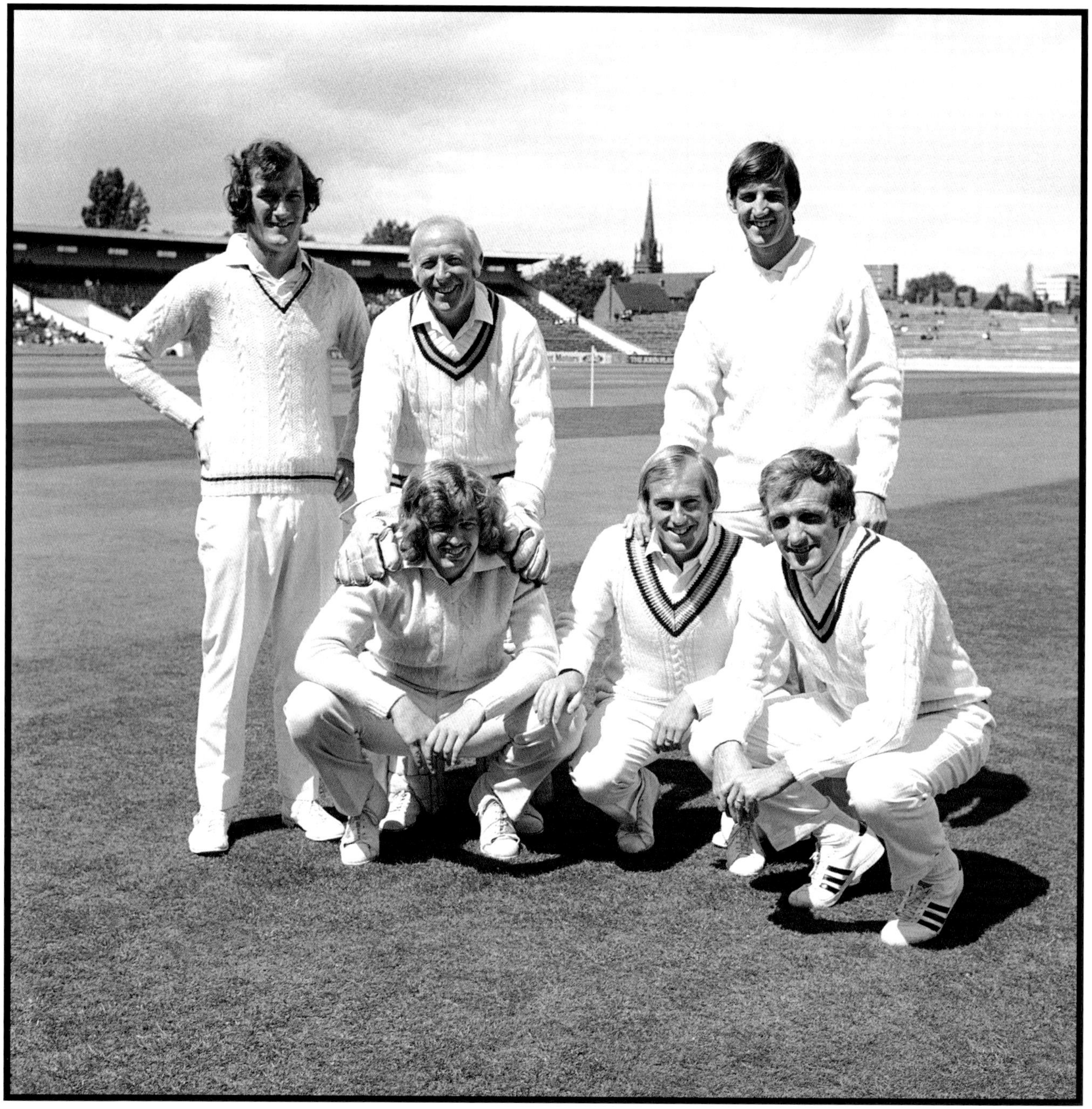

programme please

One of the most appealing aspects of going to a football match is buying a programme, particularly for young fans.

This youngster is deadly serious as he receives change from a vendor for his copy of the Villa News & Record. Who knows, it might have been his first match.

I wonder if he still goes to Villa Park today? If so, I should imagine he has a fair old collection of programmes by now!

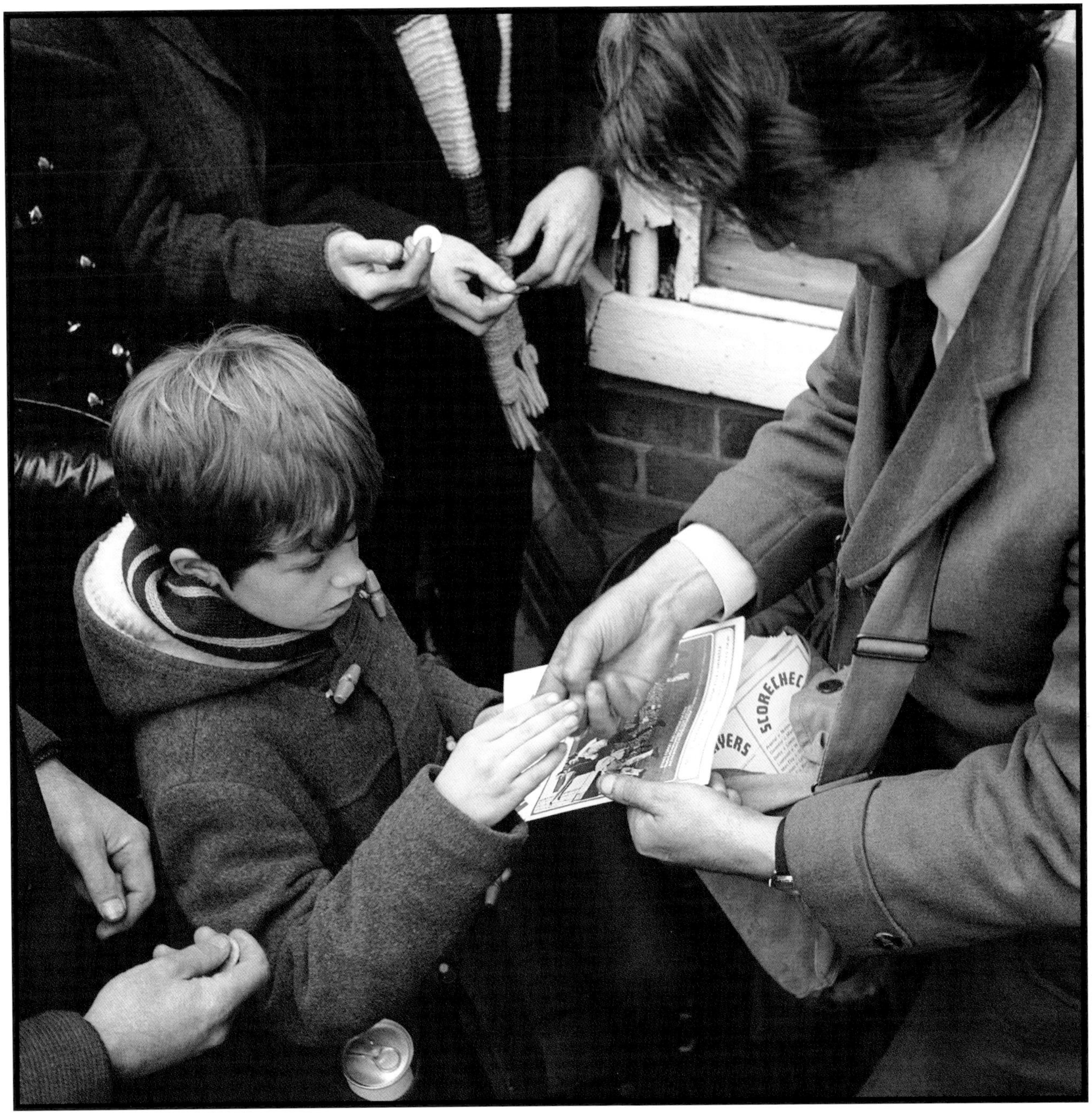

matchday

There's nothing quite like the atmosphere around a football ground on matchday, as supporters make their way to their favourite viewing positions and a sense of anticipation builds.

I always got a buzz from climbing the steps to the main stand and looking back to all the people walking down Trinity Road as kick-off time approached.

It was then, as it is now, a traffic-free zone, although you can just see a vehicle edging through the crowds. Everyone else had obviously parked some distance away.

Maybe Trinity Road should be renamed Pedestrian Way on matchdays.

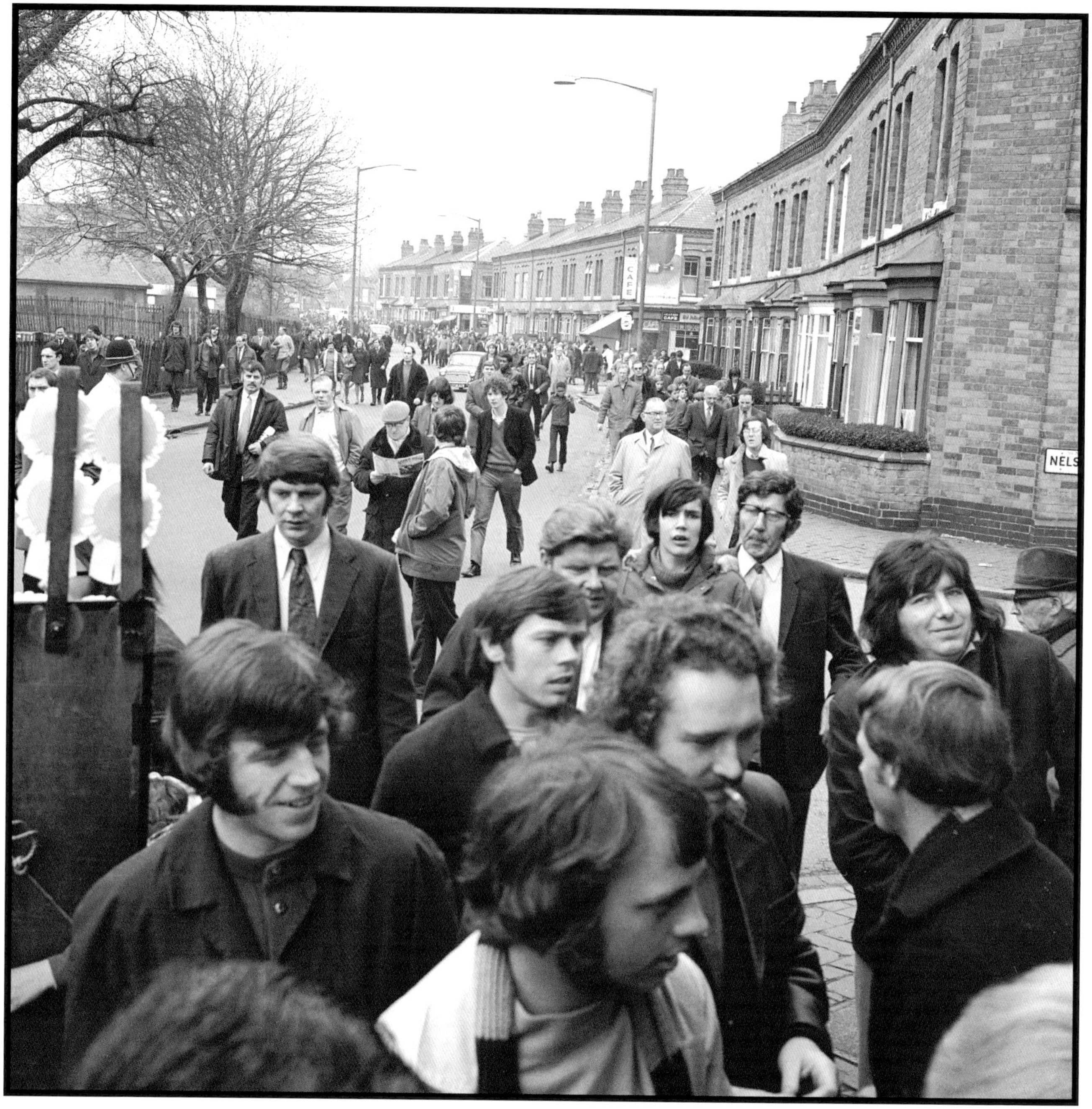

view from the top

Eric Woodward always encouraged me to adopt a roving role in my search for pictures for the official programme and one afternoon I found myself on the bank at the top of the Witton End terracing – where the North Stand is now located.

There was a wonderful view from this lofty position, even if spectators risked a real soaking on rainy afternoons and there was a danger of slipping down the bank on days when the terracing was packed.

On this particular day it was dry but cold, as you can see from the overcoats, but it must have been a compelling match – no-one bothered turning to face the camera!

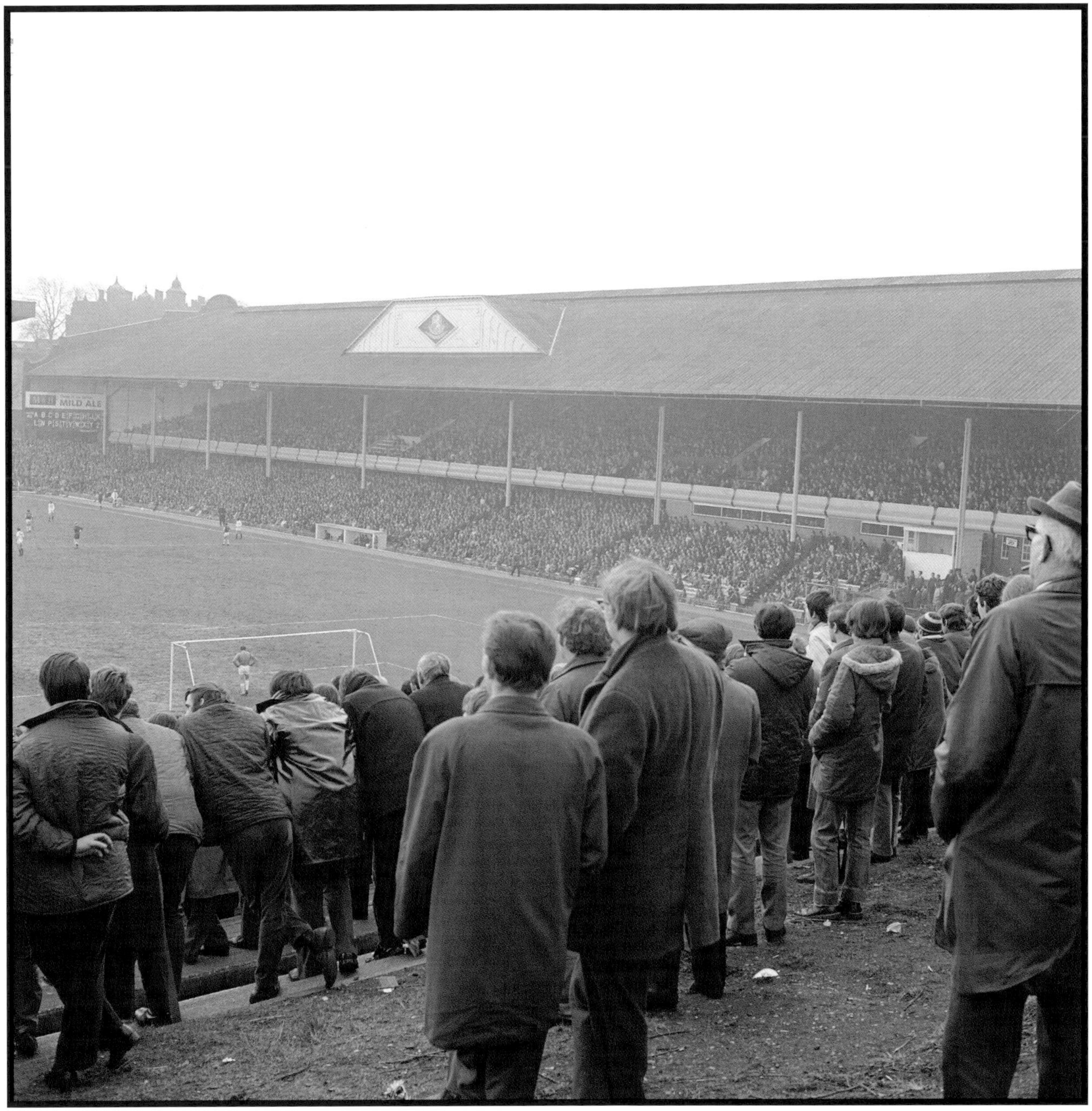

pride of the lions

The Lions Club was a den of intrigue and politics, even more so than the Villa boardroom.

All manner of functions was held at the Trinity Road venue, from dances to bingo sessions, and it was also where diehard supporters got together to enjoy a drink and air their views on events at the club.

It was also where the press corps met, both before and after matches.

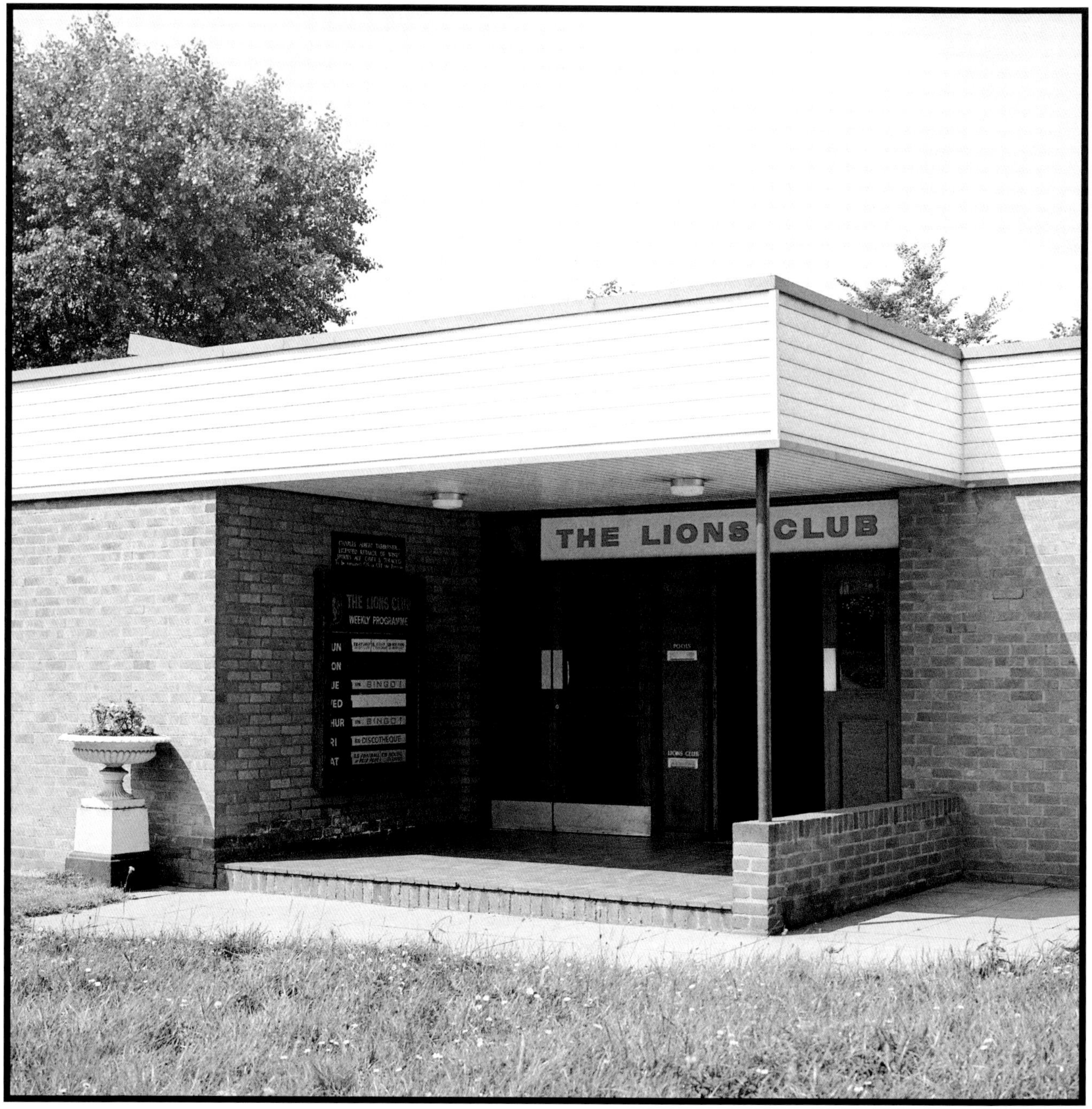

a shot in the arm

Villa received a letter from a guy who ran a tattoo studio in Erdington, asking if he could advertise in the programme, but commercial manager Eric Woodward was uneasy about it because so many people regarded the practice as distasteful.

It was suggested that we should get a photo of the artist at work before making a decision, and his client was only too happy to have the Villa badge tattooed on his right arm.

In the event, neither the picture nor an advertisement were used. Maybe a more liberal view would be taken today.

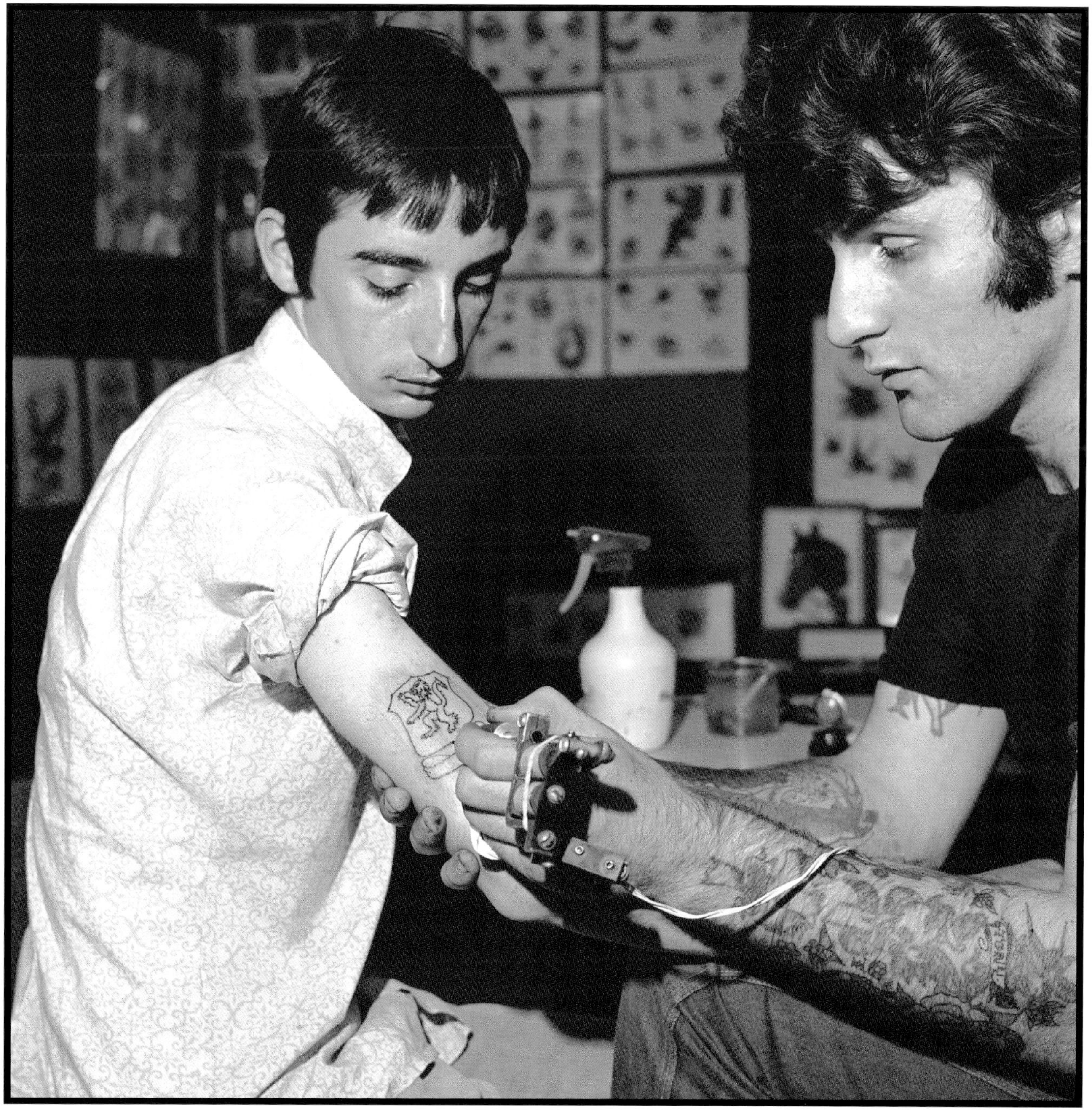

bond street

If ever you have visited Bodymoor Heath, you will know that the main driveway is called Bond Street – after this gentleman.

Bert Bond was Villa's groundsman for many years and as well as being very good at his job he was a lovely, lovely man who was respected by everyone connected with the club.

He also helped to design and build the Bodymoor complex, which was opened on 10th November, 1971, and there's a plaque commemorating the fact that he performed the official opening.

Apart from the players, Bert was the first person I got to know really well, and he always had a fascinating story to tell about life at Villa Park.

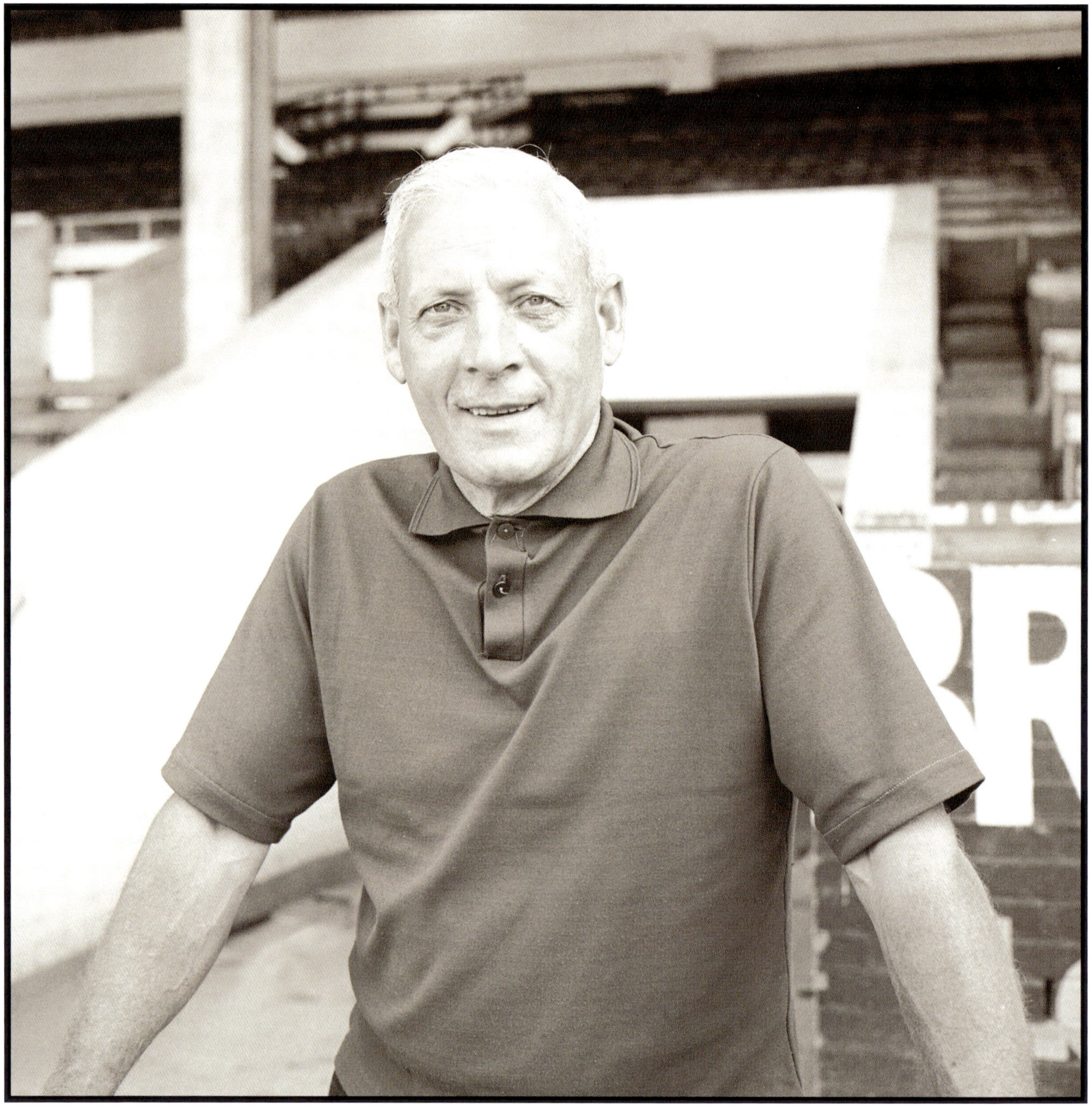

champion!

Football wasn't the only sport staged at Villa Park in the early seventies. In the summer of 1972, the club hosted the Jack Solomons - Alex Griffiths promotion of the British Heavyweight Boxing Championship between Jack Bodell and Coventry's Danny McAlinden, with the ring situated on the centre circle.

McAlinden won by a knockout in the second round, and as soon as the count reached ten, I clambered into the ring to take this picture of him raising his arms in celebration – with poor Bodell still on the canvas.

There were some really dodgy-looking characters at Villa Park that night, the sort of people you normally see in gangster films. One burly guy walked in with a blonde on his arm and I tried to take his picture, only for one of his 'minders' to tell me in no uncertain terms that the gentleman did not wish to be photographed. The evening was quite an eye-opener, although not a huge success.

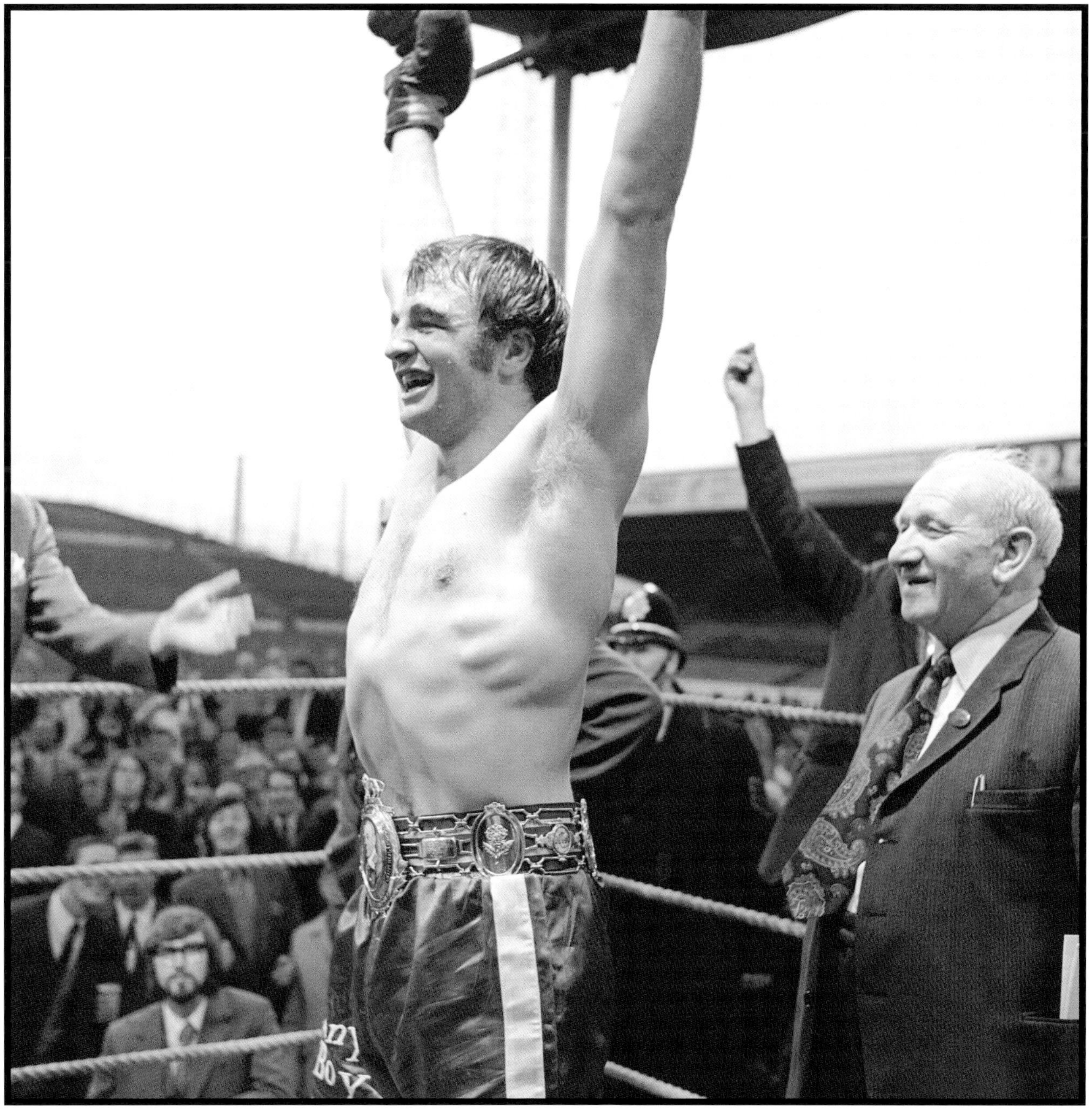

negative angle

There's far more to a photographer's job than focussing the camera and pressing the button. These gentlemen of the press, having taken their pictures at Villa Park, dashed to the Lower Grounds to develop their films before studying the negatives to determine the best picture to use.

There wasn't the convenience of wire transmissions in those days, so messengers on motorbikes were usually waiting outside to rush pictures to newspaper offices.

People take it for granted when a Villa picture appears on front of the Sports Argus within an hour of the final whistle and today's technology means it's a fairly straightforward process, but a lot of sweat and stress used to go into making the edition. There were no digital cameras then, don't forget.

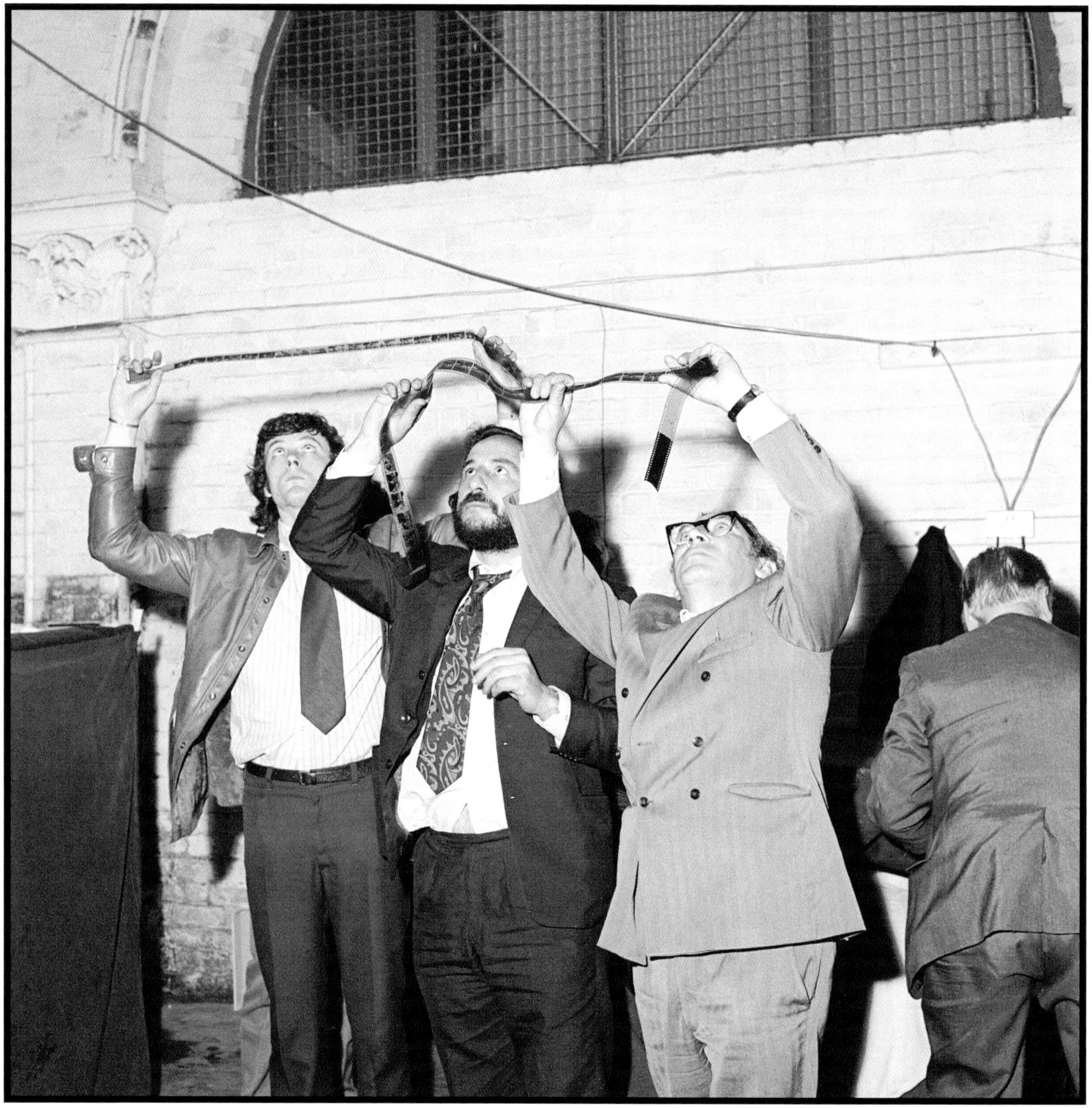

dancing lions

A typical scene on dance night at the Lions Club as young supporters enjoy a 'smooch'.

Dances were held most Saturday and Sunday evenings, and as you can see, they were very popular.

You couldn't just walk into the club, you had to become a member by going through the proper procedure of being proposed and seconded.

It was an ideal venue for a night out with your wife or girlfriend, and one night my wife Annie and I even took along my mother, who thoroughly enjoyed herself.

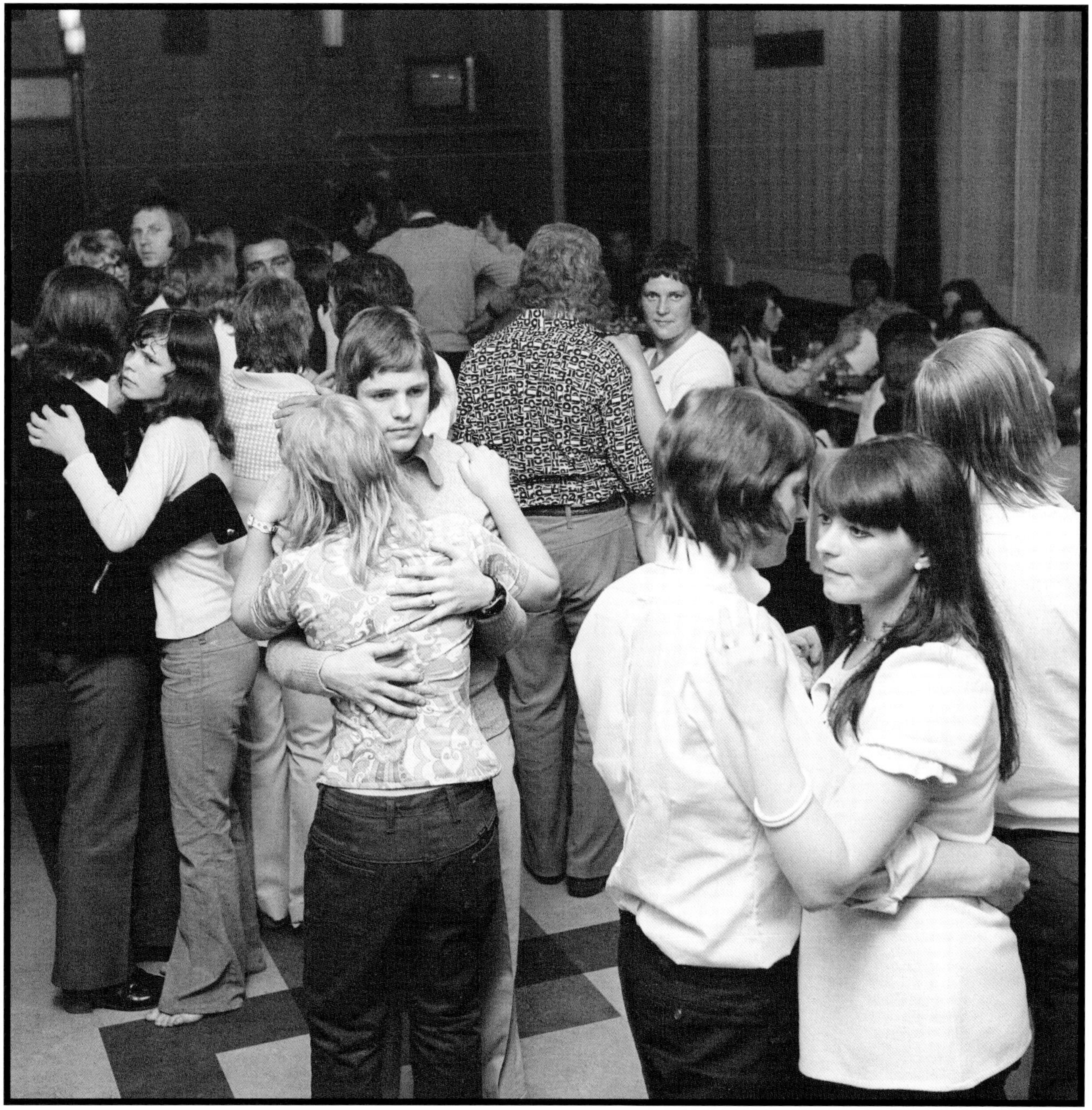

a word in vic's ear

I'm not sure exactly what chairman Doug Ellis was saying to manager Vic Crowe, or exactly when this picture was taken. Judging by the Champagne bottles on the table, though, it was obviously a happy Villa dressing room.

I was always welcome in there after the team had won, and nothing was too much trouble for the players. If Villa had lost, it was best to keep out of the way...

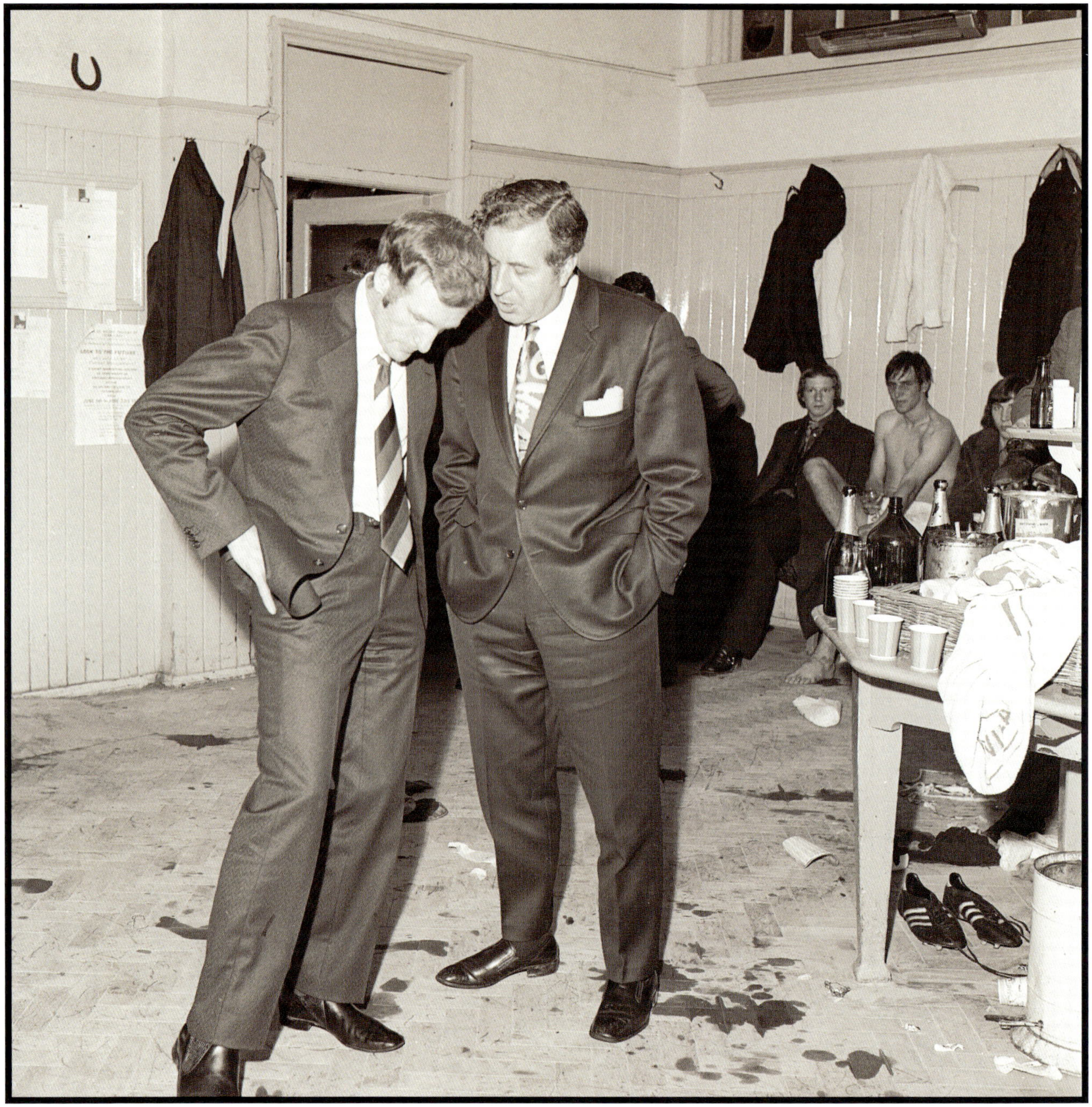

dressing down

Another happy occasion in the dressing room, judging by the bottles on the window ledge and in the foreground.

Ian Ross appears to be just a little startled as he adjusts his tie (note the 'penny round' shirt collar which was in vogue at the time), while Pat McMahon looks suitably cool – if somewhat disinterested – as he waits for his pal to finish getting changed.

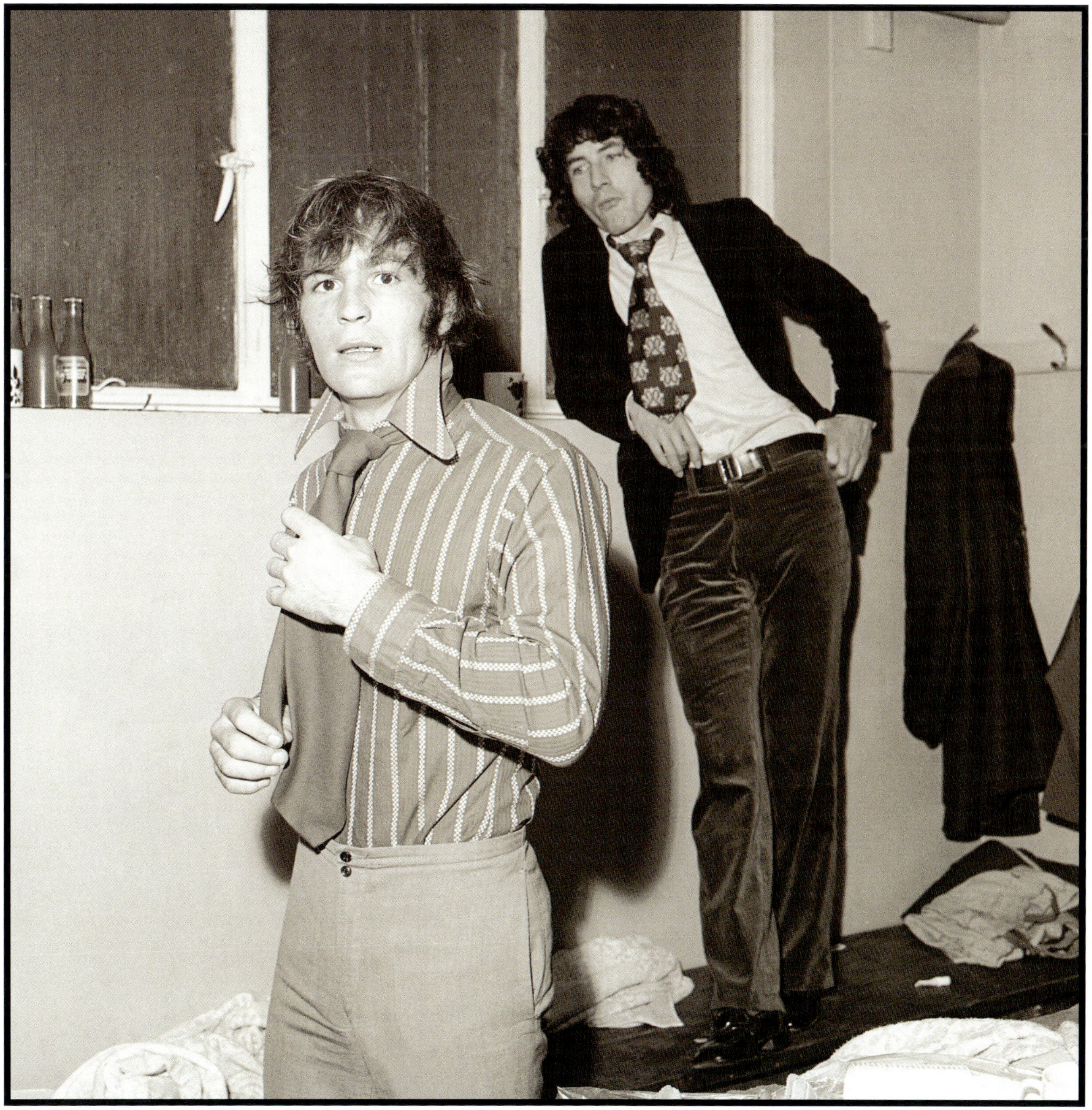

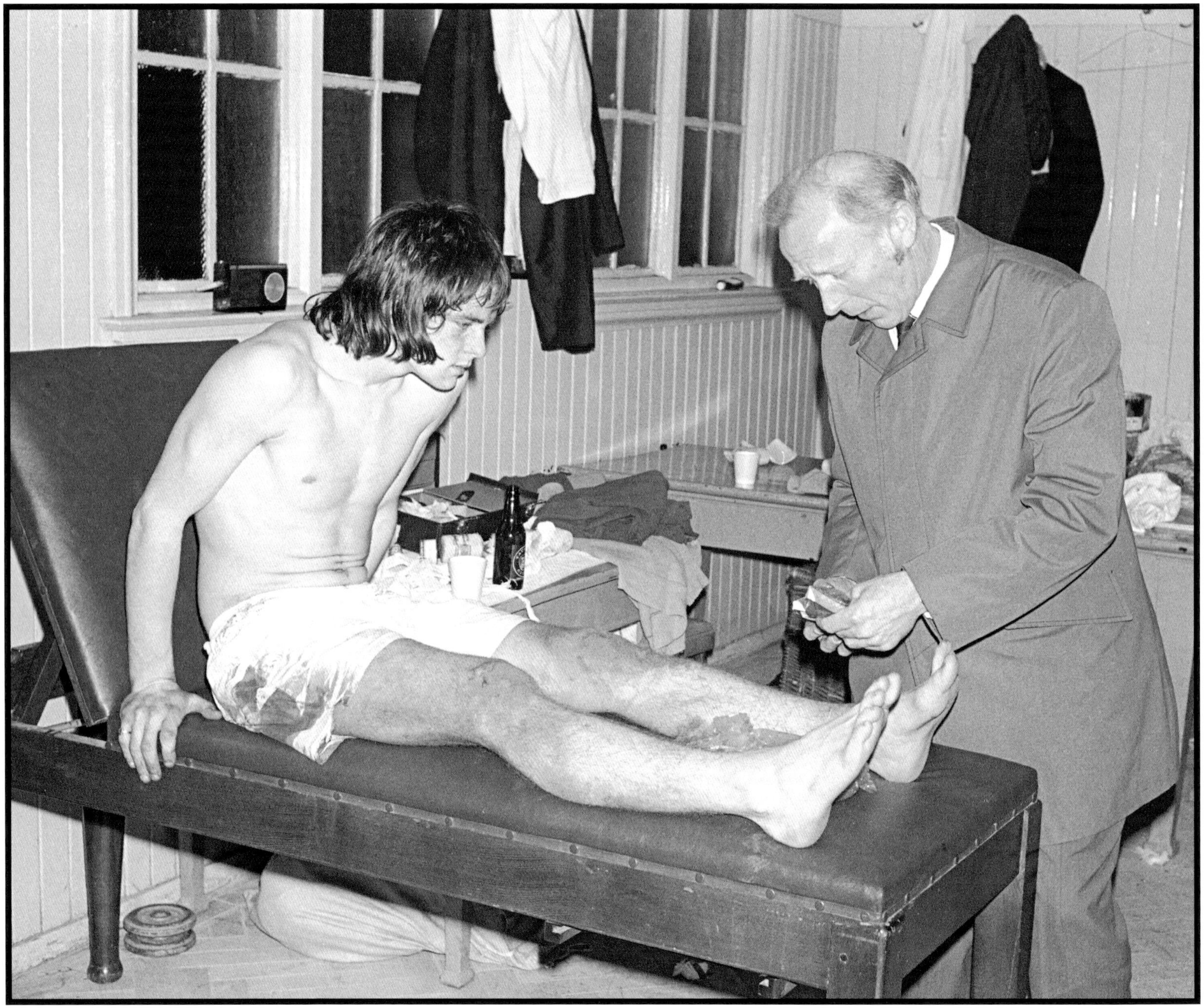

pain game

Life on the treatment table is no joke, and Brian Little is in sombre mood as he discusses an injury with reserve team coach Leo Crowther. I've seen players in tears, either because they were in so much pain or because they had just been given news they didn't want to hear. It's a sad side of football which the general public tend not to appreciate.

boy from brazil

I got home from work one evening and my wife Annie said: 'Guess who's coming to Villa Park?' I couldn't believe it when she told me she'd heard that the world's most famous footballer Pele and his Santos pals had agreed to play a friendly against the boys in claret-and-blue.

Villa Park was packed that night and we won 2-1, but Pele was only too happy to sign autographs afterwards. Director Harry Parkes (left) was among those clamouring for his signature as the legend received treatment in the dressing room.

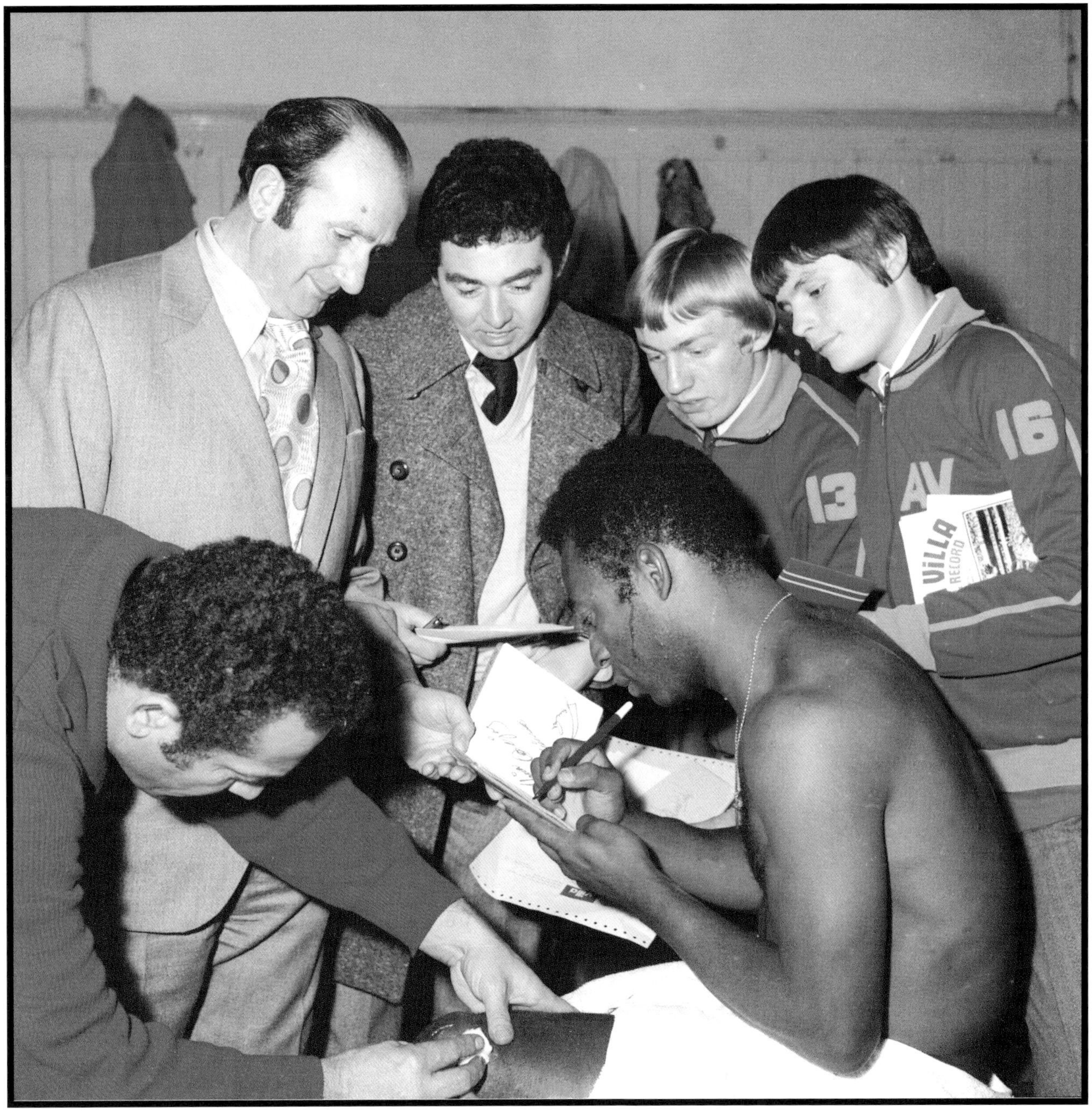

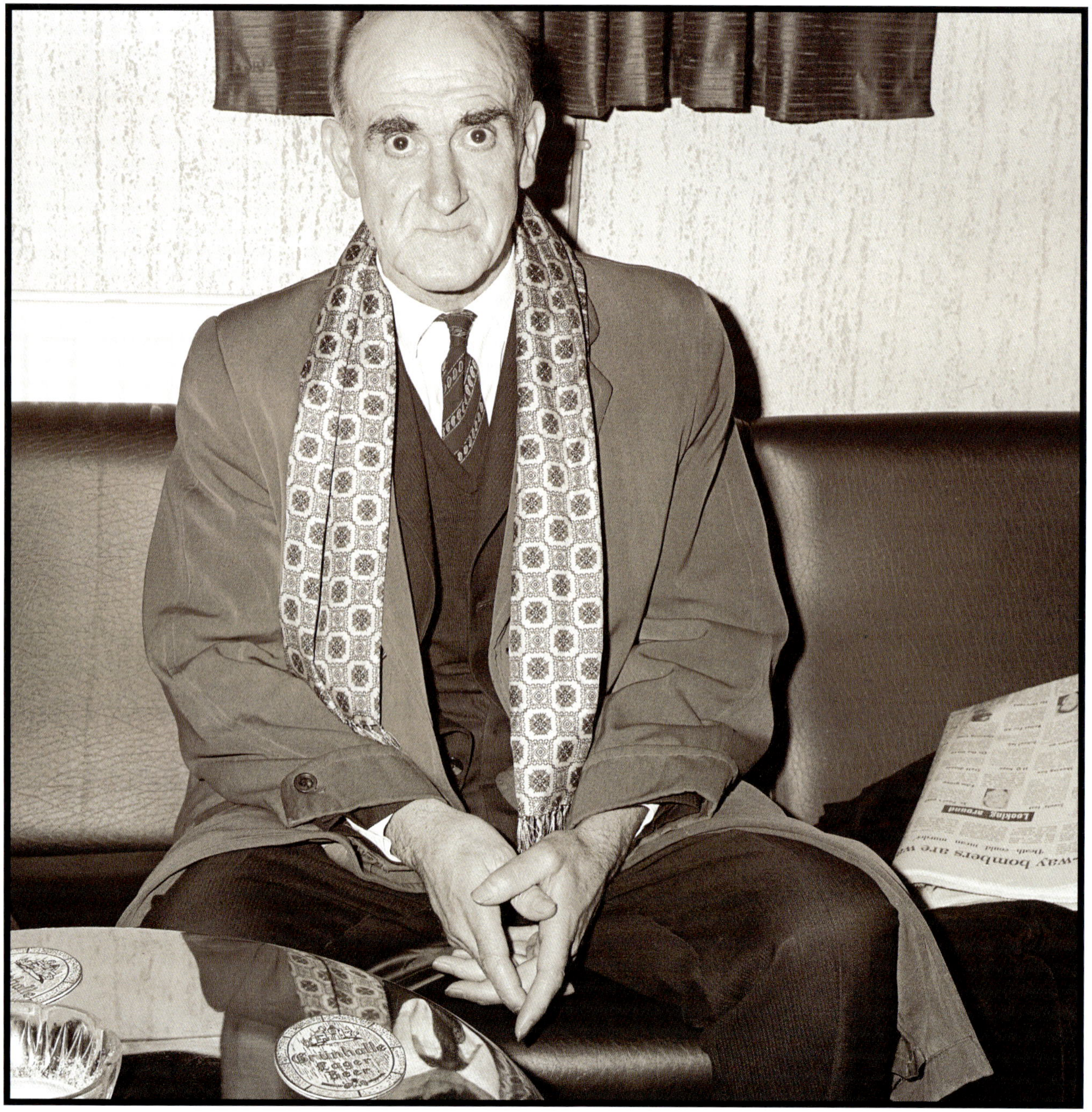

pongo waring

My father had told me all about the great Tom 'Pongo' Waring, one of Villa's finest goalscorers who still holds the club record of 49 goals in one season. Pongo was from Birkenhead, and I got to meet him when Villa played Tranmere Rovers at Prenton Park on a Friday evening in January, 1972.

I went into the Supporters Club, where I was told he would be, and asked at the bar: 'Can you tell me where Mr Waring is?' All I got in return was a shrug of the shoulders, and it was the same story when I repeated my request, adding the name Tom. It was only when I used his nickname that the steward replied: 'Oh, you mean Pongo!'

As you can see, Pongo stared suspiciously into the lens, and I was more nervous that night than in meeting any other footballer – including Pele. I was there the day Pongo's ashes were scattered over the pitch, but I didn't take a picture because it seemed disrespectful.

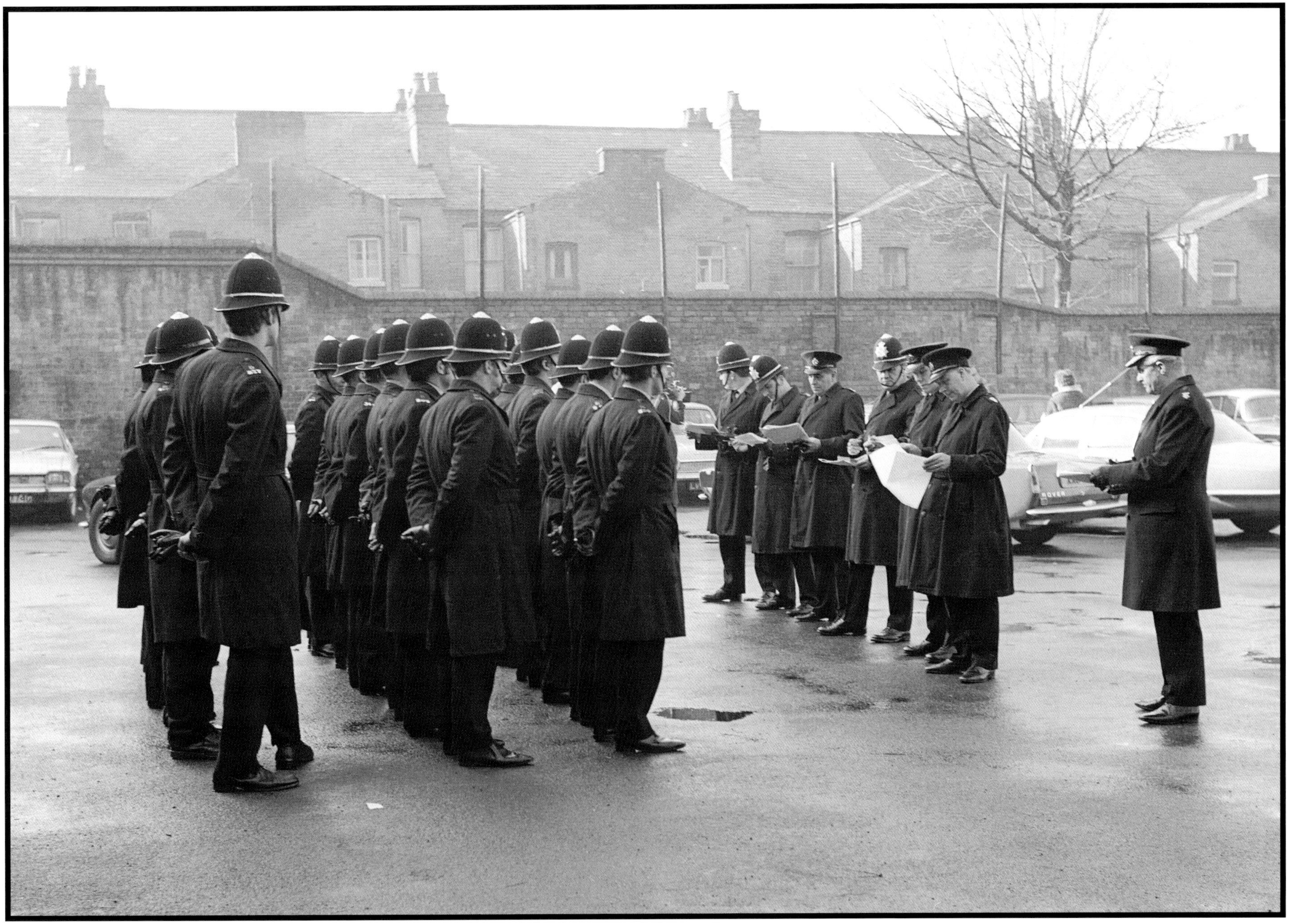

police briefing

There was a much heavier police presence at football matches in the early 70s than there is today, and the officers on duty gathered in the Villa Park car park at mid-day to receive their briefing for the afternoon.

This was another of Eric Woodward's ideas for a different angle on football, and the picture appeared on the front cover of the Villa News & Record for the Charity Shield match against Manchester City on 5th August, 1972.

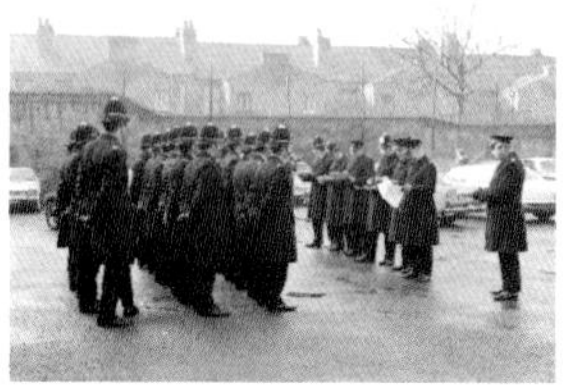

soaking in success

It's not often that visiting teams celebrate a major triumph at Anfield but Villa's youngsters did when they lifted the FA Youth Cup in 1972.

Having won 1-0 in the first leg of the Final at Villa Park, our boys really turned on the style in the return match for a 4-2 win over Liverpool on the night and a 5-2 aggregate victory.

Needless to say, they thoroughly enjoyed their soak in the bath afterwards. Coach Frank Upton is holding the cup, with John Gidman and Brian Little in the foreground. Liverpool's fans had sportingly applauded the Villa kids for their magnificent performance and it occurred to me that I might get a picture of the Merseysiders' legendary boss Bill Shankly congratulating our youngsters in the dressing room. Some hope. Shanks, who hated seeing Liverpool get beaten, had already gone home.

synchronise watches

Villa played Polish club Gornik Zabrze in a friendly and as there wasn't the pressure of a competitive fixture, I popped into the referee's dressing room before the match to see how the officials prepare.

Gordon Hill was the man in the middle and he made sure his watch was synchronised with those of his linesmen. He also displayed all the other items he would be using, including a notebook, a pencil, a coin and two whistles.

Players were booked and sent off in those days, but this was before the introduction of red and yellow cards.

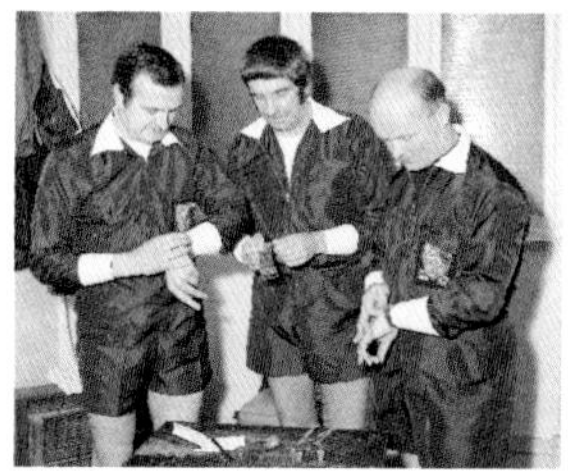

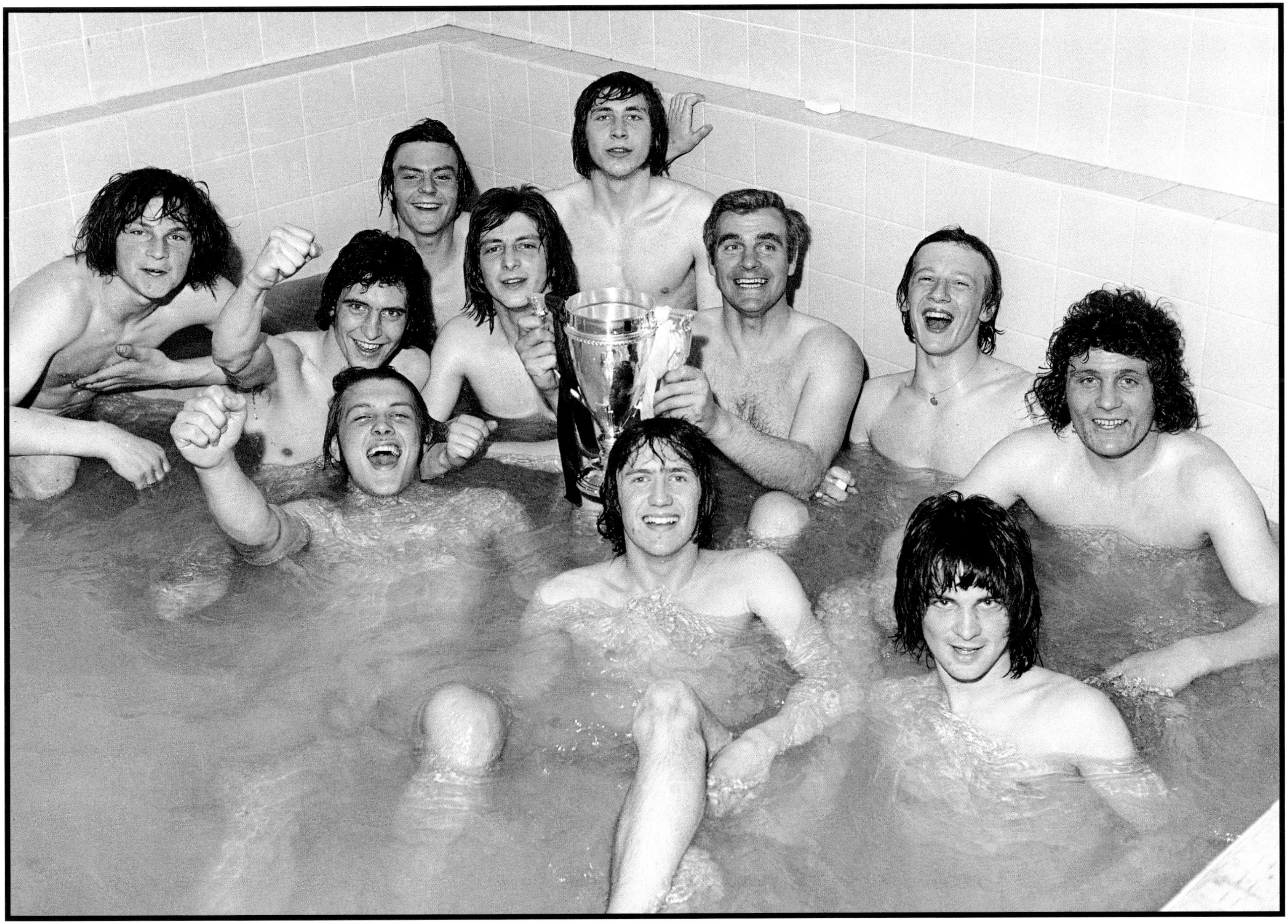

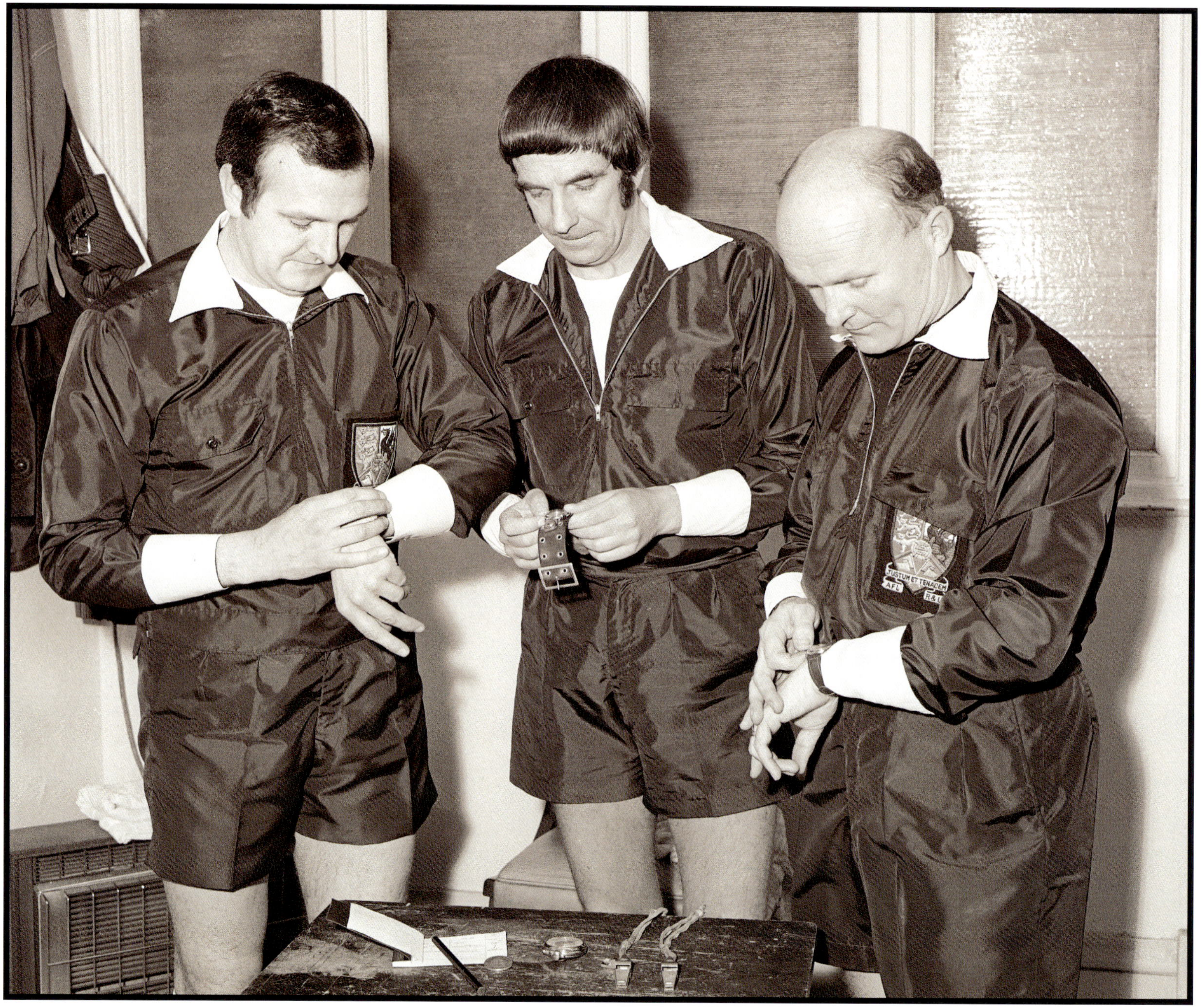
JUSTUM ET TENACEM
AFL
R&L

happy new year

Another idea for a programme picture, this one involved four youngsters wearing their shirts back-to-front to create 1972.

It didn't quite work, because this was before goalkeepers wore number one on their backs, although we eventually published a photo with the digit superimposed on the keeper's jersey.

The players featured here are Jake Findlay, Tony Betts, Nigel Dyer and Greg Fellows.

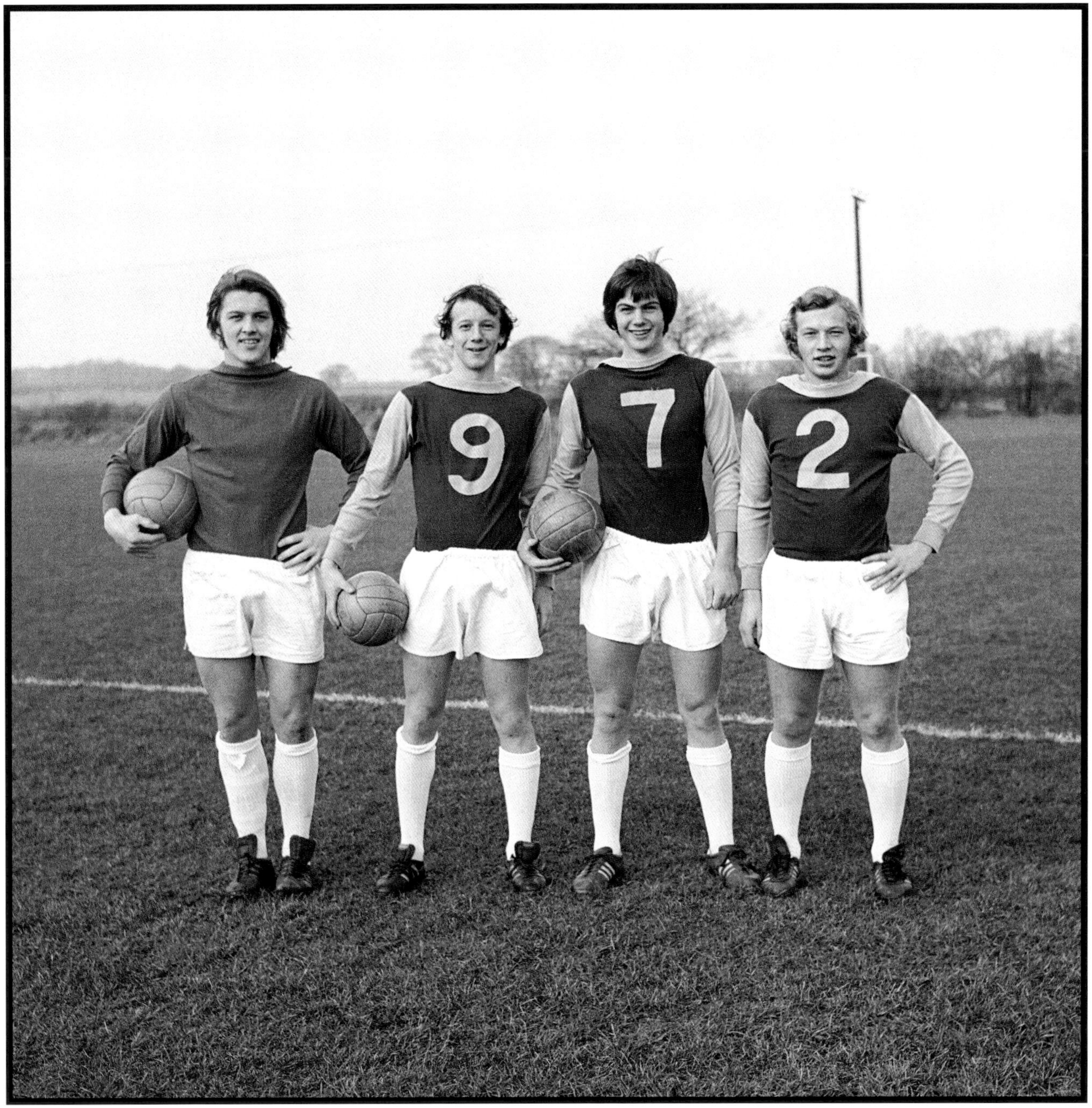

speed merchants

Athletics was far more high-profile 30 years ago than it is now, and these two guys were guests of the club for the match against Notts County on 13th November, 1971.

David Bedford (left) and Birmingham's Ian Stewart were two of the hottest properties on the scene, although they were in no hurry to run anywhere as they relaxed in the old Villa Park reception area, waiting for their tickets.

The speedy duo witnessed a home victory, too, Ray Graydon's goal ensuring a 1-0 success.

I can't recall the exact circumstances, but Bedford and Stewart were not the only celebrity visitors that afternoon. Villa were also graced by the presence of comedians Bernie Winters and the brilliant Eric Morecambe.

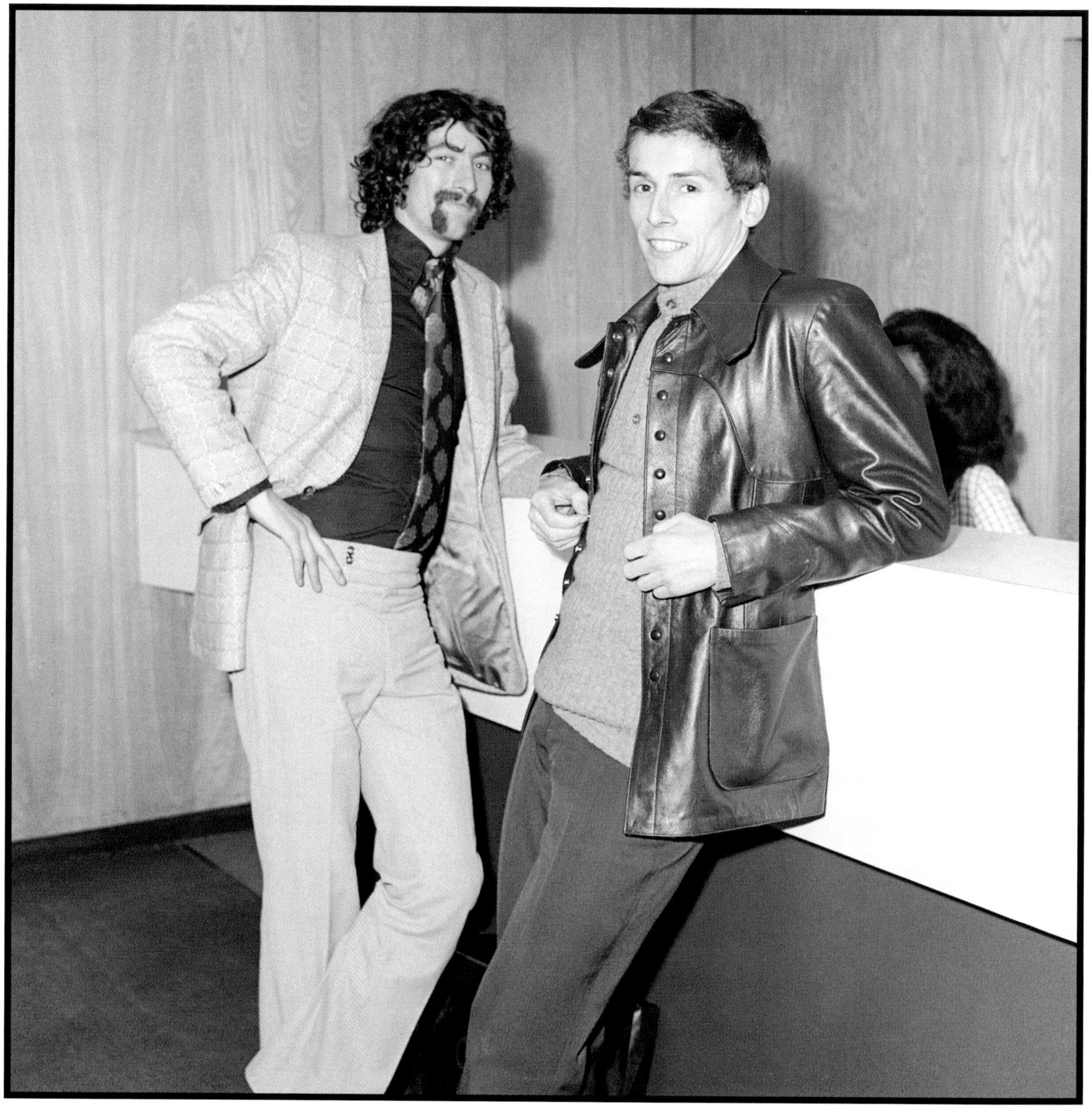

brothers in arms

The Rioch brothers, Bruce and Neil, are clearly feeling the chill wind which often cuts across Bodymoor Heath, judging by their hands-in-pockets pose.

I recall chatting with Bruce one day, when he suddenly said: 'I'd better get home, my wife's expecting.' I told him: 'So is mine.' Bruce Rioch junior made his way into the world on 9th August, 1971, with Louise Weir arriving the following day.

That gave us something in common and rather than talking football when I saw him, we used to discuss how our respective babies were progressing.

Neil, while a decent player, always tended to be in his older brother's shadow, although he has had a lot more involvement with Villa down the years, running the Old Stars team and founding the Former Players' Association.

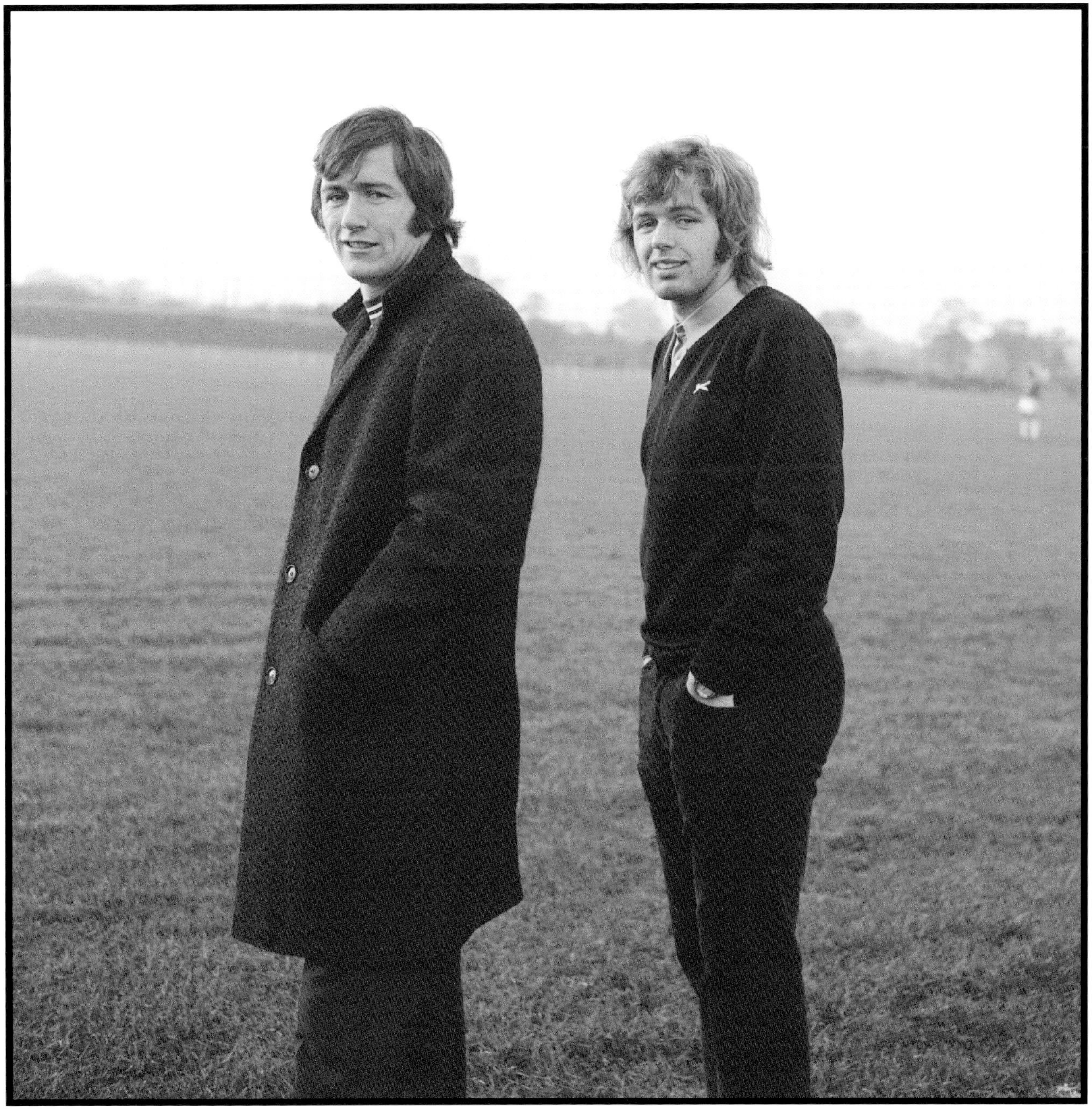

buckets of balls

David Smith never made the first team, but he did a mean balancing act with footballs – with a little help from a couple of plastic buckets.

Smith, an apprentice at the time, is seen here carrying three footballs back to the dressing room as the crowd begin to disperse after a match at Villa Park.

There's something of a guilty look on David face as he comes under the gaze of a police officer, so perhaps he was thinking of taking the balls home with him!

Walking ahead of him is Ron Wainwright, who was Villa's kit man when I first worked for the club.

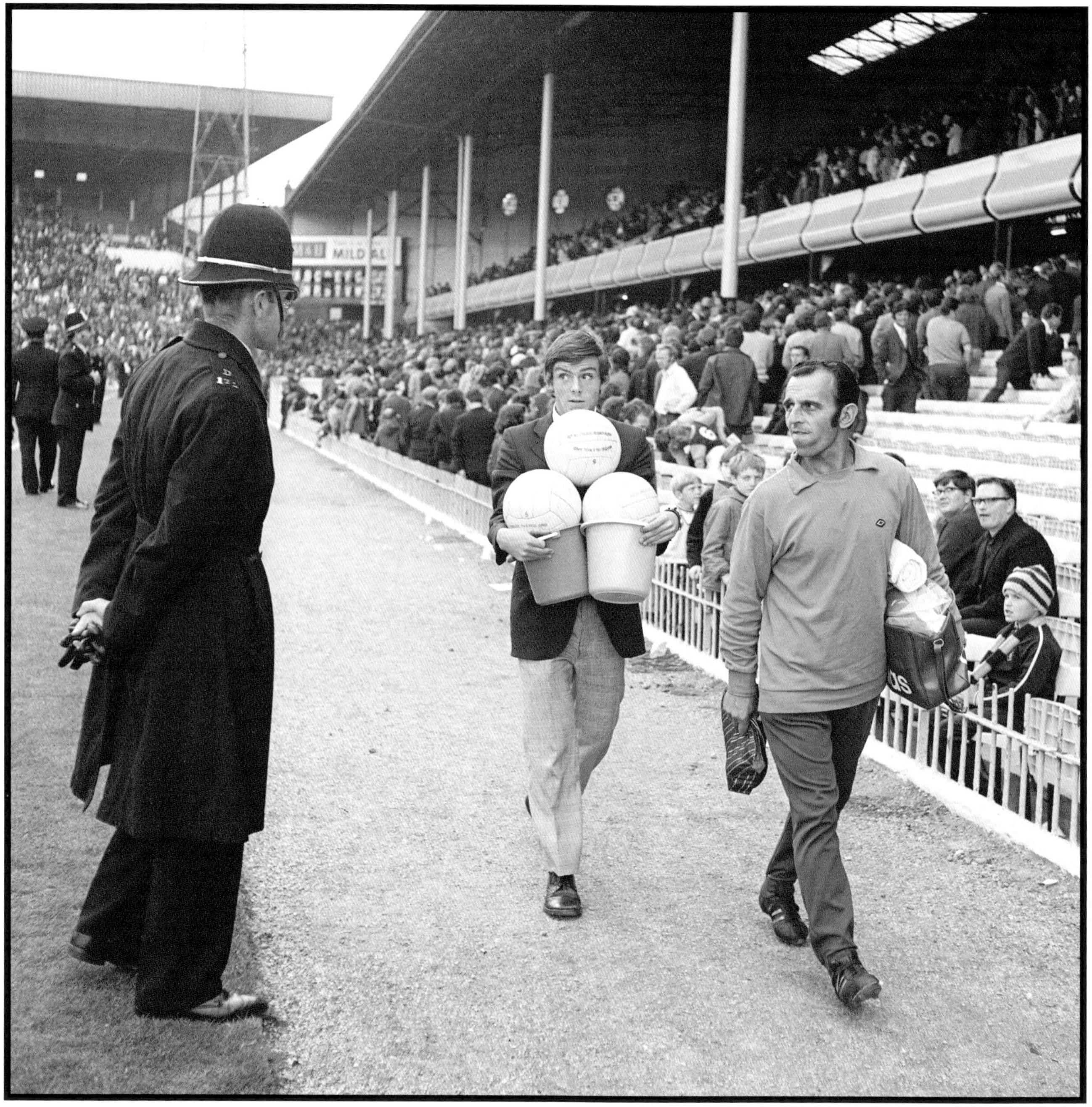

fashion statement

George Best had set quite a trend with his pin-up image a few years earlier, but if the Manchester United star was the football heart-throb of the 60s, a young pretender emerged at Villa Park in the early 70s.

The girls adored midfielder Chico Hamilton, who was as well known for his flowing locks and cheeky grin as he was for his ability on the pitch.

Like Best, too, Chico decided a boutique would be in keeping with his pop idol image, and I went along to the official opening of his shop.

Needless to say, there was no shortage of young ladies flocking to the Wylde Green establishment in search of of something new to wear to the disco.

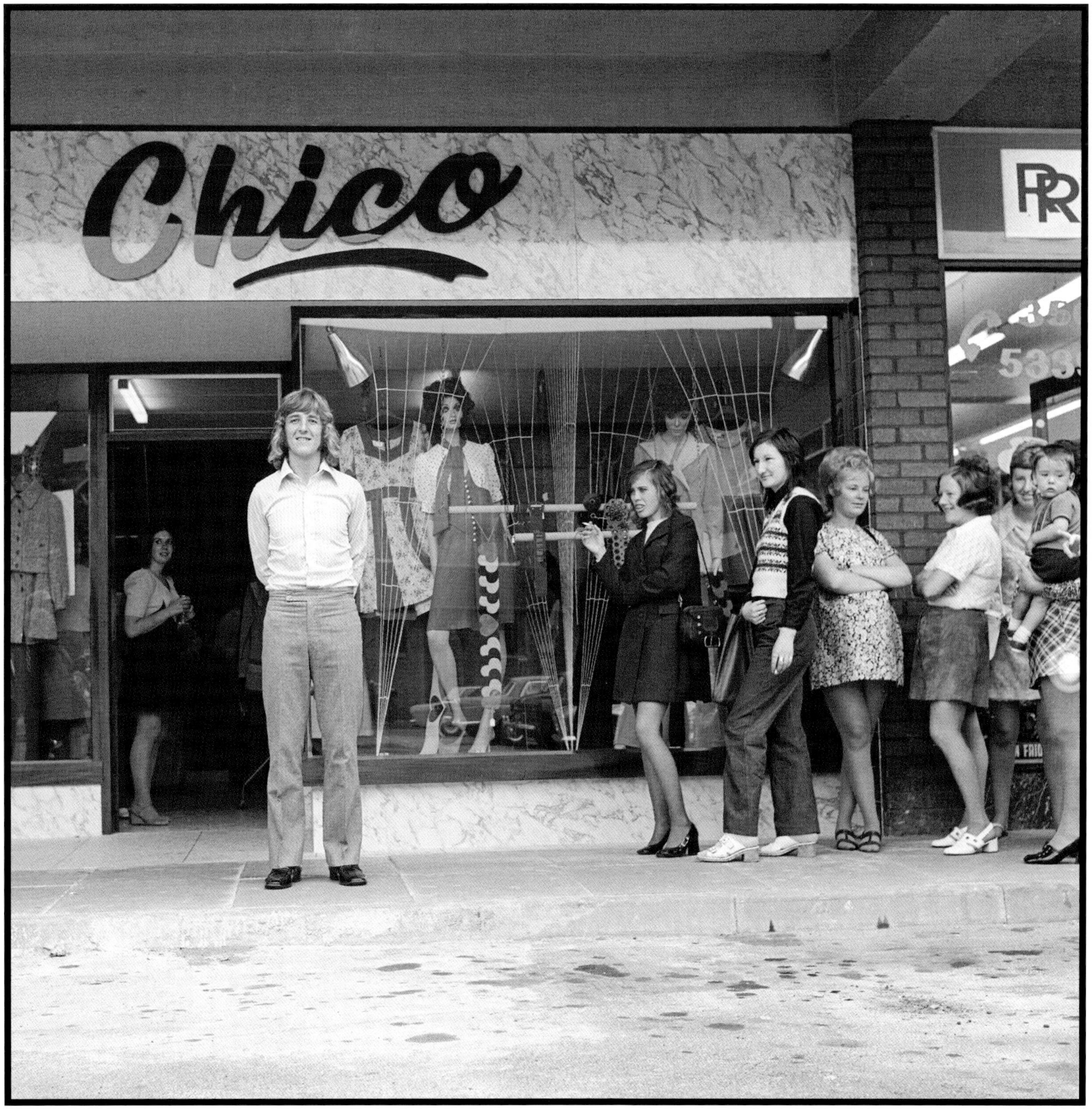

trevor hockey

Former Birmingham City players took a bit of stick if they came to Villa, and Geoff Vowden was given a particularly hard time by the fans.

But that was never the case with Trevor Hockey, possibly because he had played for Sheffield United and Norwich City since leaving St Andrew's.

Trevor spent only one season with us, playing 24 games during the 1973-74 campaign, but he was hugely popular with the Villa faithful, possibly because of his rebellious image.

Behind the long hair and the beard, though, Trevor was a really nice guy and I was sad to learn of his death in 1987, when he collapsed while playing in a five-a-side tournament in his native Keighley.

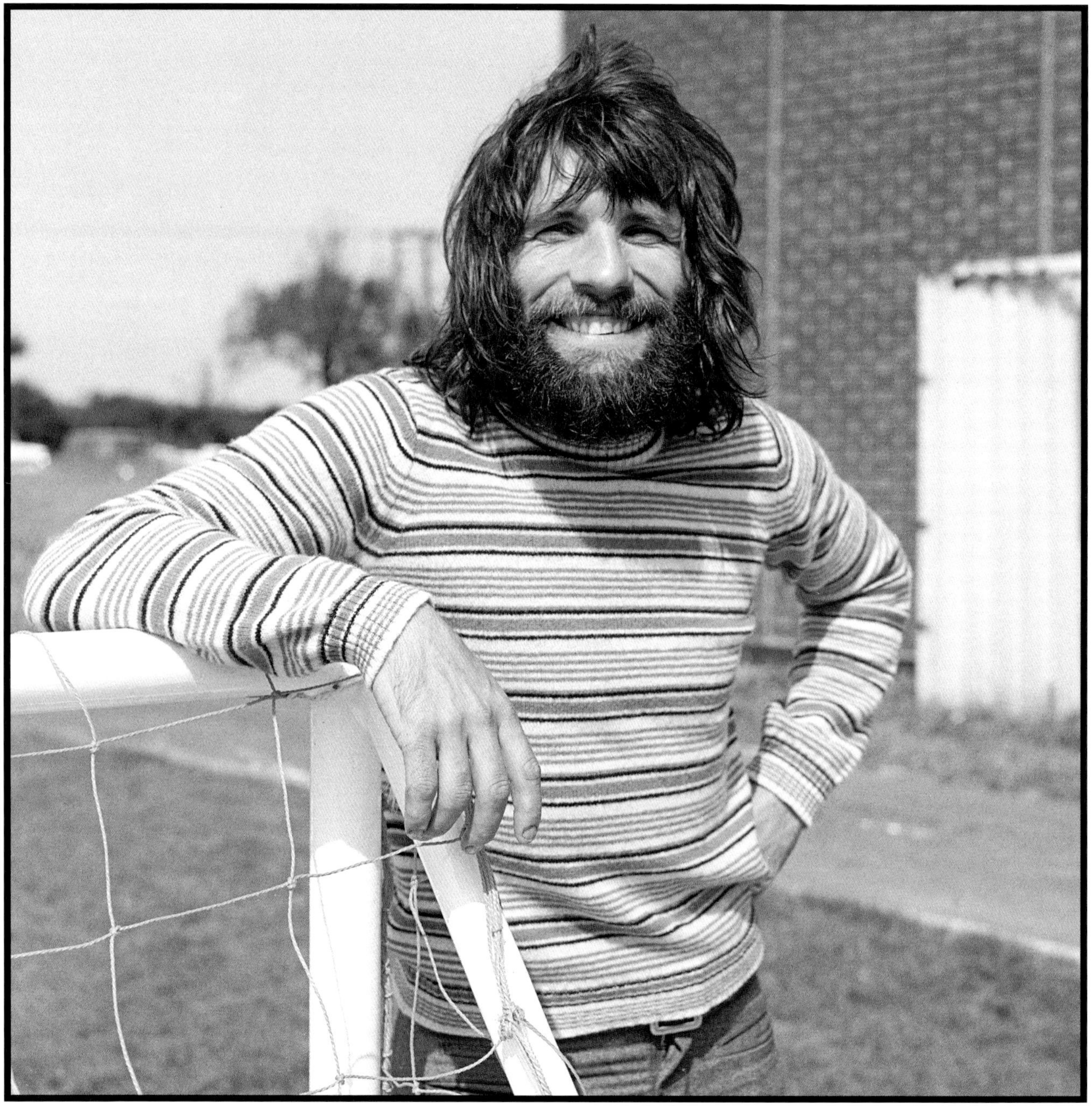

lucky horseshoe

A permanent fixture in the home dressing room over a number of years was the horseshoe which can be seen next to the mirror in the centre of this picture.

I'm not sure where it came from, but it was regarded as a lucky charm by the players over a considerable period of time.

No-one seems to know what happened to it. At one point I was tempted to pinch it for a souvenir, but I was worried some of Villa's old players might haunt me!

At the time this shot was taken, the dressing room was something of a mess because it was in the process of being refurbished. Not that it looked a great deal different afterwards – that pillar in the middle of the room meant that no great changes could be undertaken.

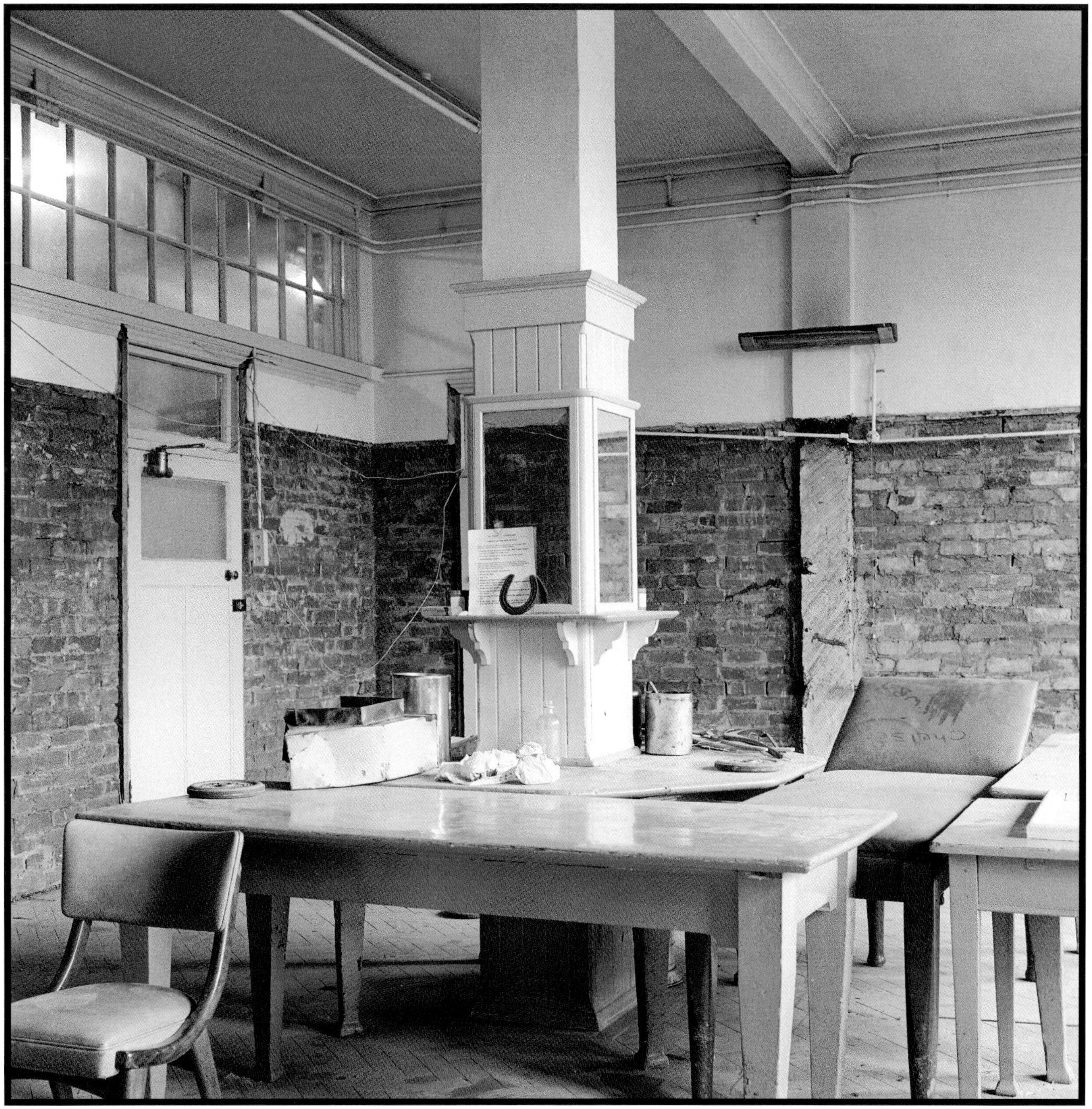

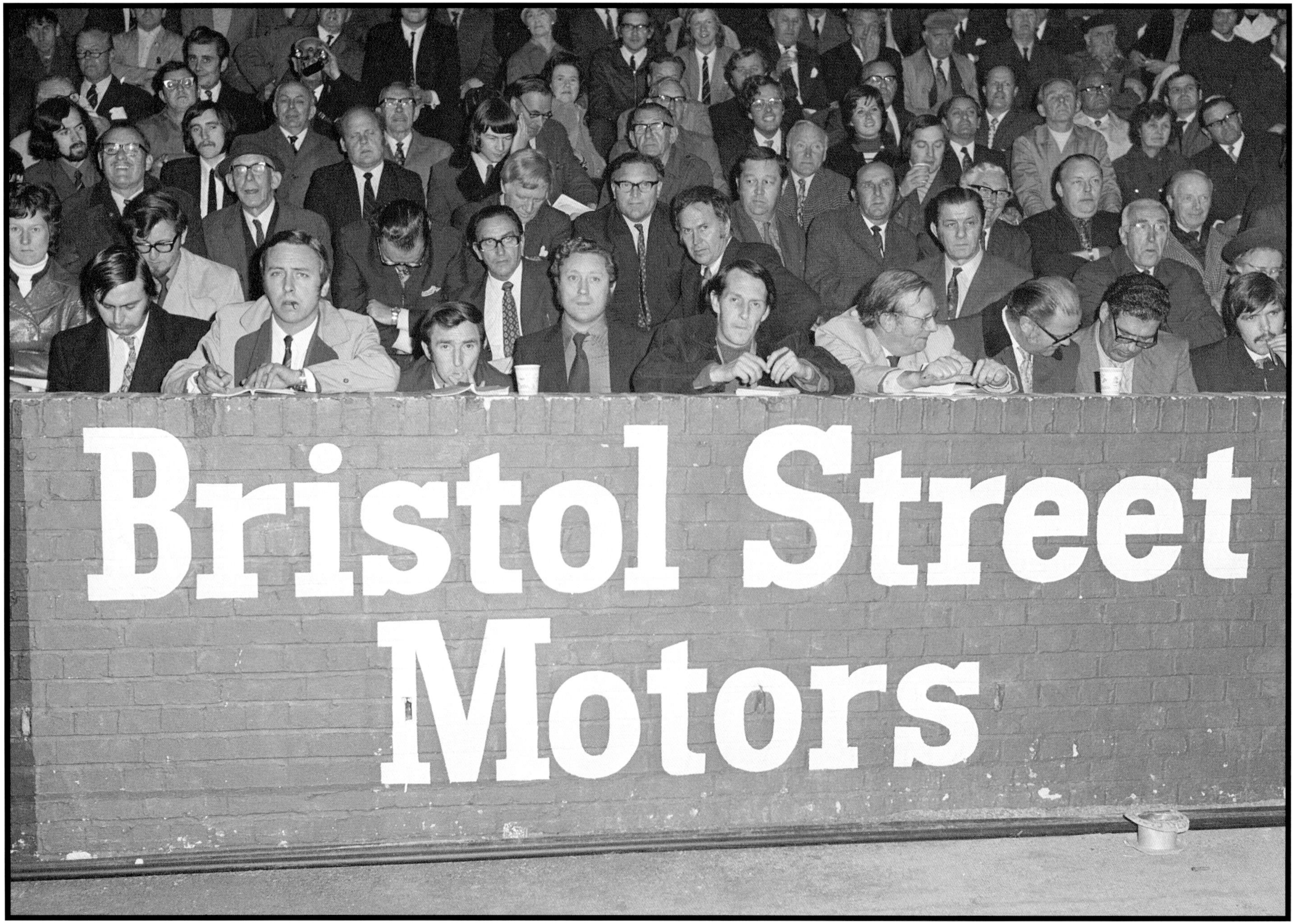
Bristol Street
Motors

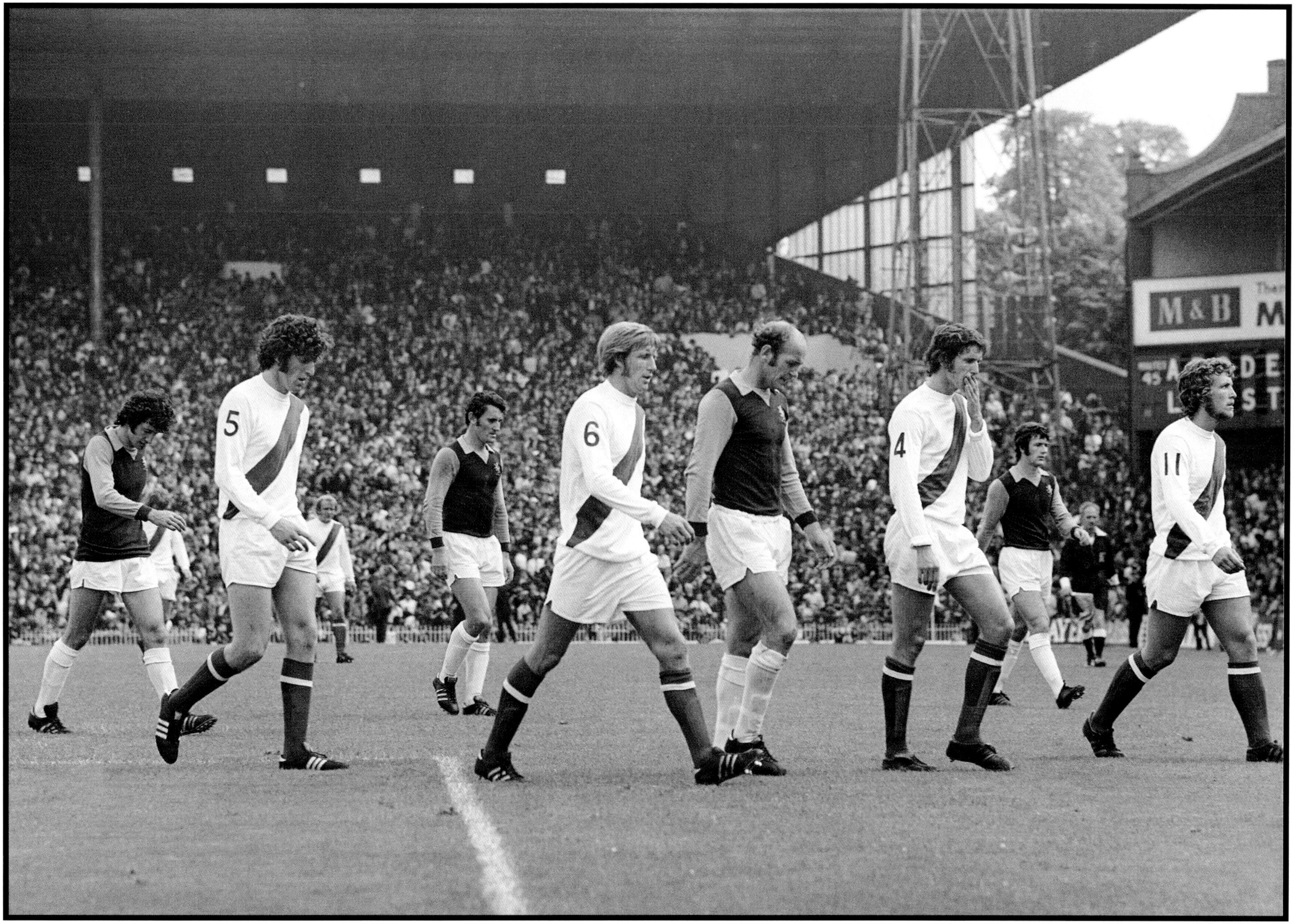
M&B

press gang

The boardroom battles of the early 70s ensured there was never a dull moment around Villa Park, and at one point there seem to be a never-ending round of meetings.

Such was the interest generated that annual meetings and egms had to be held outdoors, with a stage erected on the pitch and shareholders gathered in the old Witton Lane stand.

The media attention was high-profile, too, and reporters were usually provided with seats on the front row so they could use the wall as a desk.

The press gang featured here are (from the left): Randall Northam, Ian Willars, Neville Foulger, Denis Shaw, John Moxley, two gentleman whose names I can't recall, John Davies and Hugh Jamieson.

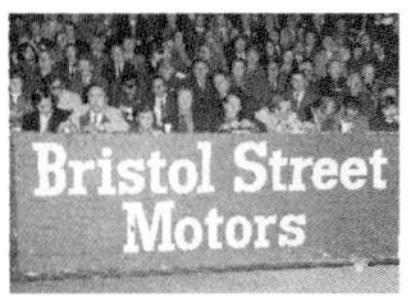

marching orders

Right lads, quick march! It was purely unintentional, of course, but I love the way Villa's players are alternating with their Manchester City counterparts as they leave the field at half-time.

The occasion was the FA Charity Shield match in August, 1972. Traditionally, the Charity Shield has always been played between the League Champions and FA Cup winners, but for a few seasons in the early seventies, the top clubs were reluctant to take part and it became an invitation event.
Having attracted bumper gates on their way to the Third Division championship, Villa were asked to stage the game against City, who were in the top flight.

The game attracted a crowd of nearly 35,000, who saw City lift the Shield by virtue of a 1-0 victory, although Villa gave a good account of themselves.

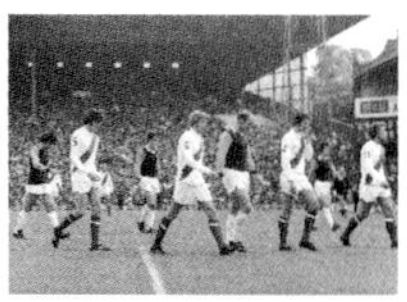

sweets at the witton

Time to own up – the only reason I took this shot was that I was near the end of a roll of film and wanted to use it up before loading a new roll in readiness for the second half.

As so often happens with an unplanned picture, though, you ended up with something which conjures up an evocative image.

This one, taken from near the old Trinity Road tunnel, captures the vast Witton End terrace as it was during our Third Division days, complete with its imposing scoreboard. The vendor, by the way, sold various types of confectionery and drinks – but not my favourite wine gums.

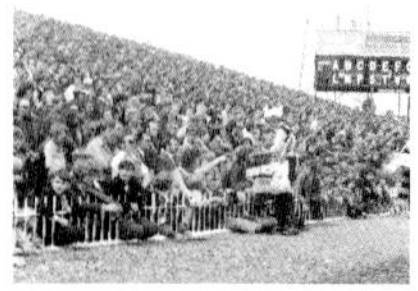

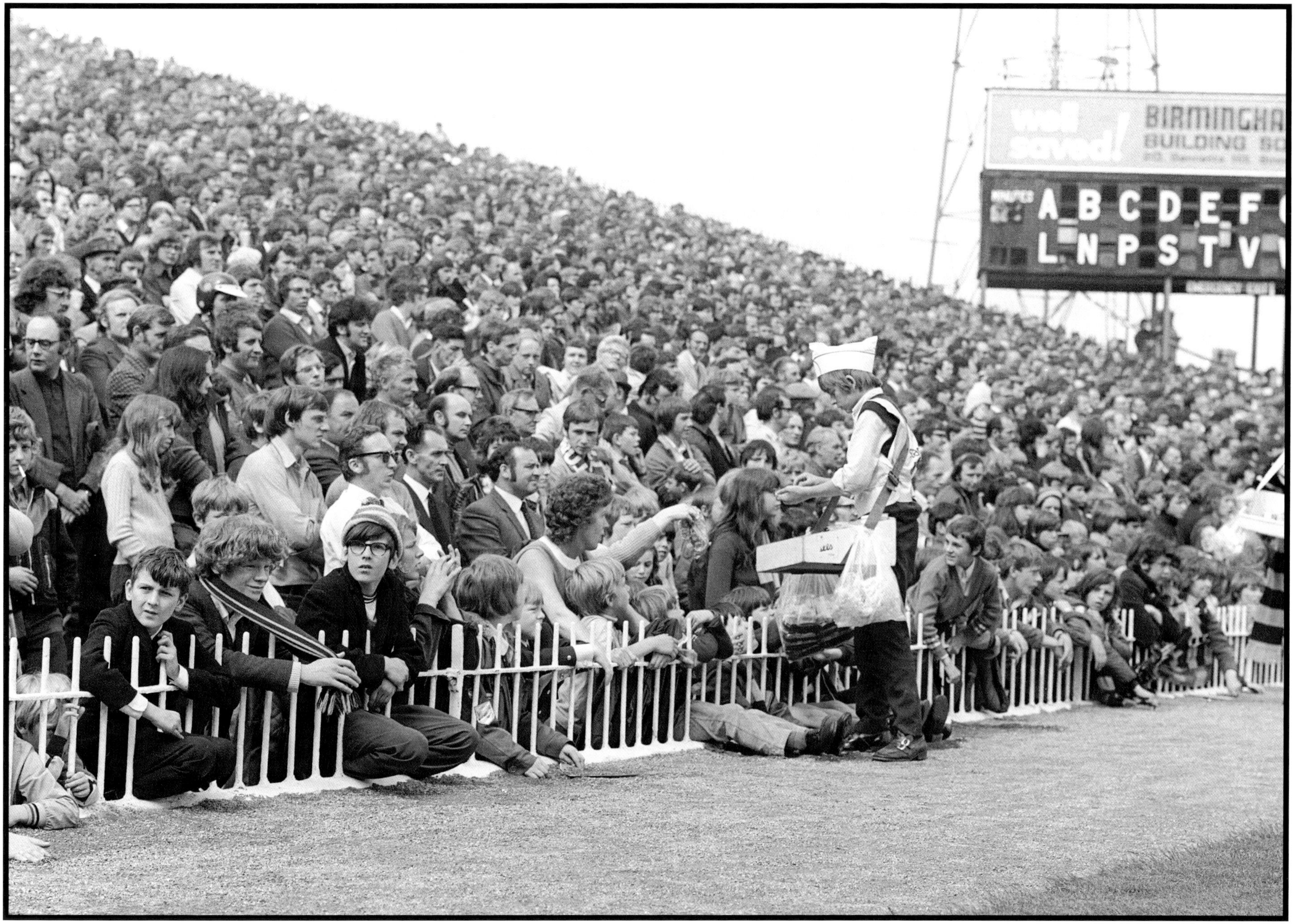
well saved!
BIRMINGHA
BUILDING SO
A B C D E F
L N P S T V

flag day

Another worm's eye view of the famous old Witton End terrace, featuring a young girl who was only too happy to fly the flag on behalf of her favourite club.

Spectators weren't supposed to step over the railings, but we made an exception on this occasion so the young lady would stand out from the rest of the crowd.

I wonder if she remembers the day she became unofficial Witton End cheer-leader?

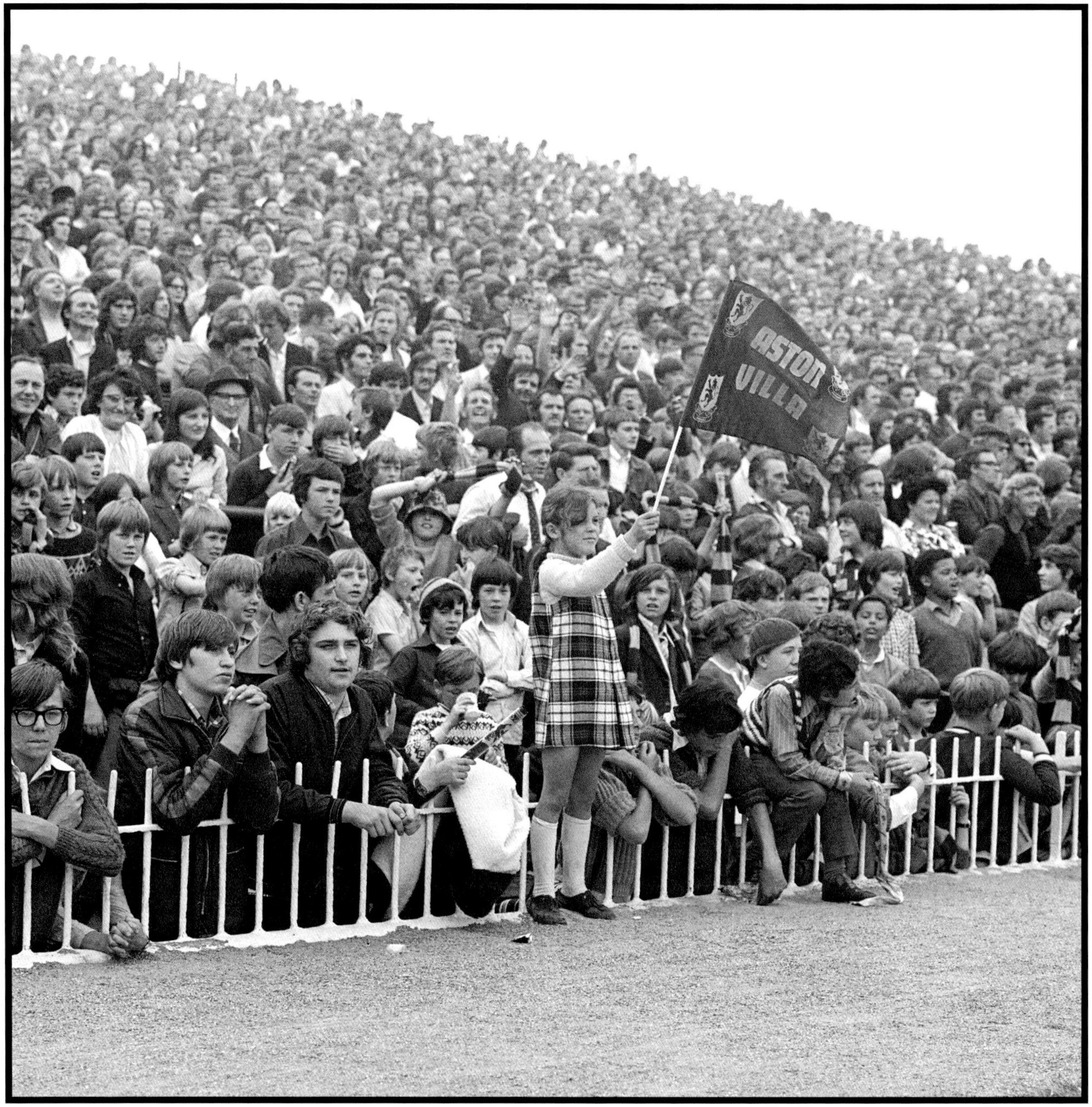

the english patient

If injuries are part and parcel of professional football, there's no doubt that players have always been afforded the best possible medical treatment.

When John Gidman had to have an operation, I went along to take a picture of him in his hospital bed. He looked pretty relaxed as he was tended by a nurse.

Not only was Giddy a fine full-back, he was a smashing lad, and it was good to see him again when he attended the Tribute Dinner to mark the 20th anniversary of Villa's European Cup triumph.

Even though he wasn't involved, he and numerous other former players simply wanted to be there for the big night, which was attended by 670 people.

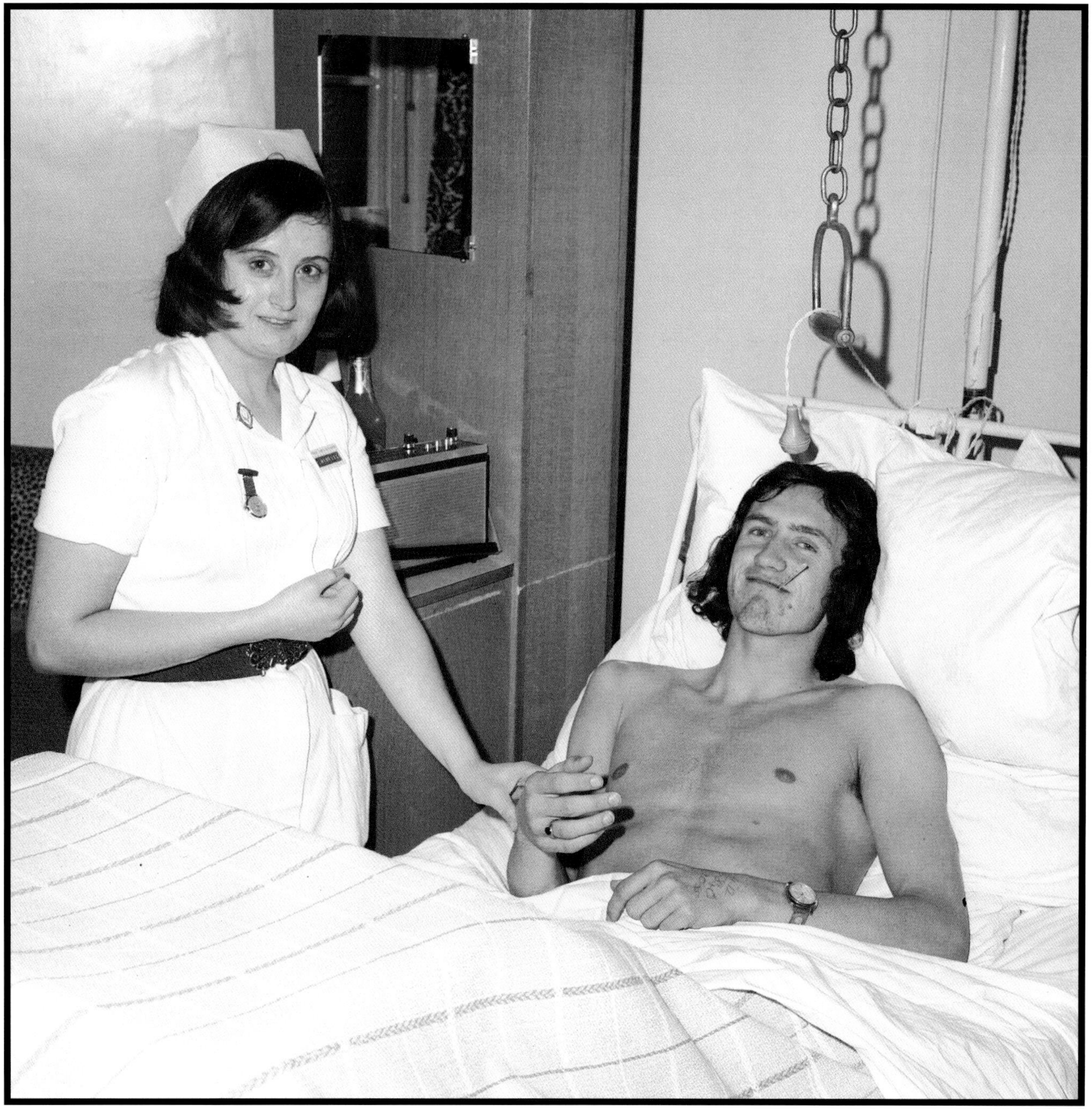

come back, dad!

The idea of this picture was to depict a family going into Villa Park, although it didn't quite turn out as intended.

The two youngsters and their Mum posed obediently, but Dad misunderstood what I was trying to do. He stepped through the turnstile – and out of the picture!

The admission prices indicate how things have changed over the past 30 years – 15p for adults and 10p for children and old age pensioners. It should be pointed out, however, that this was a Central League match, in the days when the first team and reserves played at home on alternate Saturdays.

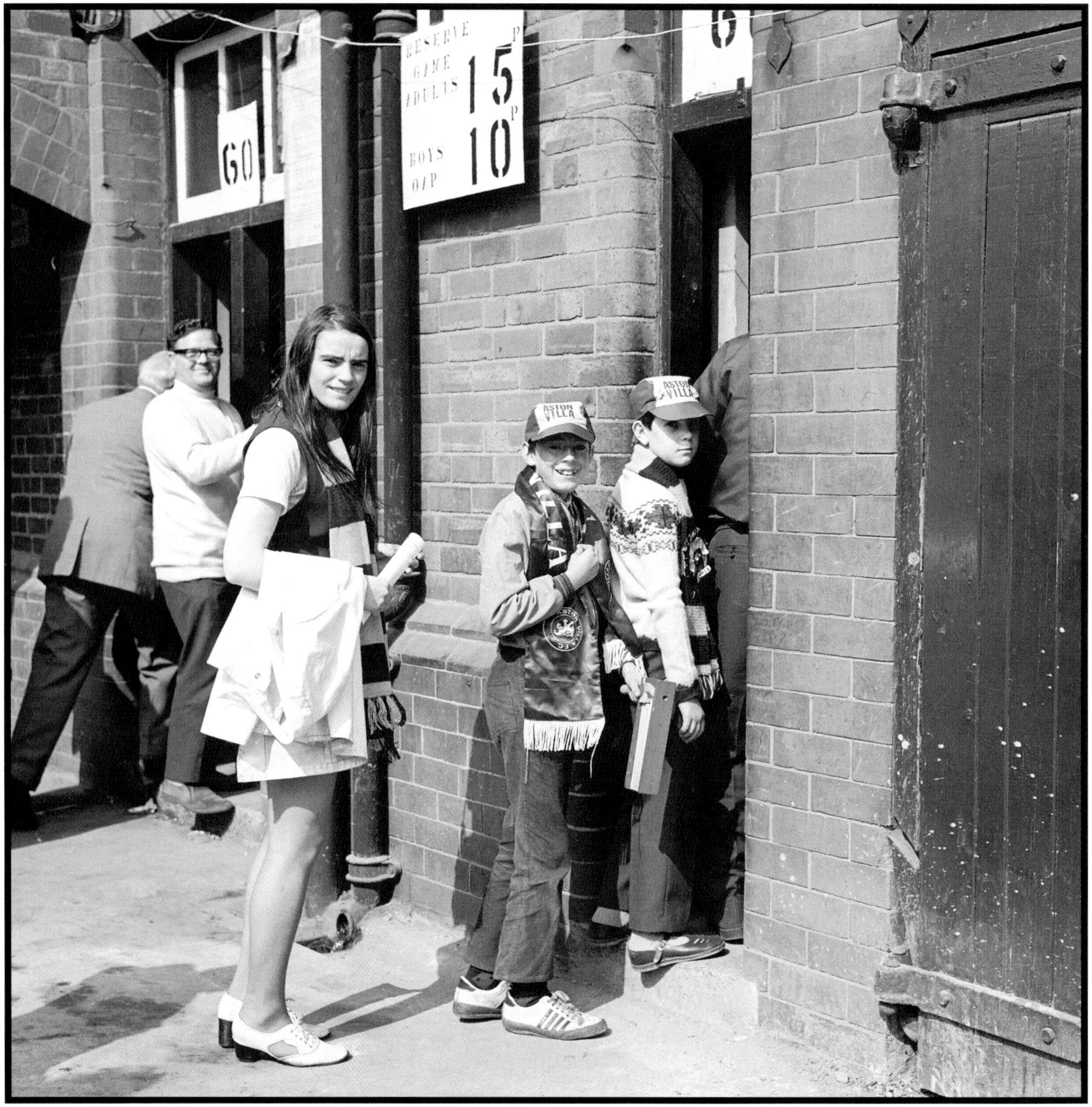

clicking in

The family turnstile photograph made the Villa News & Record, but this one didn't – much to the annoyance of one of the gentlemen featured paying their admission money.

One of them asked me why I was taking pictures and I explained it was for the programme. What I didn't say was that not every picture was used.

A while later, the club received a phone call from an irate supporter, saying I had taken his photo for the programme and it hadn't gone in.

From that moment, my stock answer was that I was snapping away for 'club records'. We didn't want to be seen to be enticing people to buy a programme under false pretences.

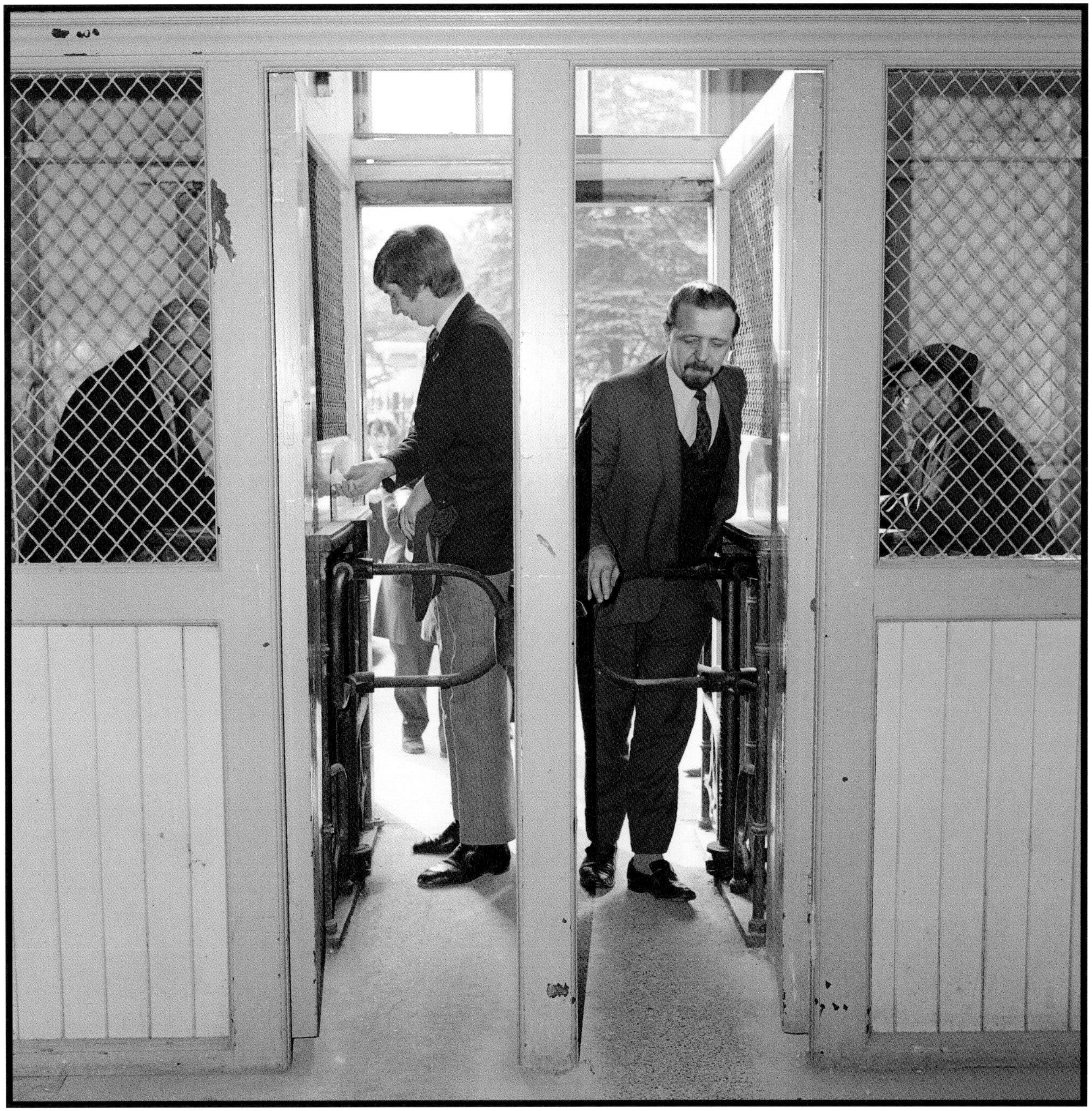

anything interesting?

If ever there was an era when ladies' fashion was popular with the lads, it was three decades ago.

The mini-skirt was all the rage, and girls were only too willing to show off their legs. This young lady certainly had no qualms about her 'revealing' pose as she read a copy of the Villa Times.

And just look at the headline across the top of the paper. Who said Golden Goals were a modern day innovation?

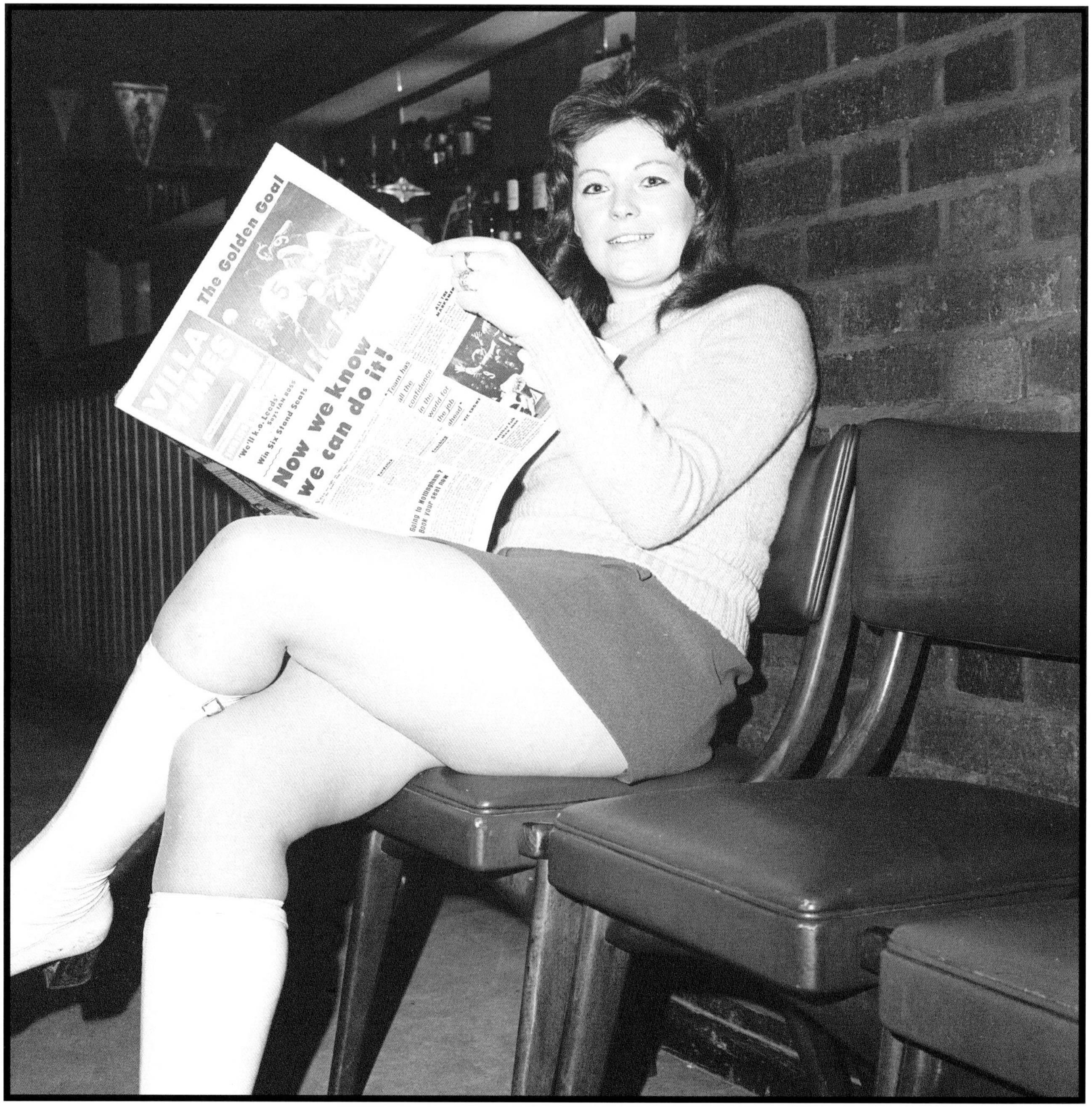

on yer bike

Want to know anything about this guy? Well, his name is John, his wife or girlfriend is called Rita, and in his dictionary, V is for Villa.

Whether he lives in Witton is debatable – it's close enough to walk to Villa Park – but there's absolutely no question about his devotion to the boys in claret and blue.

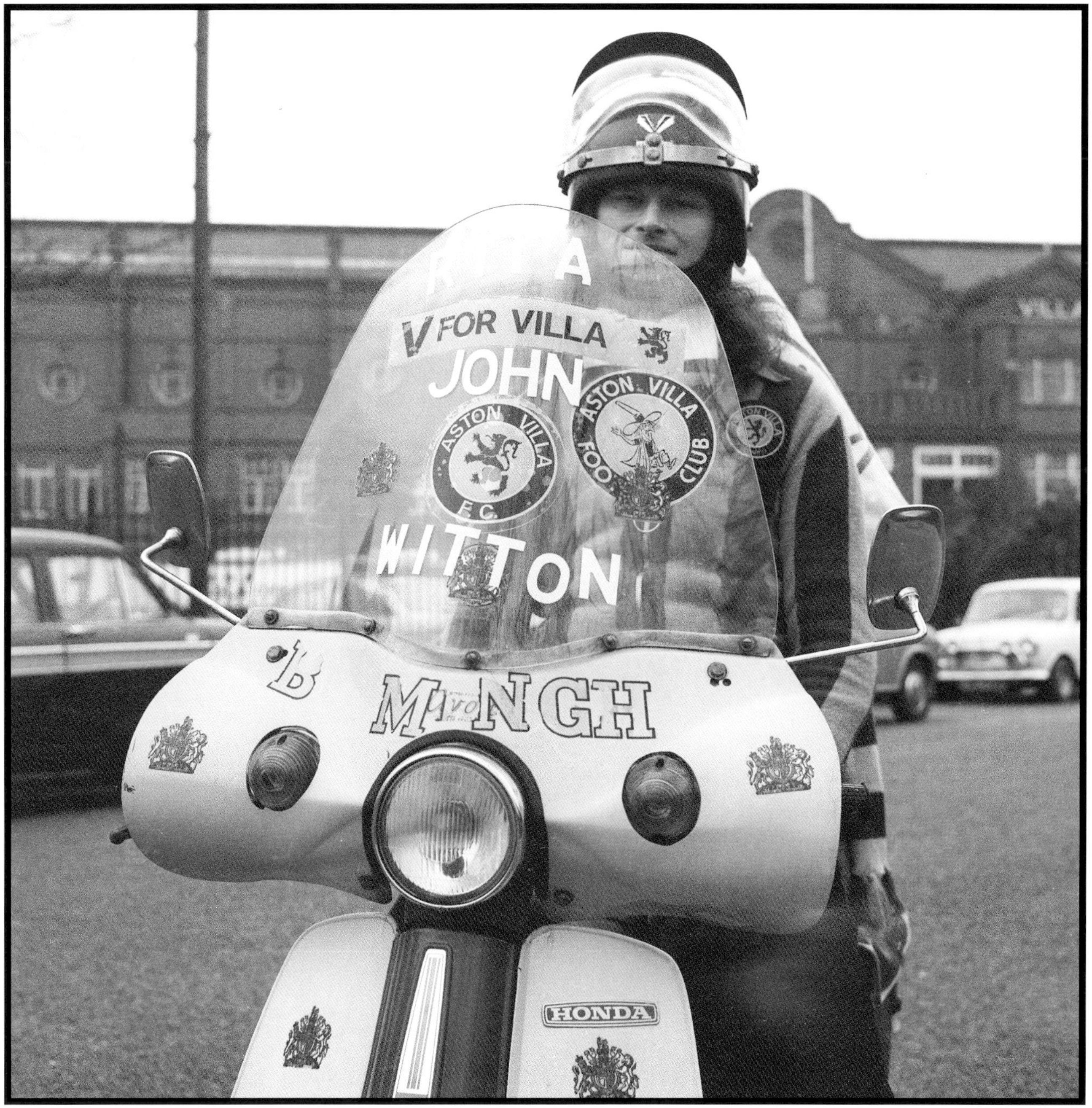

counting the cash

Once the crowd have assembled at Villa Park and the programme sellers have closed their kiosks, an important task has to be undertaken – counting the proceeds from sales of that day's Villa News & Record.

Angela Roberts is busy performing the task, with the help of a set of old-fashioned scales.

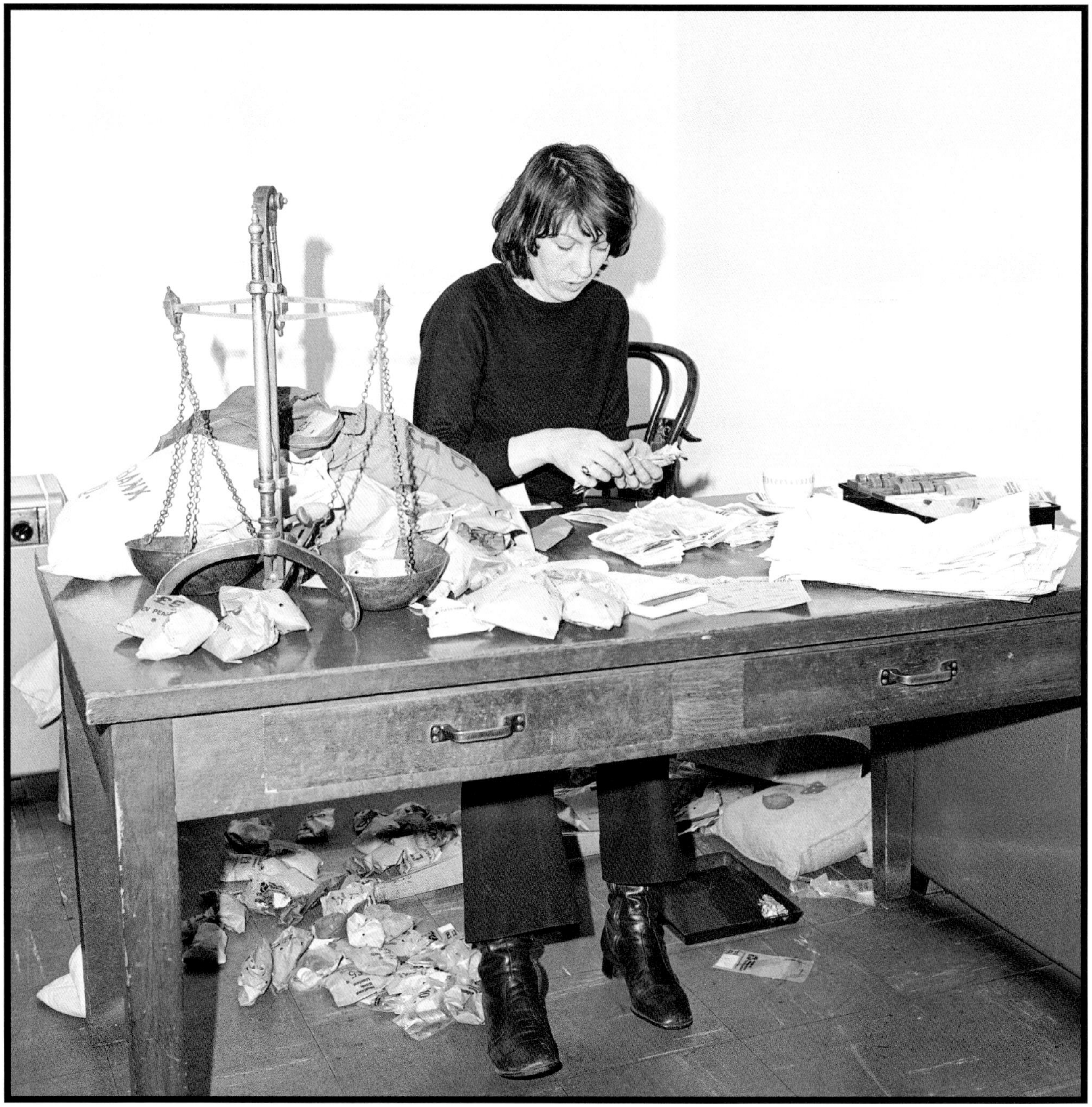

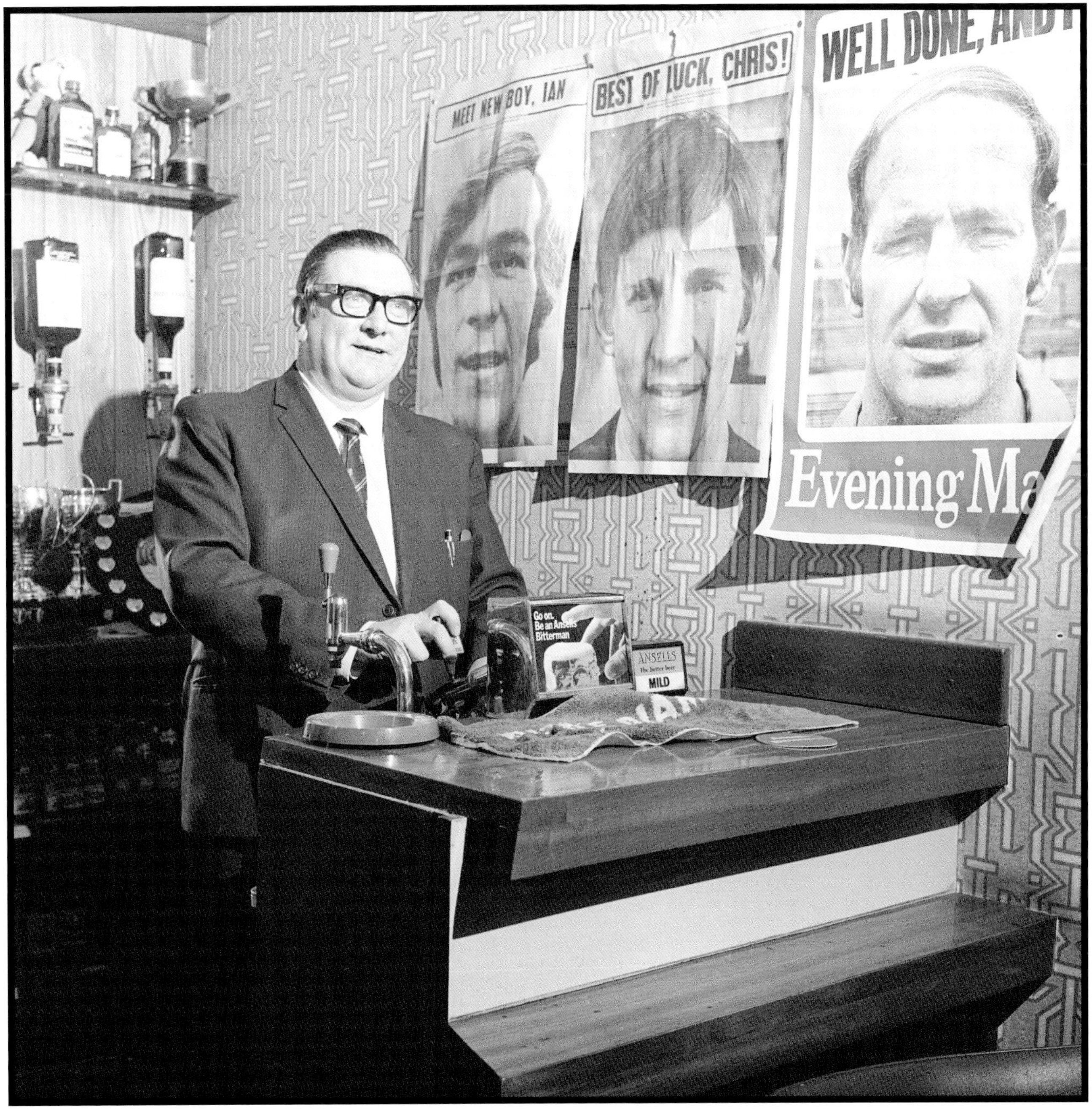

right, charlie!

This is the ubiquitous Charlie Tabberner, who ran the Lions Club with a rod of iron. Charlie was a strict disciplinarian, and if you didn't adhere to the rules of the club, you were kicked out.

To be honest, it was the only policy which was going to work in an establishment frequented by fervent football followers whose emotions sometimes ran away with them.

Charlie is pictured pulling a pint, under the watchful gaze of Ian Ross, Chris Nicholl and Andy Lochhead, whose posters adorn the wall of the bar.

we'll meet again

Villa reunions have become more and more commonplace since Neil Rioch set up the Former Players Association, but even before the launch of that much-needed organisation, old team-mates often stayed in touch when their playing days came to an end.

This group featured (from the left) Larry Canning, Jimmy Dugdale, Arthur Haynes, Stan Lynn and Roly Morris.

Arthur only made for senior appearances while Roly never played for the first team, but all the club's old boys are always made welcome.

This summer, of course, we mourned the passing of Stan Lynn, a player who had a thunderbolt shot.

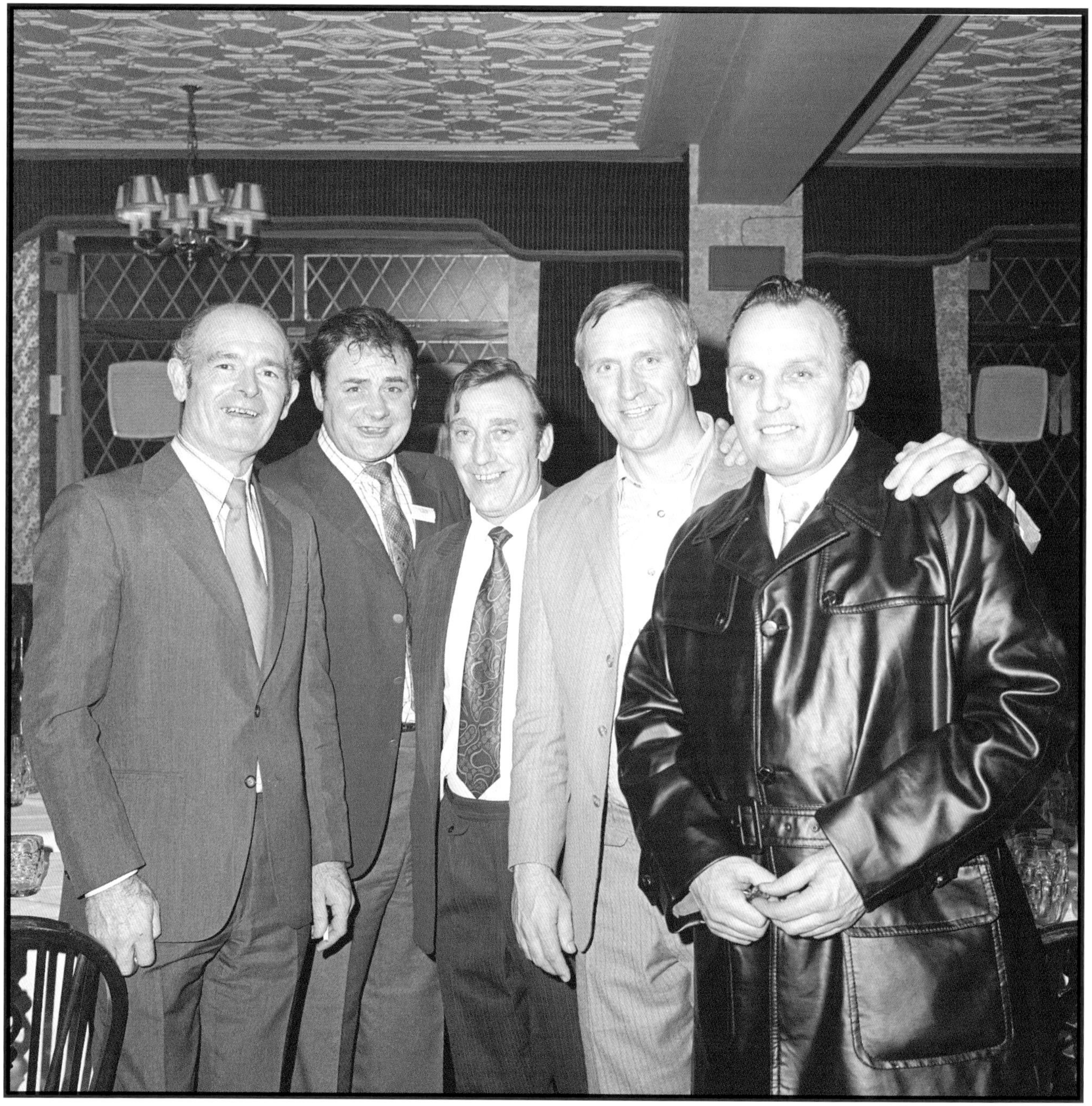

away days

Travelling to away matches has always been special, and the advent of the Travellers Club – subsequently renamed the Travel Club – meant Villa could organise transport in a proper manner.

Coaches used to leave from the Serpentine ground, now the site of the Asda hypermarket, and among the couriers was Mike Sanford, who today organises visits to Villa Park for supporters from overseas.

Mike, clipboard at the ready, welcomes John and Gill Cunliff from Sutton Coldfield and Barry and Iris Grubb from Great Barr to an excursion to Portsmouth.

I loved travelling away, and was sometimes even allowed on the team coach, although they had travelled overnight for the match on the south coast and I thoroughly enjoyed my day out with the fans.

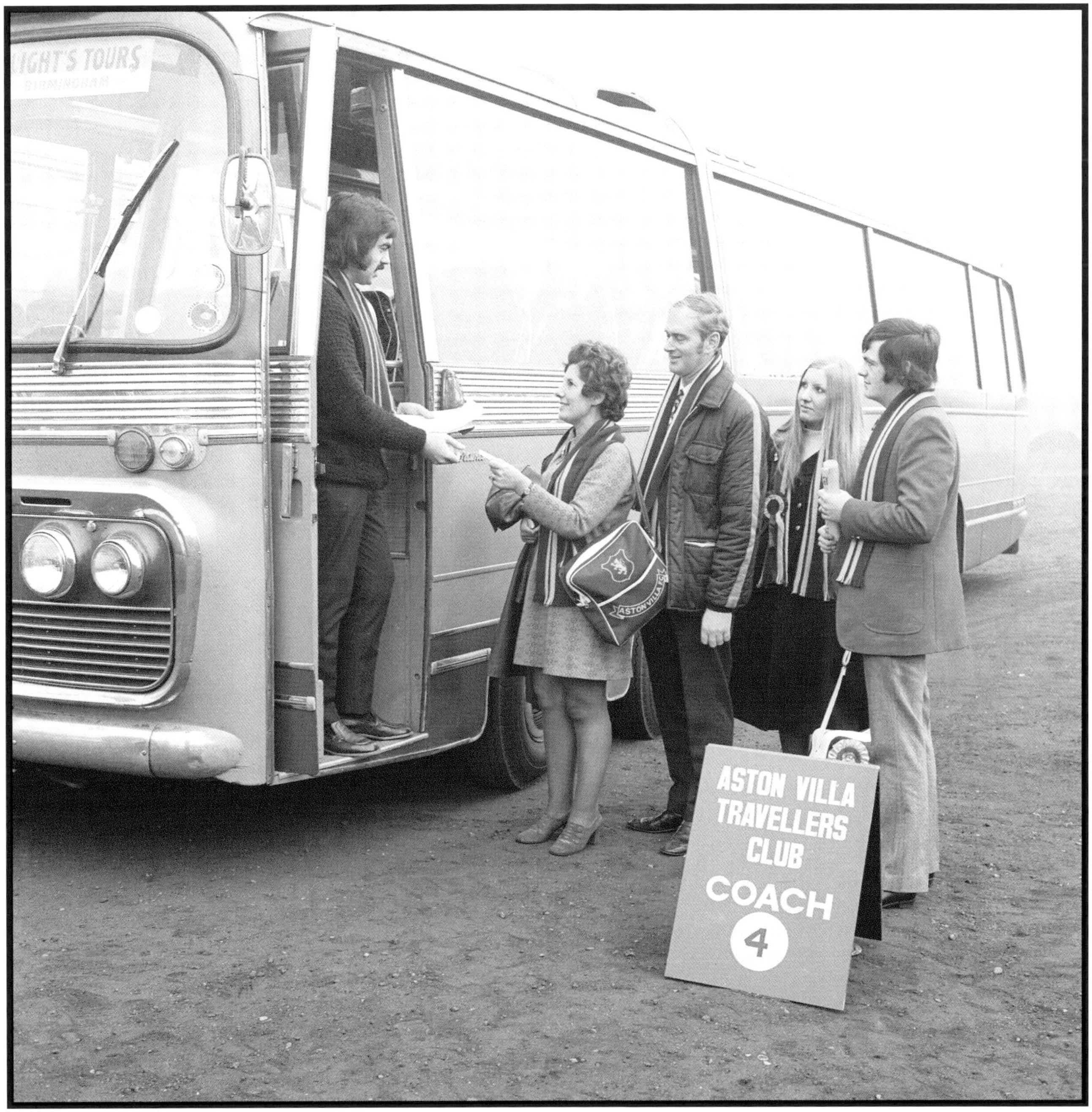

mixed support

Even when I didn't feel well, I always tried to get to Villa Park on matchday and this was one of those occasions. I had been off work all week, so it obviously wouldn't have been sensible to sit at the pitch side and make things worse.

Instead, I sat in the press box – but I couldn't resist taking a few pictures. The result was a panoramic view of the game against Queens Park Rangers, and I even managed to capture a goal – even if it was for the opposition!

You could always gauge the size of the crowd by how far people were standing towards the top of the Witton End, and if you look carefully, you can see some QPR fans celebrating. They are, of course, standing where the visiting contingent now assemble beneath the North Stand, but at that time it was very much a Villa domain

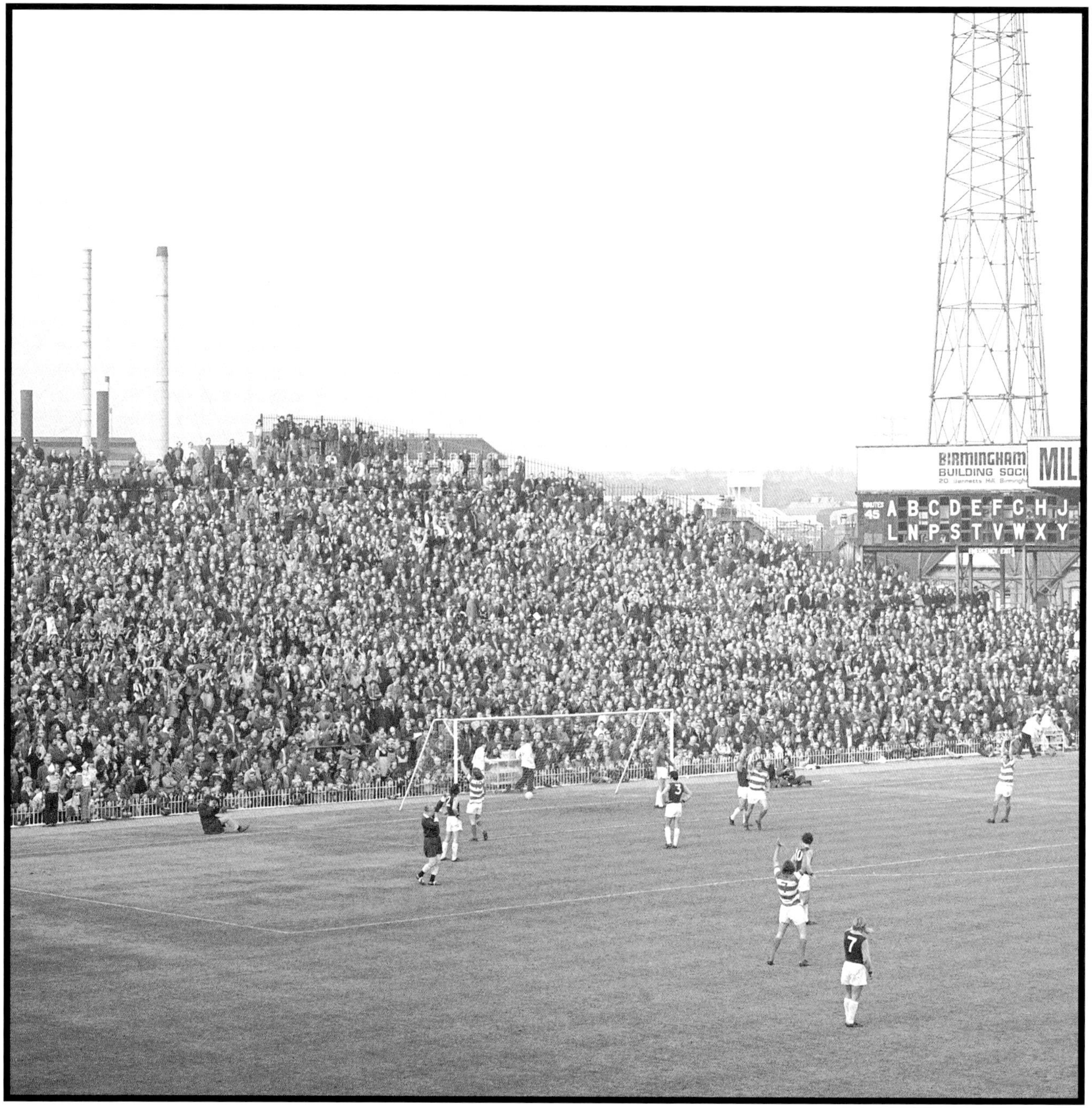

how about that!

The inimitable Eric Morecame was not only a brilliant comedian, he was also a thoroughly nice bloke and this pose epitomises his vivacious approach to life.

I had taken a photo of him with Villa directors on a previous visit to Villa Park and I reminded him of that when he returned with his beloved Luton Town.

Eric agreed to pose again before making his way up the stairs to his seat in the directors' box. He would have been in similarly jovial mood after the match, too – the Hatters beat Villa 2-0.

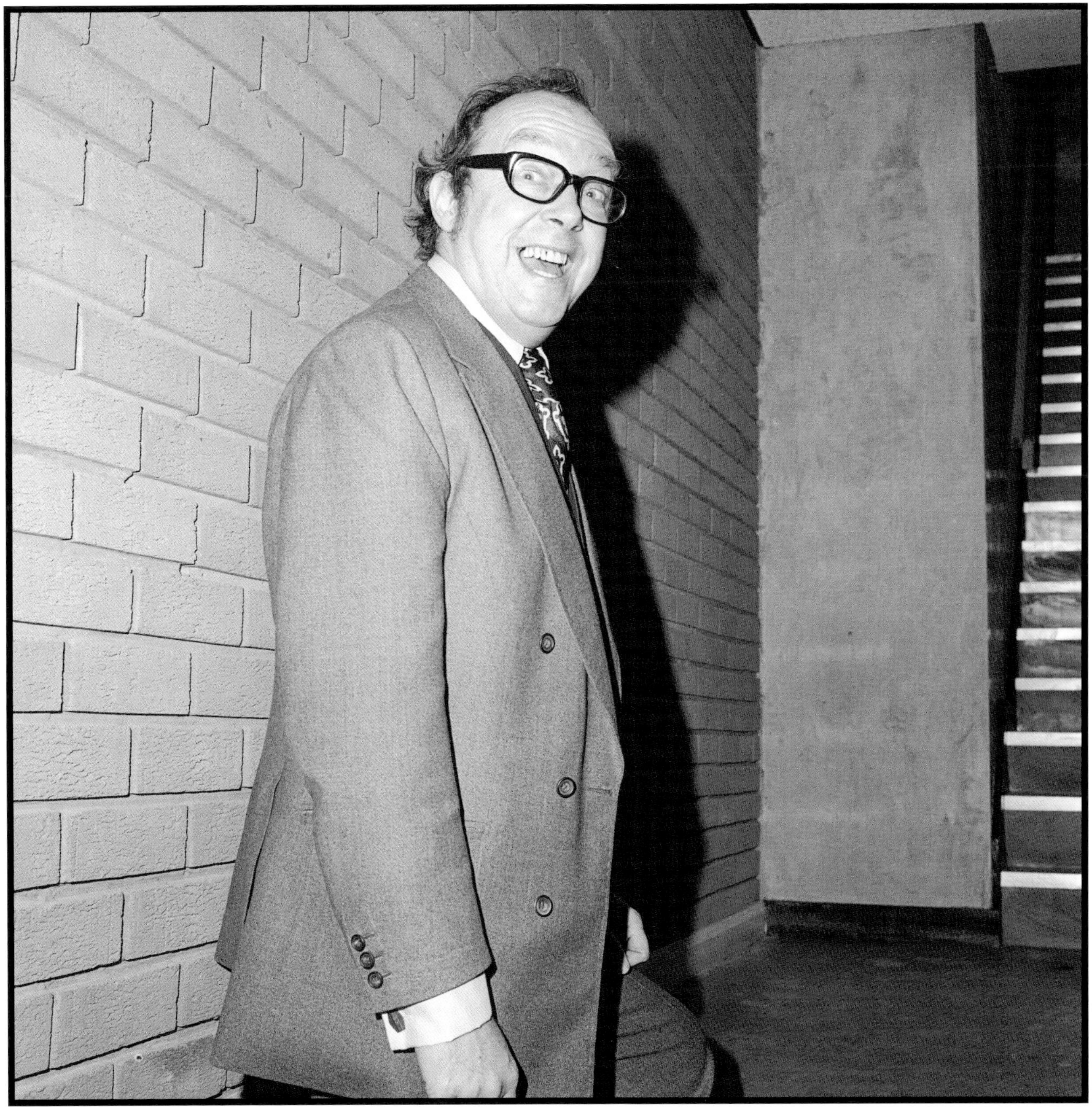

wear your colours

A familiar sight outside any football ground is that of vendors selling rosettes – often without a licence.

This lad was possibly one of them because he gave me a suspicious look as I took his picture and asked: 'What you looking at, mate?'

And if I wasn't too popular with this 'pirate' seller, the club were none to impressed when I offered the picture for possible publication in the Villa News & Record.

I was told, in no uncertain terms, that the club were not about to promote the sale of goods from which they made no money!

With the advent of official club merchandise, I should imagine unofficial sellers have a tough job drumming up trade these days.

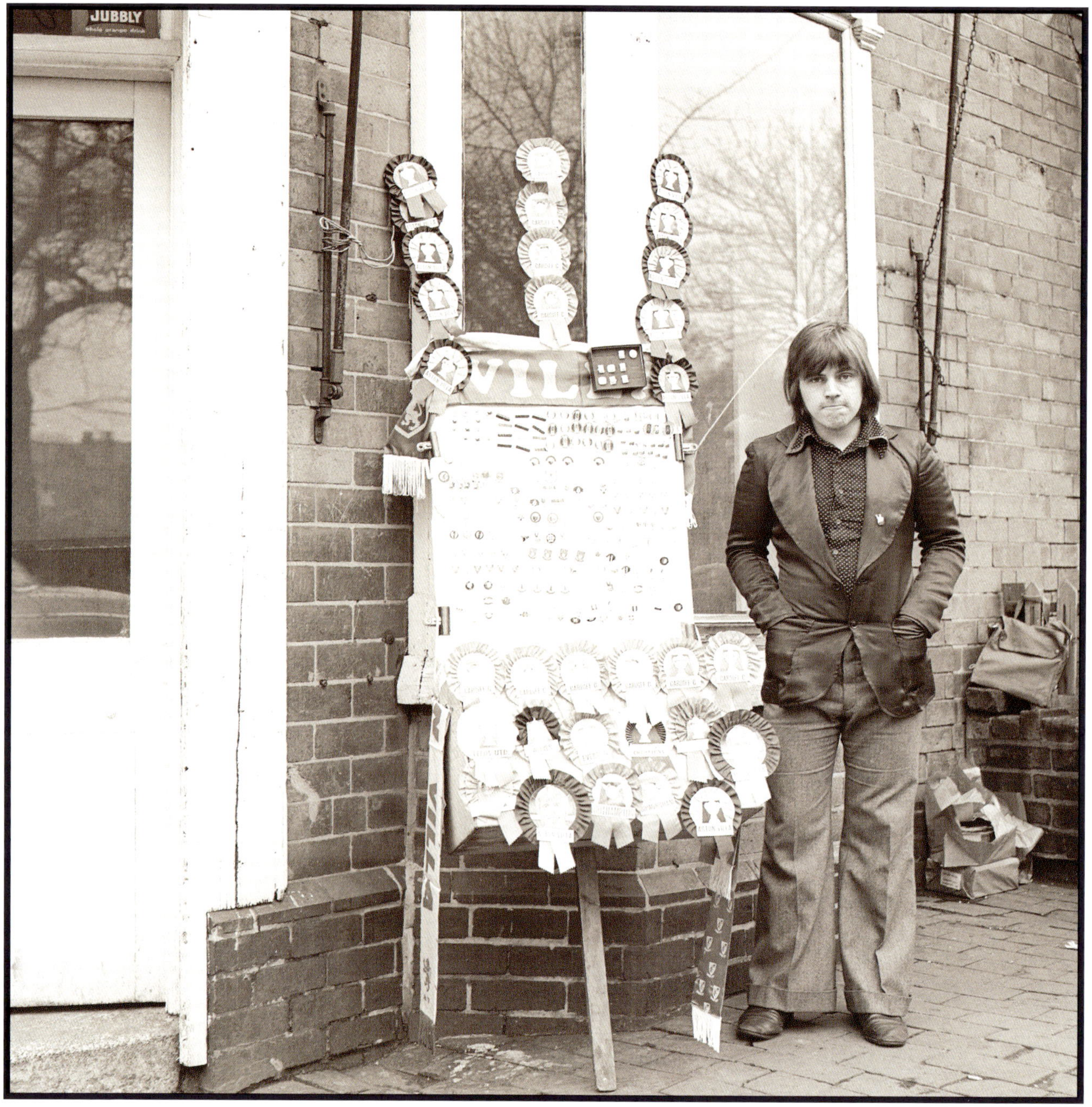

pump up the volume

Some supporters are more vocal than others in backing their favourite team, and this guy took some beating when it came to pumping up the volume.

He used to stand on the Holte End and yell 'Up the Villa' and the top of his voice, prolonging the final syllable so that it became 'Up the Villaaaaaaa'.

At times, you thought it would go on forever, and the crowd around him used to love it. He travelled to away matches, too, and kept his fellow fans amused , even when things were not going well on the pitch.

No-one can recall his full name, but I'm sure he was called Albert. Needless to say, he was quite a character.

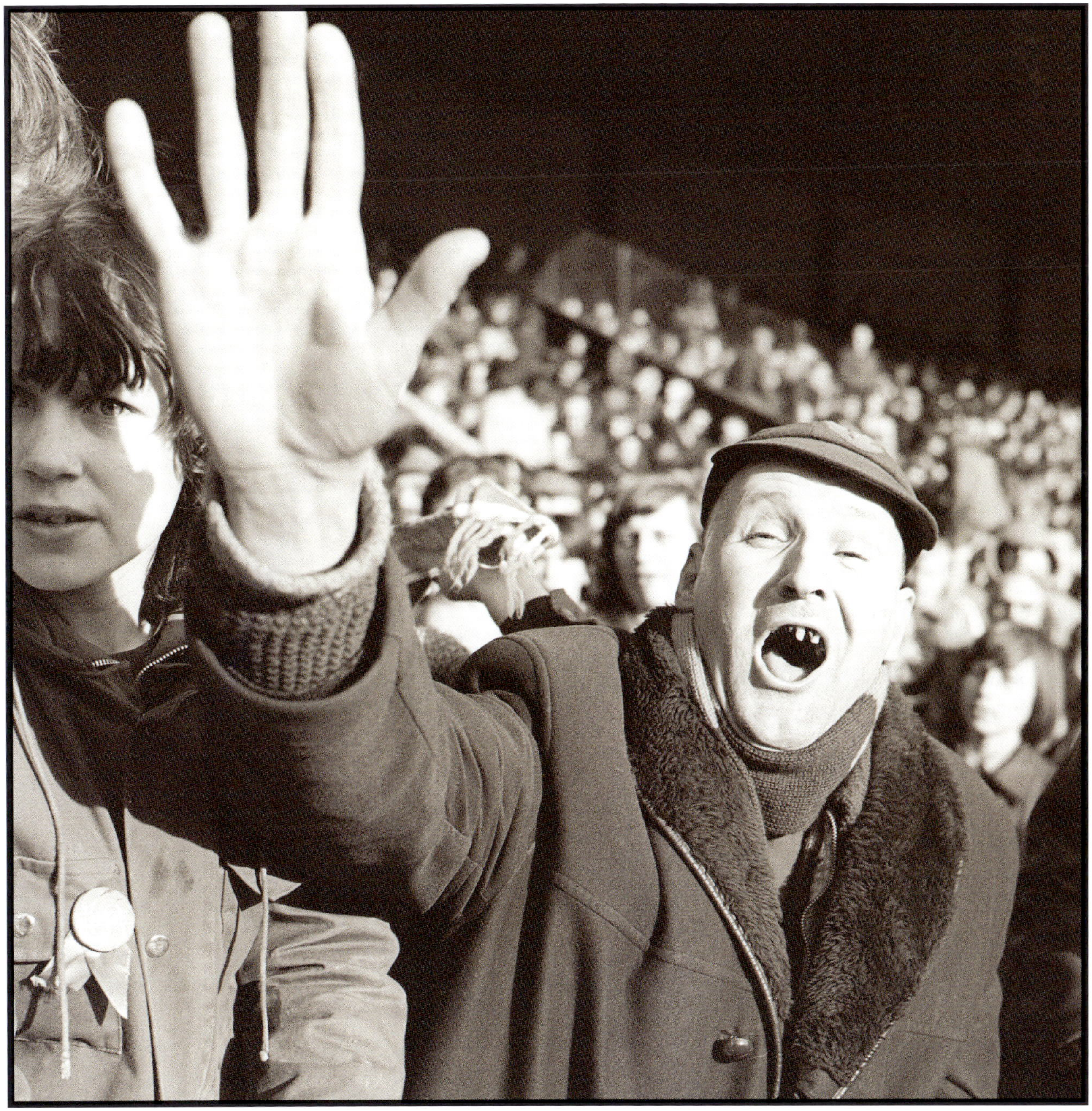

breaking glass

This was an all-too-common occurrence in the 1970s – a smashed coach window. To be sitting next to a window which suddenly smashes is a terrifying experience and I'm sorry to say it happened on a fairly regular basis during an era when football hooliganism was at its height.

Such incidents usually happened as coaches left away grounds and if it wasn't possible to patch up the damage, it was a case of travelling home with unwanted air conditioning, which was no fun at all on a cold winter evening.

On this occasion, though, the window was smashed not long after the coach had parked at White City before a match against Queens Park Rangers at Loftus Road.

I never mentioned this sort of unsavoury business to my wife Annie – she would have put the block on me travelling to away games.

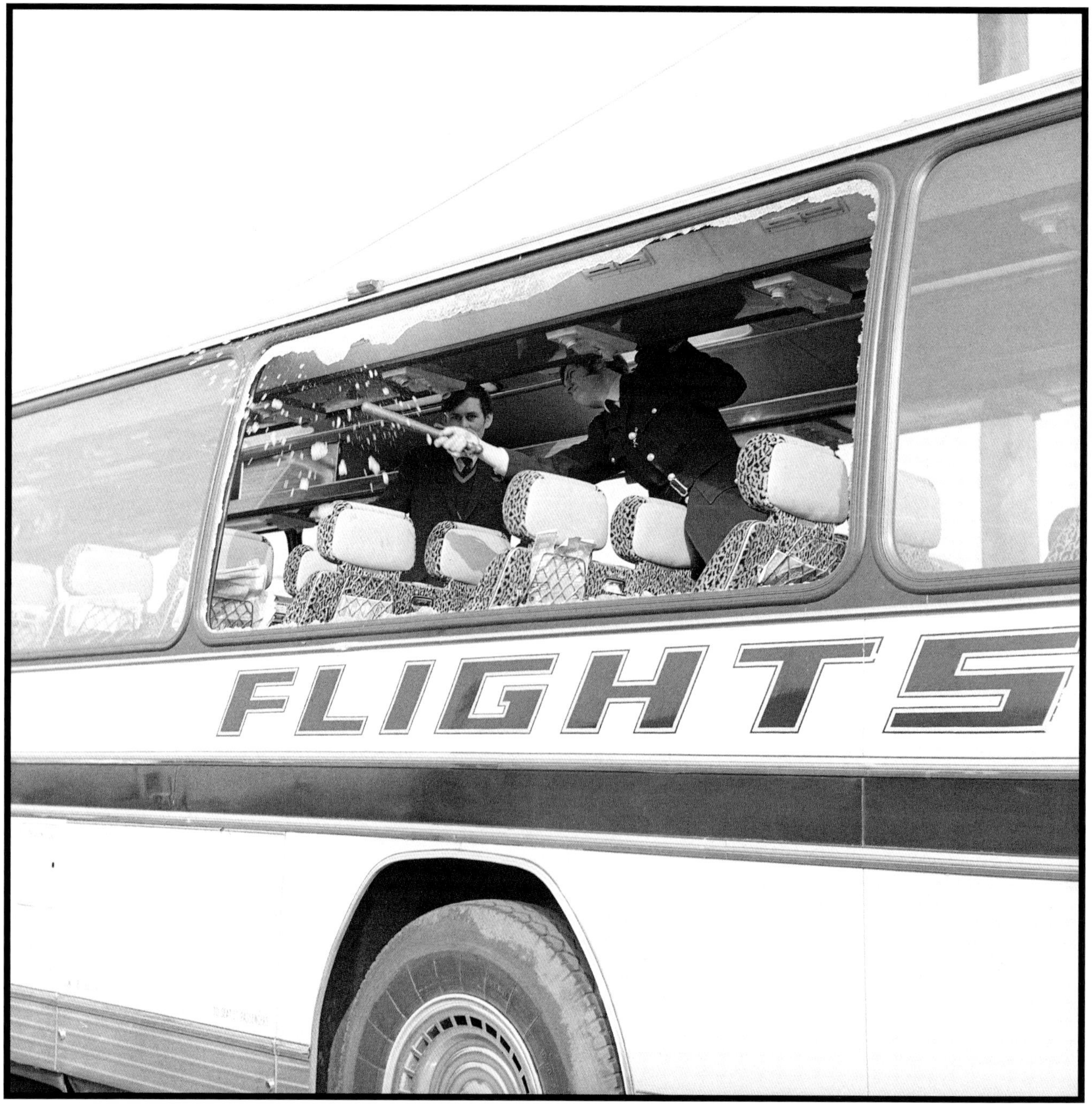

sitting tight

Policemen on duty at Villa Park and other Midland grounds usually paraded around the touchline before kick-off and then disappeared from sight unless they were required to deal with crowd disturbances.

This officer, though, sat on his plastic chair throughout the match during a Villa trip to London. I seem to recall this was the Clock End at Arsenal when it was still an open terrace and although the policeman has a rather serious expression on his face, he at least engaged in a touch of banter with me.

When I told him he had the best job in the country, he said that was rich coming from me. 'Yes,' I said, 'but I'm not on double time!'

I couldn't help but feel sorry for the youngsters standing behind him. These days, they would have paid a reduced admission charge for their restricted view.

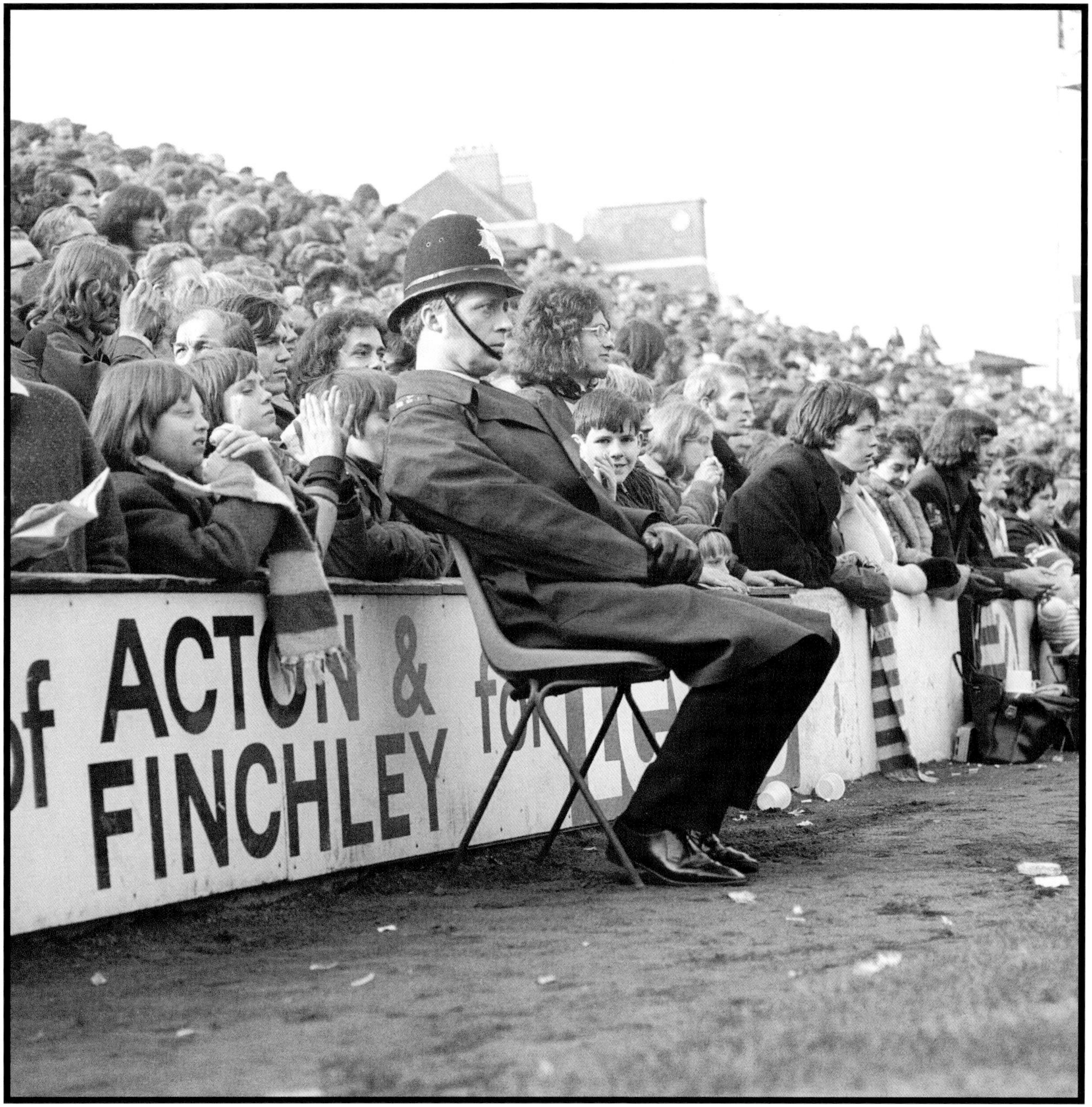

the name game

Supporters sometimes take their devotion to extreme lengths, like the couple from Oldbury who decided to name their son after the whole of the Villa team.

The young man in question, pictured here with his mum during the 1973-74 season, looks somewhat bewildered by the sight of all the wording on his passport details – Ian, Thomas, James, Christopher, Alan, Michael, Victor, Charles, Raymond, Ronald, Bruce, Jeffrey, David Smith.

His father was Private Ken Smith of the Worcester and Sherwood Foresters Regiment, and the passport details – featuring Villa players and managers – were submitted to the British Consulate in Berlin, where Ken was based.

As a wedding photographer, I'm aware of just how embarrassed Ian must have been if he got married and all his names were read out at the ceremony. At least Ken didn't fall into the trap of using players' surnames, which some fans have done over the years.

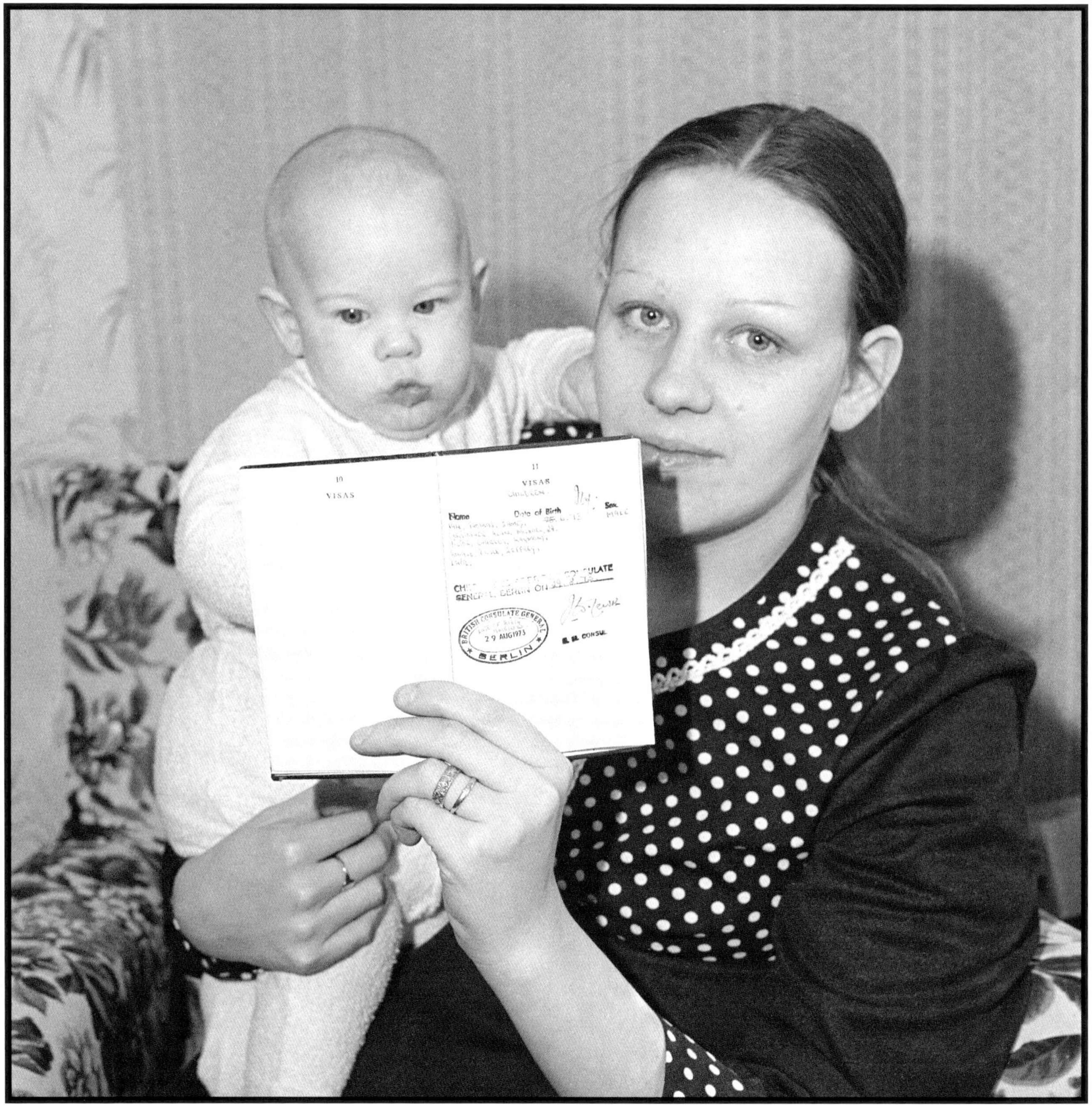

a question of light

Holte Enders might be a little miffed that my crowd shots invariably feature regulars at the Witton End, but the reason is perfectly simple.

Before kick-off, I was always situated near the tunnel in readiness for presentations and other promotional events, and Villa invariably kicked that way in the first half – as they still do today, of course.

By the time I got to the Holte End for the second half, the light wasn't so good, and photographic conditions were not helped by the shadow from the roof of the stand.

This attractive young lady, resplendent in wild west gear, was throwing sweets to supporters. It wouldn't happen now – there are regulations about not throwing missiles into the crowd!

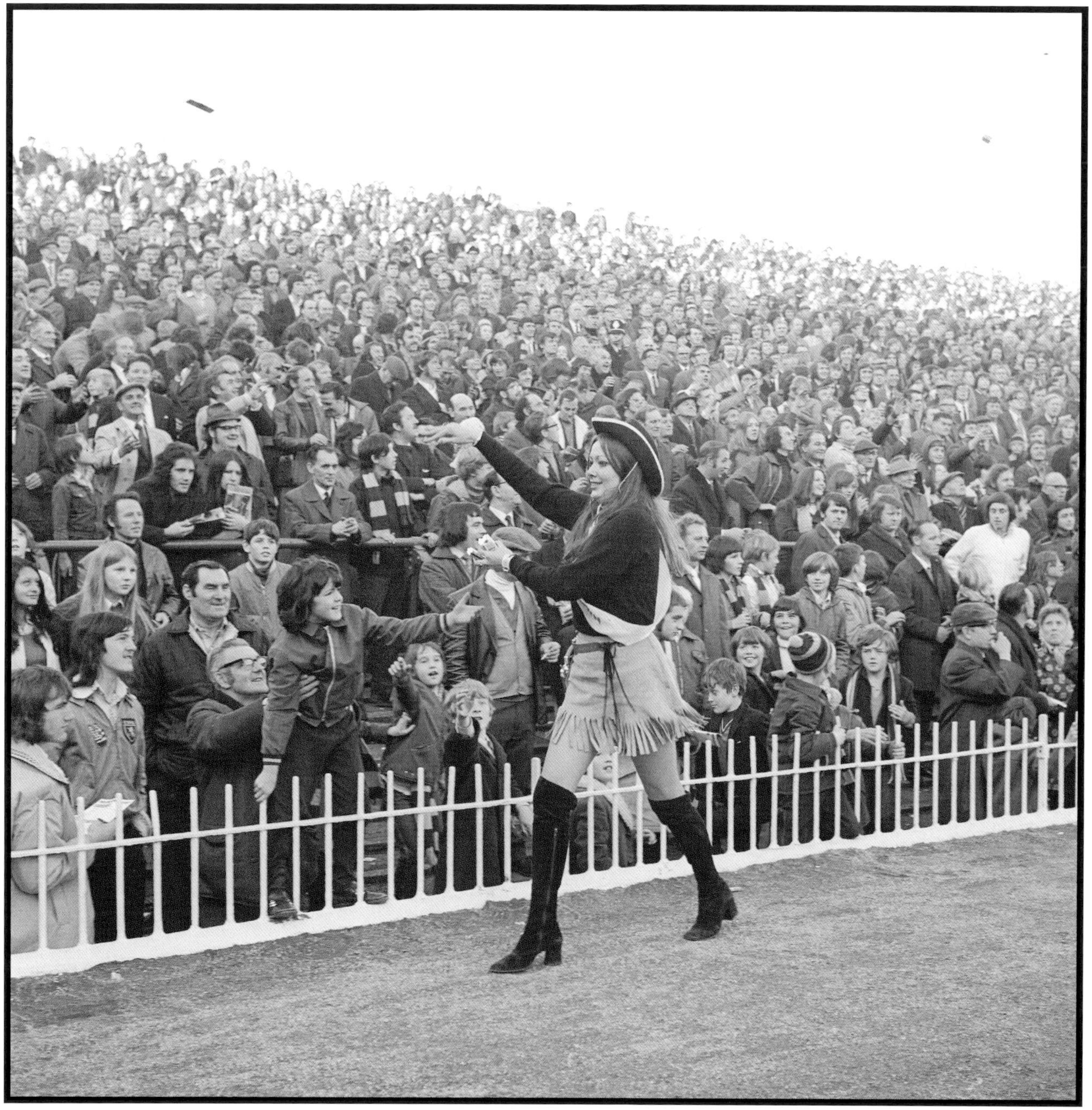

germany calling

In January, 1973, Villa landed quite a coup when Bayern Munich came to Birmingham for a friendly. At that time Bayern were undoubtedly the top side in Europe, while we were in the old Second Division.

On the Monday evening, I went along to Birmingham Airport (the old terminal at Elmdon) to get pictures of the Germans arriving on British soil, and I captured striker Gerd Muller with his bag of duty free goods. Muller, of course, was the man who knocked England out of the 1970 World Cup with his extra-time goal in the Mexico quarter-final.

Two other German legends, Franz Beckenbauer and Uwe Seeler, were also among the visiting party and I got them and Muller to sign a Villa programme – a souvenir I still have today.

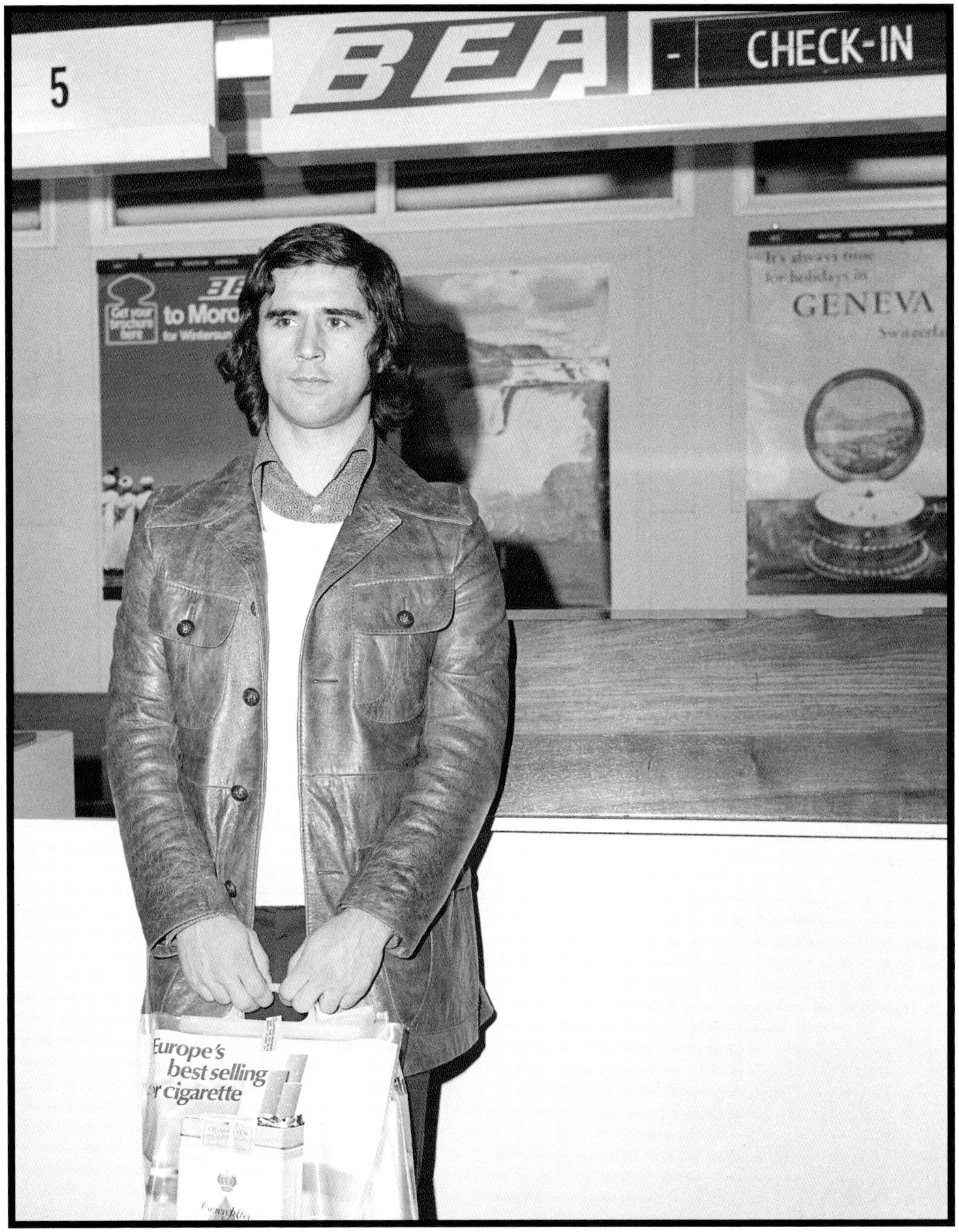

kings of the road

Villa's support, both home and away, was absolutely phenomenal during the early 1970s, and the sight of dozens of coaches in convoy was incredible.

Numerous clubs had to put up the 'sold out' signs when Villa went visiting for Third Division matches.

The line of coaches stretching down Trinity Road, in the shadow of the Holte End, seems endless as the claret and blue army prepare for another day out.

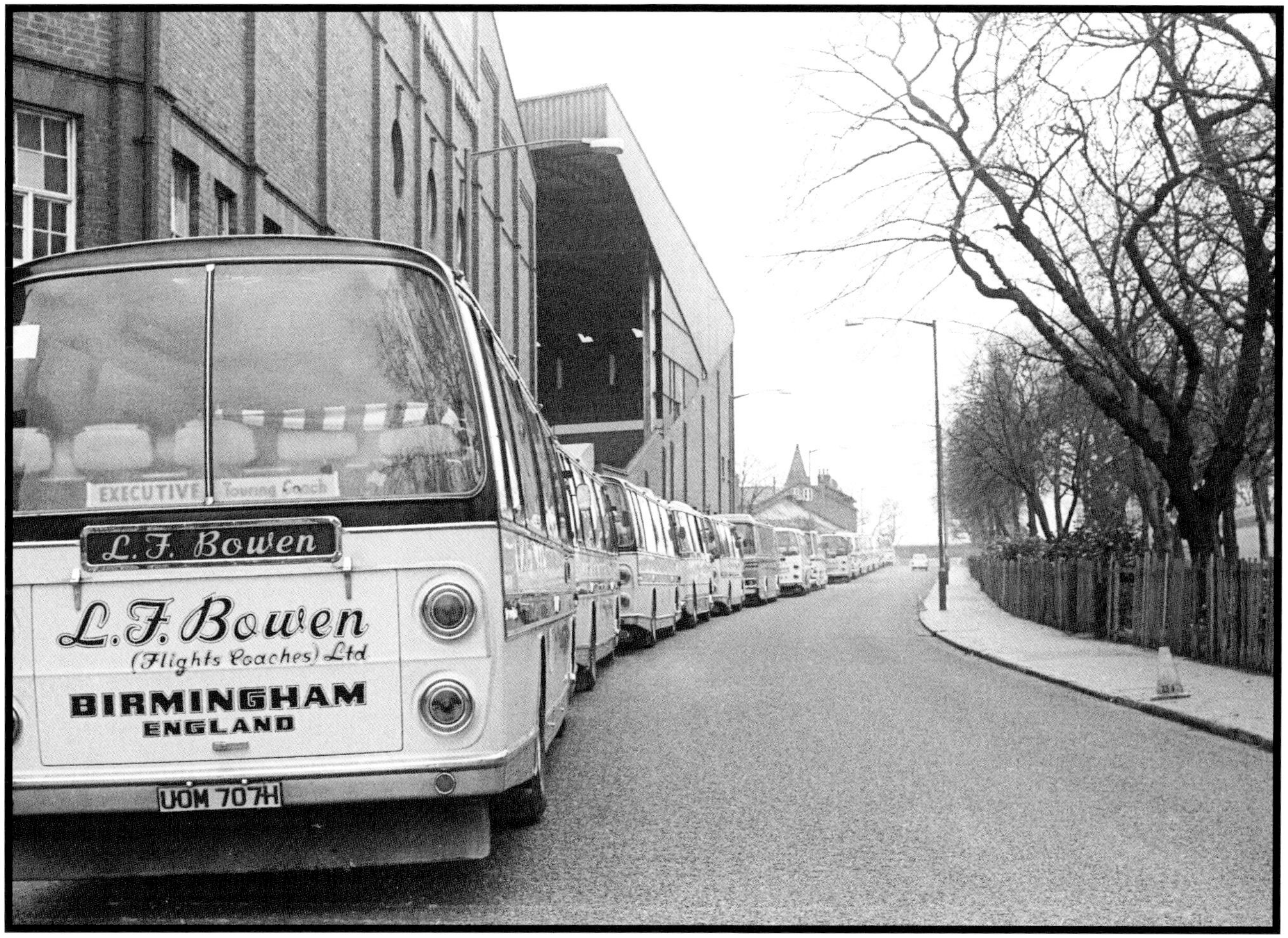

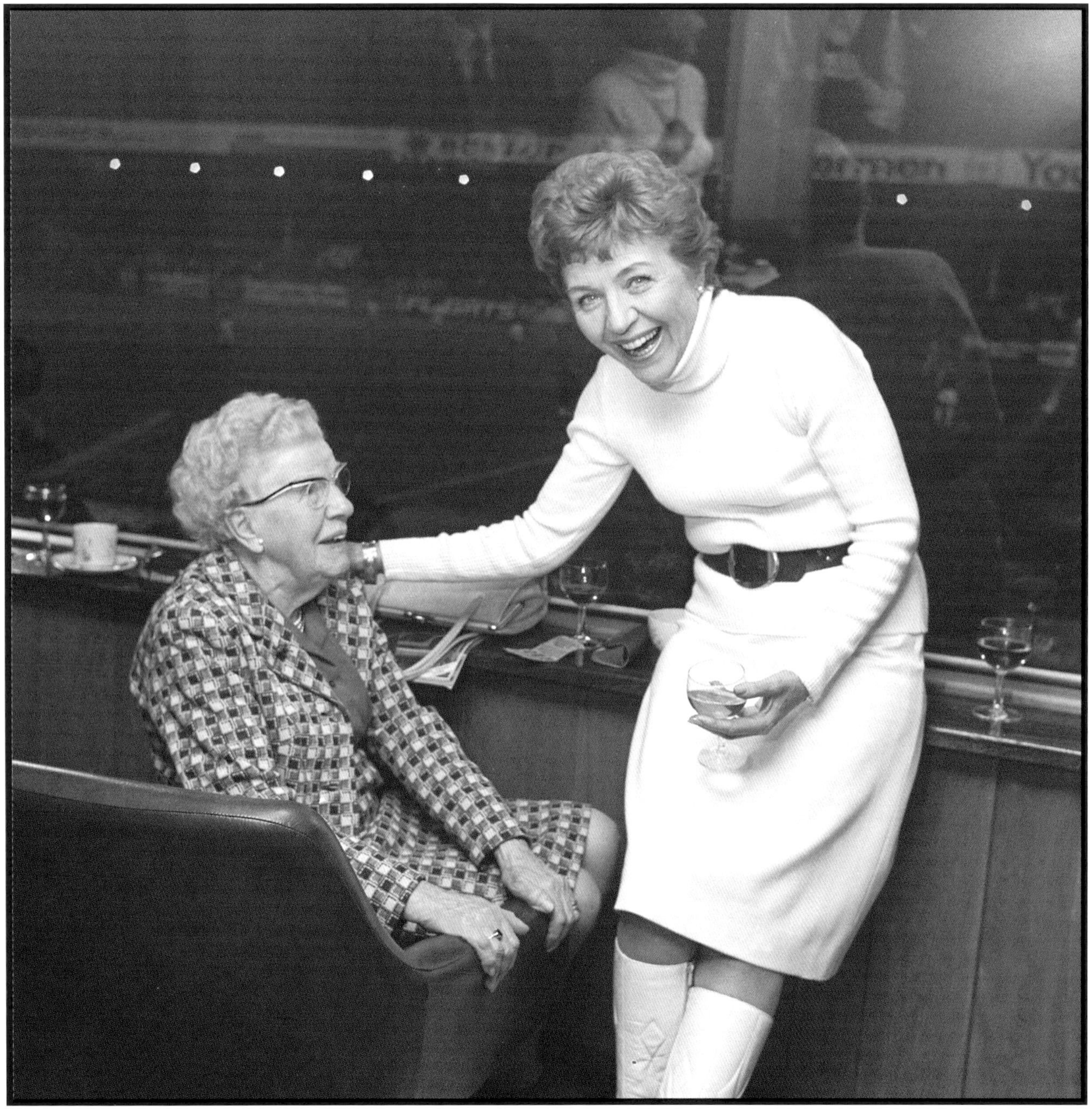

at the crossroads

The divine Noele Gordon was the duchess of the Midlands in her role as Meg in Crossroads during the 1970s and she was also a frequent visitor to Villa Park – usually as a guest in the executive box used by Pauline and Bob Jones of Sutton Coldfield.

A West Ham supporter who adopted Villa, Noele is pictured enjoying a post-match drink with her mother. She was a lovely, lovely lady, who left us far too soon.

leap to it

It's the first day of pre-season training at Bodymoor Heath, and this quartet of players, with Bobby McDonald on the left, are engaged in a spot of leaping practice.

Either that, or Ron Saunders had stamped his foot so hard that the shock forced this group to almost jump out of their skin! Bobby McDonald and Charlie Young are the two players facing the camera, but I have to admit I'm struggling to identify the other two high-fliers. Any suggestions?

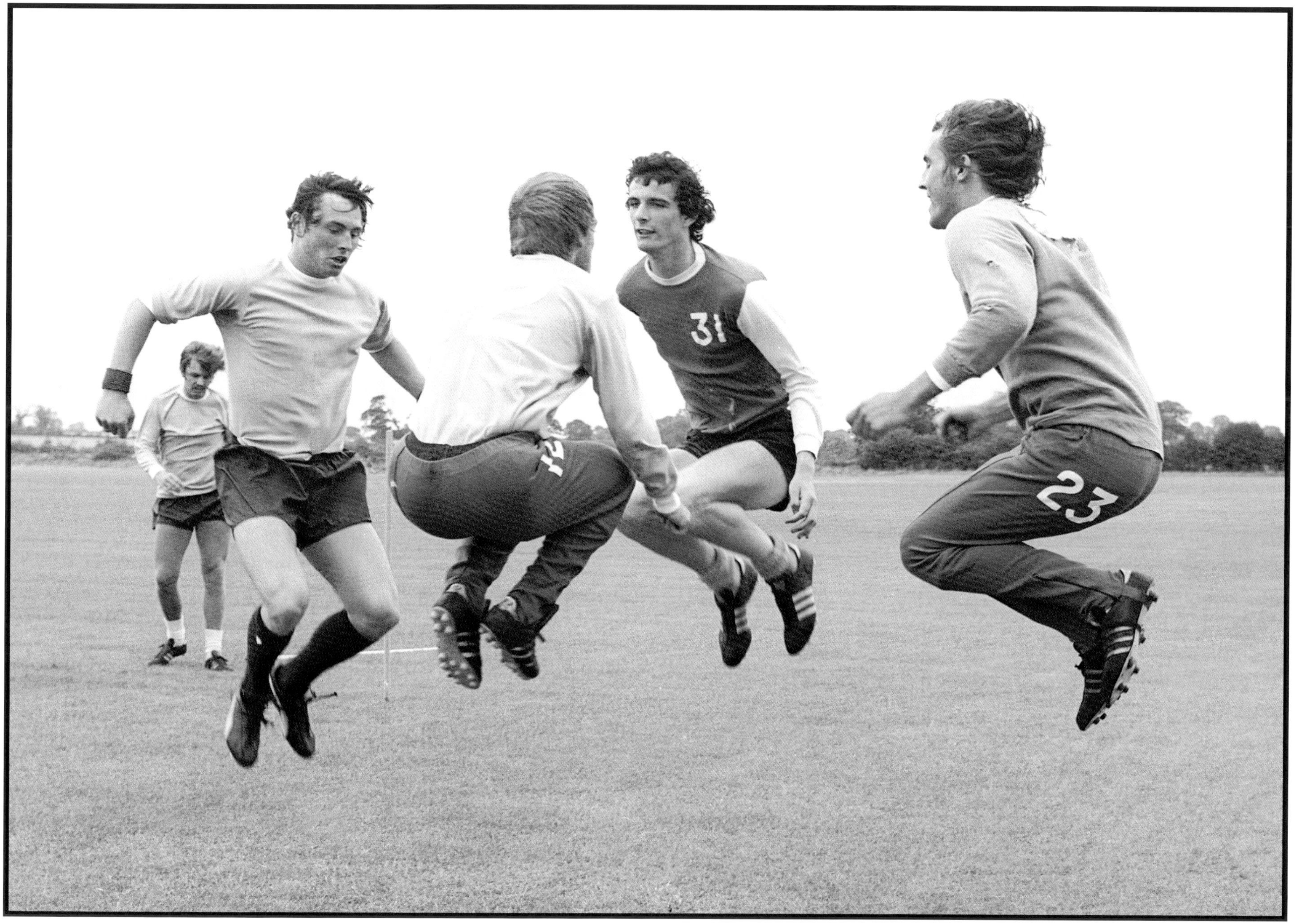

toes in the water

The winter of 1971-72 was a grim time for this country, dominated as it was by the miners' strike, the three-day working week and frequent power cuts.

The energy crisis meant that everyone was encouraged not to be wasteful, even when it came to using hot water. That's why youth players John Overton (left) and Tony Betts are soaking their feet in the same bowl as they relax after a match.

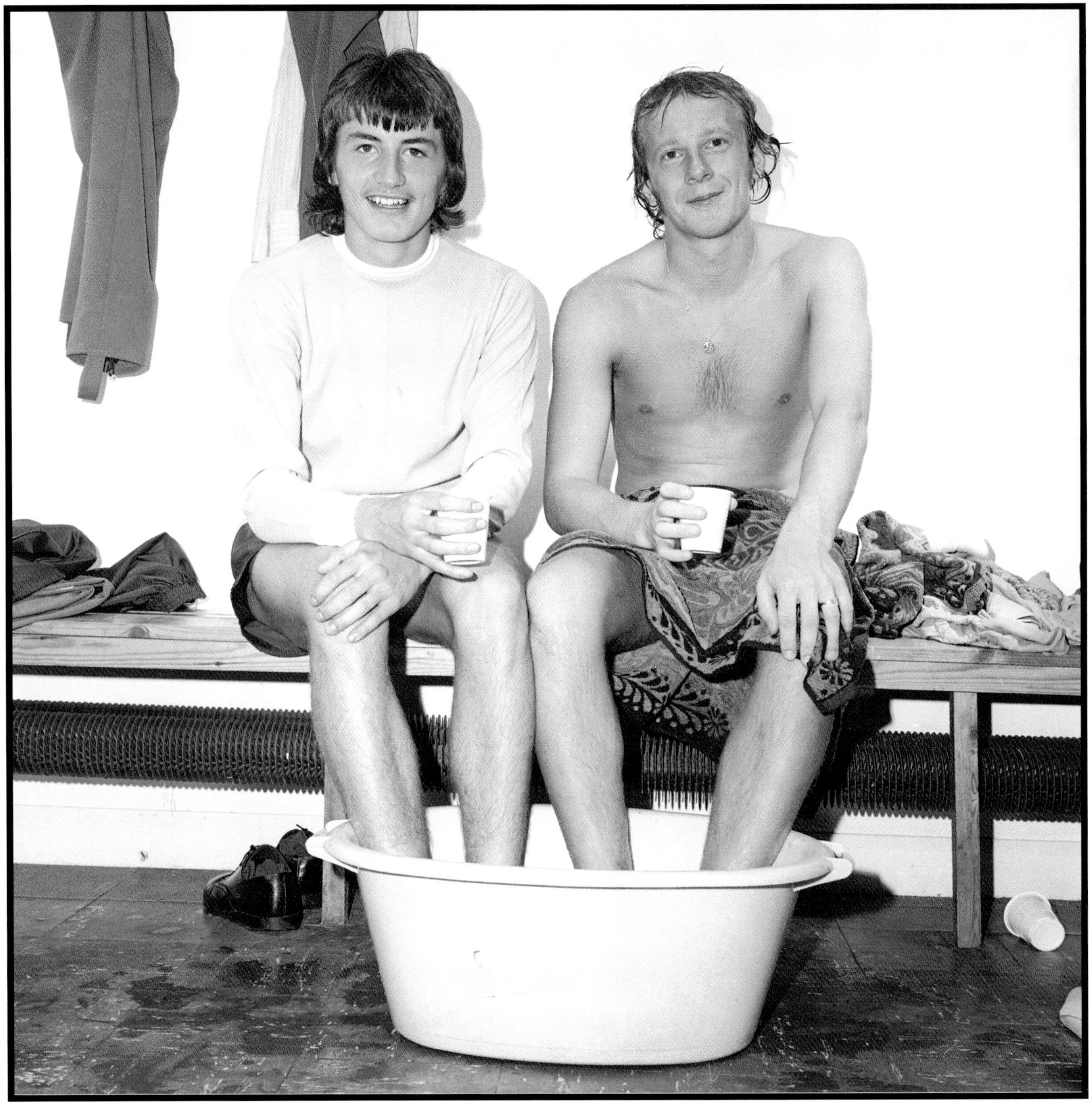

in the dug-out

The dug-out is an area which invariably attracts a lot of attention from youngsters who are almost as interested in what is happening on the sidelines as as they are in events on the pitch.

This shot at a Villa away match features physio Fred Pedley, manager Ron Saunders and striker Alun Evans, who obviously didn't make the squad that day.

Presumably, the curious quartet of young lads leaning on top of the dug-out settled down before kick-off. If not, I'm sure Mr Saunders would have had a word or two to say to them!

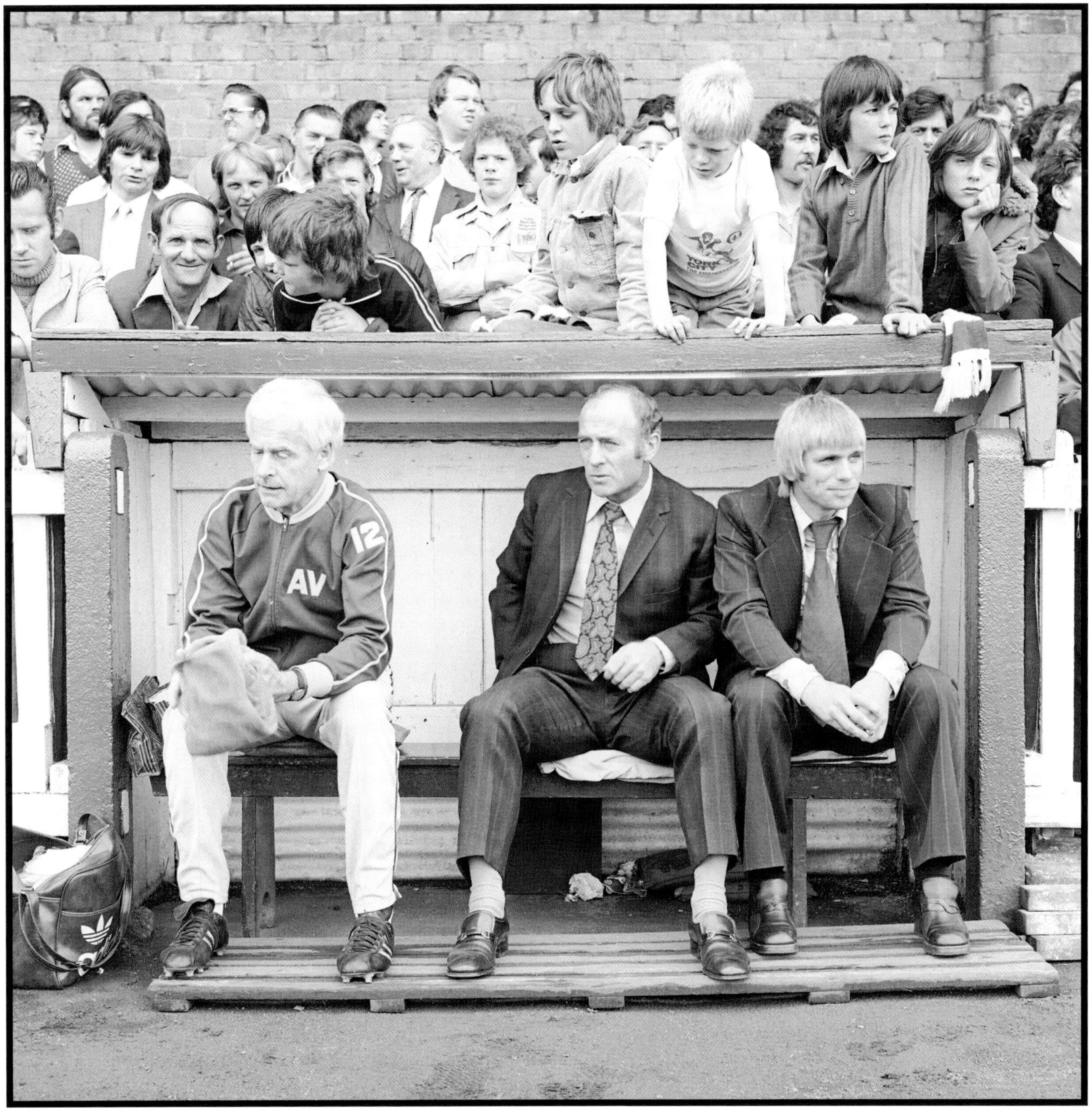

a stolen moment

A famous landmark in Villa's history – the shop in the centre is the one from which the original FA Cup was stolen in September, 1895.

At that time the shop, in Newtown Row, Birmingham, belonged to William Shillcock, a boot and shoe manufacturer, but by the time I took this shot the building was due for demolition.

My father was born about half a mile away from this famous site and my mother was born even closer to it. Dad used to tell me the story of how the Cup was stolen and as a boy I actually went into the building with my mum, when it was a butcher's shop.

Aware that the bulldozers would soon be moving in, I decided the run-down building needed to be a part of my photographic collection.

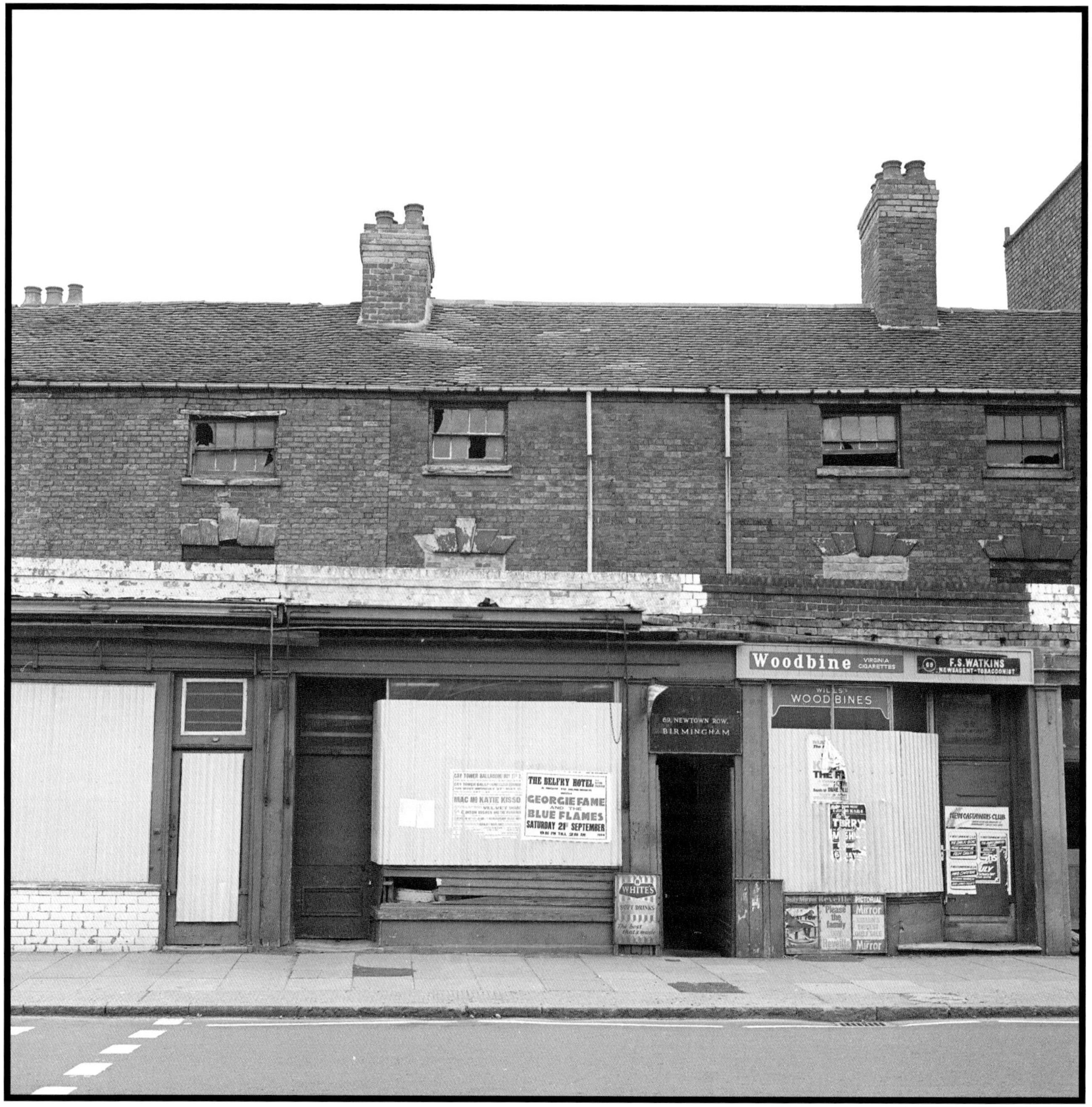

hey, baby!

Proud father Chris Nicholl, a key figure in Villa's defence during the mid and late 1970s, proudly shows off his baby daughter Cathy just a few days after she was born.

Photographs of babies always have an obvious appeal, although they can sometimes create problems.

Very often, when a picture of a player with his son or daughter appeared in the programme, it would cause discontent among the wives of other players whose babies had not been featured. With a squad of 20-somethings, there were inevitably a fair few births, and there was always the risk that one or two would slip through the net.

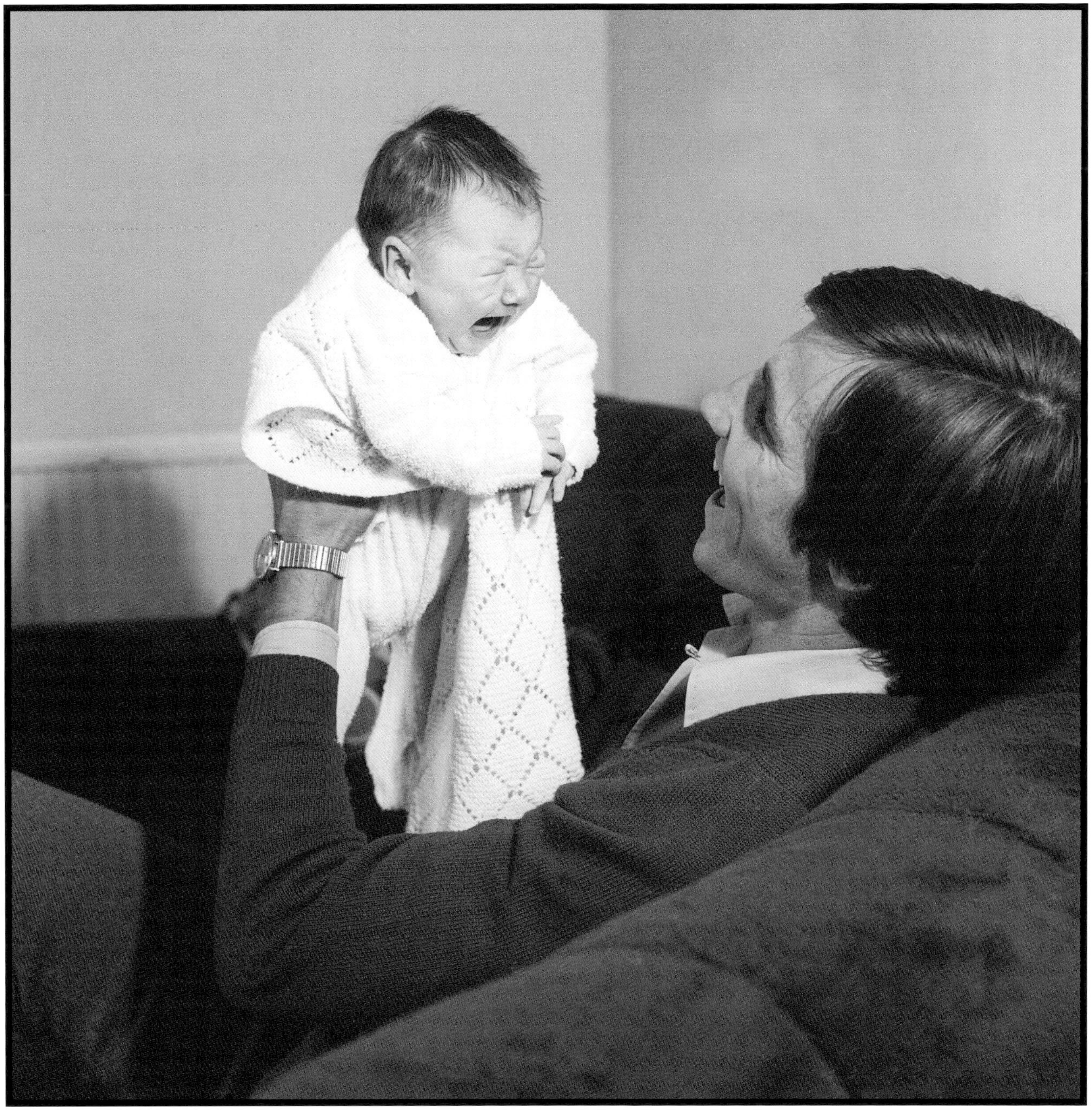

top gear

A lady phoned the club one day to say she had spent hours knitting a Villa jumper for her son, and would we like to take a photograph?

The obvious picture was a 'full frontal', but we decided it made more sense to take a rear view shot which displayed a footballer design together with the words Aston Villa.

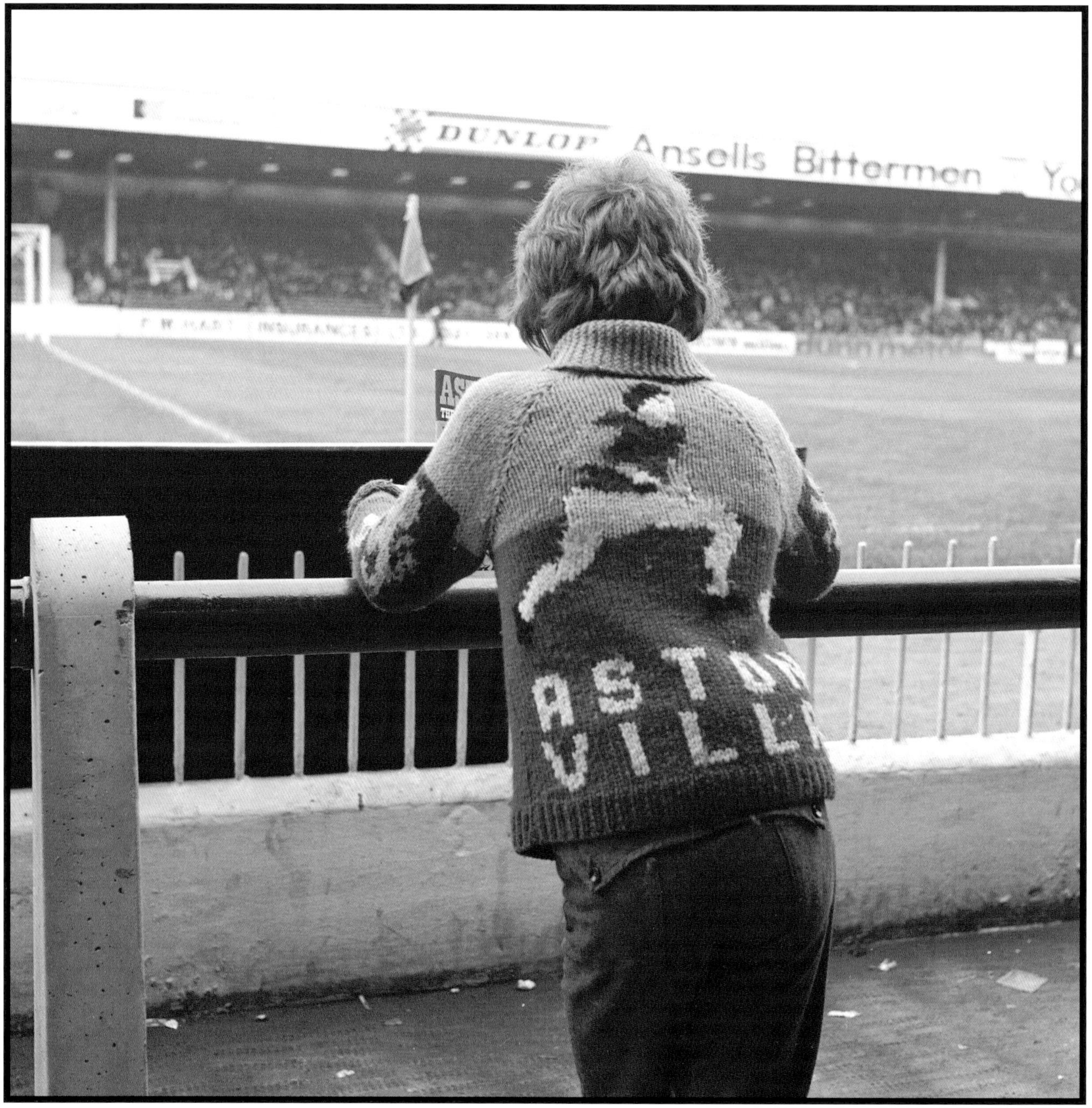

star gazer

Alan Price has the broadest Geordie accent I've ever heard, but for some reason he had strong connections with Fulham, and I captured him relaxing during a Villa match at Craven Cottage.

Alan had made his name as a member of the group The Animals in the 1960s and later forged a successful career as a solo singer.

As a jazz fan, I wasn't particularly overwhelmed at meeting him, but it was a different story when I came face to face with Bobby Moore just before kick-off. Moore, England's captain when we won the 1966 World Cup, willingly agreed to pose for me when I explained I worked for Villa.

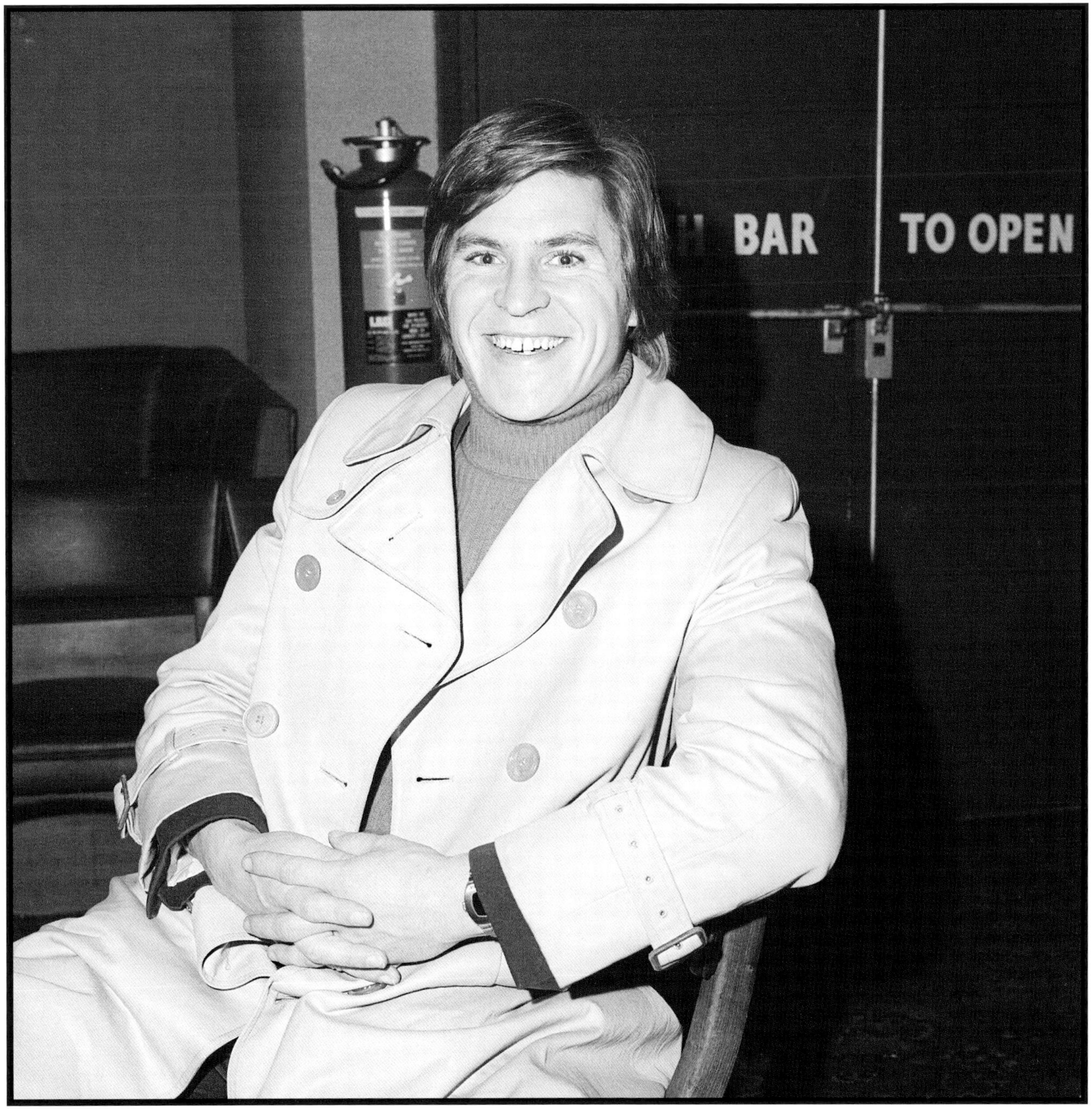

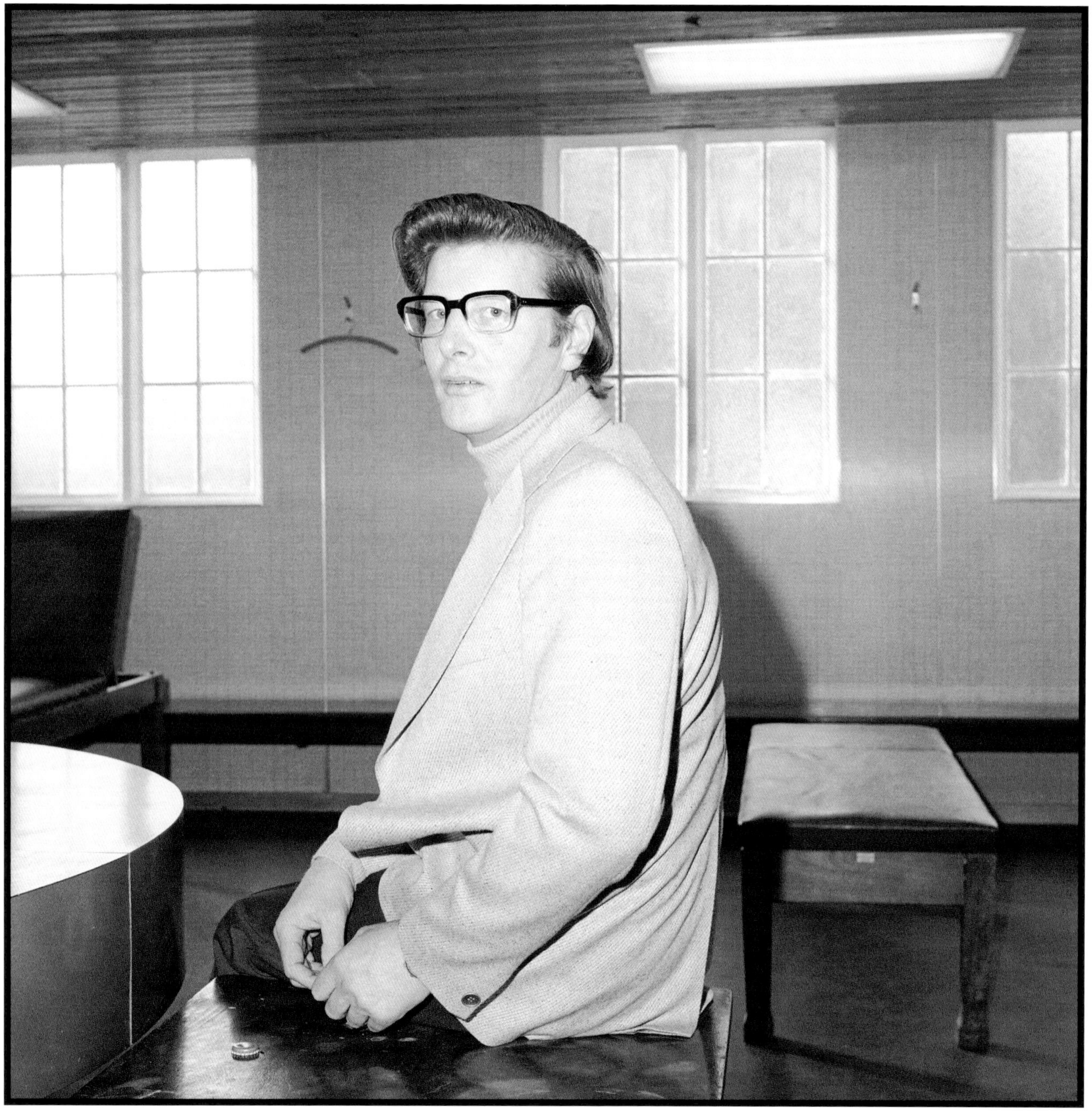

what's up, doc?

Doctor David Targett was Villa's medical officer, primarily concerned with the welfare of the players, but he always took time to enquire after my health. He often told me I was overdoing things and suggested that I should take things a little easier.

A smashing guy, who loved telling and listening to jokes, Doc Targett was hugely popular with the players and everyone else on the staff, and was particularly close to Steve Stride.

It was a great tragedy when he died in May, 1997, suffering a brain haemorrhage just after returning from a match at Middlesbrough.

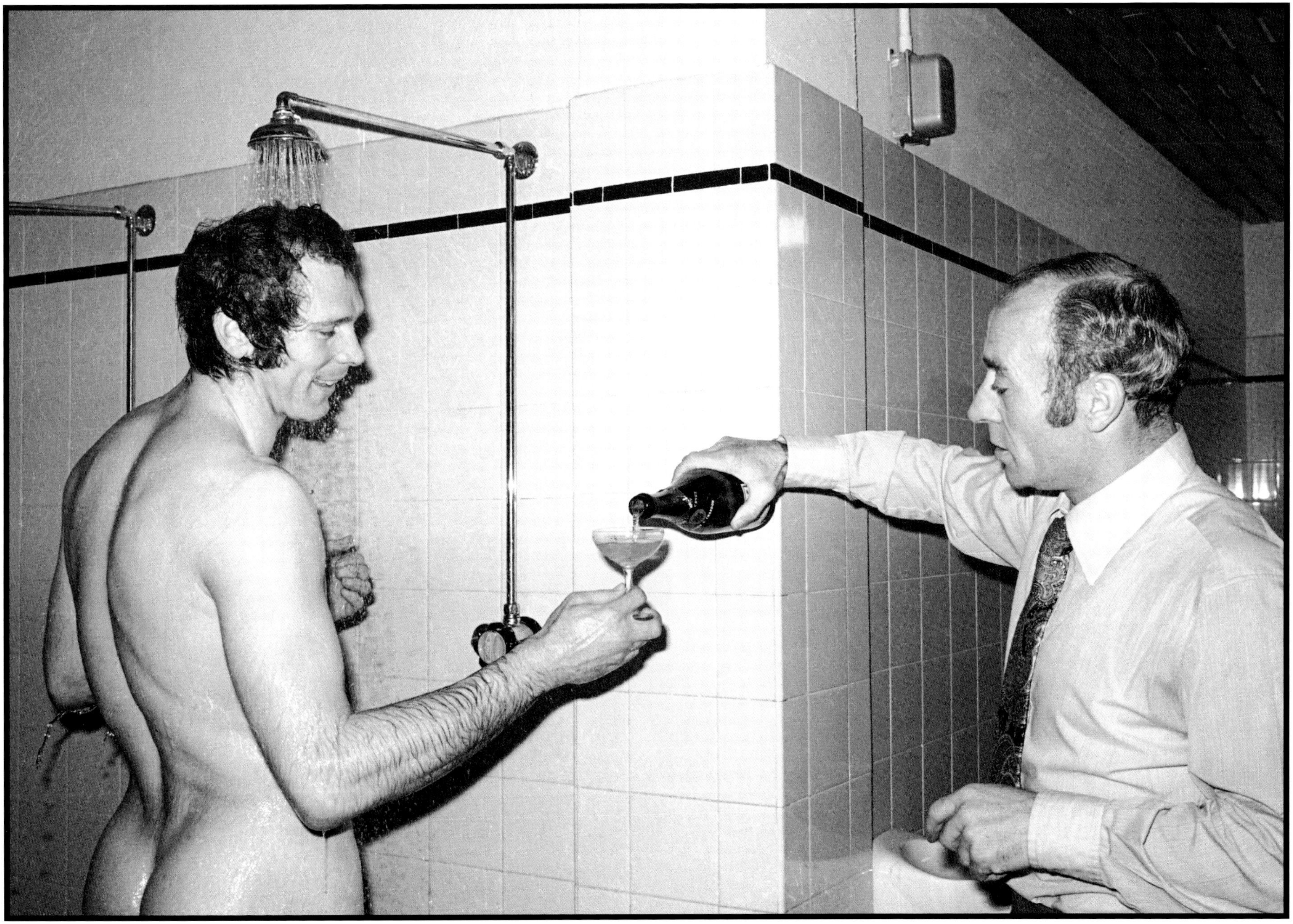

champagne celebration

We're on our way to Wembley, and what better way to celebrate than with a good soaking – both inside and out?

Villa had just beaten Chester City the 1975 League Cup semi-final, and goalkeeper Jimmy Cumbes couldn't wait to celebrate, so manager Ron Saunders obliged by pouring him a drop of bubbly in the showers.

I reckon I could have made a bob or two from this picture – at that time Playboy magazine were offering good money for candid shots of people in the news.

A few people have also suggested we should have published the picture full length, but Mr Cumbes would not have taken kindly to that. Bottoms up, Jimmy!

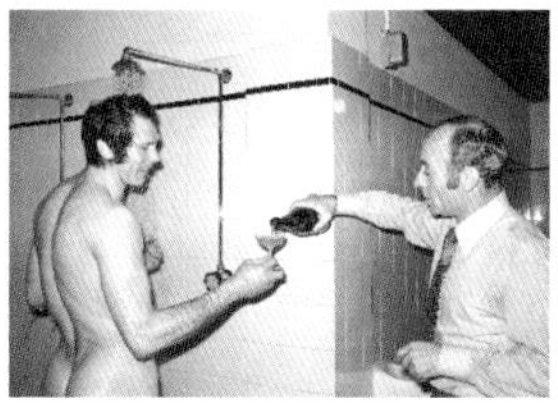

terrace tots

If I was asked to compile a Top Ten of my photographs, this would definitely be in there – both for artistic and sentimental reasons. Whenever I look at the faces of these young supporters, it reminds me of when I was first taken along to Villa Park.

If you've ever stood down at the front of the terracing peering through the railings (or over the wall in later years) you will know how this angelic-looking duo must have felt.

This is where so many youngsters have literally cut their teeth as Villa supporters, many of them having had a chew of the railings while watching the match!

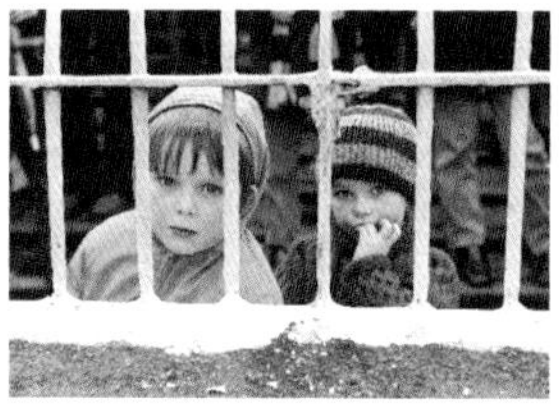

posing in the park

This group picture was taken in Aston Park during the build-up to the 1975 League Cup final against Norwich City.

By that stage, I'd got to know the players very well, and I just told them to turn up in casual clothes for a photo which was used in their souvenir brochure for the big game. They won 1-0 at Wembley and went on to win promotion to the top flight, playing some exciting football.

From the lack of leaves on the trees, you can tell that it's still wintertime, and this enabled me to get the image I wanted, with Villa Park in the background.

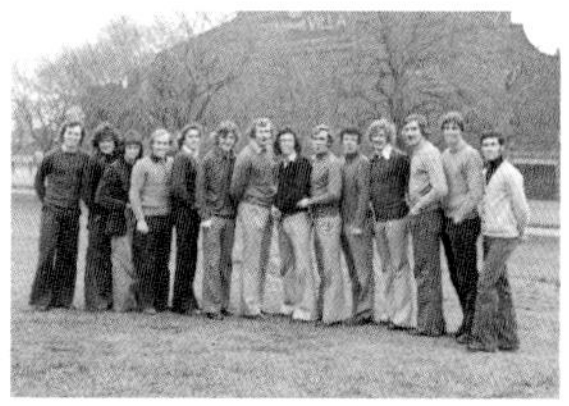

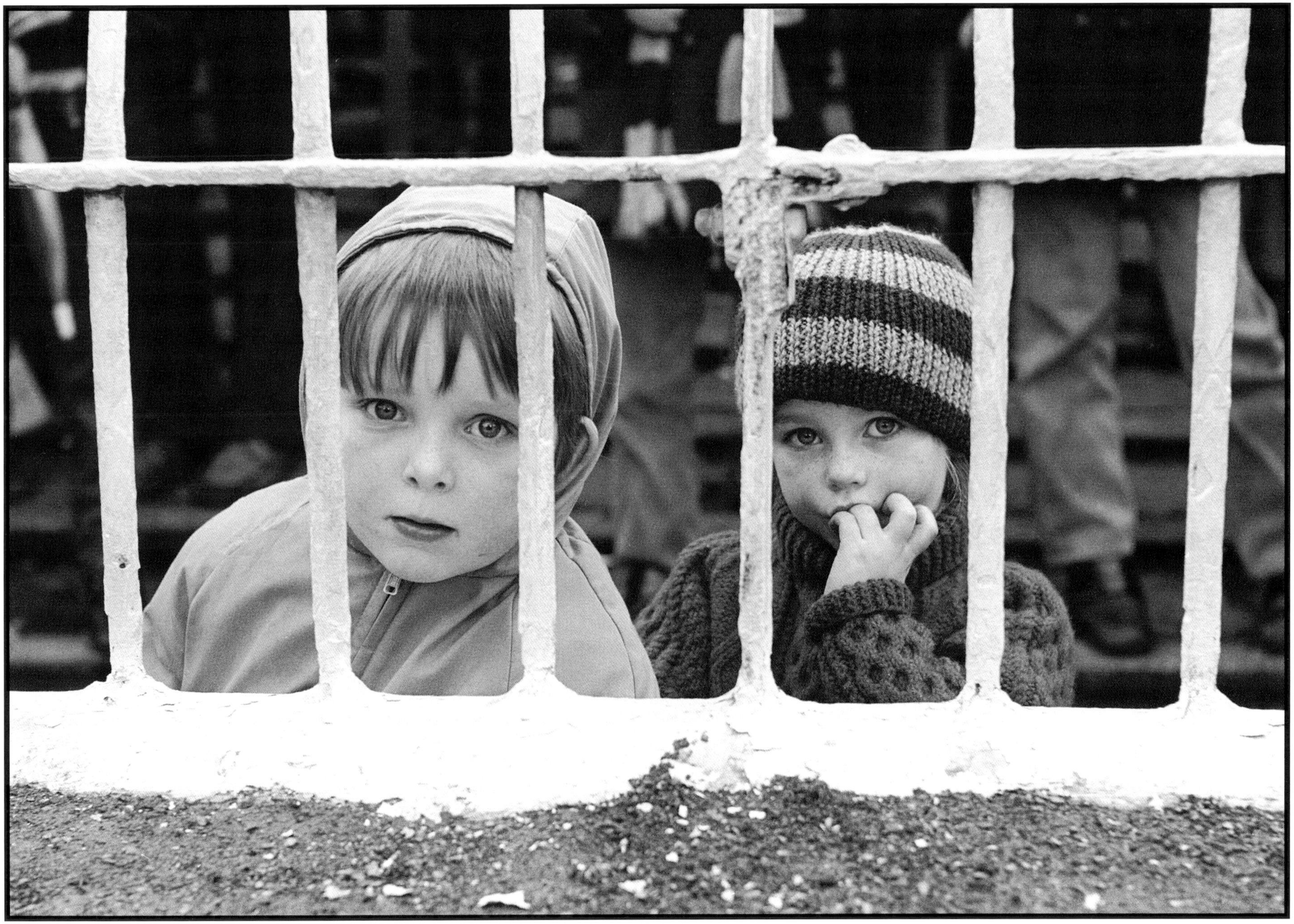

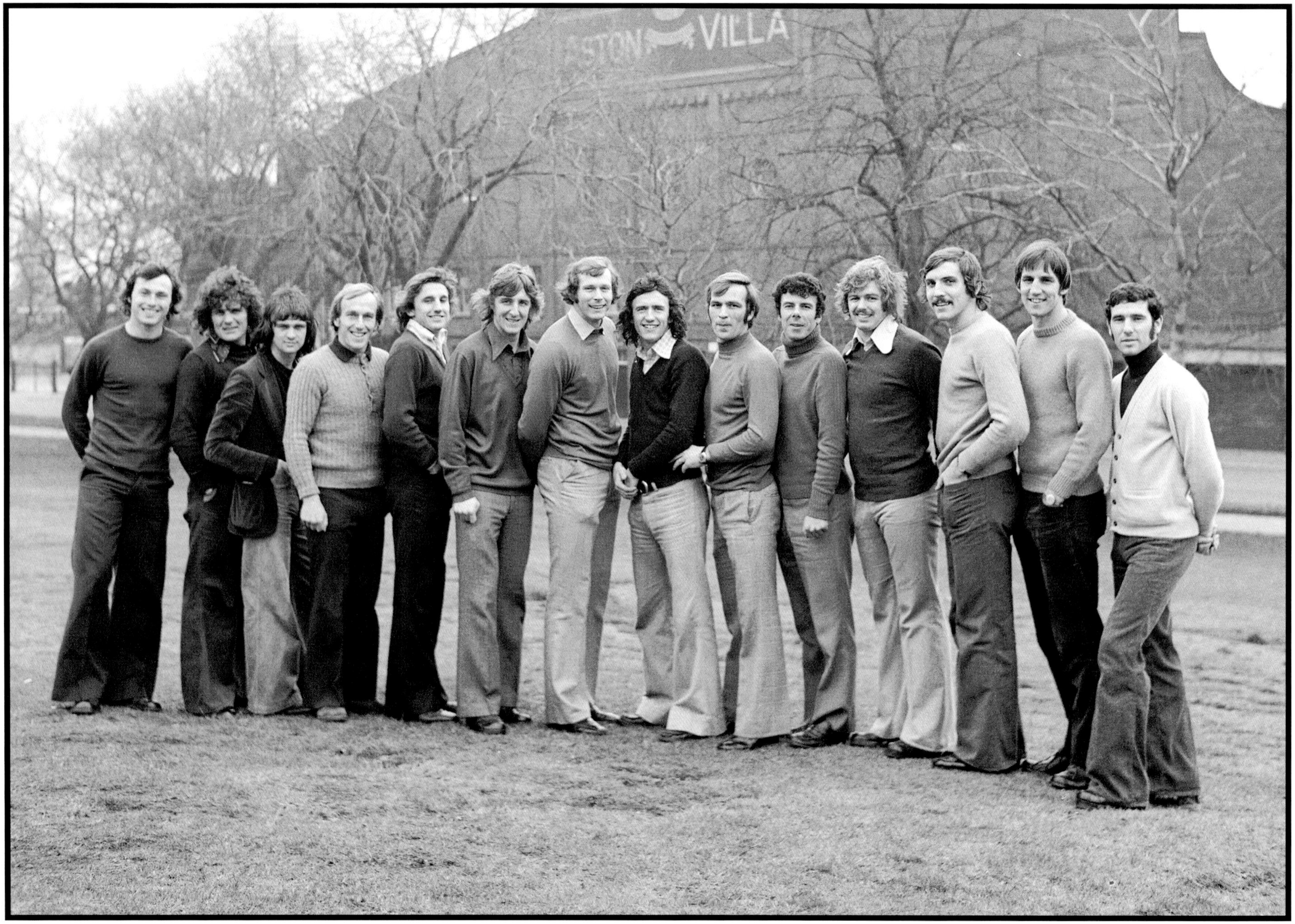

VILLA

the ironmongers

I called these lads The Ironmongers – because they had more metal on them than the local steelworks!

Their collection of badges was pretty impressive, no question about that, but it's surprising the guys weren't weighed down by them.

This picture was taken at the old Serpentine car park just before the coaches departed for an away match in the early seventies.

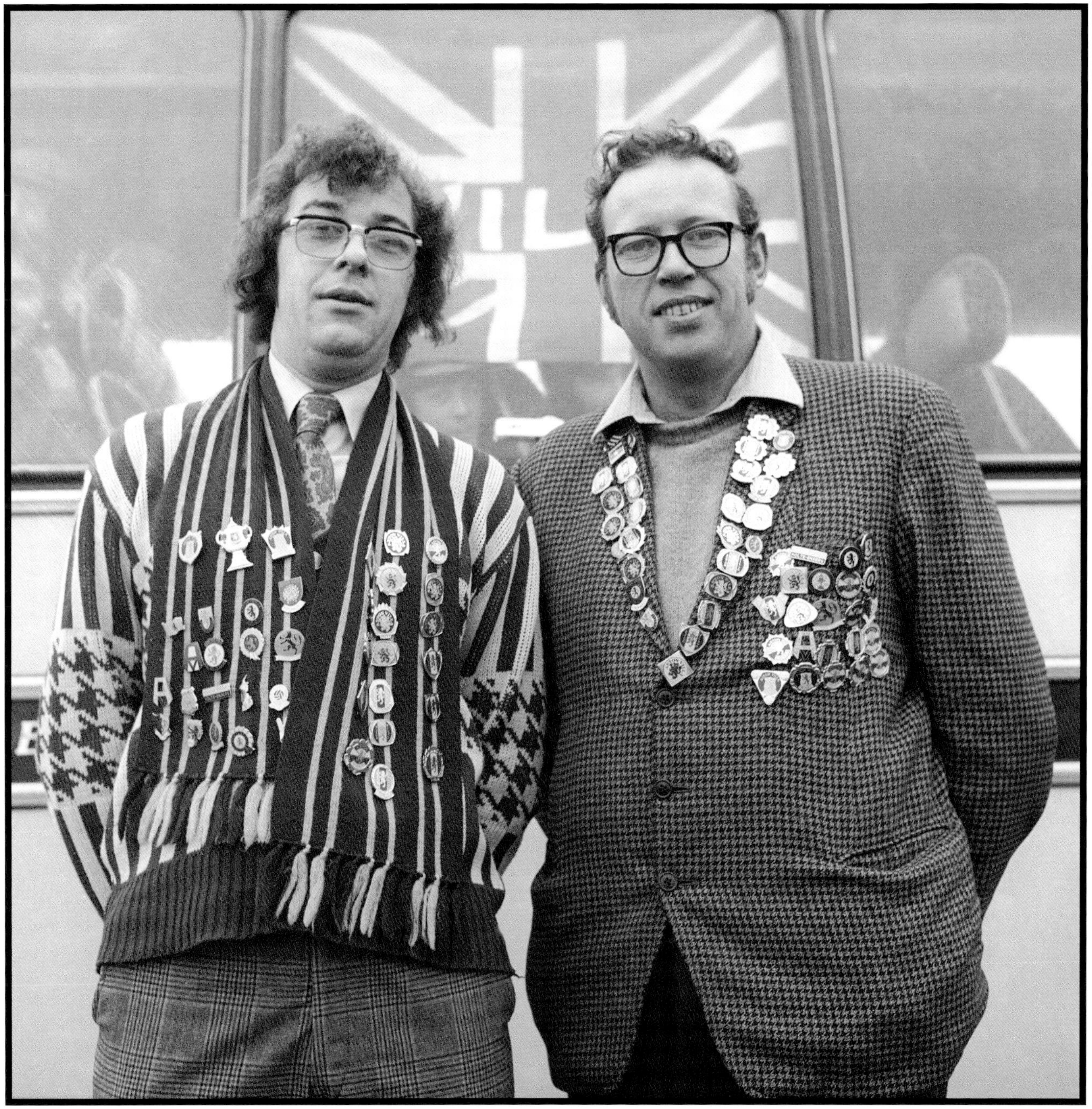

board meeting

Important announcements from the club are accompanied by full-blown press conferences these days, but things used to be rather more relaxed.

When Ron Bendall was appointed to the board in February, 1975, for instance, a group of reporters and photographers were invited into the boardroom, where the news was discussed around a table – once Bendall and chairman Doug Ellis had posed for pictures, of course.

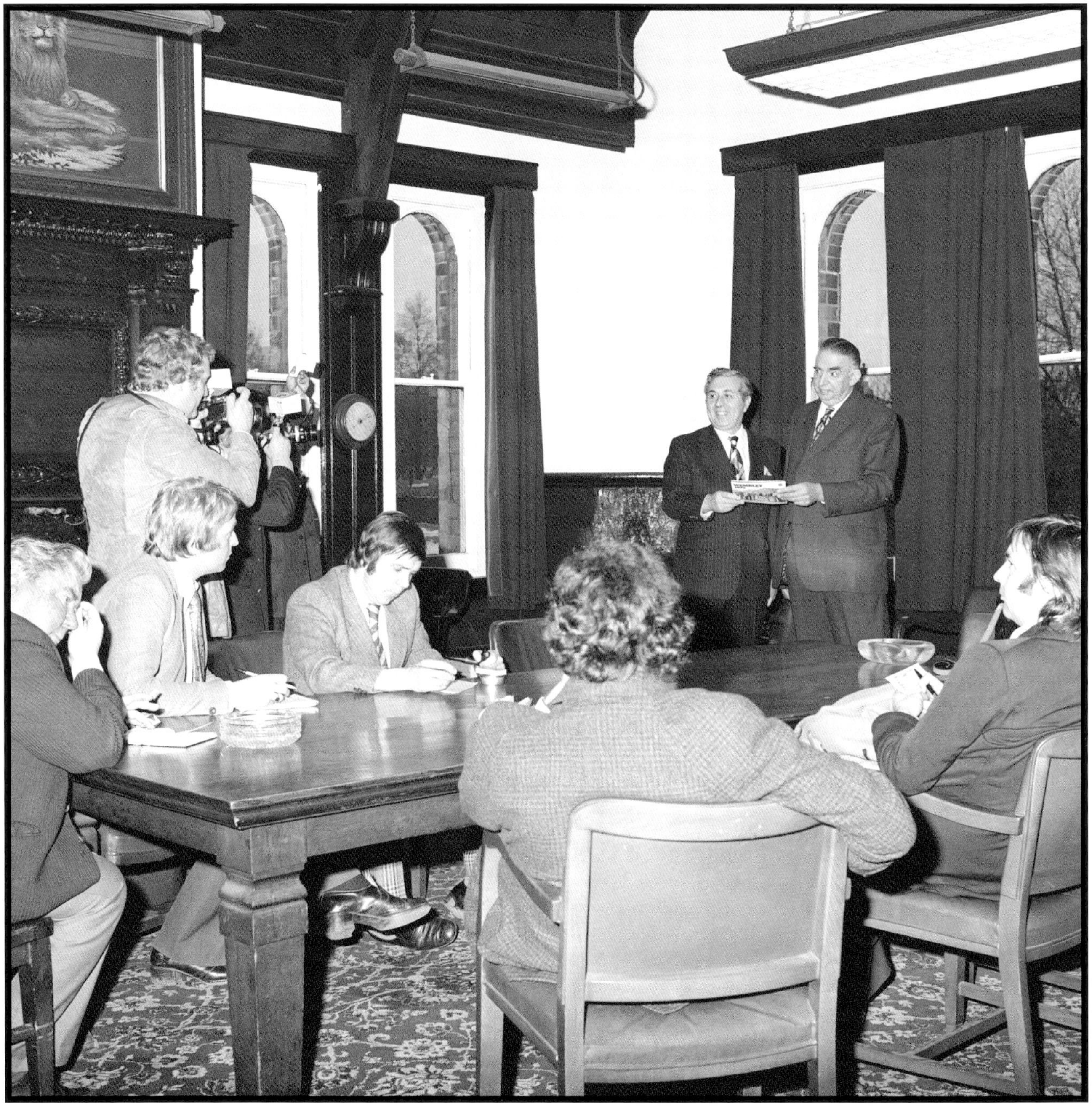

hold the front page

It's celebration time at London's Savoy Hotel after the 1975 League Cup final victory over Norwich City.

The couple on the left are Mr and Mrs Eric Cheadle, who were prominent members of Villa's Vice-Presidents' Association, together with Ron Bendall and his wife.

The younger guy displaying the front page of that afternoon's Sports Argus is Donald Bendall. Copies of the Argus had been sent down to the post-match reception by motorbike.

Bendall and son, of course, would savour even greater glory as chairman and vice-chairman a few years later...

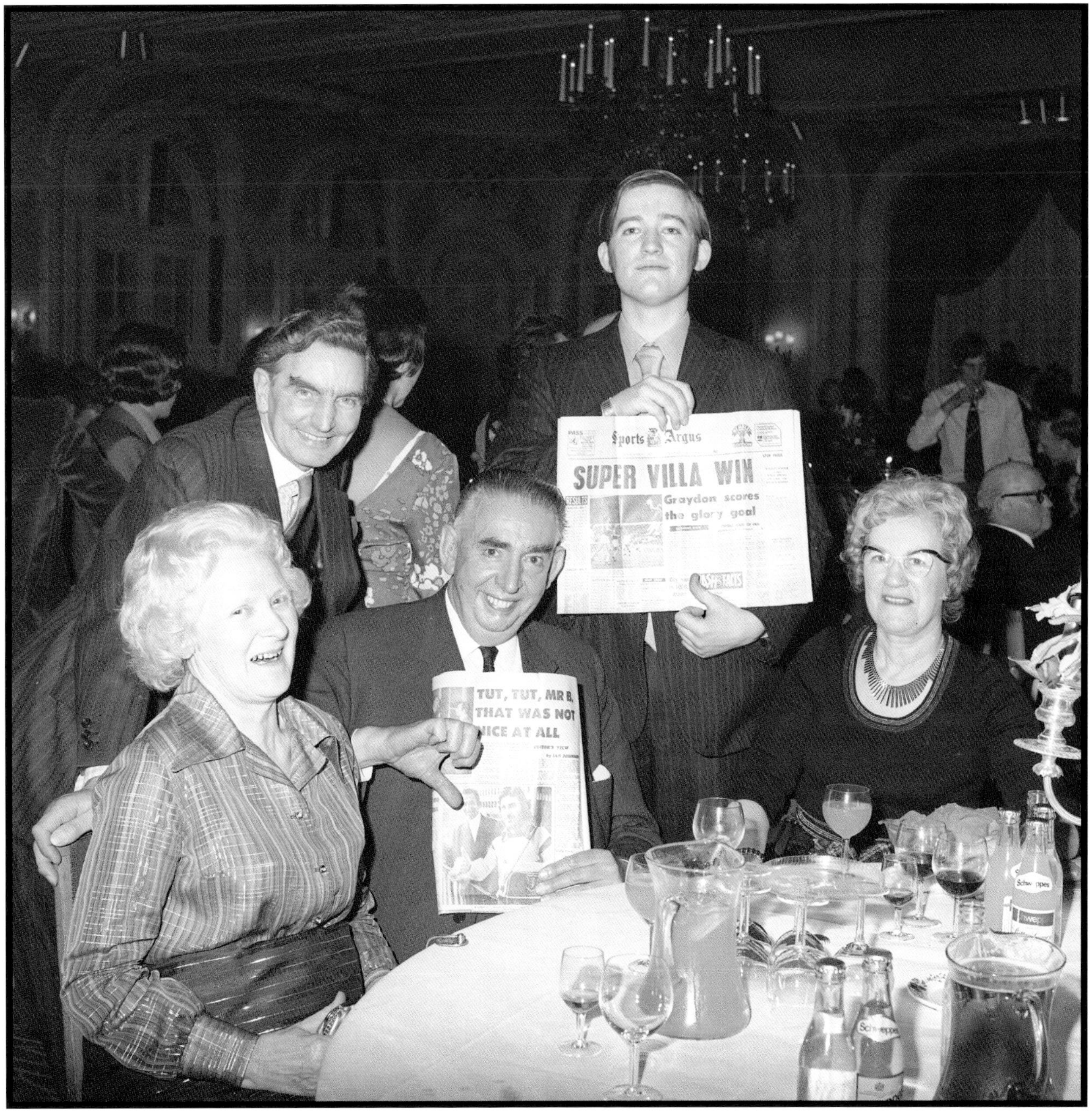

ball boy to manager

Ball boys perform a task which often goes unappreciated but undeniably helps the flow of a football match as they ensure that delays are kept to a minimum.

This team group of ball boys was taken during the 1974-75 season, and features someone who has since assumed a high-profile role at Aston Villa. Abdul Rashid (front row, second left) went on to become the club's Commercial Manager.

His affection for Villa has rubbed off on his three daughters, Tanya, Lisa and Lauren, who all followed in his footsteps by becoming ball girls.

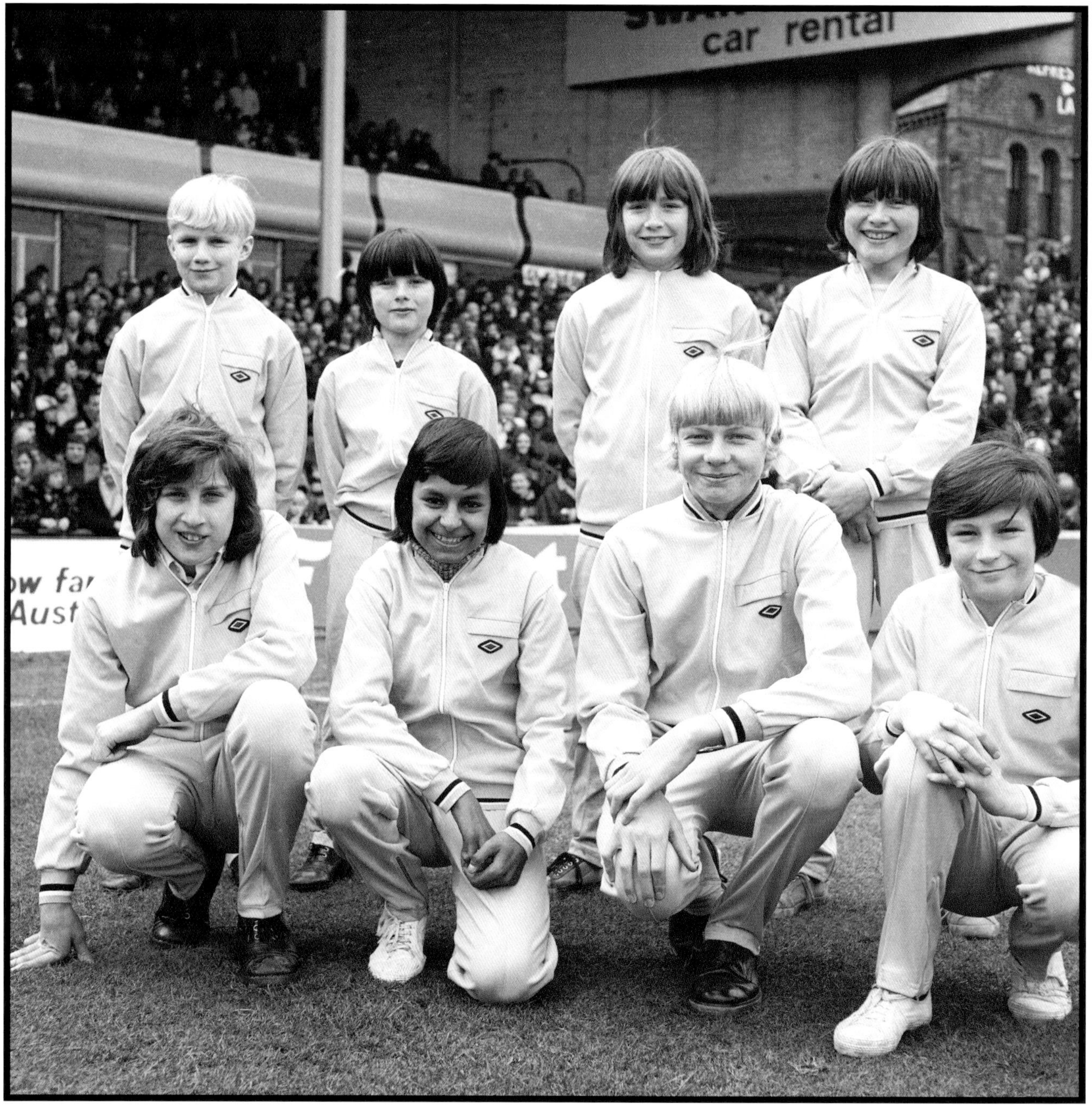

massie magic

Charlie Tabberner frequently held get-togethers with Villa personalities for members of the Lions Club.

Former player and manager Eric Houghton was in the chair the night Alex Massie faced questions from the audience and I had quite a thrill to be in the presence of a man who was in the Villa team when I first slipped into Villa Park to watch the closing minutes of matches in the early 1940s. Alex was the star of that team and later went on to become manager.

One thing baffles me, though. Eric was English and Alex Scottish. Where was the Irishman on St Patrick's Day?

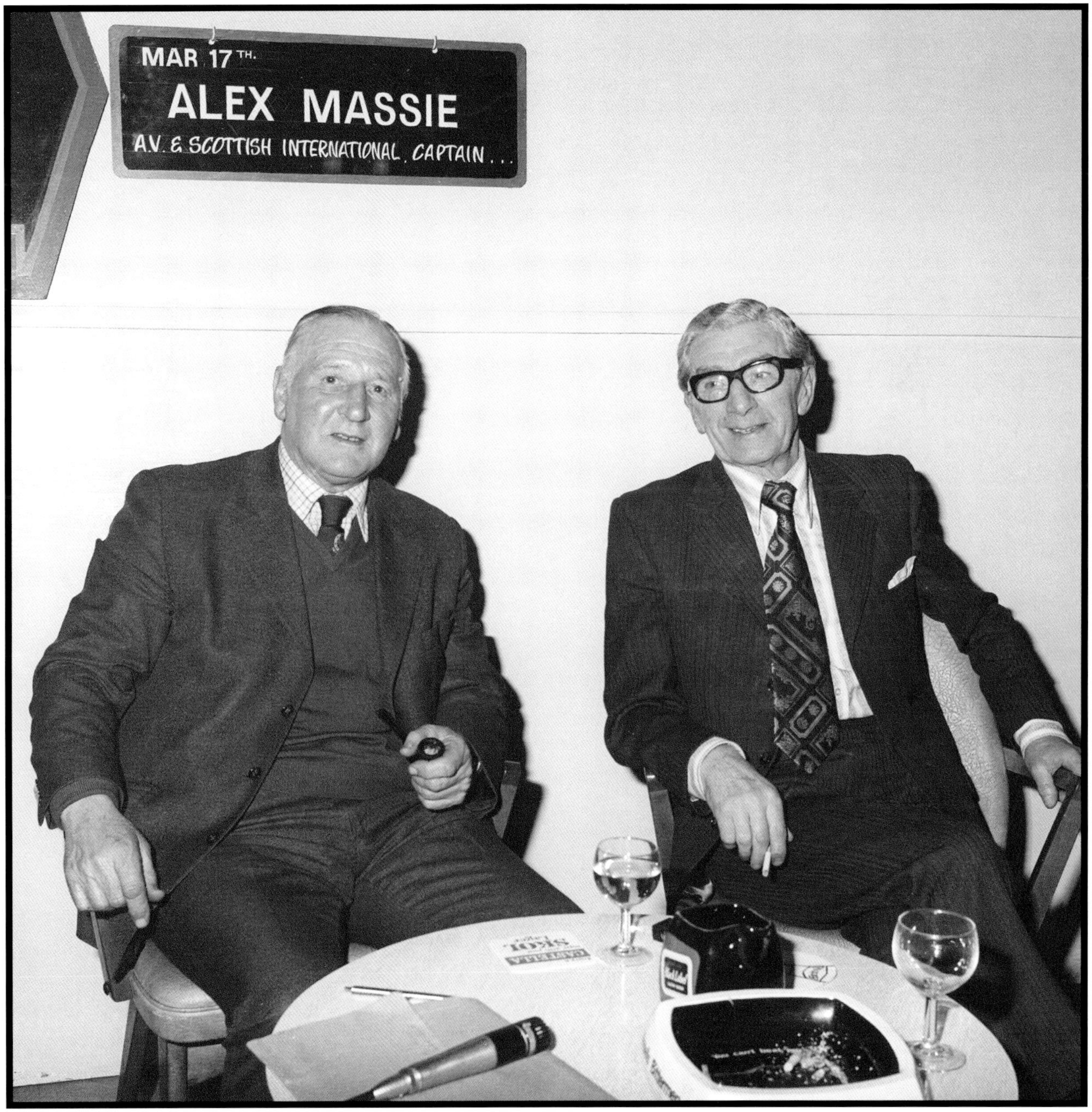

kit cowans

Gordon Cowans is one of the biggest names in Villa history, but his father also had an important job – that of kit man. Walter Cowans originated from the north east and was in charge of Villa's kit during Gordon's formative years as a midfielder.

He later bred greyhounds and I once went to a meeting and put a bet on every one of his dogs running that night. Not one of them won.

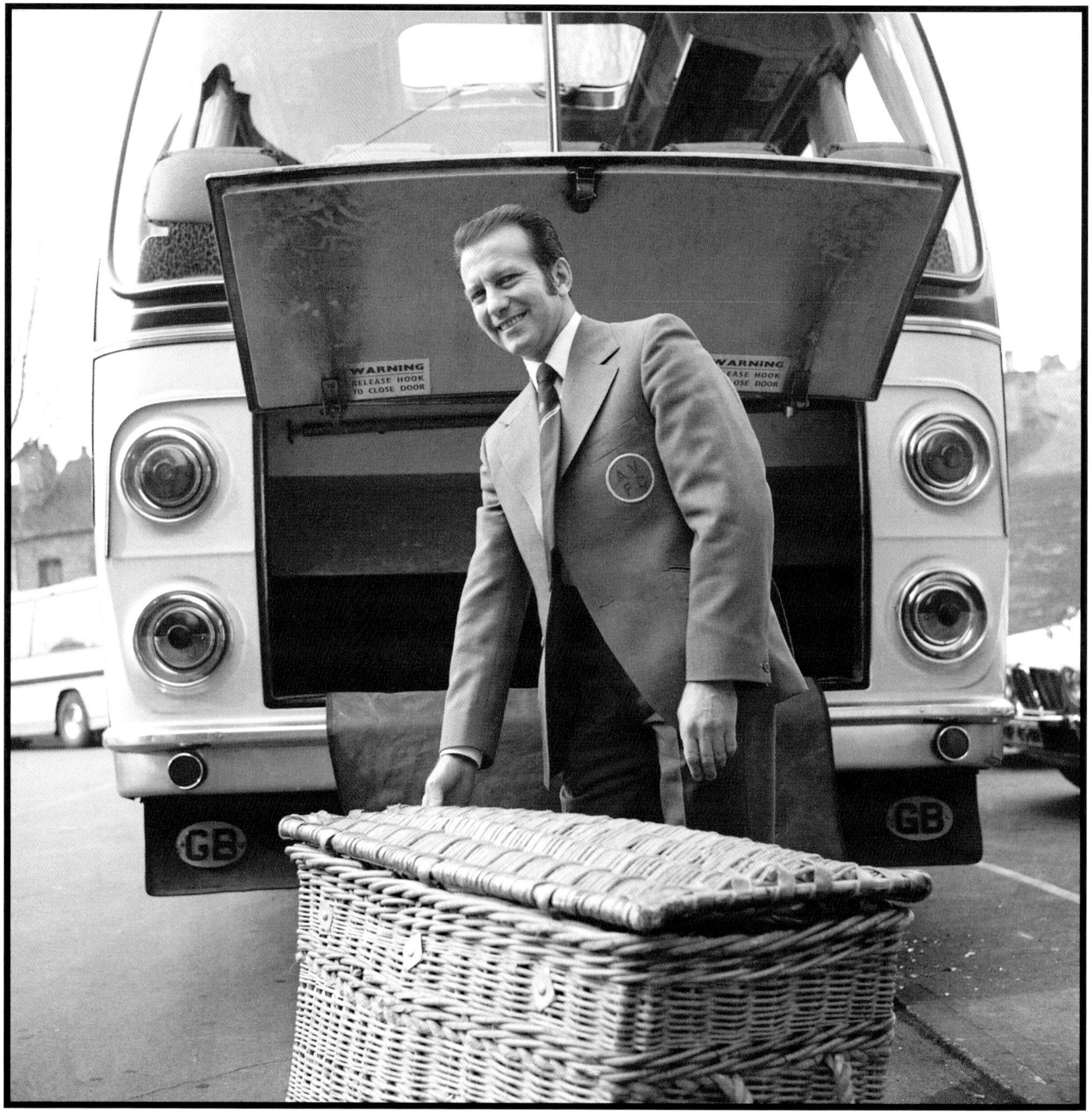

a wet weekend

Doug Ellis and Harry Cressman got more than they bargained for when they went into the dressing room at Hillsborough on 23rd April, 1975.

The purpose of their visit was to congratulate Villa's players on securing promotion to the top flight with a 4-0 victory over Sheffield Wednesday, but both gentlemen ended up being thrown in the bath.

They are seen here ringing out their jackets, although there was no chance of the garments drying out before the journey back to Birmingham.

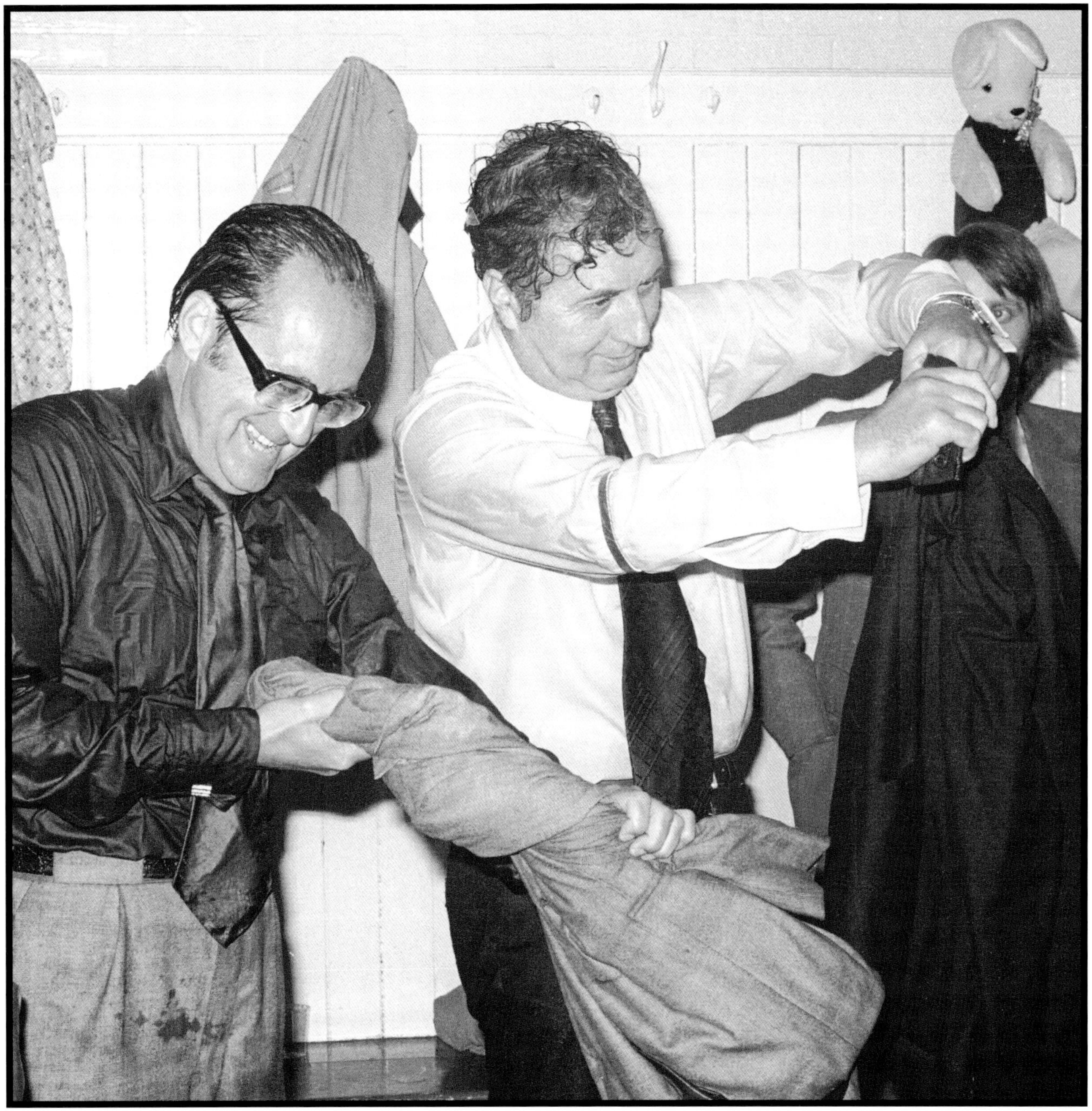

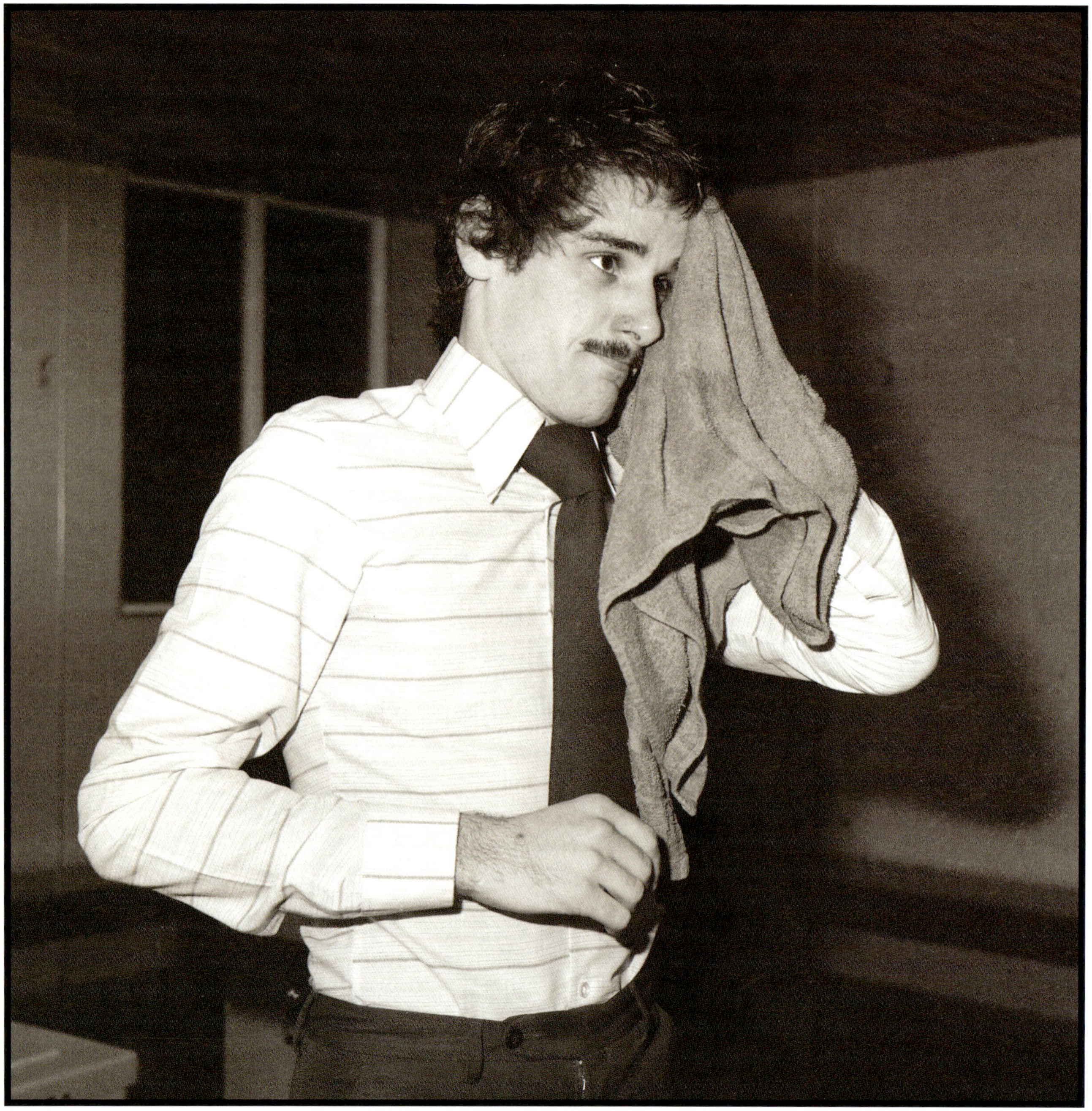

first time around

John Gregory has been best known in recent times as Villa's manager, having occupied the hot seat for nearly four years between February 1998 and January 2002. But he also served the club as a competent midfielder before moving to Queens Park Rangers.

There aren't a lot of offbeat pictures of JG during his first spell at Villa Park, but I managed to capture him in the dressing room, drying his hair after a match.

wembley winners

It must have been the greatest feeling any footballer could experience – holding a cup aloft at Wembley in front of thousands of adoring fans.

Ian Ross savoured the moment in 1975, lifting the League Cup after Ray Graydon's penalty rebound goal had clinched a 1-0 win over Norwich City.

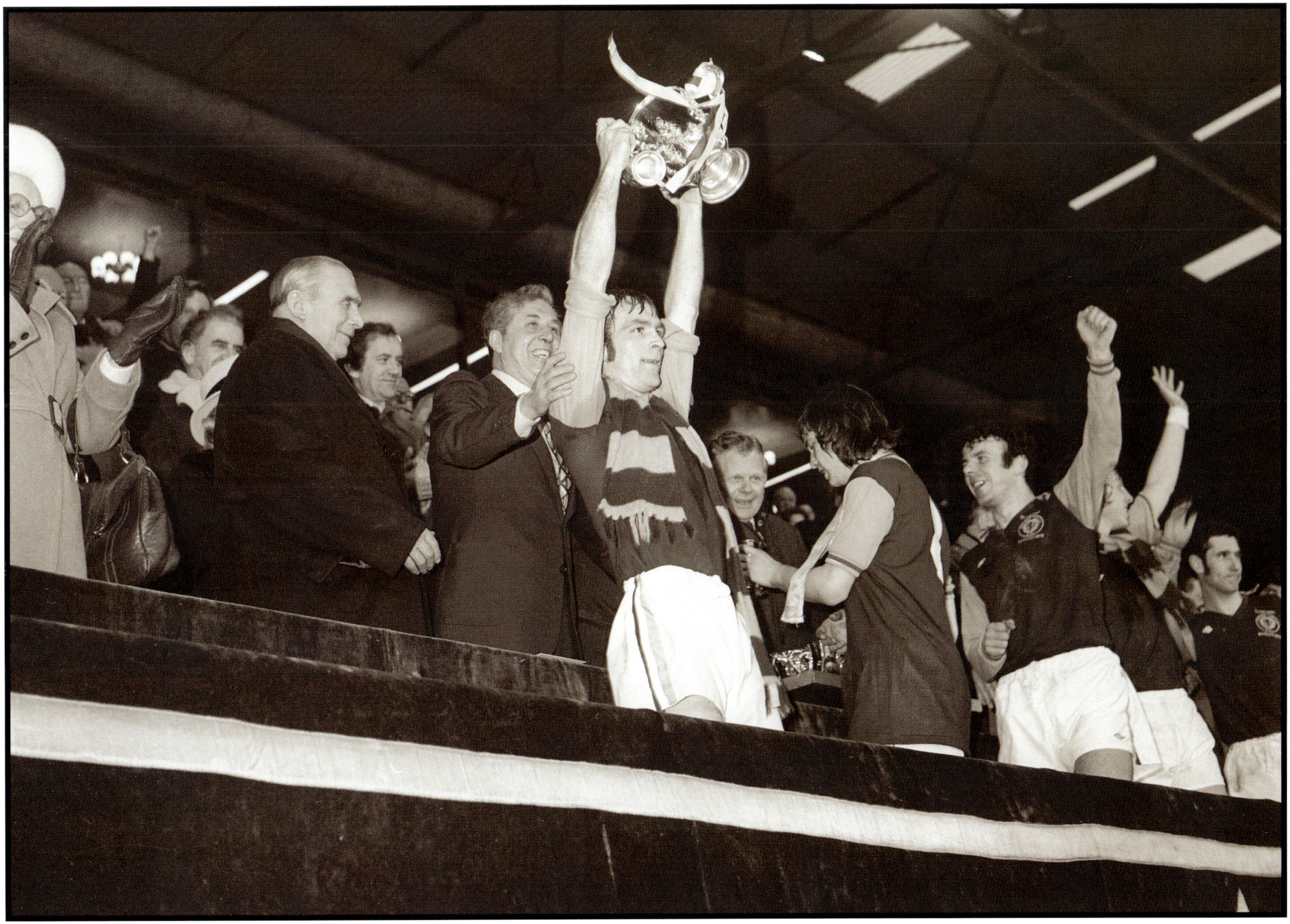

going up

Three days after clinching promotion, Villa beat Sunderland 2-0 in their final home match, in front of a crowd of 57,266.

Not unexpectedly, after such a long time out of the top flight, thousands of supporters ran on to the pitch to celebrate at the final whistle.

Had I remained in my position behind the Holte End goal, I would have been caught up among them, which wouldn't have been a problem because I was as happy as anyone in the ground that day.

But there was work to be done. Ten minutes from time, I headed down the tunnel, made my way up to the directors' box and was well placed to capture the celebrating fans.

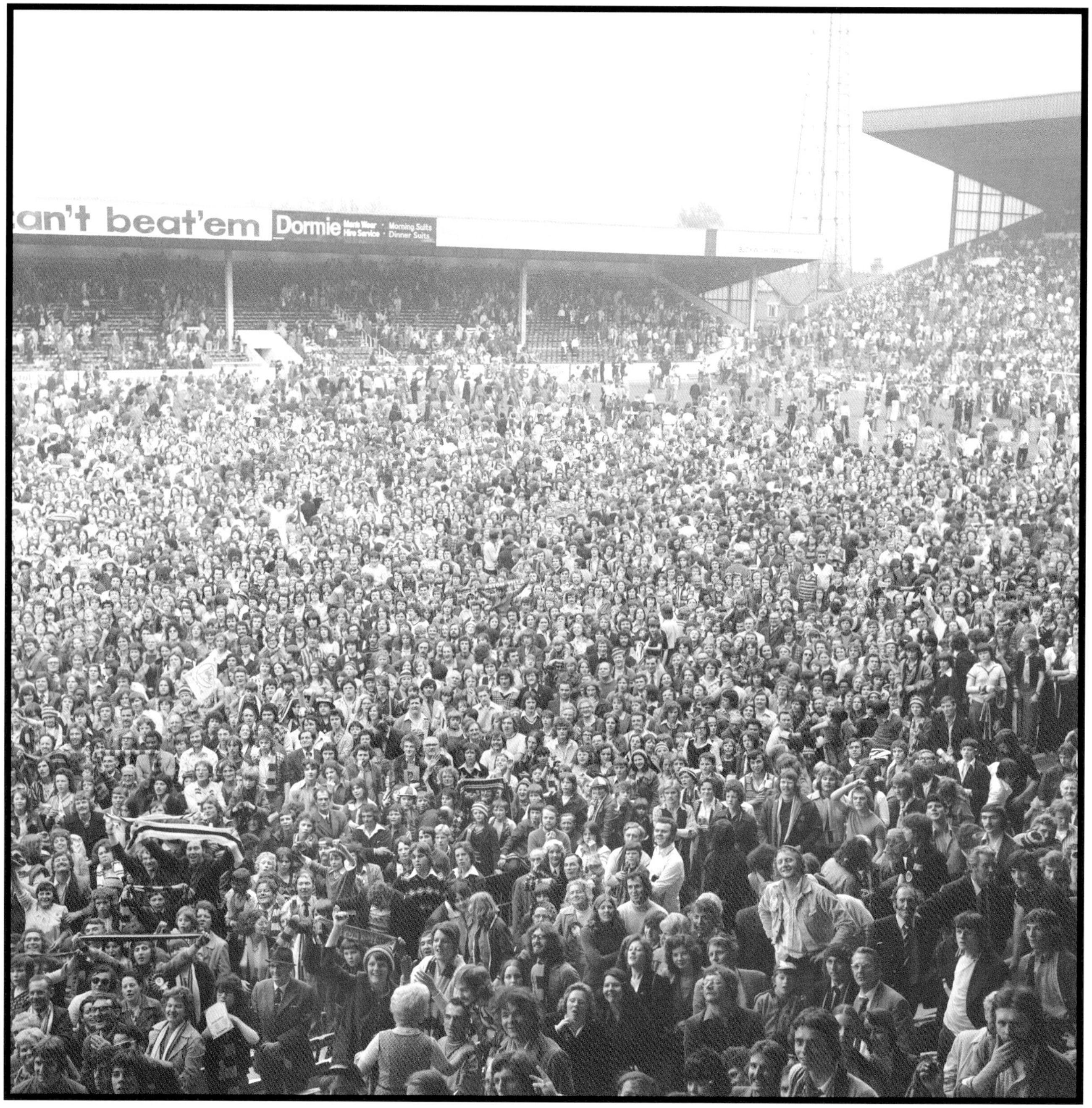

magic spray

There was a time when physiotherapists were called trainers and the 'magic sponge' was the answer to many an injury.

By the mid-1970s, though the magic sponge had given way to the magic spray, which Fred Pedley is seen administering to Keith Leonard's right knee during the 2-0 home win over Sunderland on 26th April, 1975.

Keith recovered from this one, but wasn't so fortunate when he suffered a more serious knee problem against Arsenal early the following season. That one ended his career.

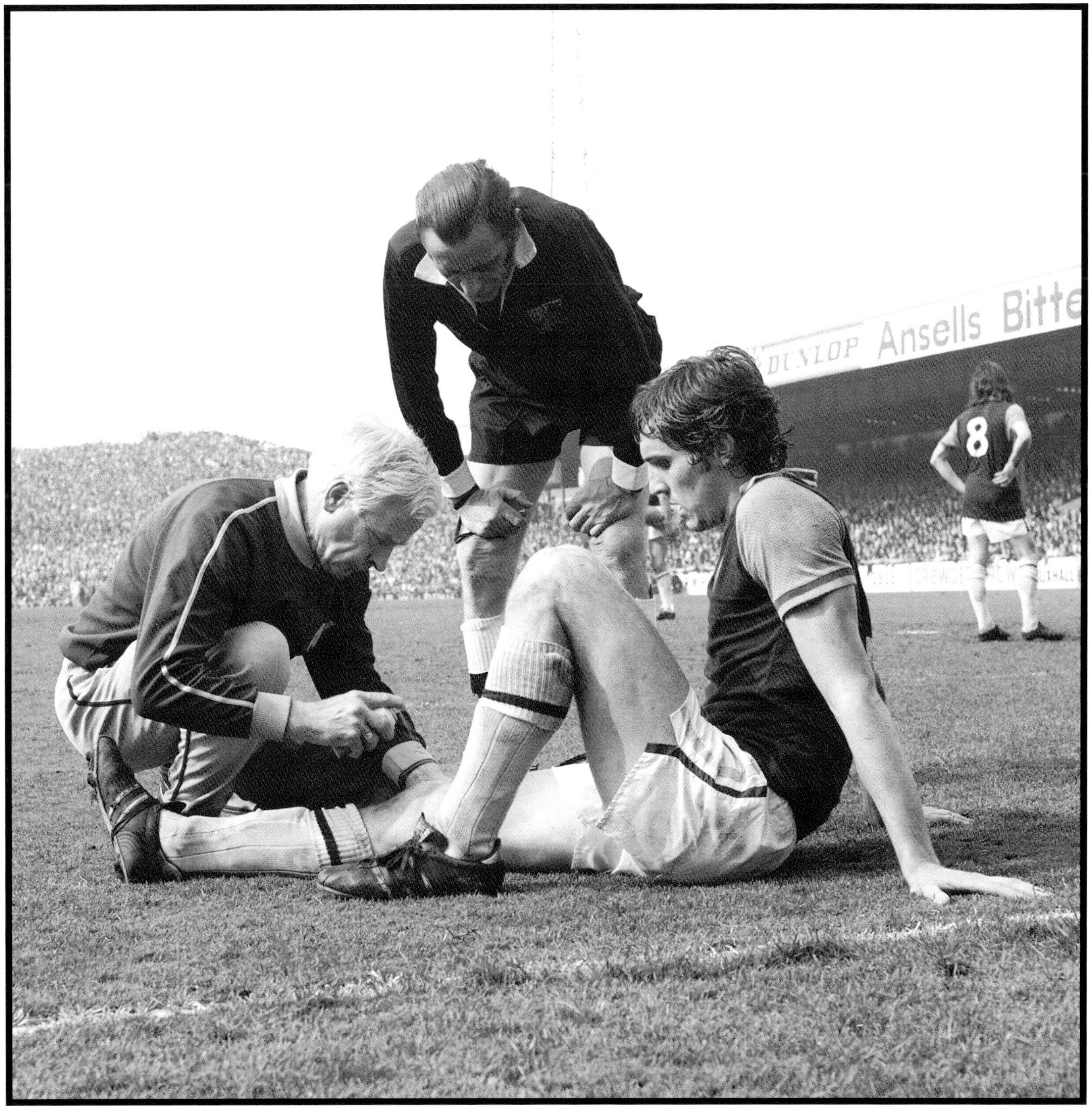

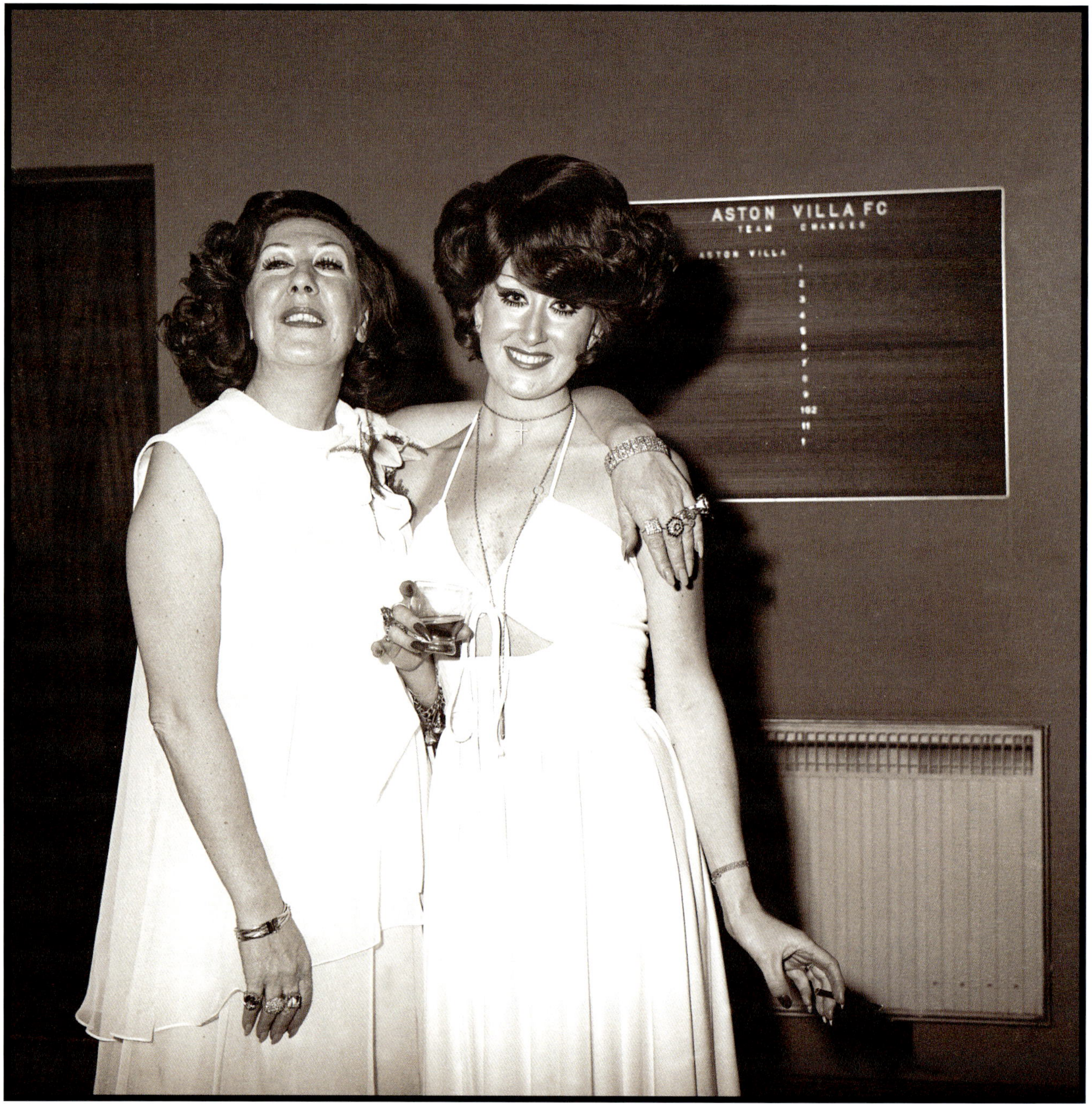
ASTON VILLA FC
TEAM CHANGES

backstage with barry

Being backstage at some of the pop concerts staged at Villa Park was always quite an experience. When Barry White performed at the Witton End, I met the owner of the agency who organised the event and the lady in question is pictured (left) relaxing with her daughter.

If my memory serves me correctly, the show made a huge loss because it was an awful night and the attendance was nowhere near what had been anticipated, but at least the girls gave me broad grins when I pointed the camera in their direction.

As for Barry White, he was in rather more pensive mood before going on stage, but there was no lack of energy once he got there. With the backing of three gorgeous backing singers, he performed non-stop for two hours, and looked as if he had run a marathon when he came off.

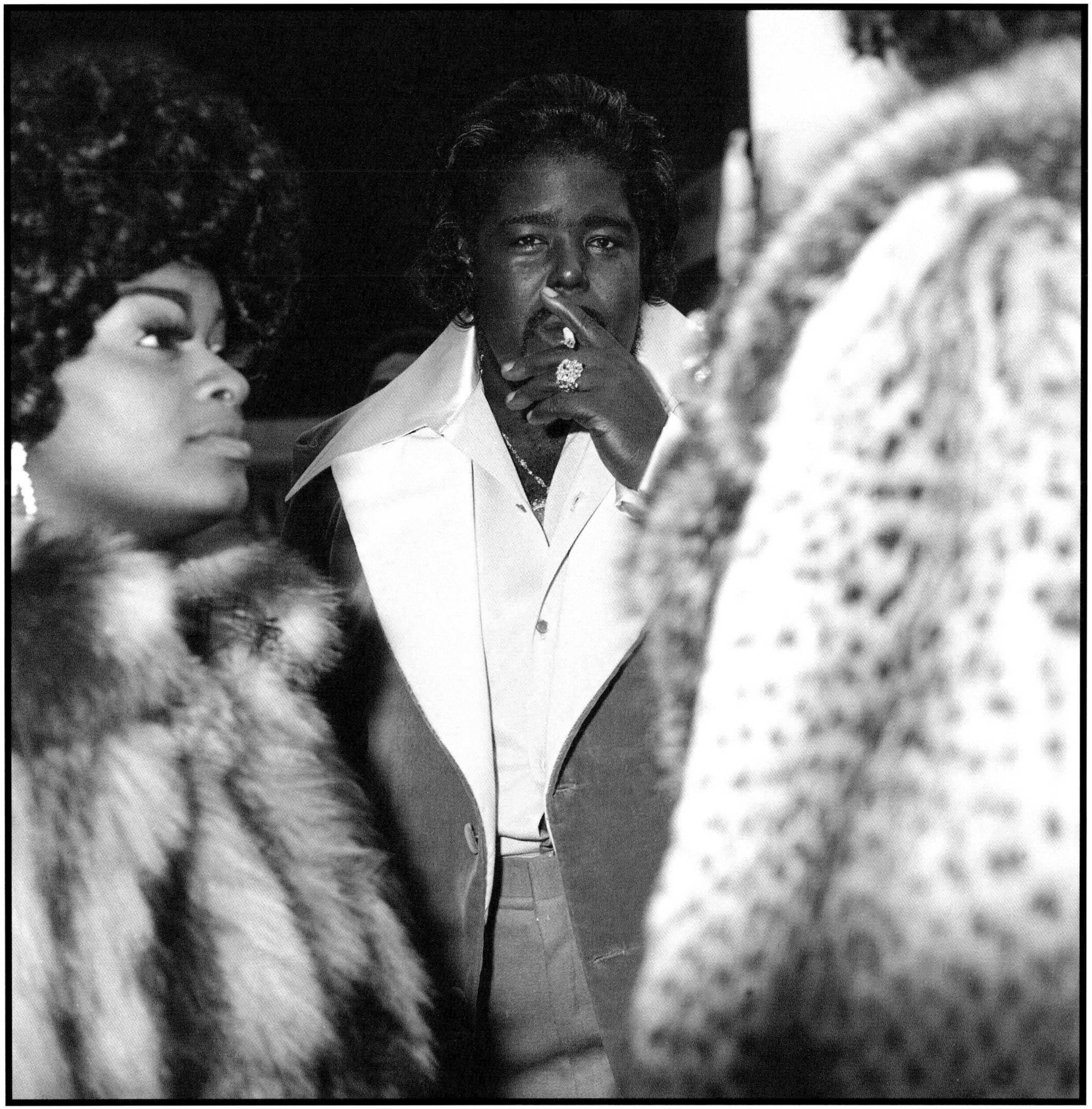

power of the press

Like Doug Ellis and Harry Cressman, journalist John Moxley also received a good soaking while fully clothed in the Hillsborough dressing room. But I will never forget how he emerged from the water still clutching his press pass, which he is holding in his left hand as broadcaster Jim Rosenthal and coach Roy McLaren enjoy the moment.

The players also tried to throw me in, but I persuaded them otherwise because I had my cameras around my neck.

It's just as well they resisted the temptation, or these pictures would never have seen the light of day.

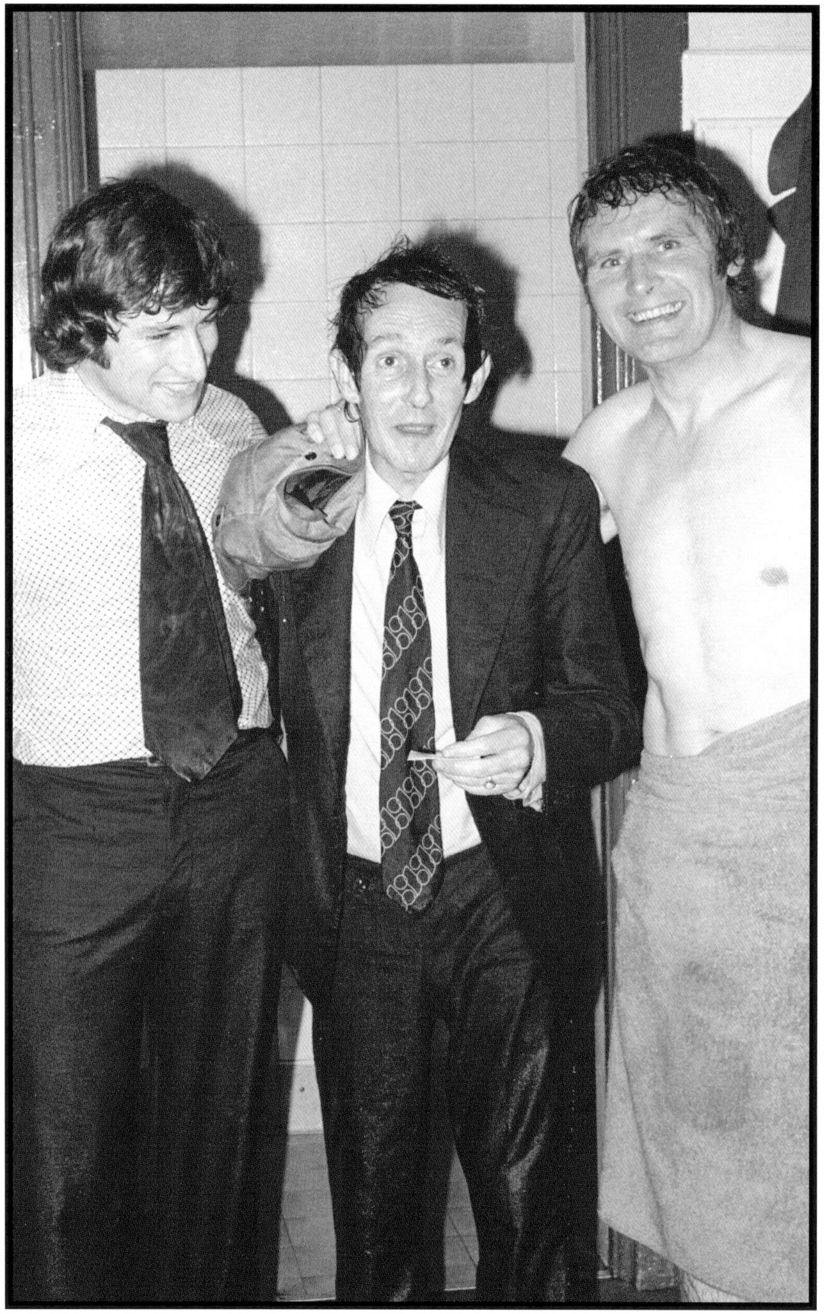

belgian bus stop

Before Villa ventured into Europe for the first time in 1975, I'd never been abroad, not even on holiday, so I had to purchase my first passport.

I went on the official party for the UEFA Cup-tie against Royal Antwerp, but I spotted a group of supporters at a bus stop outside our hotel and persuaded John Gidman to pose for a picture with them – making sure the advertising board was prominent to show we were in a foreign land.

On the day before the match, I went to the ground with Ron Saunders and Roy McLaren and Roy borrowed my raincoat while I took a picture of the them. I've never had it back!

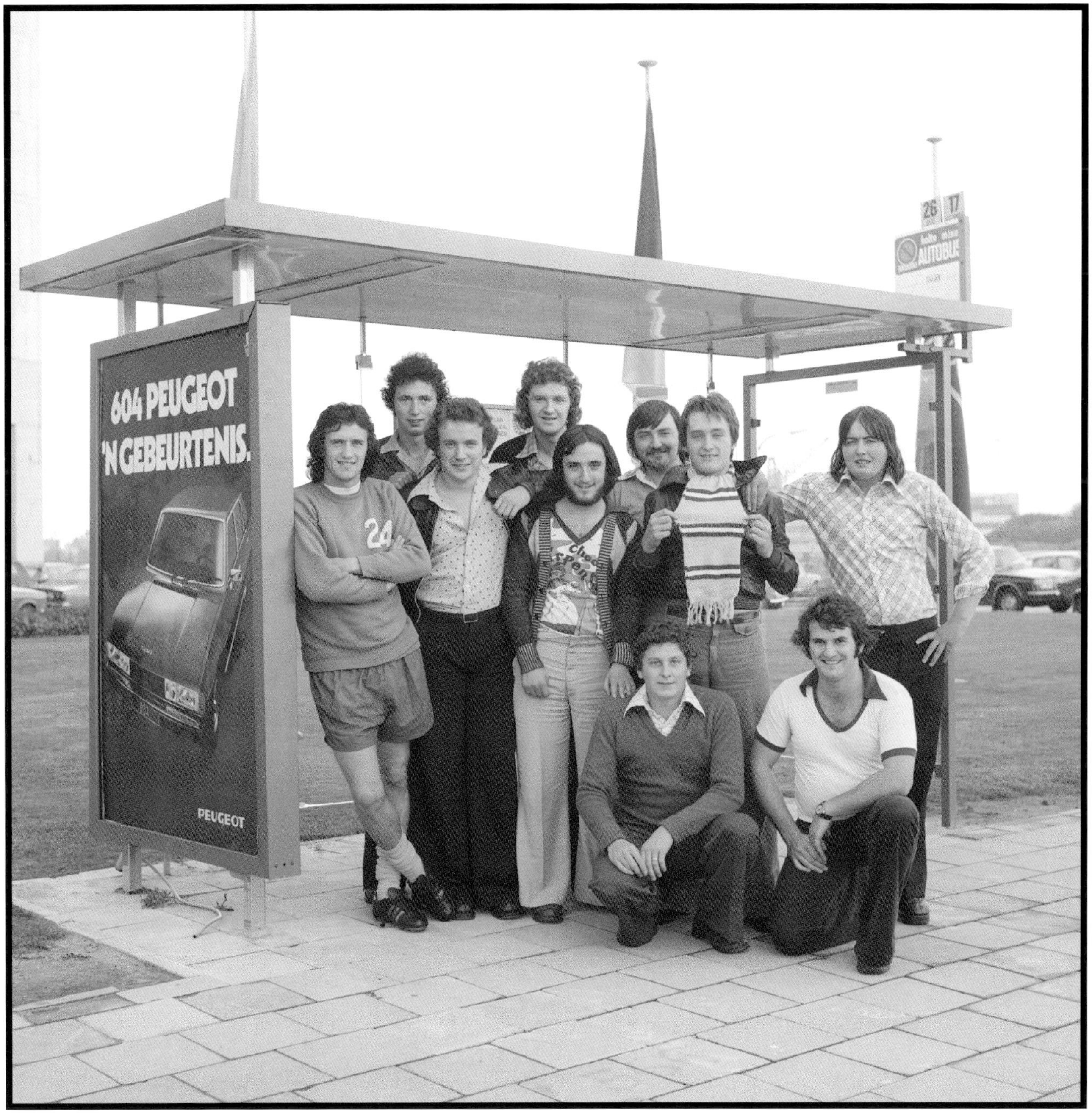

love thy neighbour

It wasn't just the home dressing room which produced memorable pictures. When Manchester United won 2-1 in a League Cup tie at Villa Park in October, 1975, TV personality Jack Smethurst joined in their post-match celebrations.

Jack, star of the comedy programme Love Thy Neighbour and a keen United fan, ended up in the bath with Sammy McIlroy and Brian McClair, a player who had been on Villa's books as a youngster.

I could have made money from this picture because the press boys from Manchester wanted to publish it, but I couldn't let them have the film because my Villa stuff was on it. Such is life.

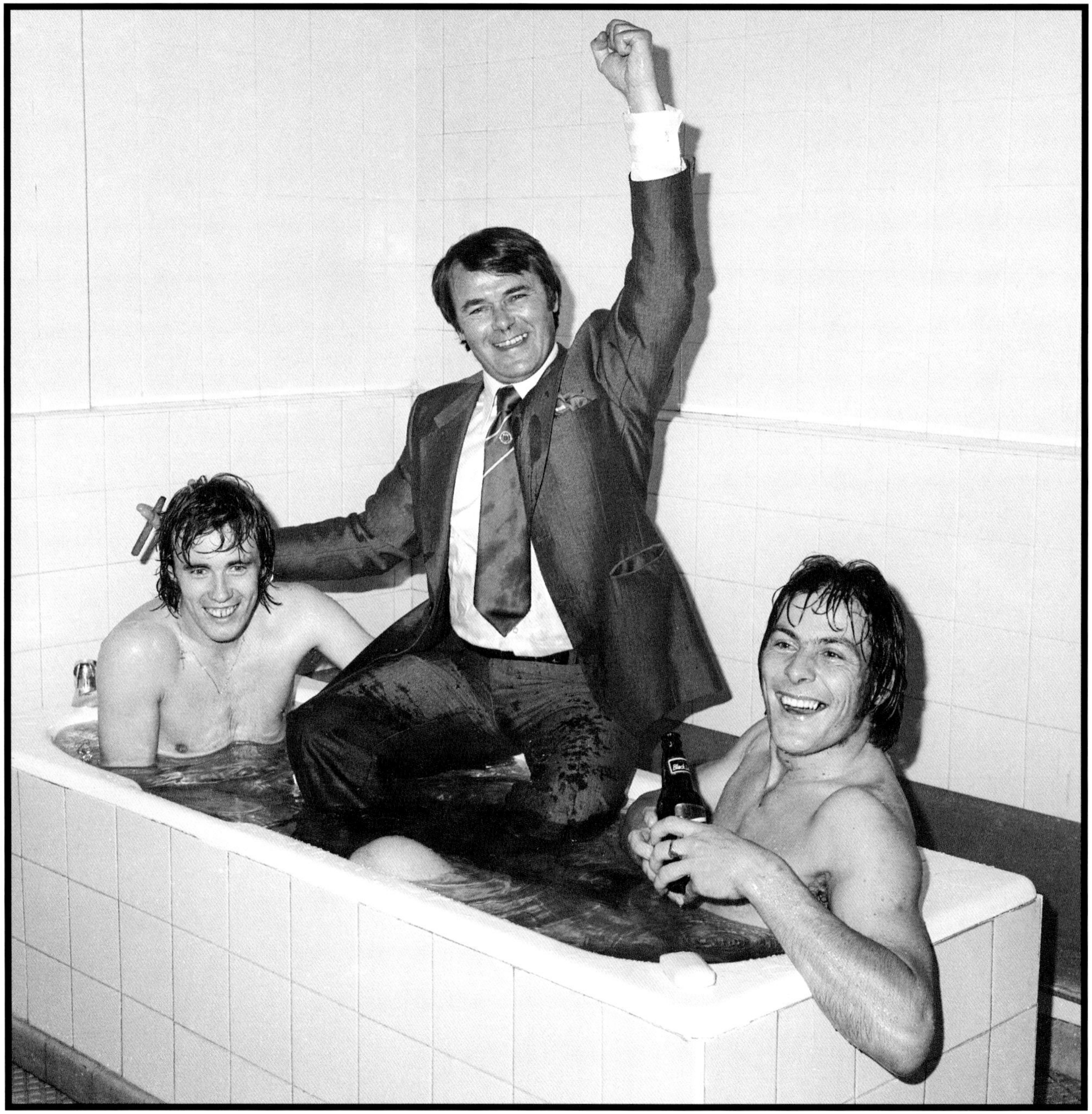

hanging around

This shirt has been hanging around for a long, long time – it was one of those worn by Villa players during the early 1930s, when football attire was known as jerseys rather than shirts.

You get the impression it would have been ideal in the middle of winter, but I'm sure modern day players would have found it a touch restrictive in warm weather.

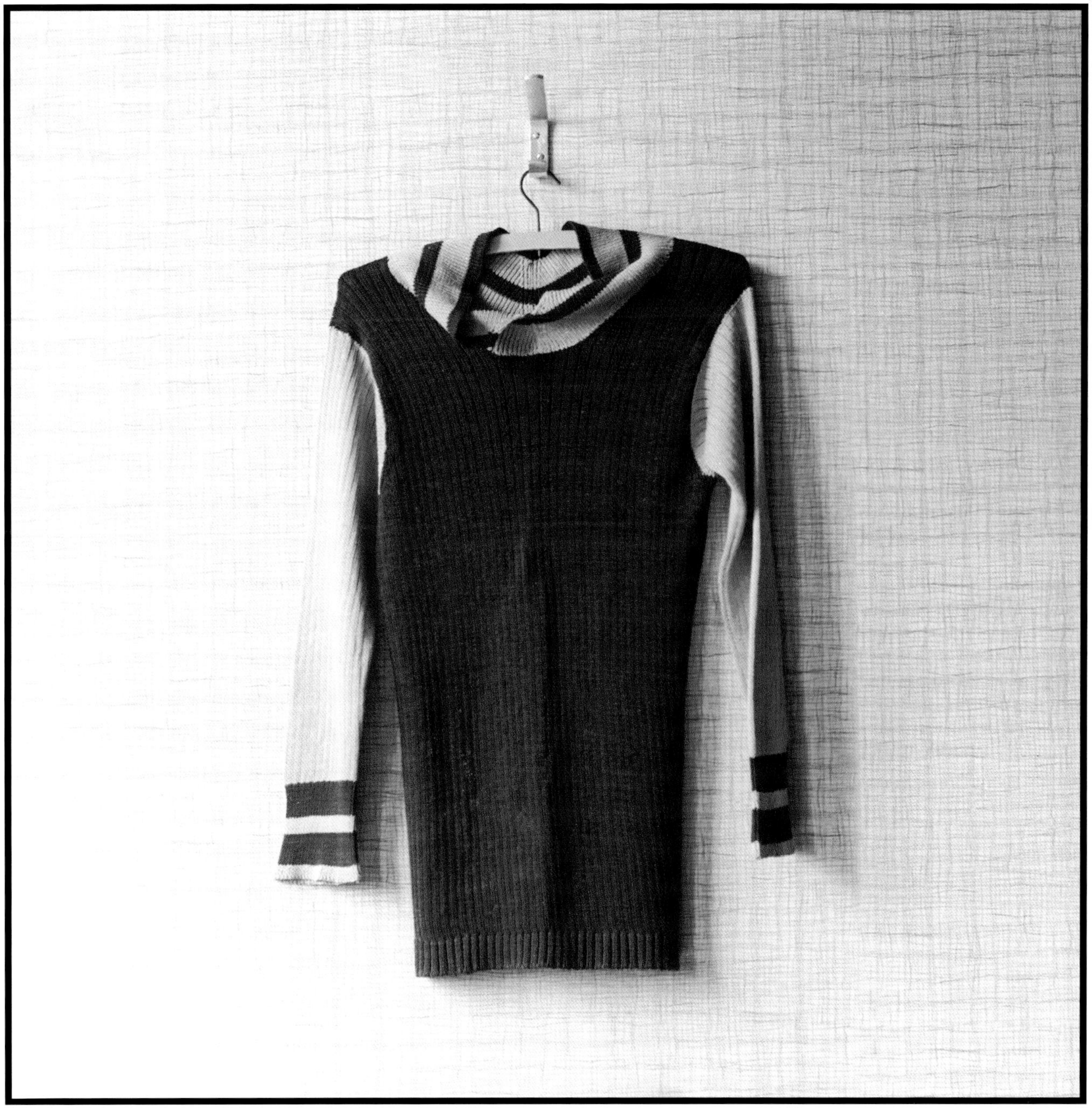

rock on

Young players who lived at the club's hostel regularly brightened up their rooms with pictures of pop stars in an attempt to make it home from home.

Tony Coles (left) and Micky Buttress were obviously keen on rock music, judging by the posters of Pink Floyd, Status Quo, Jimi Hendrix and The Who, although I'm willing to bet they had to keep the music at a reasonable volume!

On odd occasions, first team players stayed overnight at the hostel, although the senior guys weren't so keen on observing the rules.

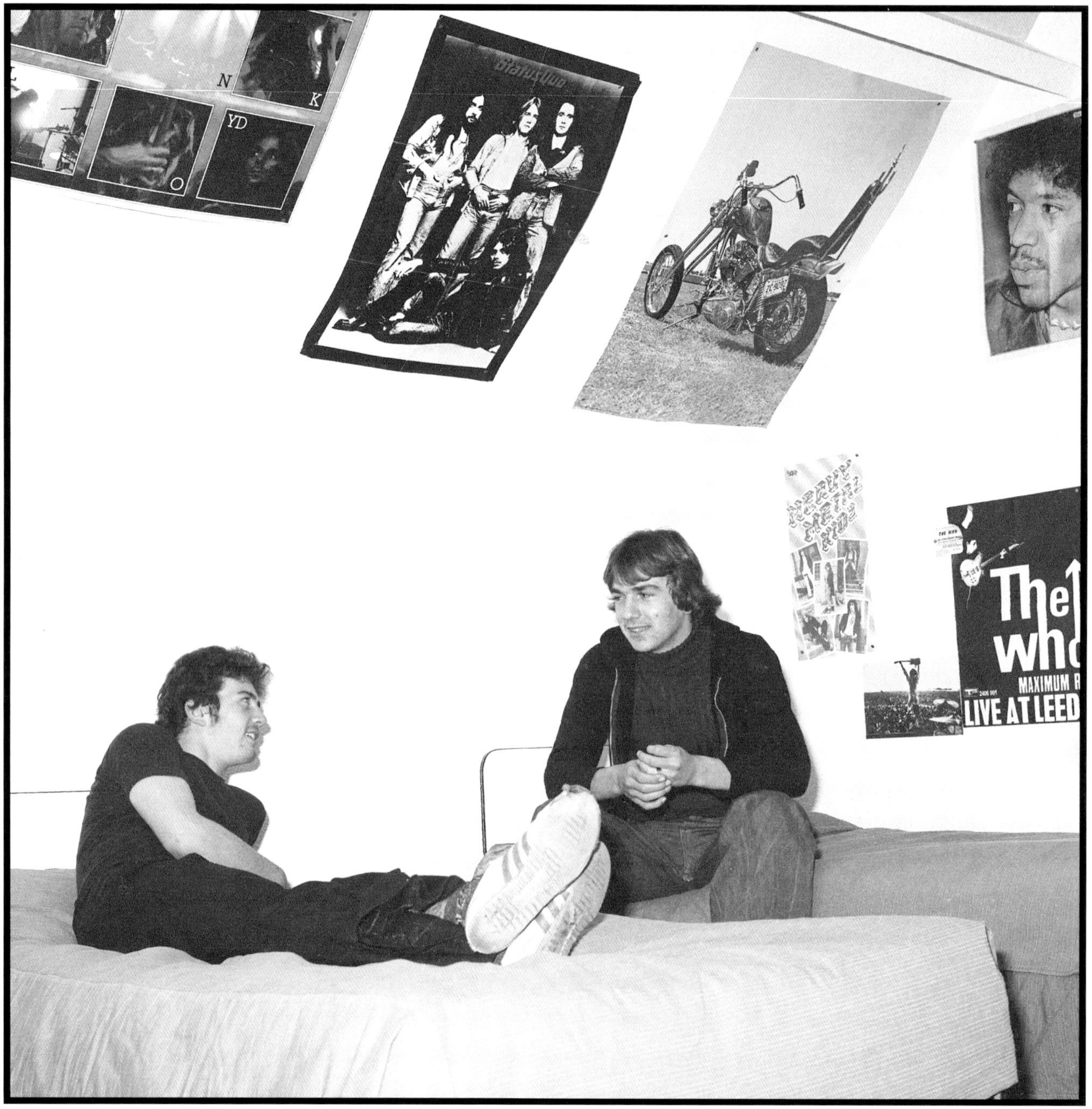

relaxed times

The men behind the League Championship and European Cup triumphs of the early eighties – manager Ron Saunders and his assistant Tony Barton, who took over after Ron had resigned in February 1982.

I have a feeling this was the first time I'd met Tony, who went along to the club's hostel with Ron to meet some of the younger players. Ron could be a fearsome character at times, but he was clearly relaxed on this occasion.

From the decorations around the room, it was Christmas time, and the boss and his assistant had gone along to a party organised for the youngsters.

On odd occasions, first team players stayed overnight at the hostel, although the senior guys weren't so keen on observing the rules.

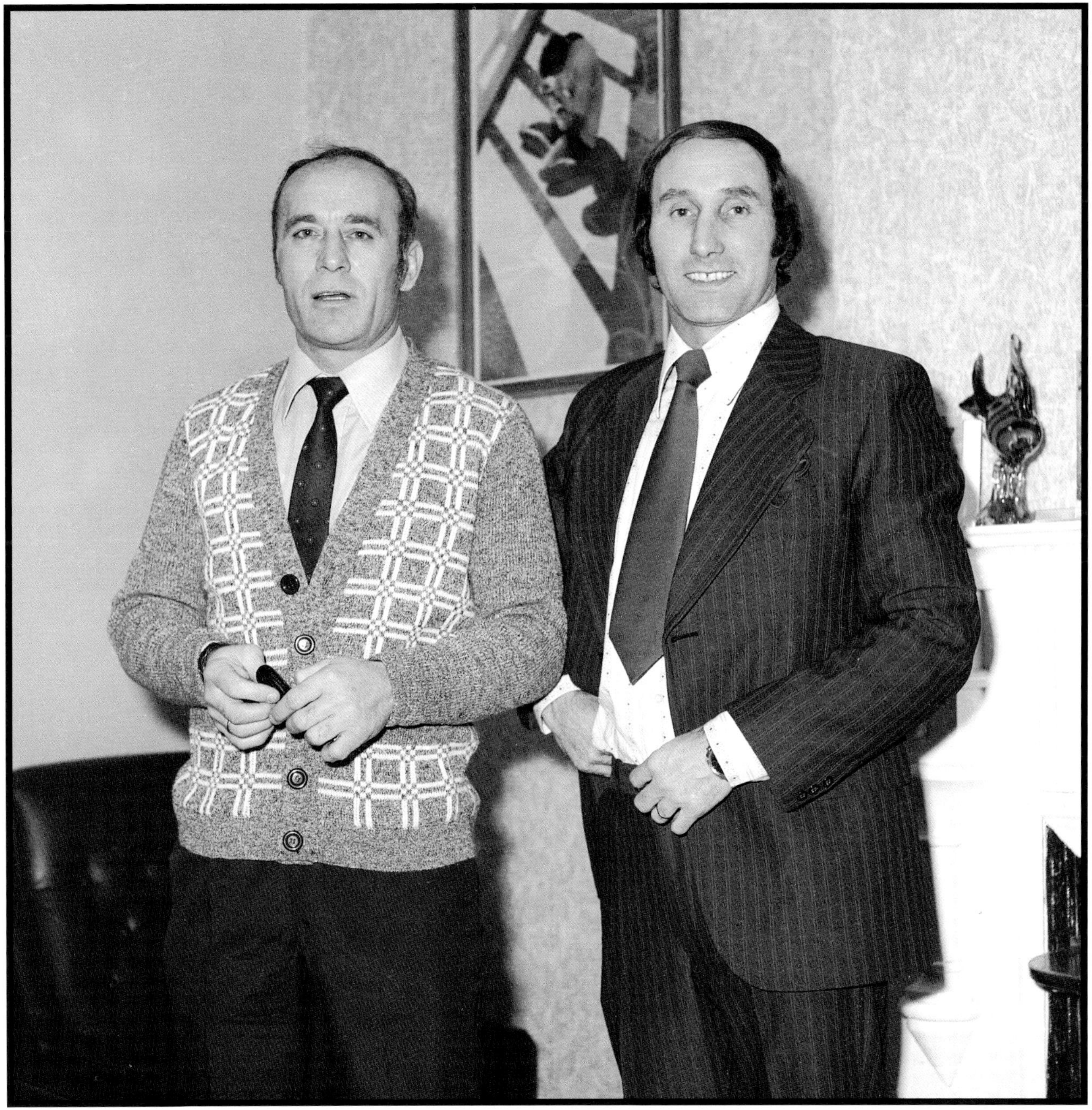

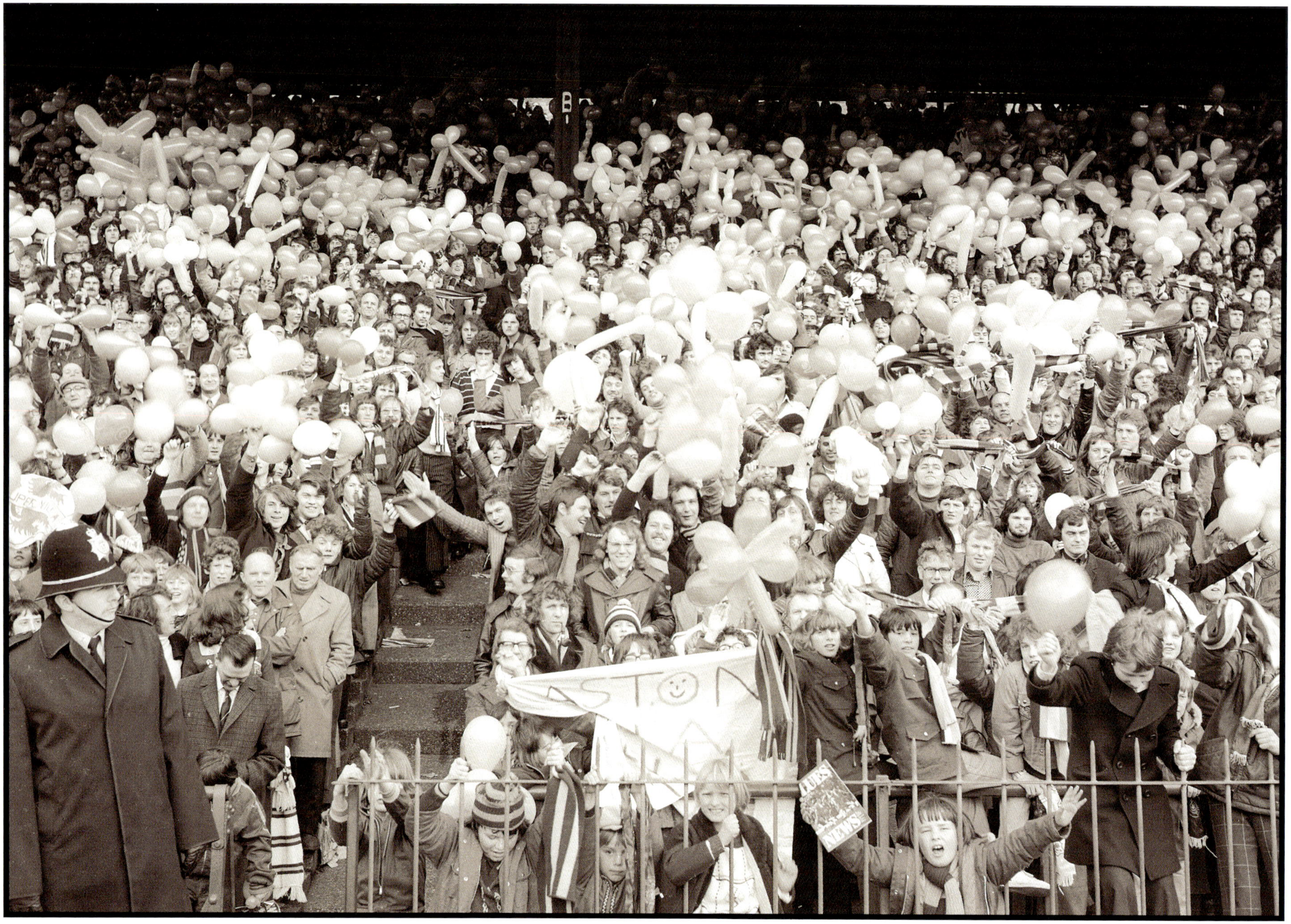
ASTON

balloons on the holte

Football went through an era when balloons were in abundance, and the fans who massed at the Holte End were no exception, as this shot illustrates.
That end of Villa Park is now an impressive double decker stand, but I was sorry to see the end of it as a terrace.

laughing policeman

A policeman's lot is not always a happy one at football matches, but this one seems to be enjoying himself!

I took this picture to commemorate the final day of duty at Villa Park for this officer, who was due to retire from the force..

It was always nice to see the Laughing Policeman on match days and I certainly wasn't going to turn down his request for a photograph – I like to keep on the right side of the law!

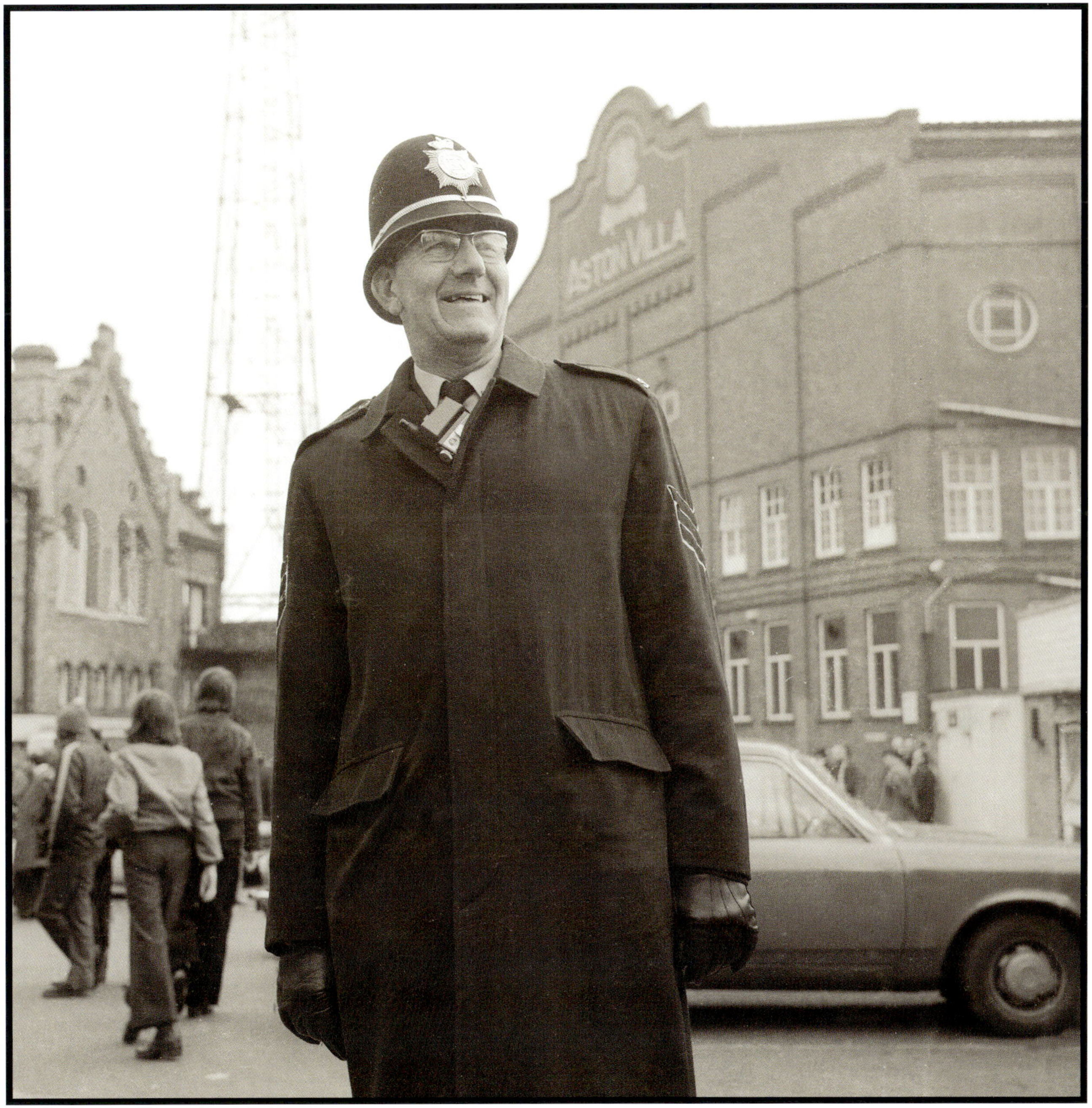

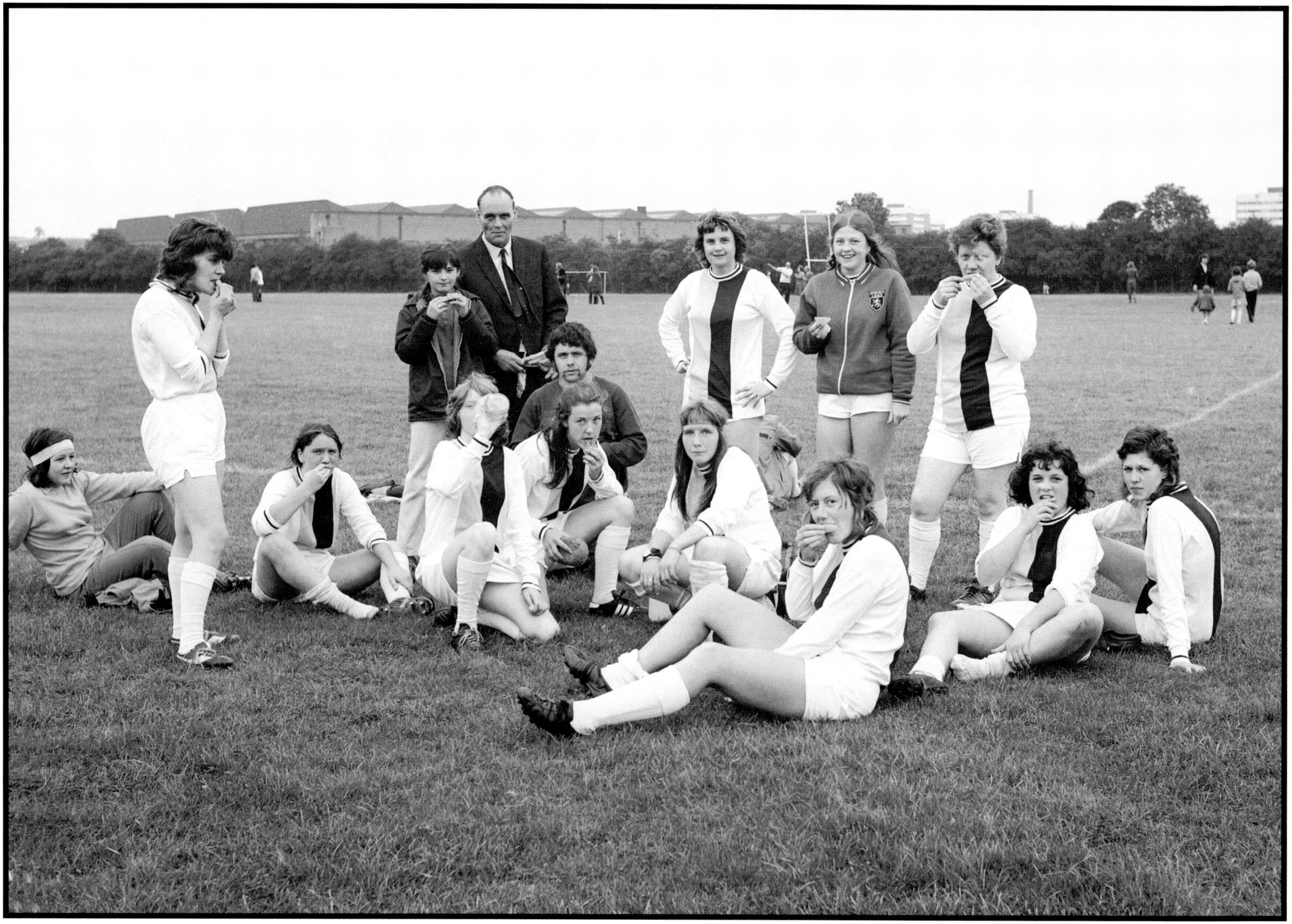

ladies' day

Respect for ladies football has increased considerably in recent times, but even back in the seventies the standard of the Aston Villa Ladies team was pretty high.

I went along ready to make fun of the girls, but left impressed with what I'd seen – although not with what I'd heard. Some of the language would have embarrassed hardened professionals. As you can see from these faces as they indulged in their half-time oranges, the girls took it very seriously.

boom time

Back in the top flight in 1975-76, Villa's league attendances soared to an average of 38,874, the club's highest figure since 1951-52, and one which has not been bettered since. Crowds of 40,000-plus were a regular feature of that campaign, with the 50,000 mark surpassed for some.
This scene along Trinity Road was common throughout that season, even though we finished a modest 16th.

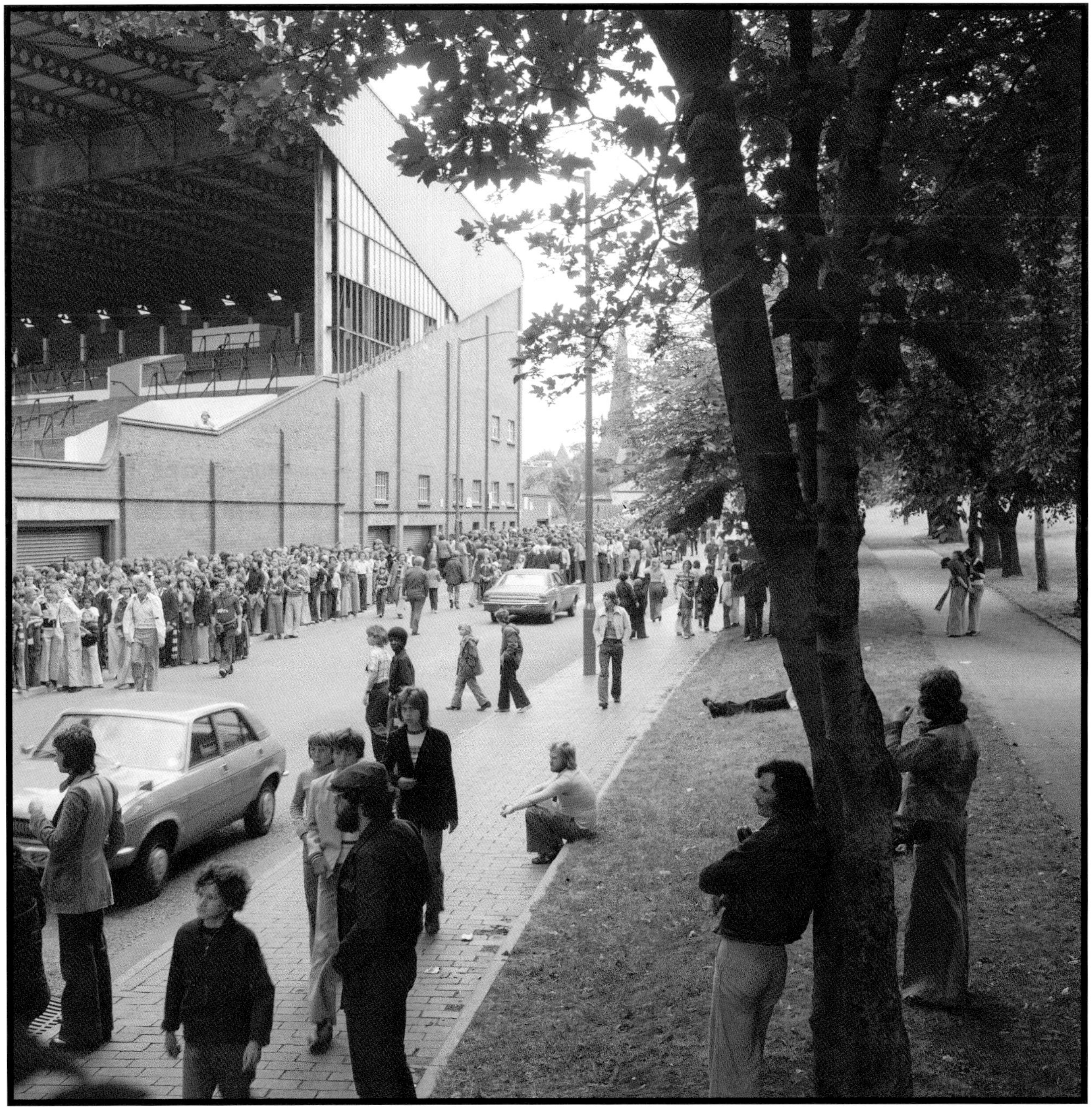

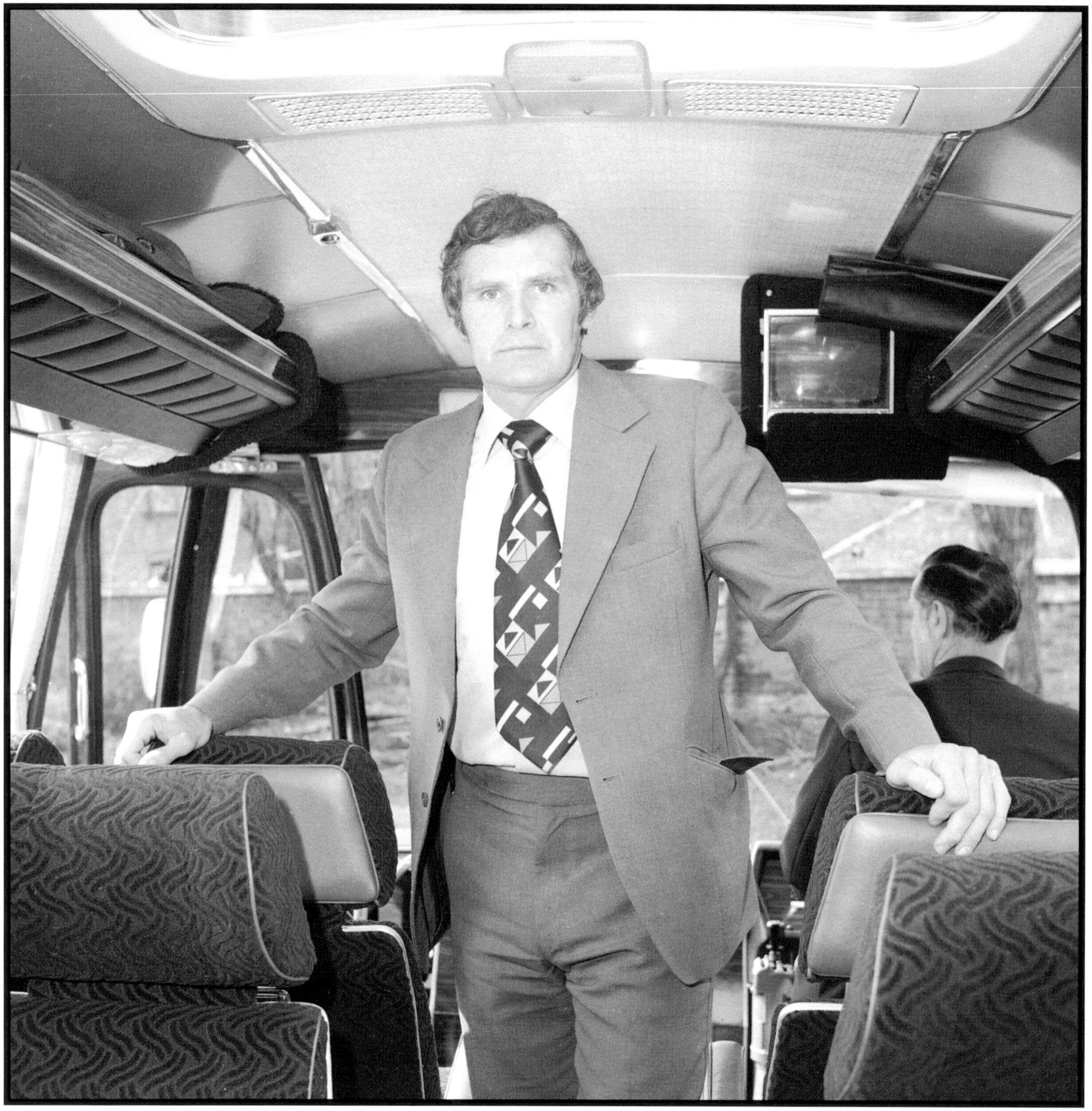

coach on the coach

Coach Roy McLaren boards the team bus as Villa prepare to head home from an away match.

Roy, who moved to Australia after leaving the club, was an underrated figure at Villa, and the players who won the title in 1981 and the European Cup the following year will tell you just what an influential figure he was, even though Ron Saunders and Tony Barton took most of the credit.

I photographed both of Roy's daughters' weddings – at reduced rates because he's a Scot!

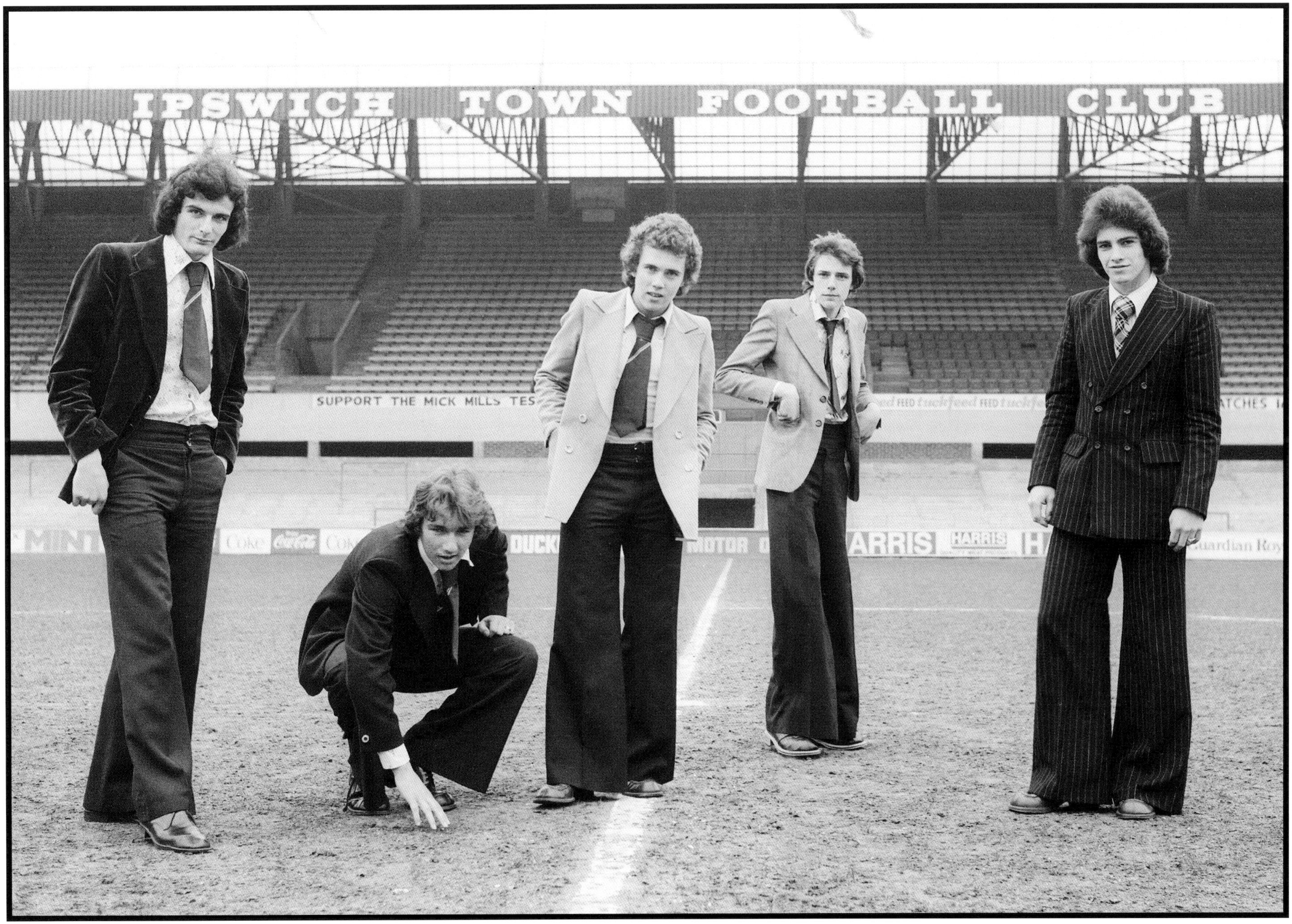
IPSWICH TOWN FOOTBALL CLUB
SUPPORT THE MICK MILLS
HARRIS

youth stars

Between the FA Youth Cup triumphs of 1972 and 1980, Villa were also dominant in the Southern Junior Floodlit Cup – and they always seemed to be facing Ipswich Town in the final.

They overcame the East Anglian youngsters over two legs in 1973, 1975 and 1976, and there was certainly a confident look about the youngsters as they took a look at the Portman Road pitch before the second leg in the last of those finals.

The quintet are (from the left) Charlie Young, Micky Buttress, David Hughes, Michael Parsons and David Evans.

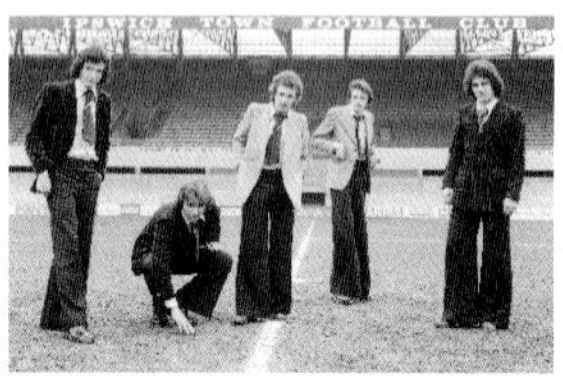

just one more

When footballers aren't kicking a ball, they love taking photographs. John Gidman and Dwight Yorke were two, in particular, who couldn't resist grabbing my camera and snapping away at anything that took their fancy.

When Villa's players gathered for the traditional photo-call before the 1977-78 campaign, the players decided it would be nice to take a 'team group' of the photographers, who duly took up their positions on the benches provided for group pictures.

On the far right is Dennis Mortimer, who always said he would have loved to be a sports photographer. I reckon he was better off as a footballer!

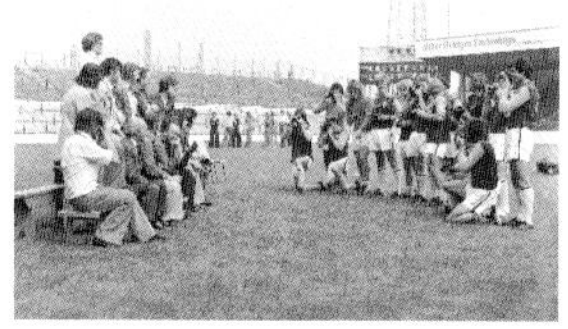

team talk

The first team may have been his priority, but Ron Saunders was always aware of the importance of bringing young players through the ranks.

He is seen here addressing the youth team, together with coach Frank Upton, who was in charge of the kids.

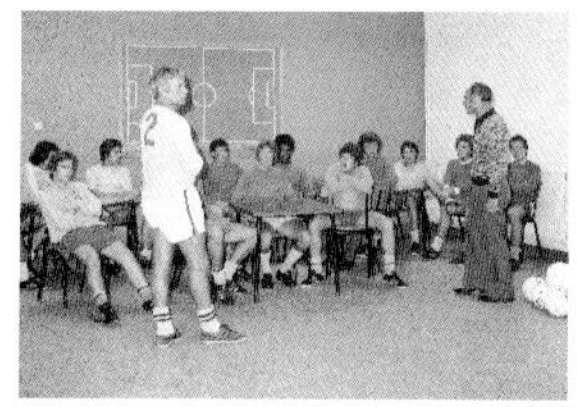

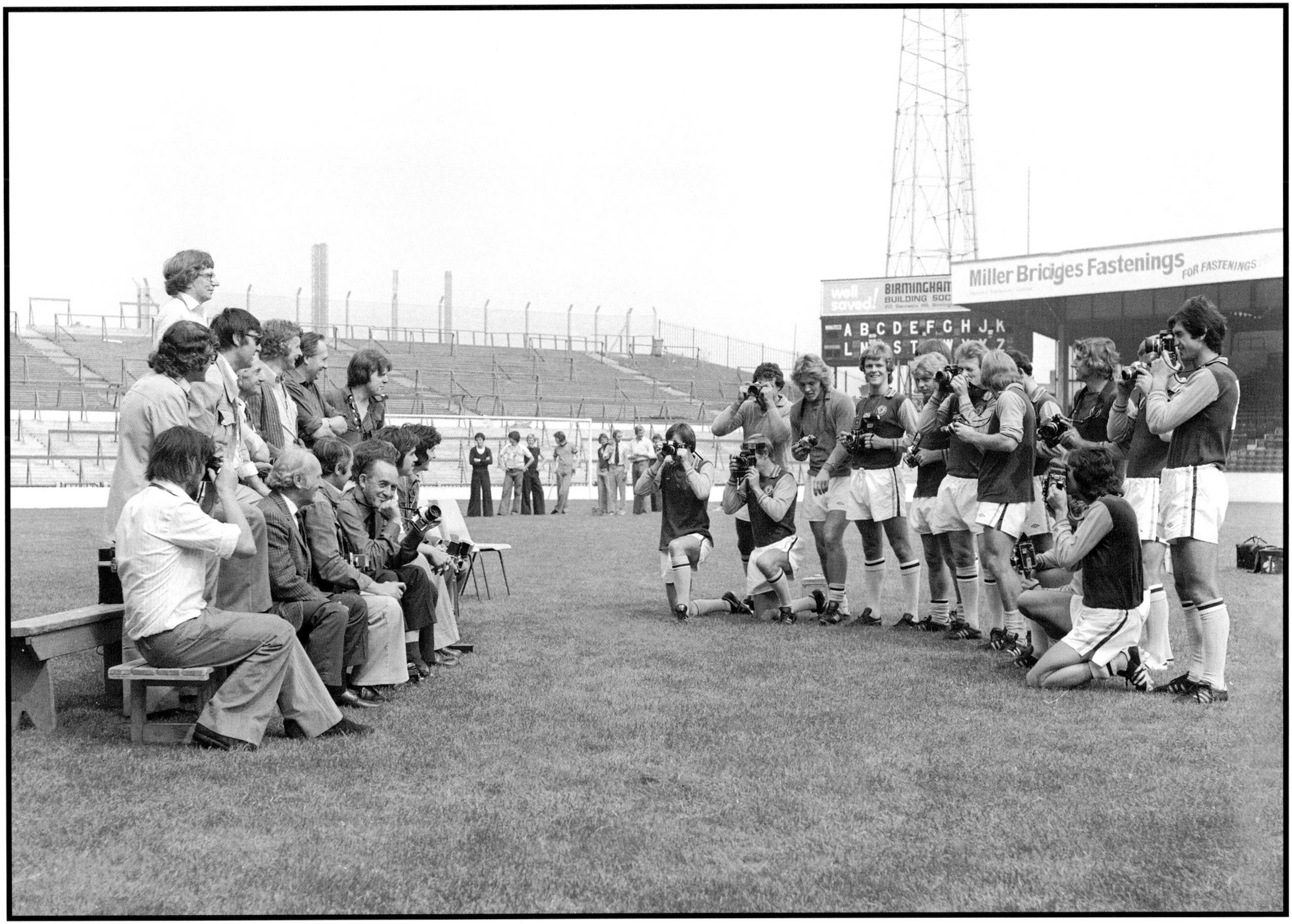
Miller Bridges Fastenings
FOR FASTENINGS
BIRMINGHAM
BUILDING SOC
well saved!
A B C D E F G H J K

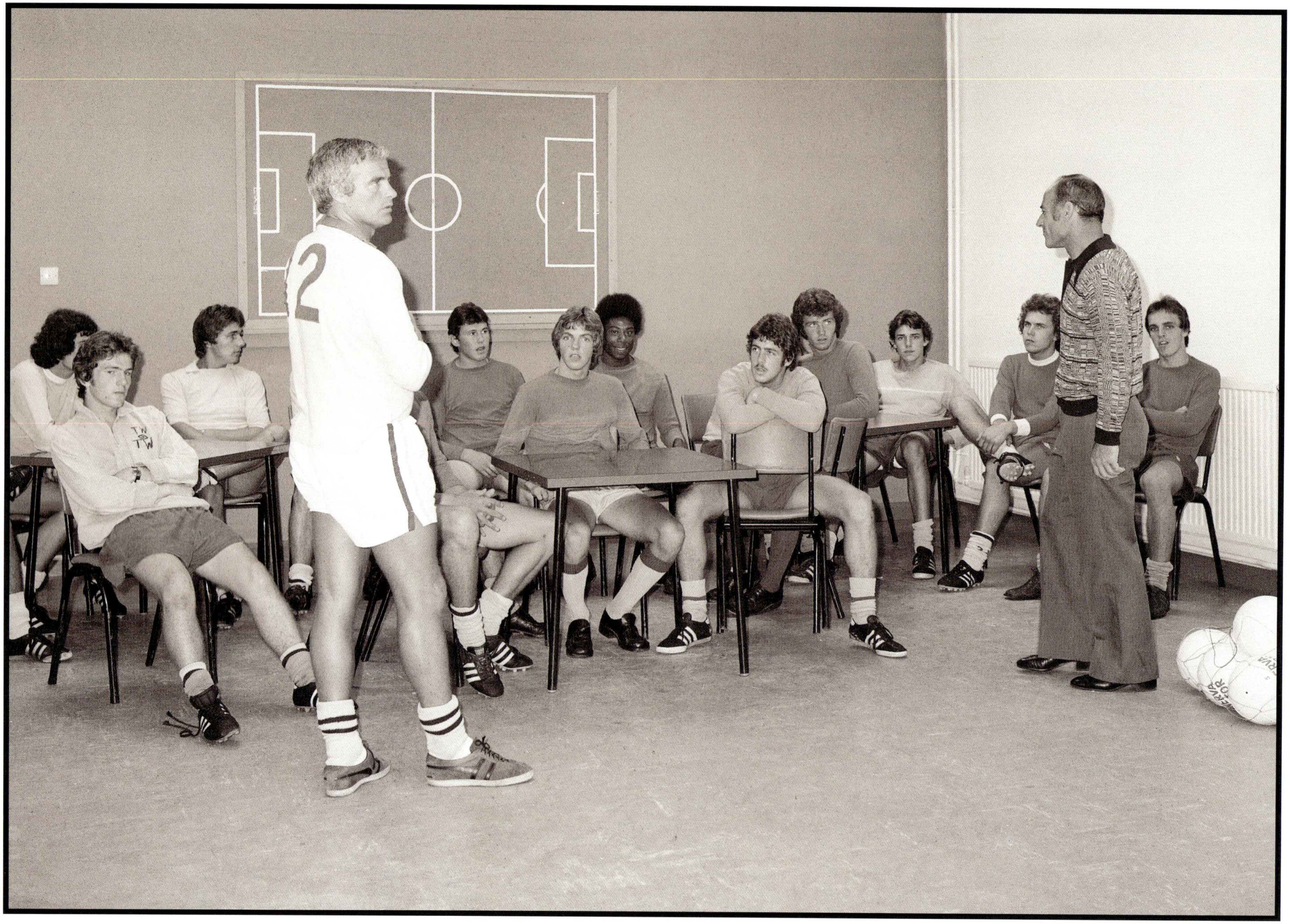

witton end

It's the beginning of the end for the Witton End, the vast open terrace which gave way to Villa Park's North Stand. At the time, of course, the North Stand was the newest feature of the ground, but it has since been superseded by three other stands.

The Witton was hugely popular with a lot of supporters, but it had become outdated and had to go. Apart from having no cover, it was also dangerous for anyone standing at the top of the terrace. I've seen one of two people slip backwards and fall down this steep bank.

Note the houses in Witton Lane, which also gave way to the bulldozers.

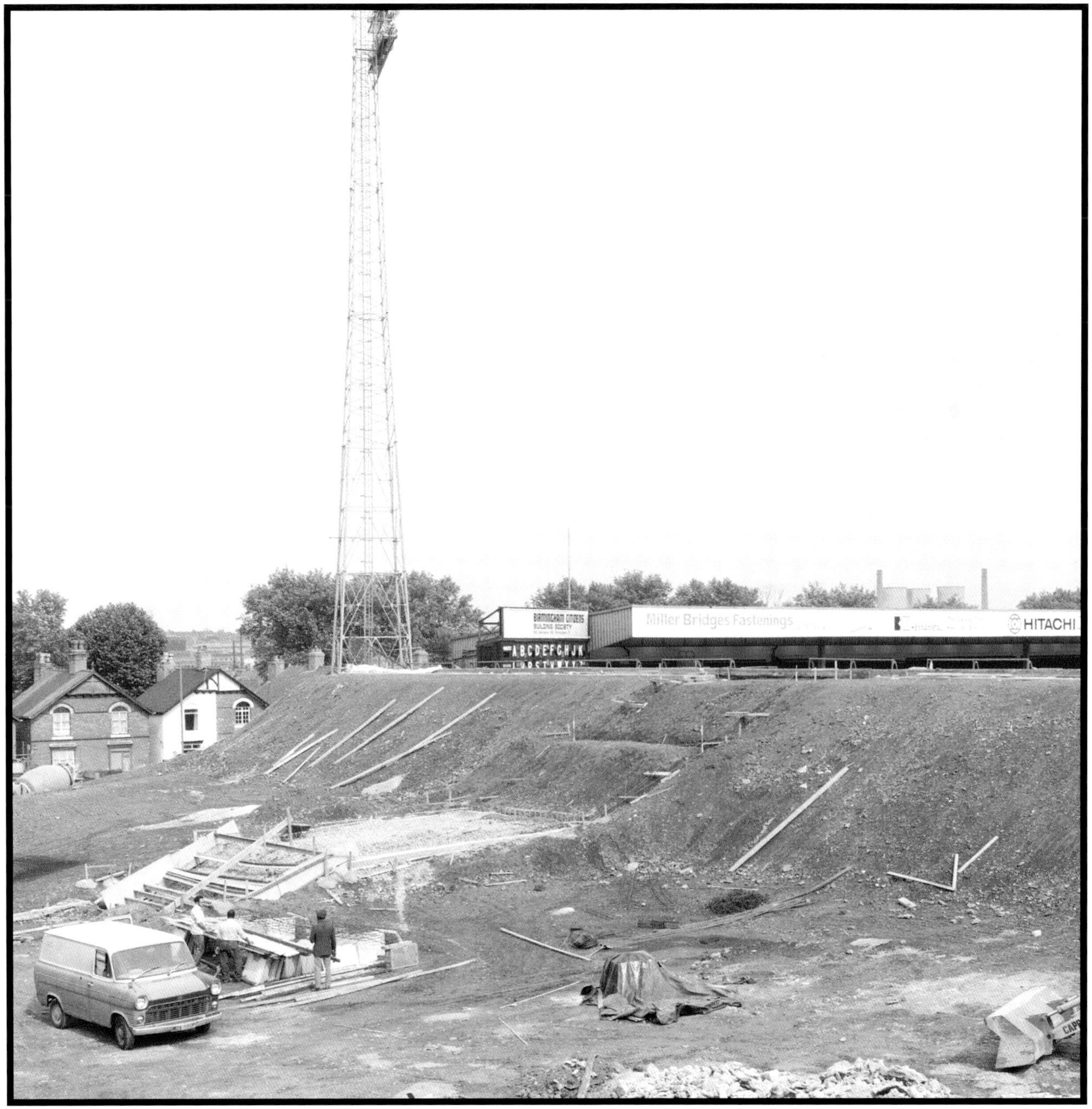

monkey business

We stopped off for a pre-match meal on the way to Manchester City, and I couldn't believe it when John Gidman came into the restaurant and said there was a monkey in the foyer.

This was a picture not to be missed, although my original plan didn't quite work out. The owner was quite happy for Giddy to hold her chum, but the monkey was having none of it. Obviously he'd been told not to go to strange men!

I settled for the next best thing, or no-one would have believed the story, and the lady happily obliged. To this day, I have no idea what they were doing at the hotel.

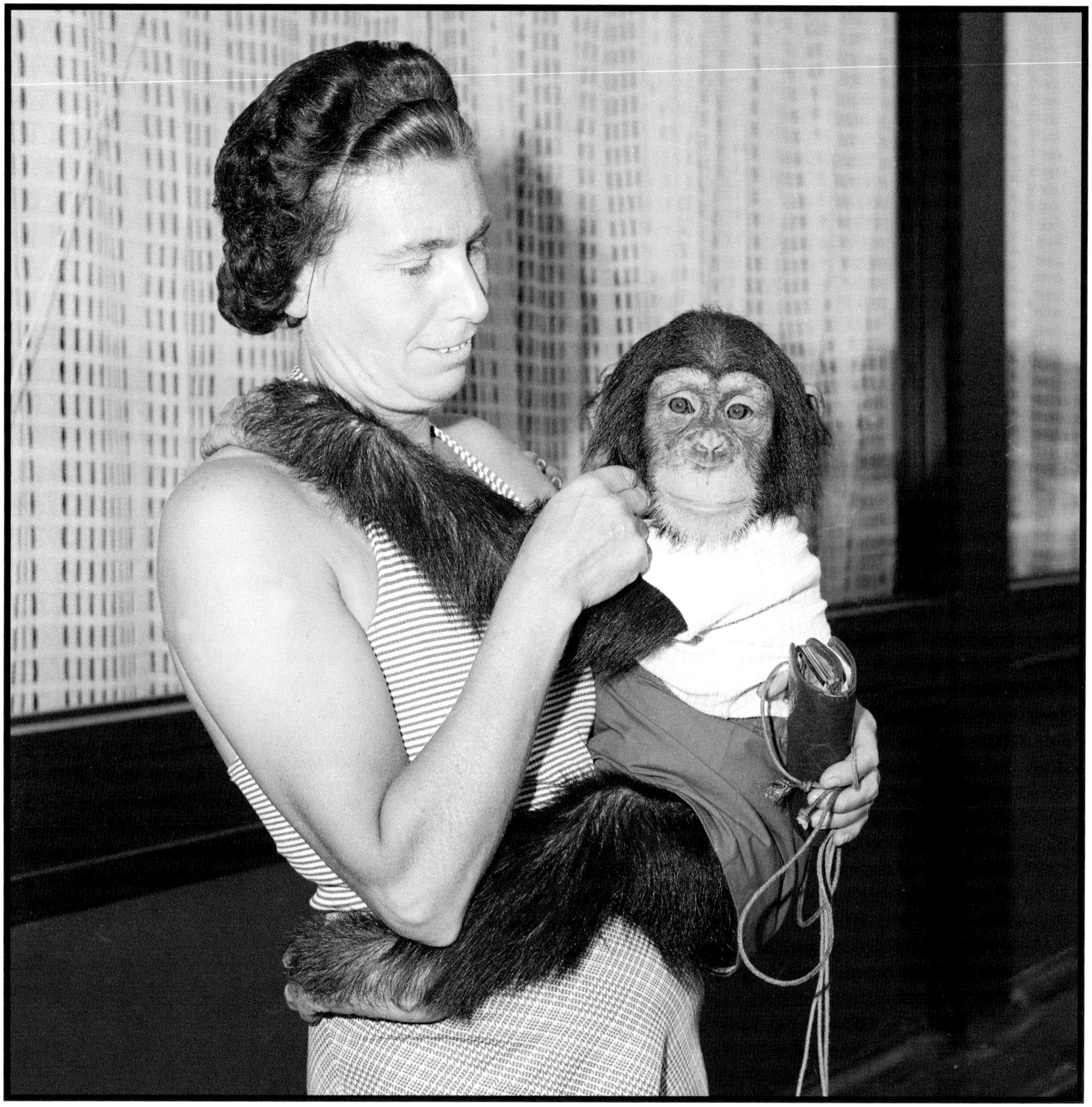

like a ballerina

Few players had the agility of Brian Little, who almost resembles a ballet dancer in this attempt at goal during a match against Everton at Goodison Park. I'm surprised he didn't do himself an injury.

If the ball had gone in, I would have regarded this as one of my best pictures, but with no end result, it falls short of that category.

If he failed to score on this occasion, though, he is still among my all-time Villa favourites, along with Gordon Cowans, Gary Shaw and Paul McGrath. That should tell you how I like my football.

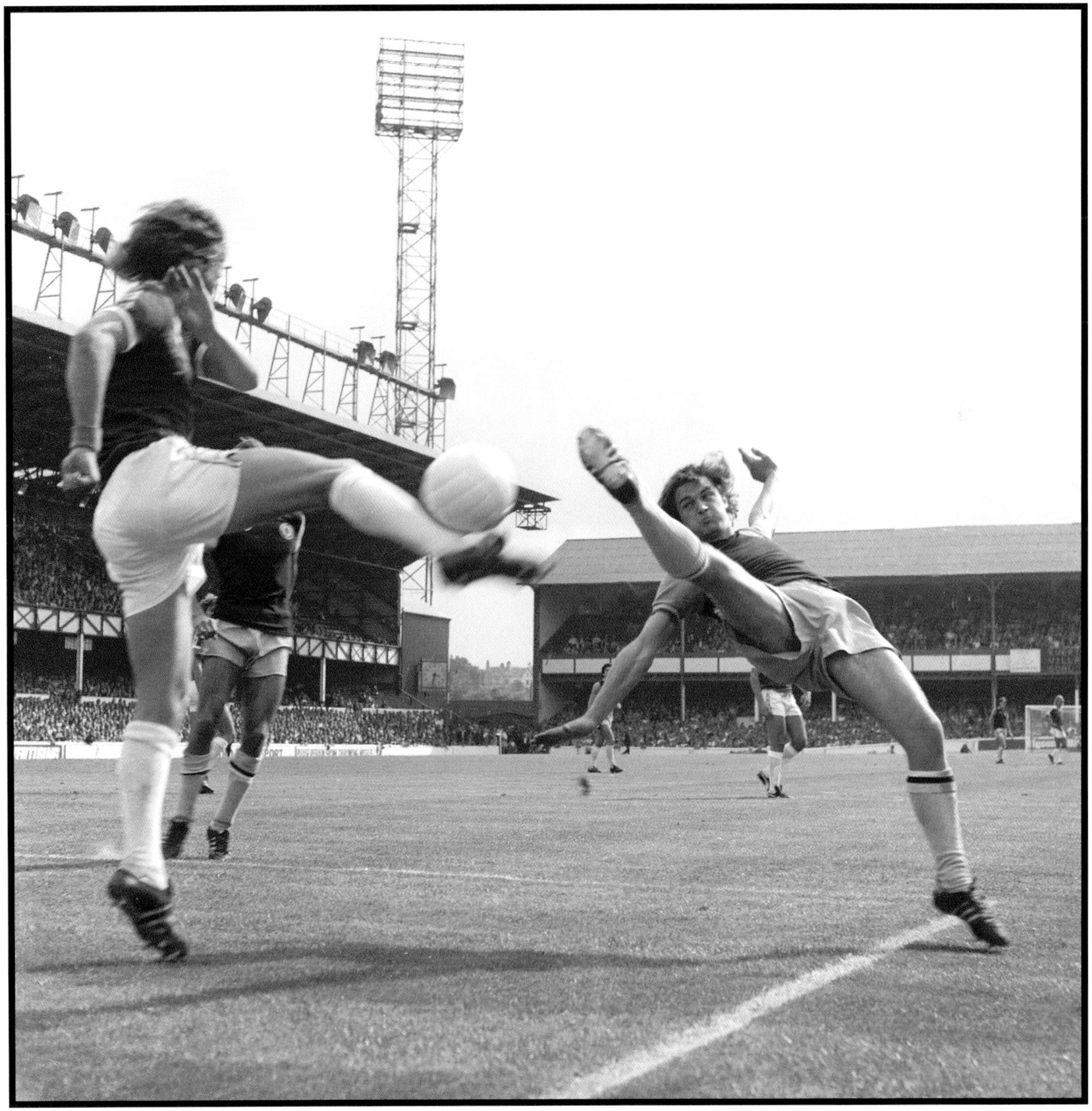

wise move

It was quite a bold move when Villa appointed Eric Woodward as their first commercial manager, but it was one they certainly did not regret.

Eric introduced a whole range of projects which generated funds for the club, including that never-to-be-forgotten friendly against Brazilian giants Santos – Pele and all.

Eric, a former reporter with the Birmingham Evening Mail, also used his journalistic expertise to good effect, transforming the Villa News & Record into an award-winning programme.

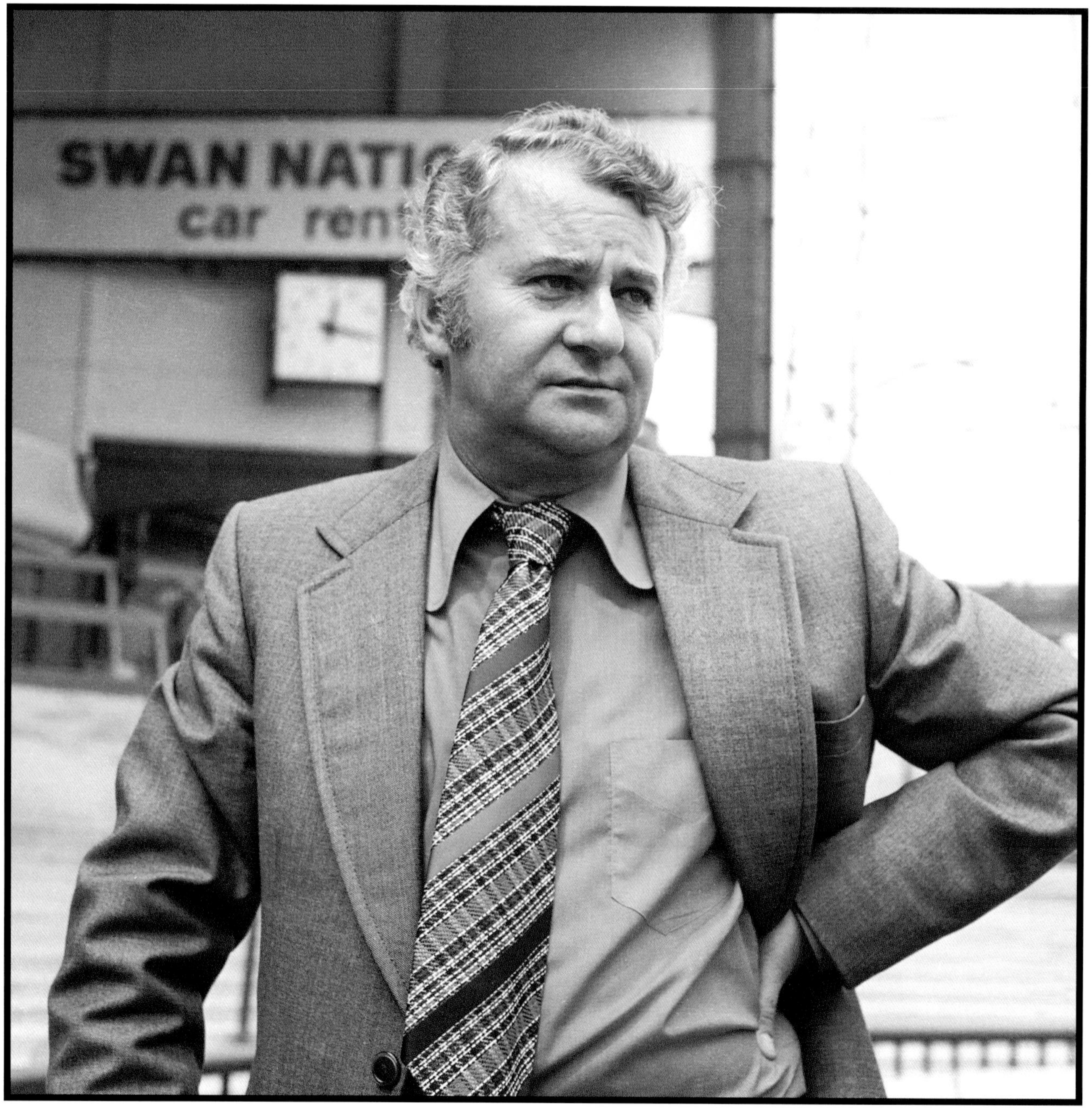

white horse

Wembley is famous for the 'White Horse' Cup Final, but Villa Park also boasted a white horse at one stage.

He is pictured here with his policeman rider, trotting along Trinity Road before a match, although there obviously wasn't much need for a police presence for this particular fixture.

It was a wet, miserable afternoon and there clearly wasn't going to be a very big crowd.

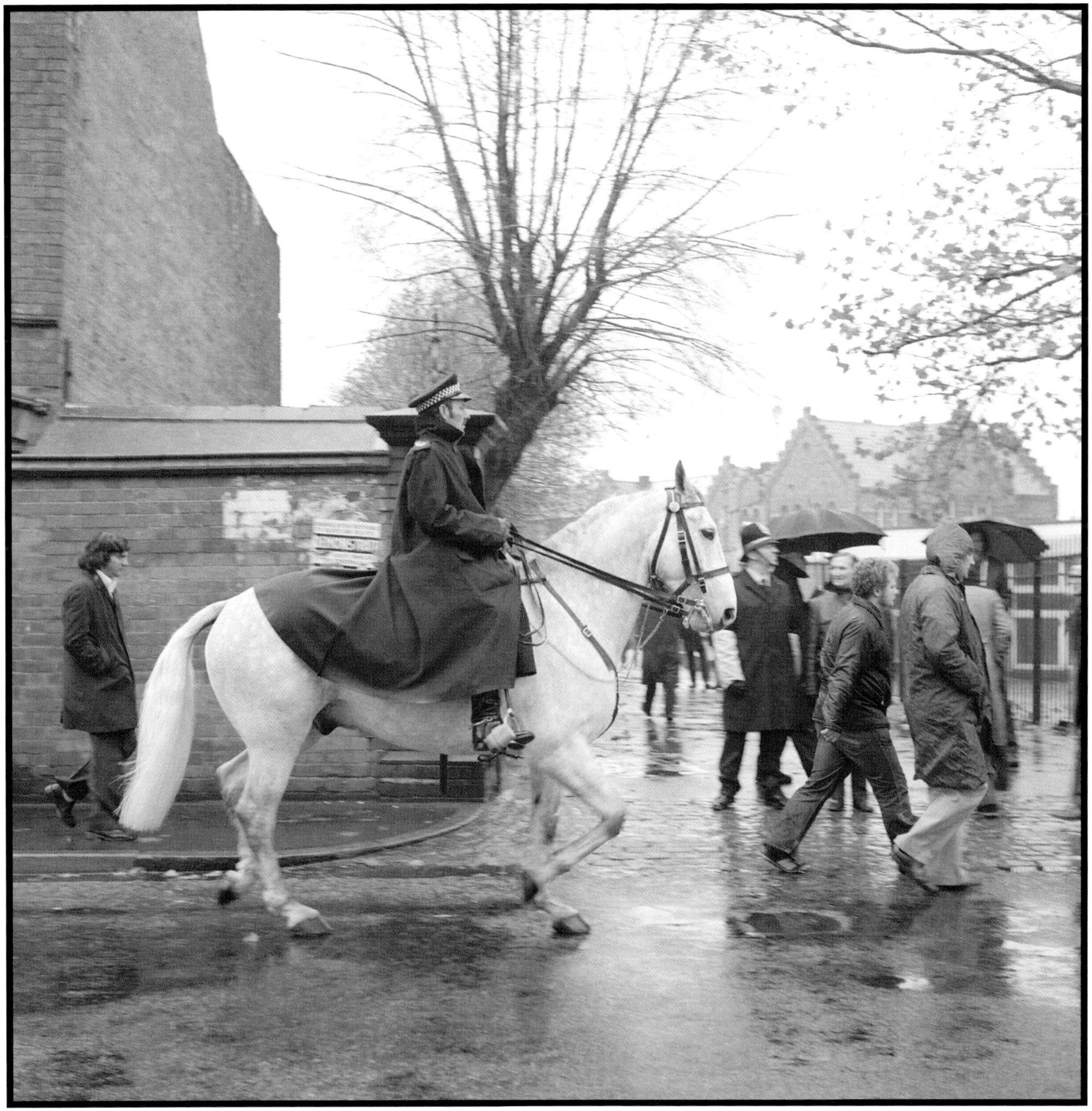

frank flanned!

Footballers are frequently requested to attend functions, but Frank Carrodus must wish he had given this one a miss. Frank, a midfielder who would run and run, was a celebrity guest at a fete in Dartmouth Park, West Bromwich, and had to stand still when he found himself as a target on the mud-slinging stall.

It wasn't real mud, but I would imagine his suit needed dry cleaning afterwards. In hindsight, he would have been wiser turning up in T-shirt and jeans.

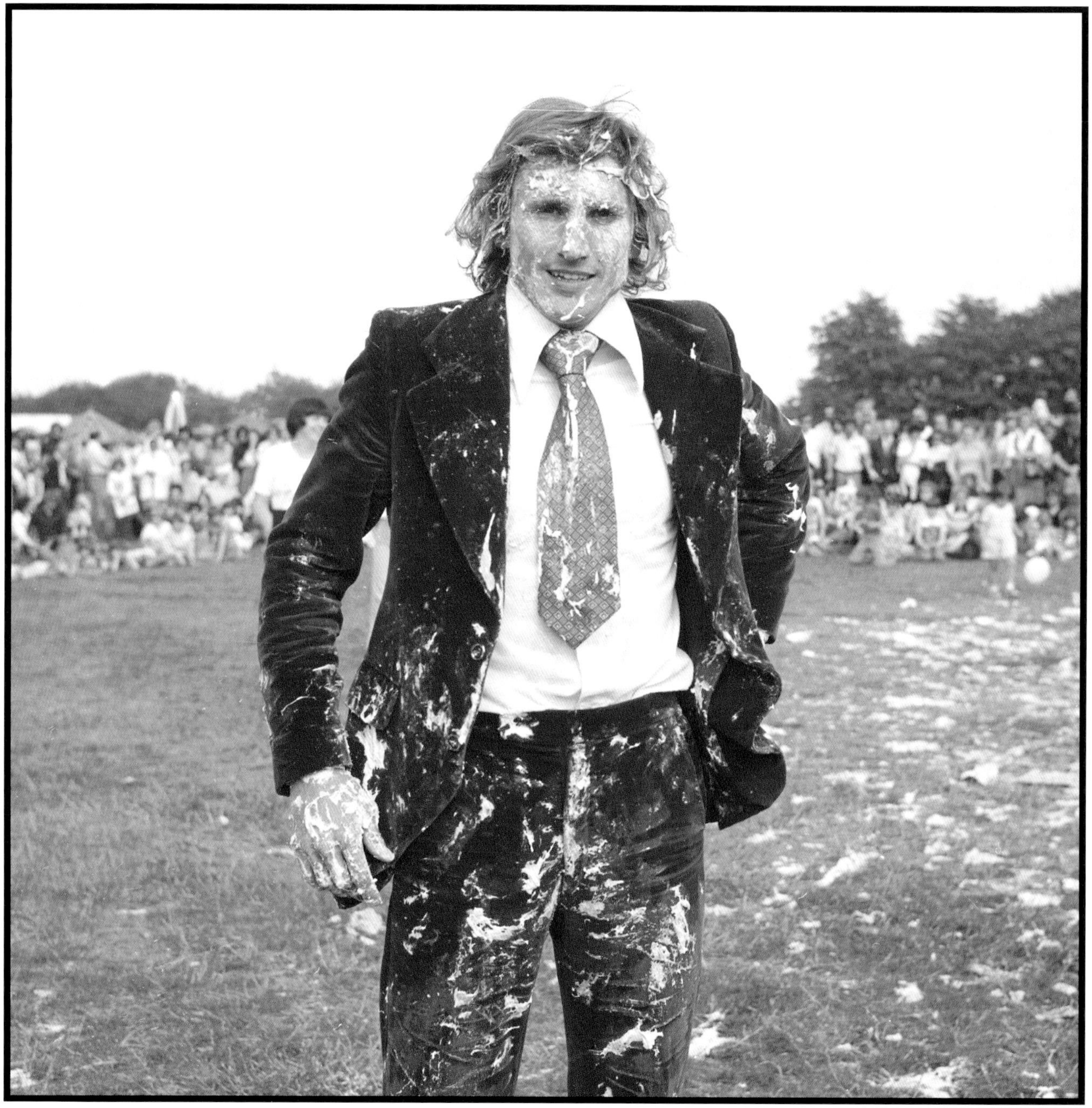

champagne charlies

Wembley, here we come! Villa have just beaten Queens Park Rangers 3-0 at Highbury in the 1977 League Cup semi-final replay, and Dennis Mortimer, John Burridge, Chris Nicholl and Andy Gray toast the team's success with a drop of bubbly on the team coach.

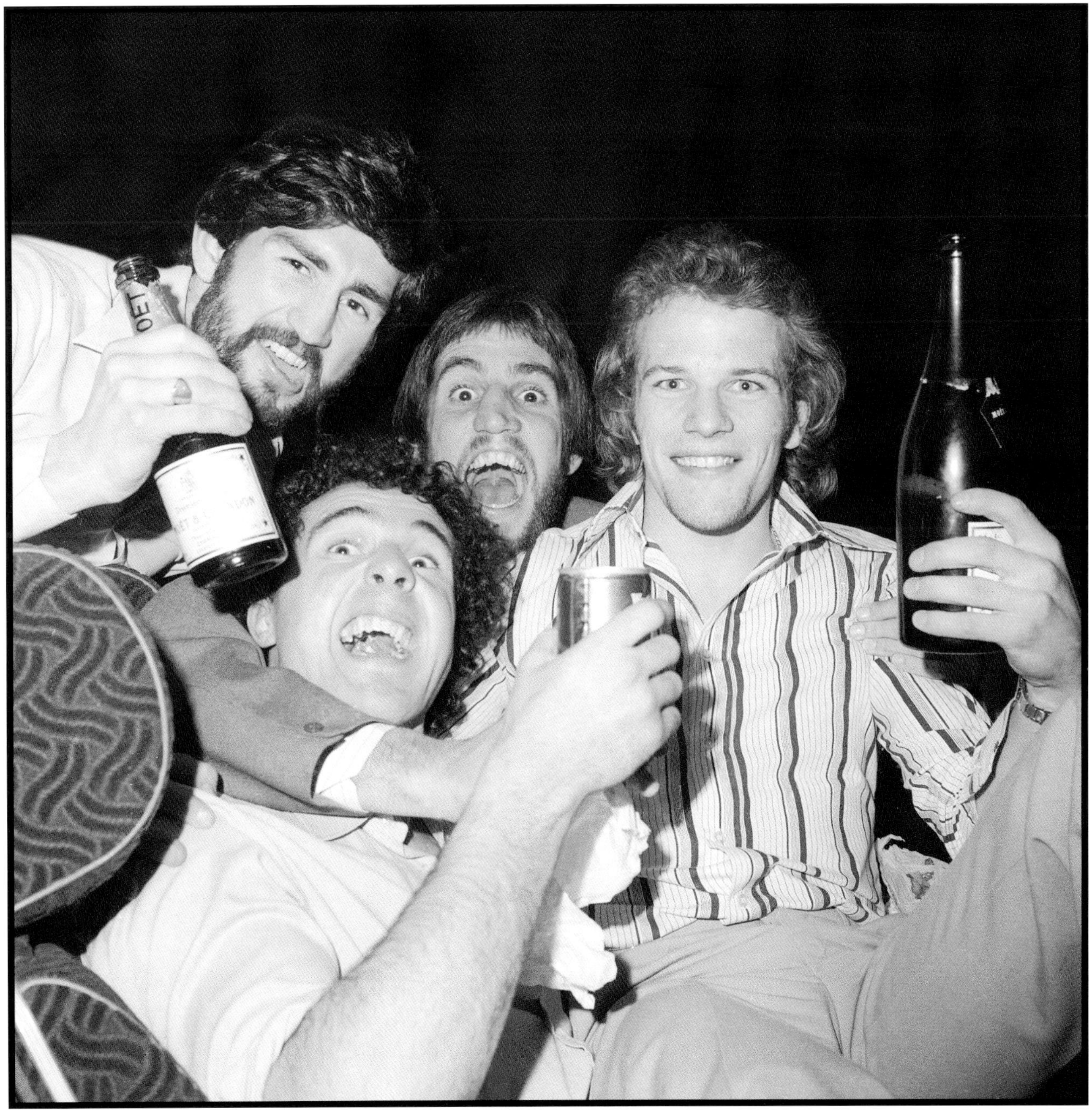

enterprising bruce

The game's financial rewards were nowhere near as great in the 1970s as they are today, and many players established themselves in business in readiness for when their playing days were over.

Bruce Rioch opened this shop in Hawthorn Road, Kingstanding, selling bathroom fittings, although I seem to recall it didn't stay open very long.

Not that it really mattered, because Bruce enjoyed a lengthy career as a footballer and subsequently moved into management, making a name for himself as boss of Arsenal.

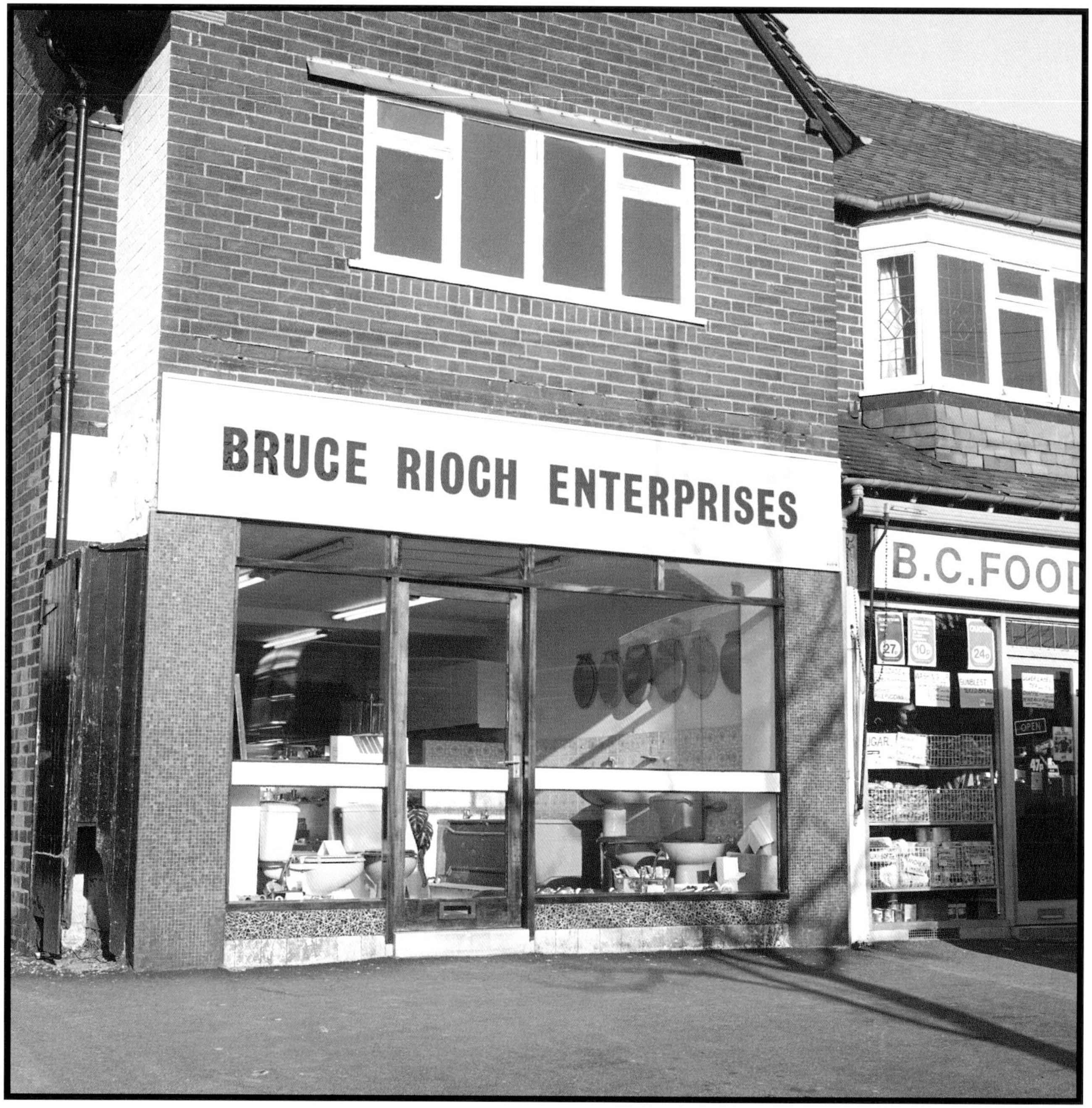

tunnel vision

This youngster is well and truly ‘Up for the Cup’ as he perches on the wall above Wembley's famous tunnel before the 1977 League Cup final against Everton.

He and the rest of the Villa fans didn't have a great deal to cheer that day, the game ending in a drab goalless draw, while the replay at Hillsborough also finished all square at 1-1 before Villa won the third game 3-2 after extra-time at Old Trafford.

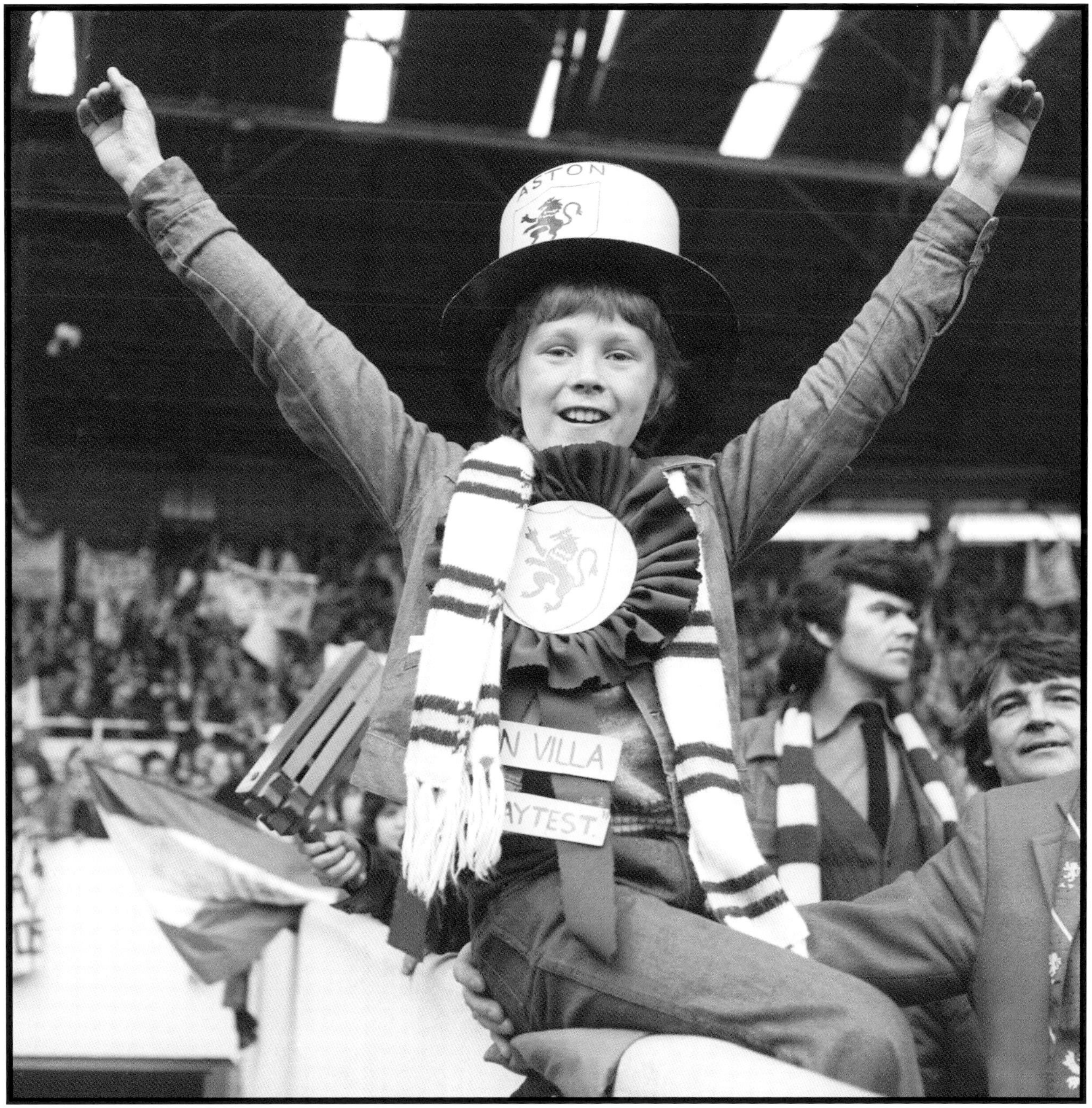

father frank

Youth coaches have to think about more than just football when they take youngsters overseas. For the duration of the trip, they have to be the players' mother, father and nursemaid.

Frank Upton underlines the point by giving physio treatment to one of his young charges during a youth tournament in Holland in the summer of 1977.

Such trips are important to the development of young players, both from a football point of view and in terms of widening their horizons.

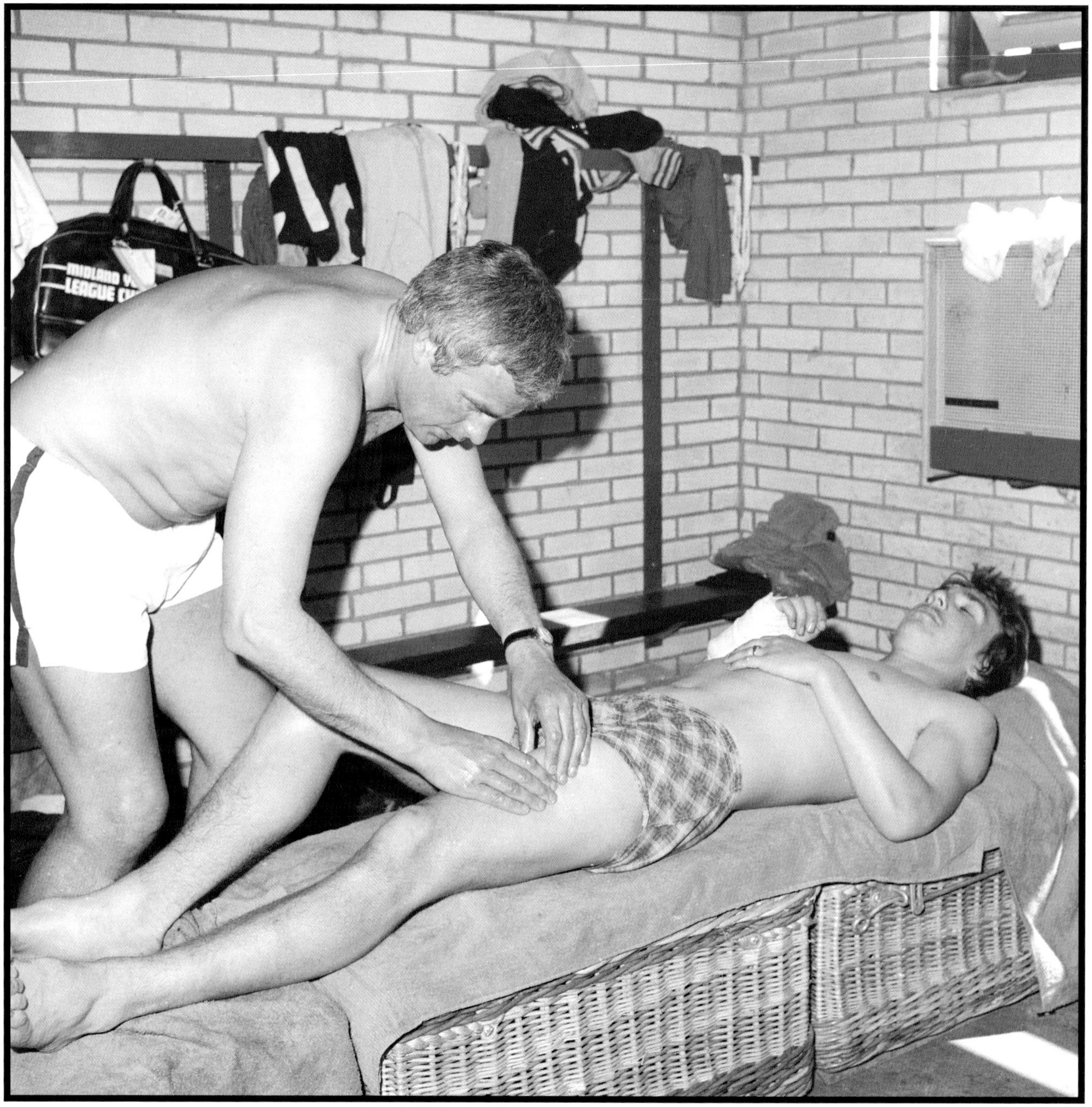

hostel hosts

Jim and Sylvia Paul were the couple who ran the hostel, making sure young players stayed on the straight and narrow.

Sylvia cooked the kids some wonderful meals and also fended off the endless stream of young ladies who called to see the up-and-coming young footballers.

Jim, of course, has been Villa's kit man for the best part of three decades. People take it for granted when the team run out in smart, clean shirts and shorts before a match, but a lot of work goes into making sure the players look the business.

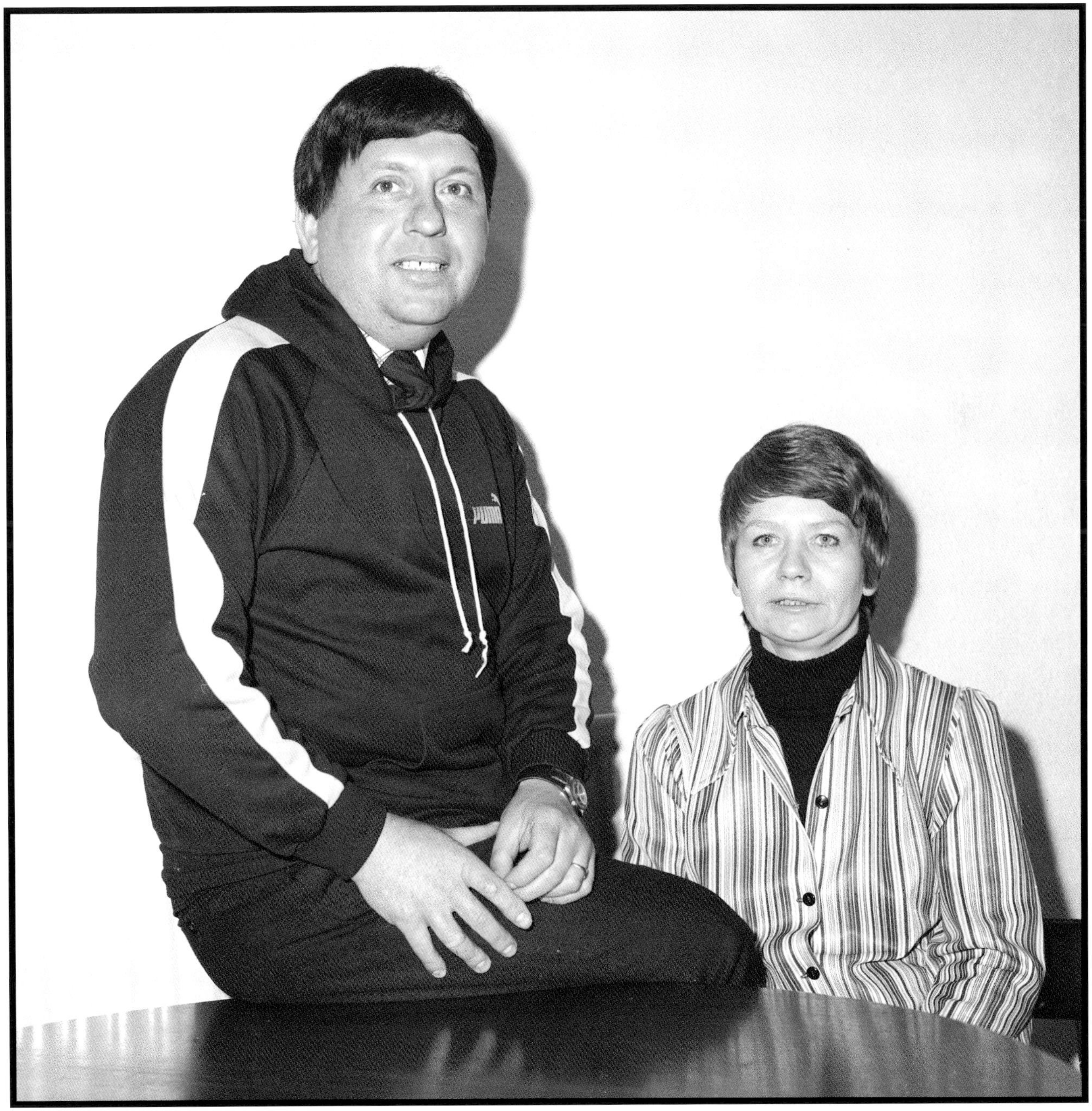

young hopefuls

Five young hopefuls are welcomed to Villa Park in July, 1977 by the club's Youth Development Officer Dave Richardson.

The quintet had just signed apprentice forms, but only one of them went on to make a name for himself. A 16-year-old Gary Shaw (second left) is easily identifiable, but I wonder what happened to the other lads?

That's the sad fact of football life. For every young hopeful who makes the grade, there are dozens who fall by the wayside.
For the record, the other players pictured are (left to right) Lee Jenkins, Alan Ollis, Glen Beech and Ian Ward.

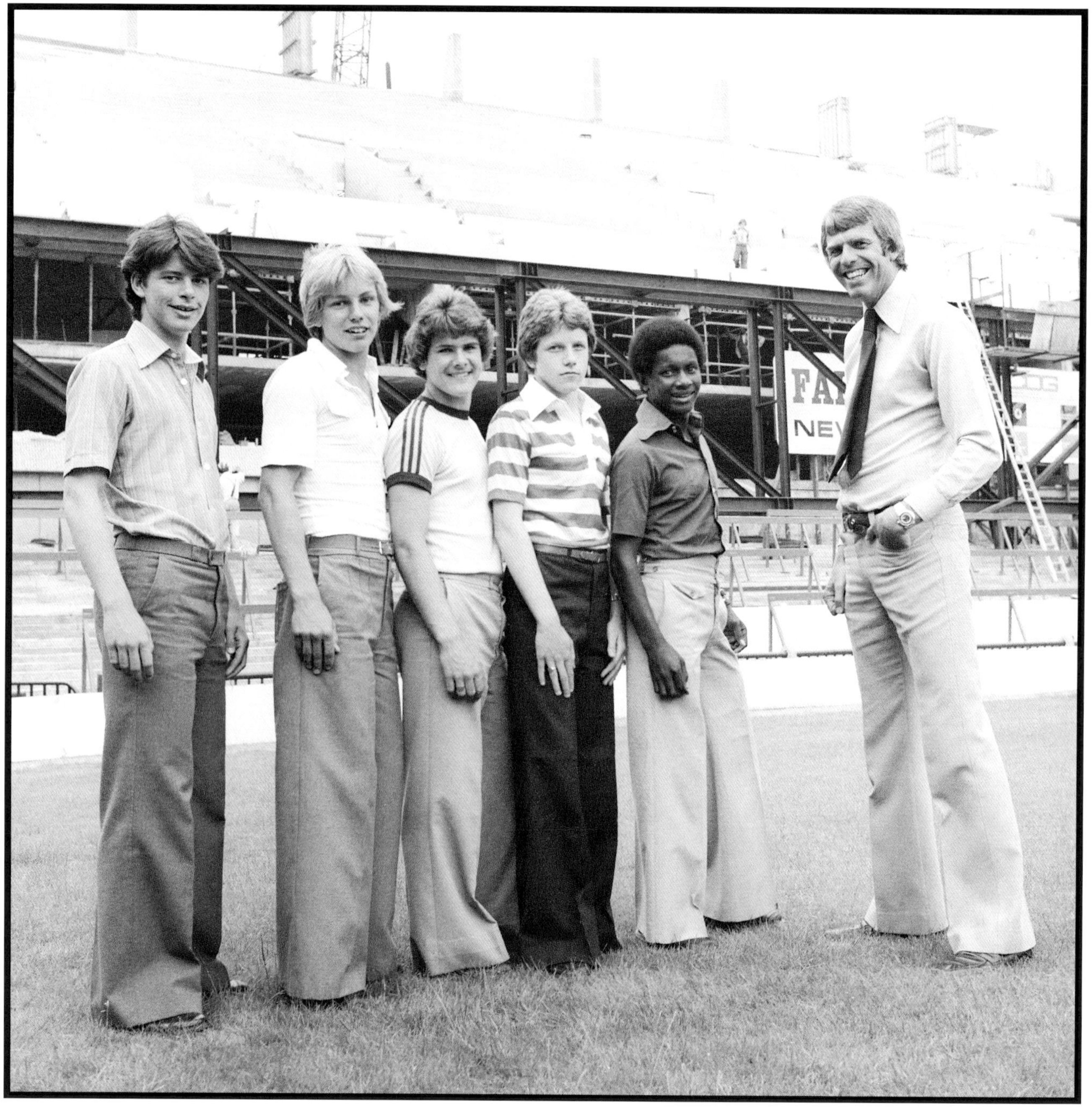

a cap for sid

Gordon Sidney Cowans is as quiet and unassuming today as he was when he first broke on to the scene as a promising youngster, and has never allowed his reputation as one of the greatest passers in Villa's history to go to his head.

He was a great footballer with tremendous vision and a lot of players benefited from his immense talents. David Platt, for one, has always acknowledged how important Gordon was in the development of his career.

This was taken at his home near Tamworth, just after he had won an England cap, and I was also delighted to take the photographs at his wedding.

For some reason, 'Sid' never received the international recognition he deserved. He won eight full caps, but it should have been nearer 80.

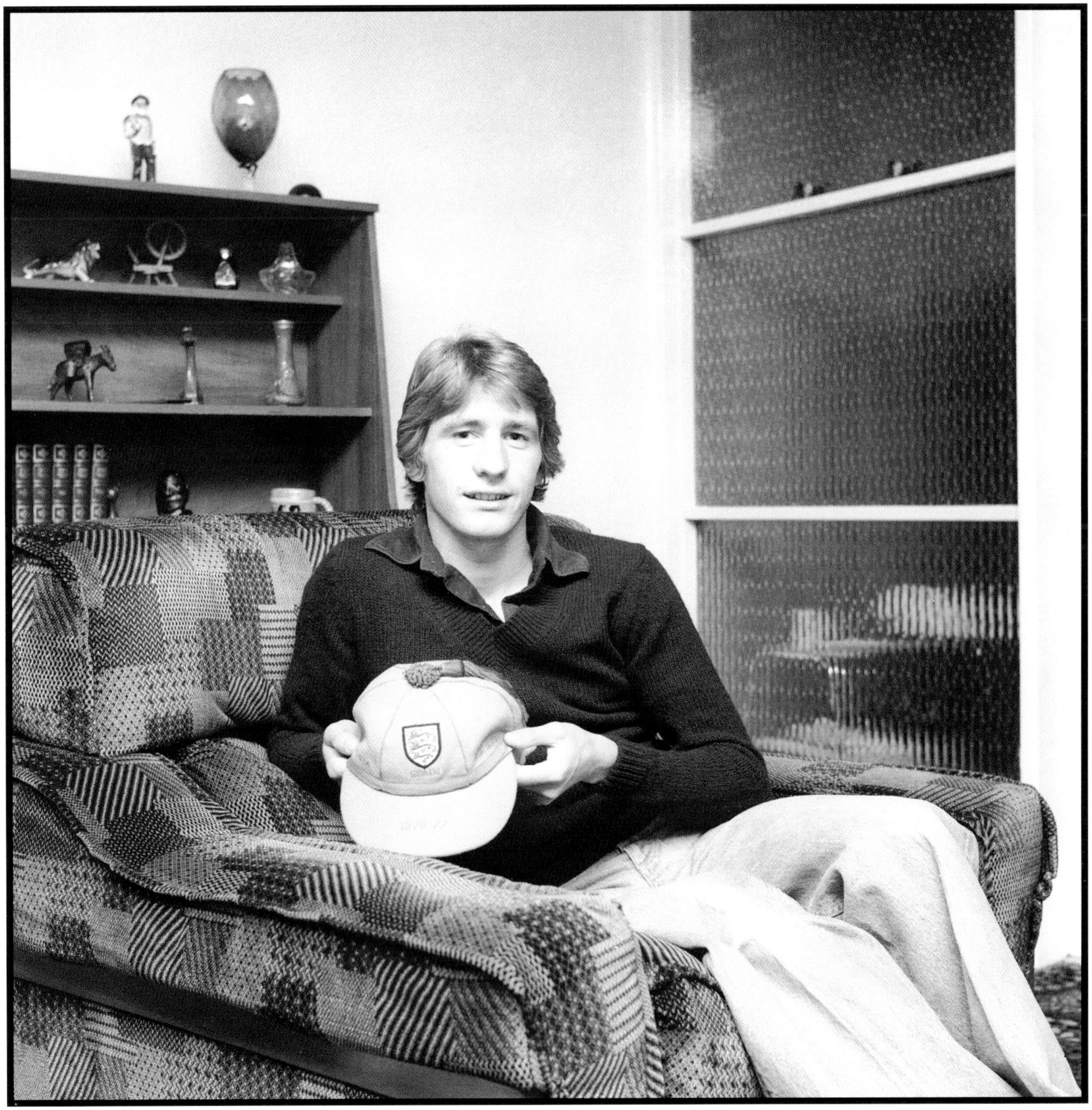

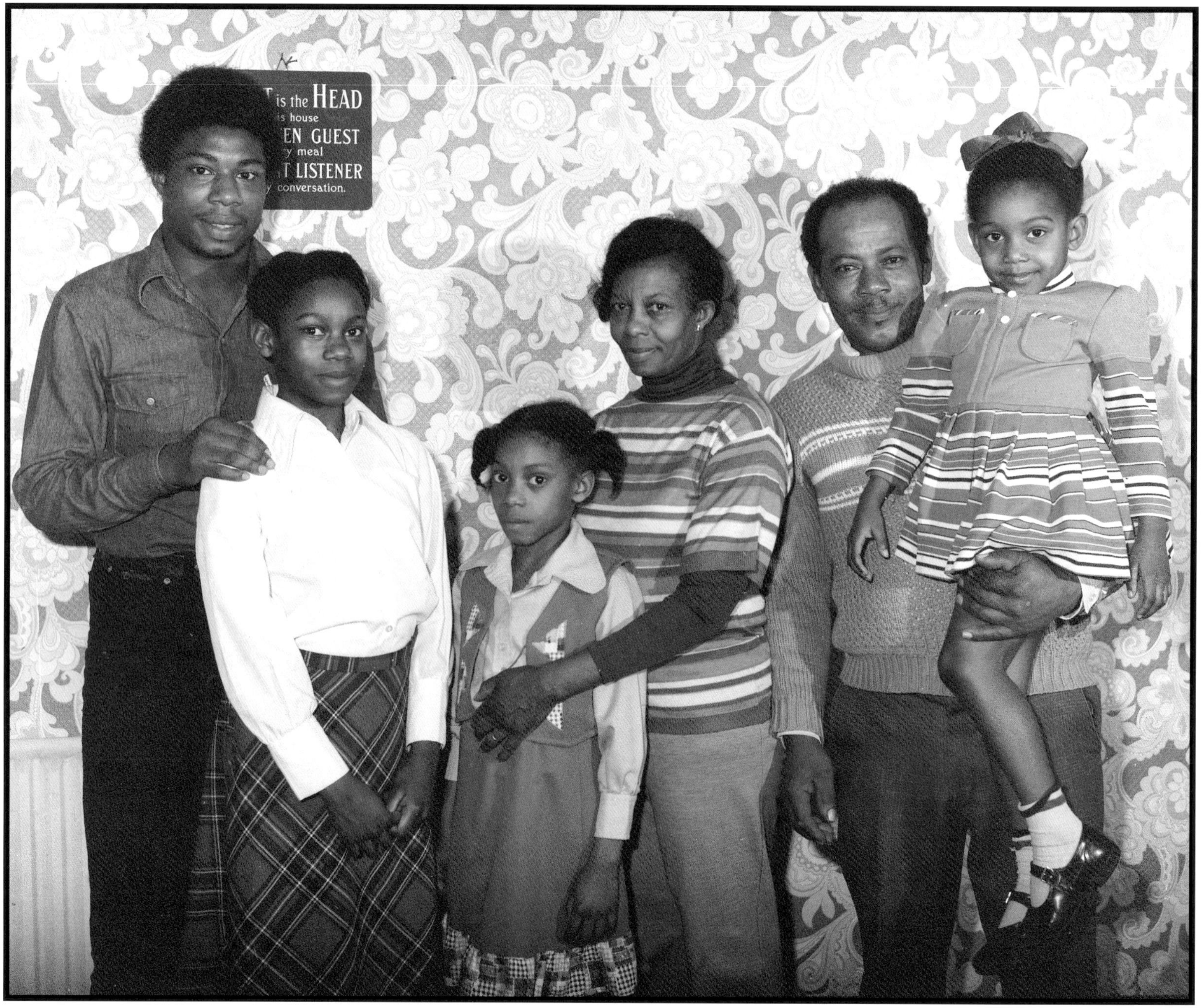
is the HEAD
house
GUEST
meal
LISTENER
conversation.

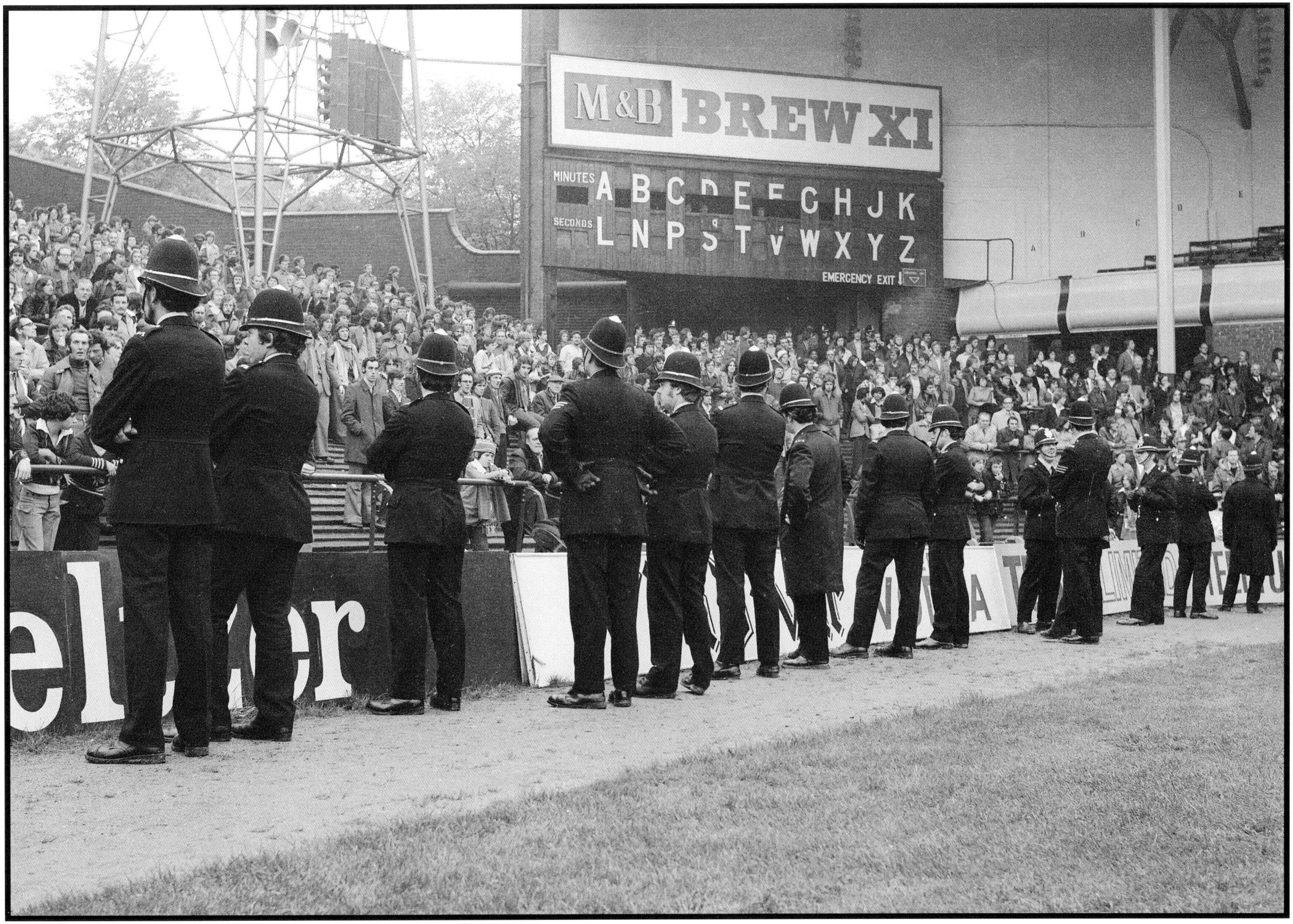
M&B BREW XI
MINUTES A B C D E F G H J K
SECONDS L N P S T V W X Y Z
EMERGENCY EXIT

smile please

Try as I might to get huge grins from Ivor Linton and his family, it simply didn't work. They dutifully stood in line to face the camera at their home in West Bromwich but, with the exception of the little girl on the right, they barely raised a smile.

Ivor never made a get impact at Villa, although he went on as substitute in the 2-1 European Cup win over Dynamo Berlin in 1981 and was unlucky to concede the penalty from which the Germans scored their goal.

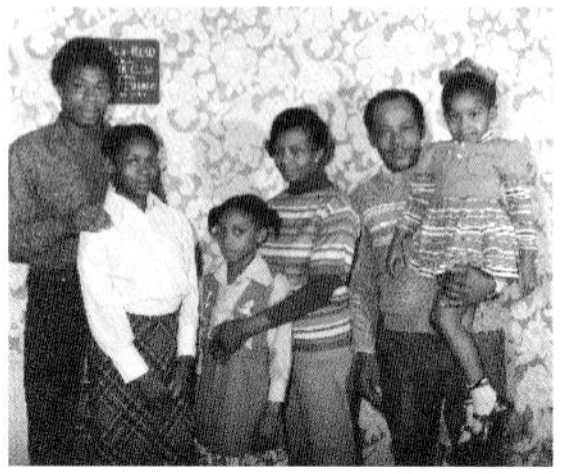

the blue line

This sight was all-too-common in the seventies – police officers lining up along the touchline to ensure that fans did not run on to the pitch.

The bobbies on duty in front of the Holte End appear to be fairly relaxed on the occasion, although the mood wasn't always so sedate.

Anyone who was at Villa Park in October, 1976 will recall with horror the terrifying scenes as thousands of drunken Scots invaded the pitch and other areas of the ground, causing the abandonment of the ill-fated 'friendly' against Glasgow Rangers.

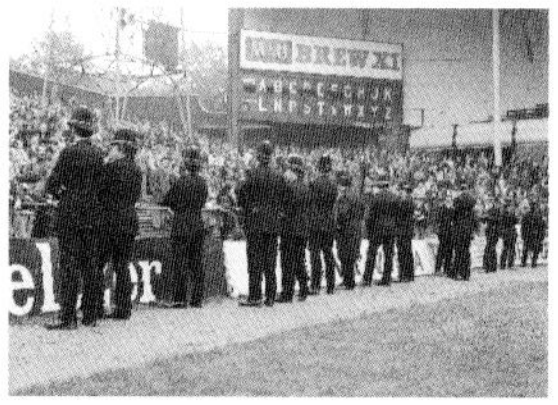

goal kick

Brian Little rates this as the best picture ever taken of him, and one of the best football photographs he has seen.

It was taken at Ashton Gate on 3rd September, 1977, and Brian is scoring a spectacular goal in a 1-1 draw against Bristol City. He actually had time to let the ball drop, but decided to try something out of the ordinary – for which I am eternally grateful.

The picture was taken with a camera I had borrowed, one which was normally used for studio work and to be honest, it wasn't really suitable for football.

Even so, it captured this memorable moment and when I printed 150 copies for a charity event not long afterwards, they sold out in no time.

People often come up to me and say: 'I still have your picture of Brian Little.' It always gives me a thrill.

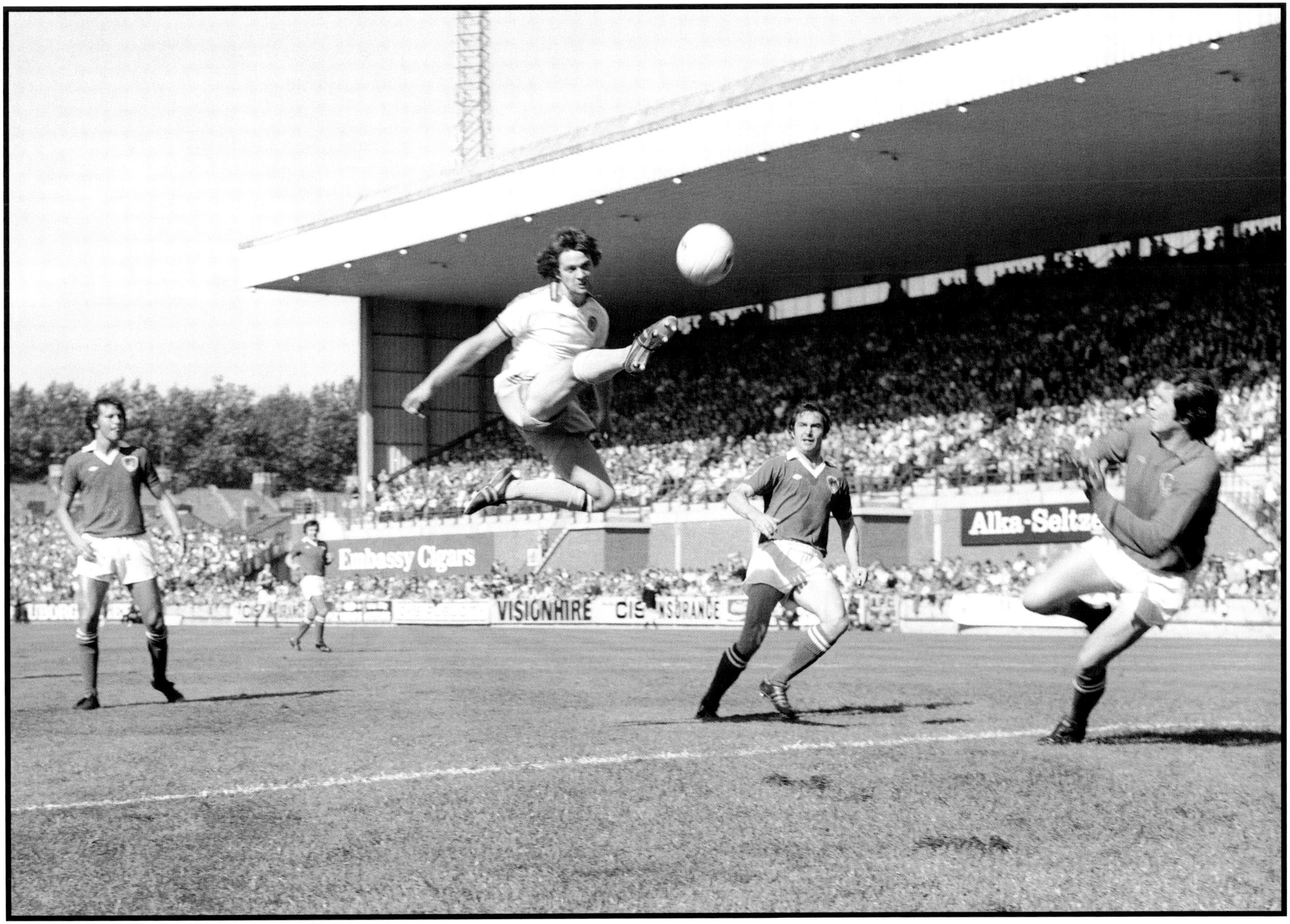
Alka-Seltze
Embassy Cigars
VISIGNHIRE
CIS INSURANCE

the boot room

When I first worked as Villa's club photographer, I couldn't get used to the idea of the senior players having their boots cleaned for them.

That's the way it is, though, with apprentices expected to perform the task as part of their football education.

At least this young player managed a smile as he got to work with the dubbin in the boot room at Bodymoor Heath.

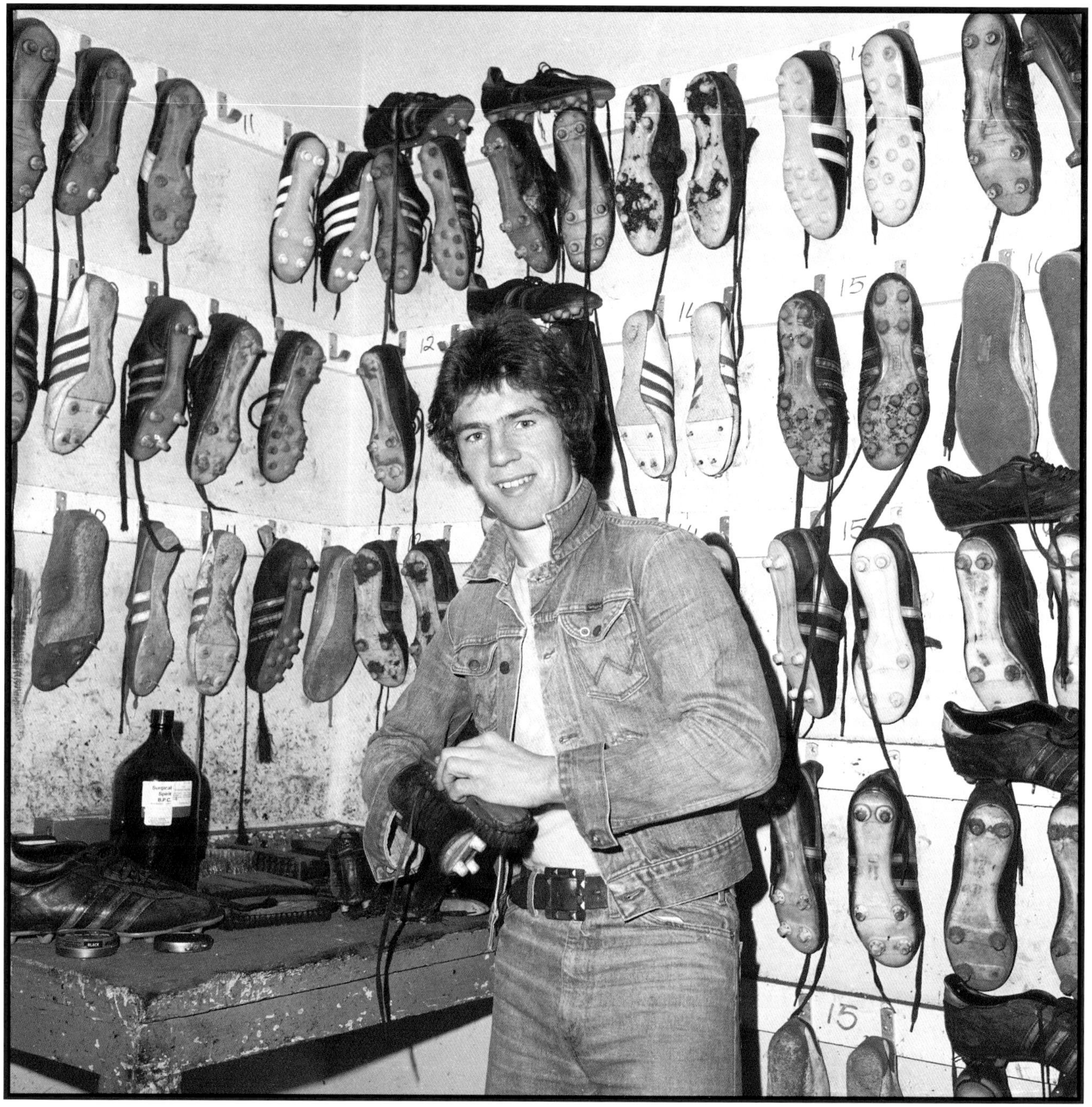

bill's beret

Sir William Dugdale was well-known for his unconventional dress sense, so when he was given a Basque beret as a present during a UEFA Cup trip to Bilbao, he didn't hesitate to wear it.

When Sir William joined the Villa board, it was the first time I had met anyone from the landed gentry. I asked how I should address him and he said that on a one-to-one basis, he was happy to be called Bill, but that protocol decreed I should use his title if we were in company.

Although I'm a Socialist, I have to say he was one of the nicest people I've met. When I met him recently at a party, he nudged me in the back and said: 'Hello, Bill here!'

Full of honesty and integrity, Sir William belonged to an age that is sadly gone.

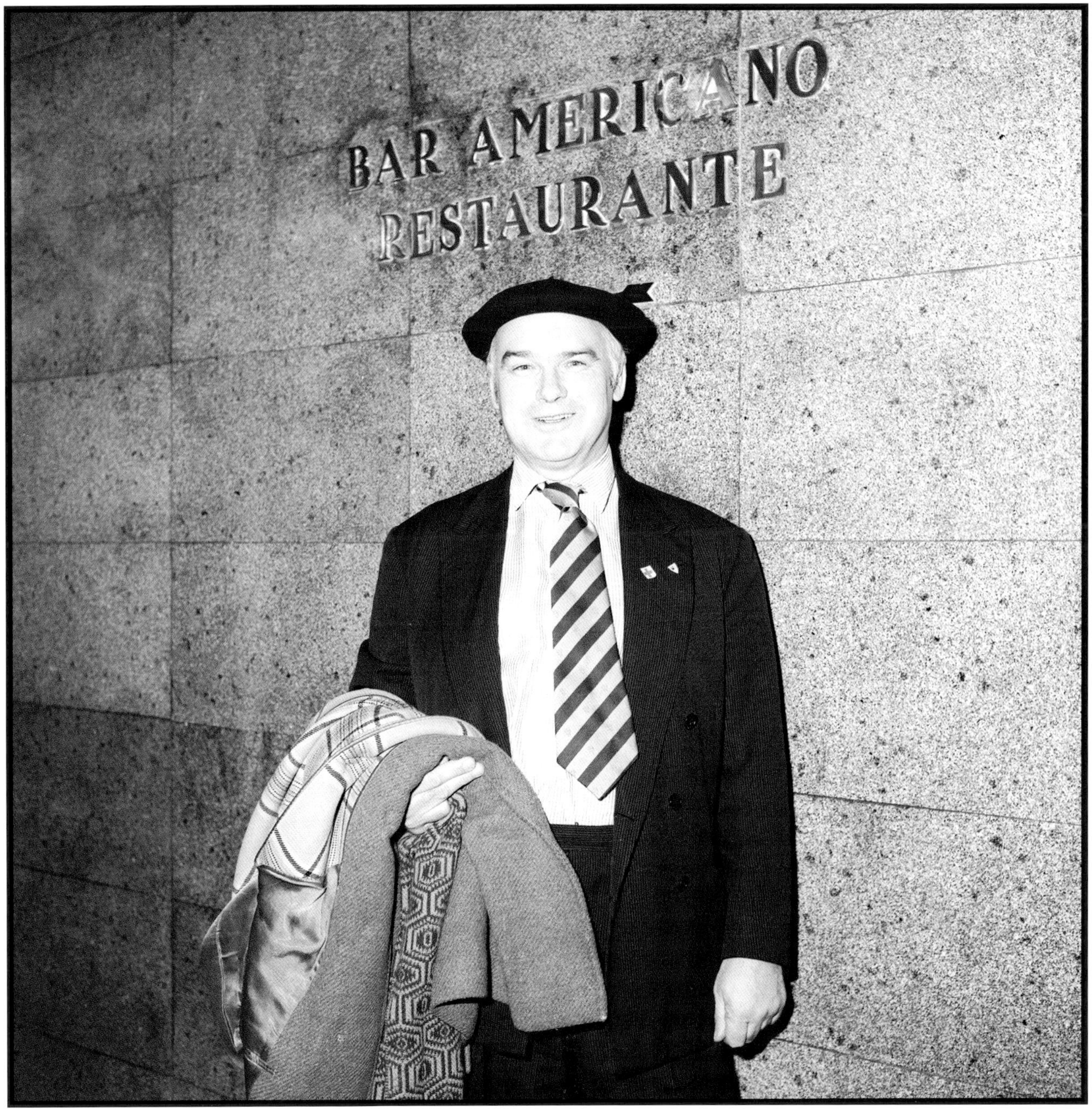

tea with pop

'Pop' Ward was Villa's dressing room attendant, making sure the players had everything they needed and preparing their half-time cups of tea.

A jovial character, he was forever telling stories about legendary figures like Harry Hampton and Joe Bache, and frequently quoted former players he had known.

Pop fought in the First World War and when we went to Antwerp it was an emotional experience for him because several of his friends had been killed during fighting in that region.

Pop died in 1980, just short of his 85th birthday, and the club closed down so that everyone could attend his funeral.

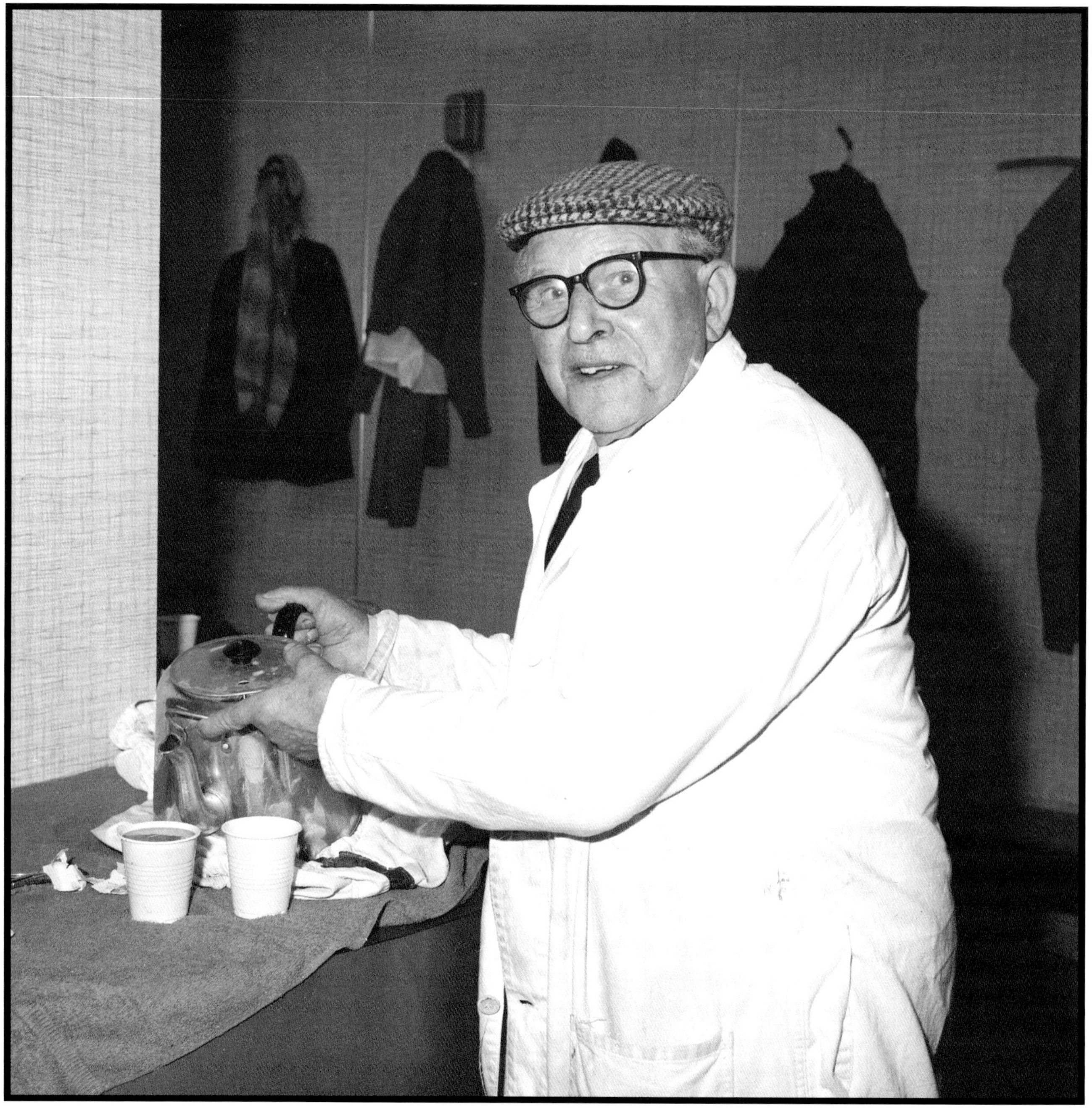

villa at the villa

Argentinian star Riccardo Villa was a sensational footballer, as he proved with his amazing solo goal for Tottenham in the 1981 FA Cup final replay against Manchester City.

Long before his Wembley wizardry, though, Villa donned a Villa shirt for John Robson's testimonial match in 1978.

It was my idea to get him pointing at the badge, but the other photographers quickly moved in, and the picture was all over the national press the following day.

My son Michael also worked as a photographer at that time, and when I saw him later his coat was ripped. When I asked how it had happened he said a shot from Villa had struck him while he was snapping away behind the goal!

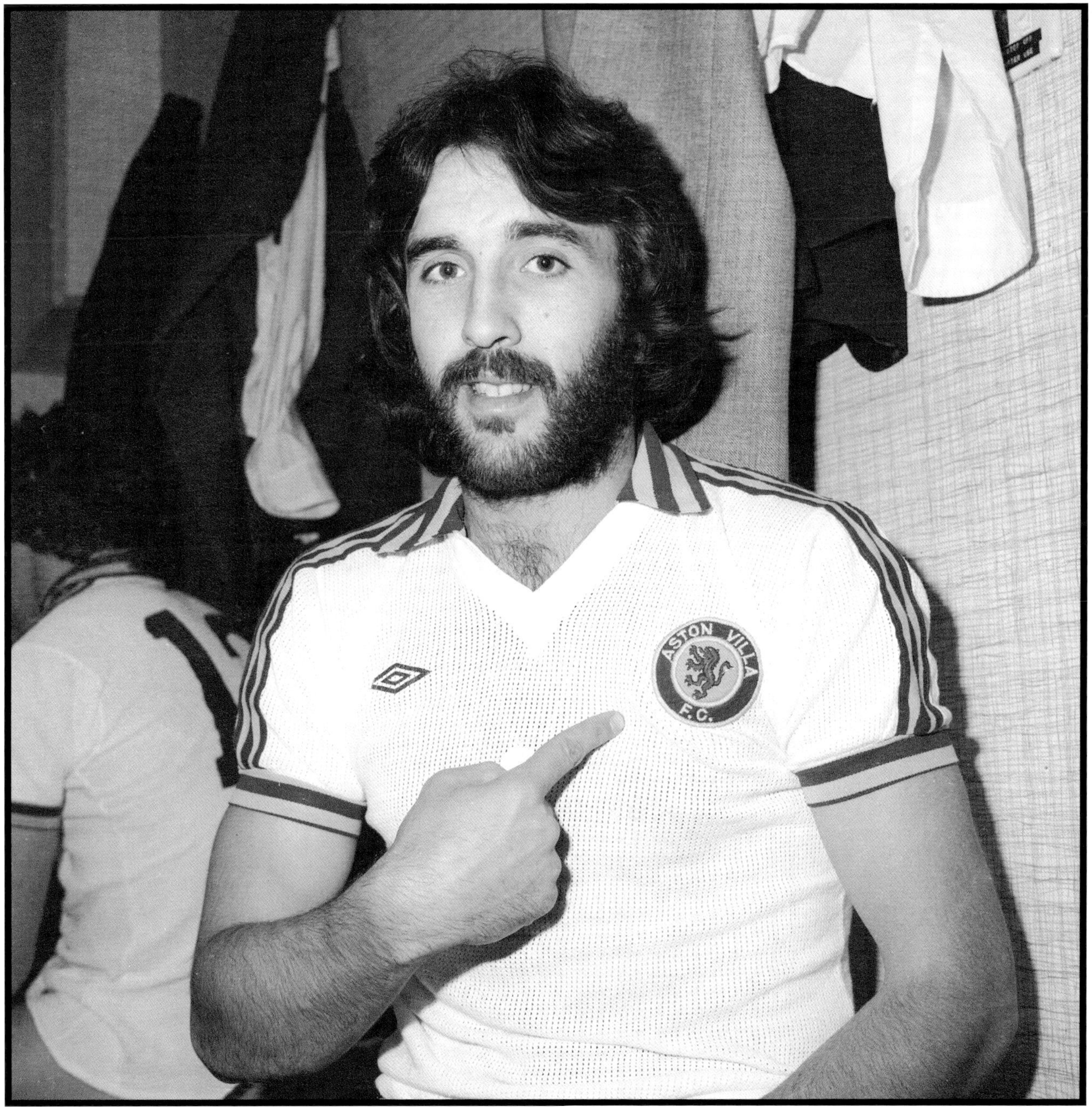

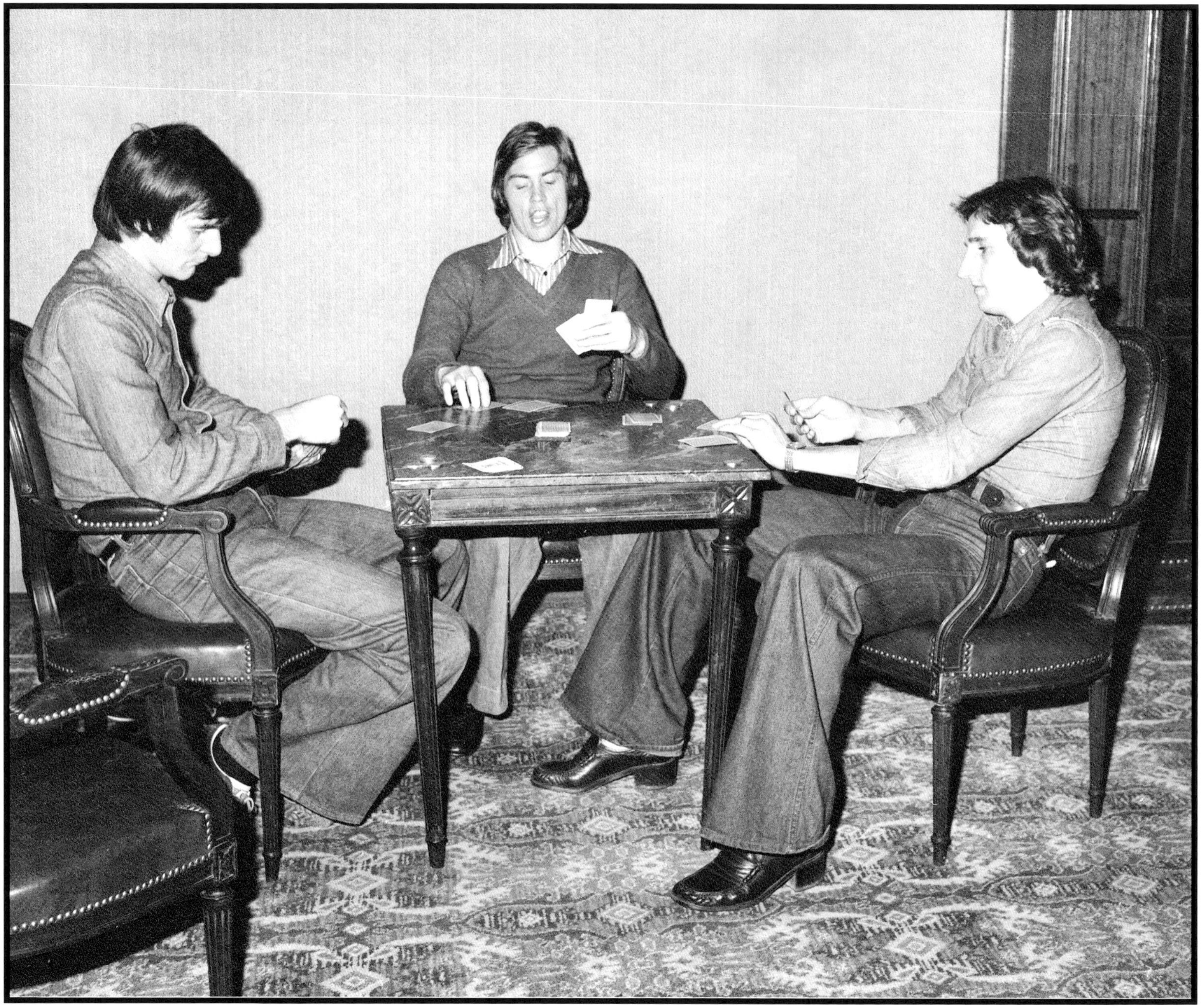

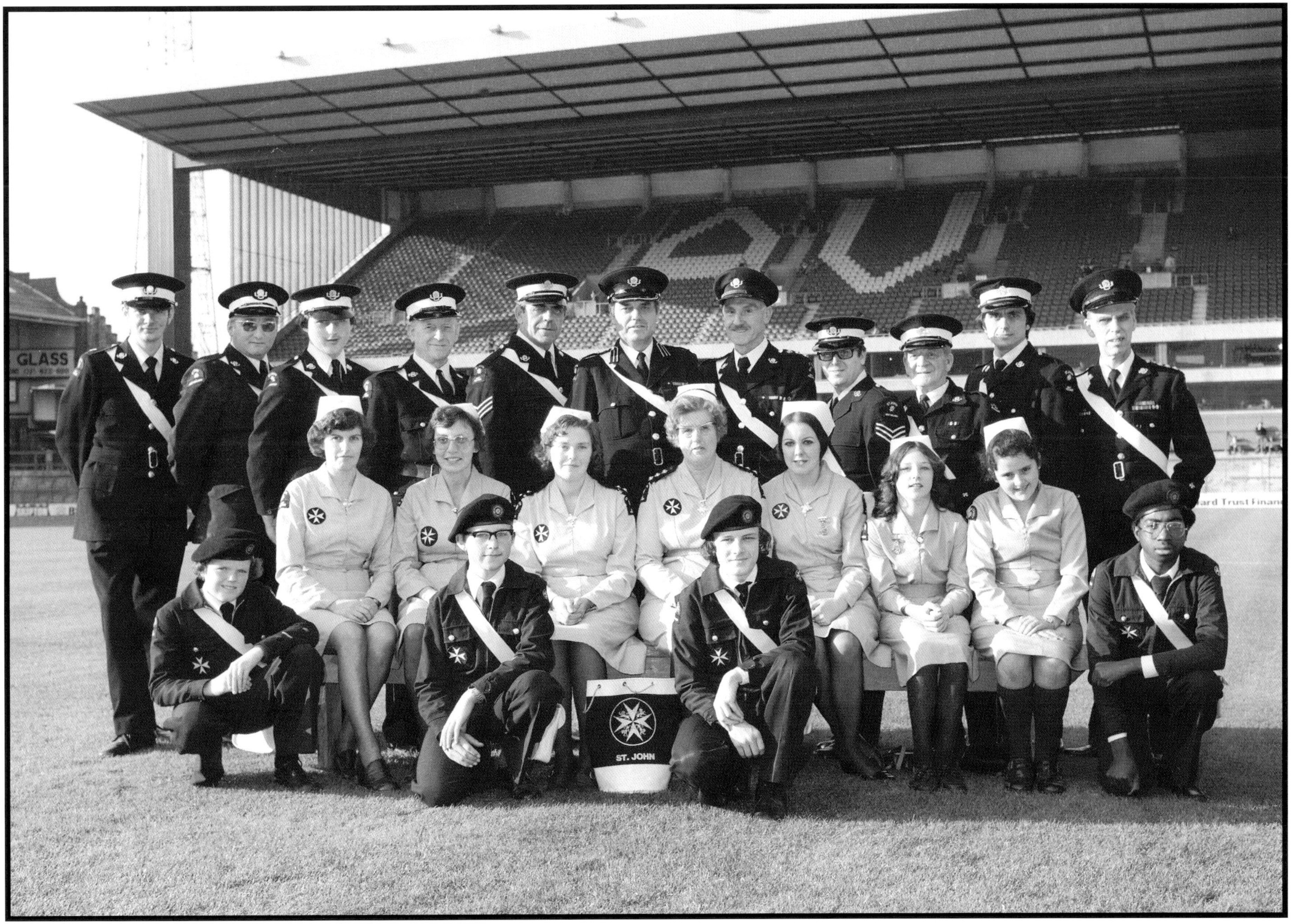
GLASS
ST. JOHN

mark my card

Wherever footballers gather, you will find a pack of cards. Normally, it happens on the team bus, travelling to away matches, but games sometimes continue in the hotel following a pre-match meal.

I've seen lots of money won and lost on the turn of a card down the years, and members of the card schools were often on the coach an hour before we were due to depart.

The trio deep in concentration here are Leighton Phillips (left), Alex Cropley and Frank Carrodus.

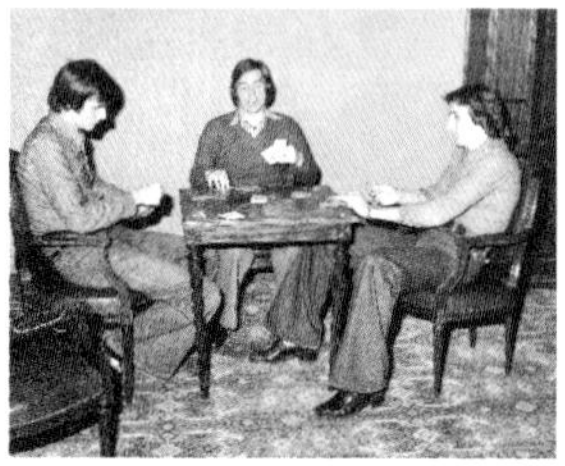

support team

One of my favourite team groups – without a footballer in sight. These good people are the ladies and gentlemen of the St John Ambulance, who play such an important role on match day.

A lot them became good friends over a number of years and several of them attended to me on the three or four occasions I suffered accidents.

Their counterparts are Millwall also once patched me up after I had slipped and cut my head on a railing at The Den, and even took the trouble to phone the following week to check that I was okay.

Lining up this particular shot, taken at around mid-day, earned me a ticking off from the groundsman. But it was worth it!

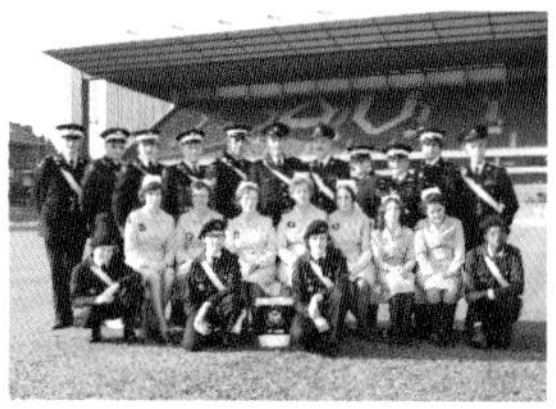

bus stop

Pop stars who visit Villa Park don't always get away with quietly watching the match from the Directors' Box. Sometimes they are introduced to the crowd before a game and possibly even interviewed.

That was the fate which befell The Hollies when they came calling, although they look here as if they are waiting for a bus, rather than standing on a football pitch. Didn't they sing a song about that back in the 60s?

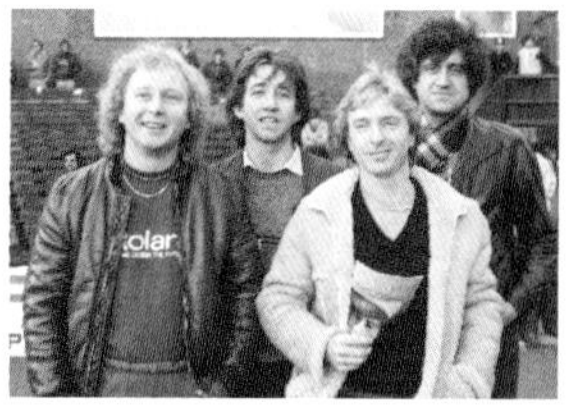

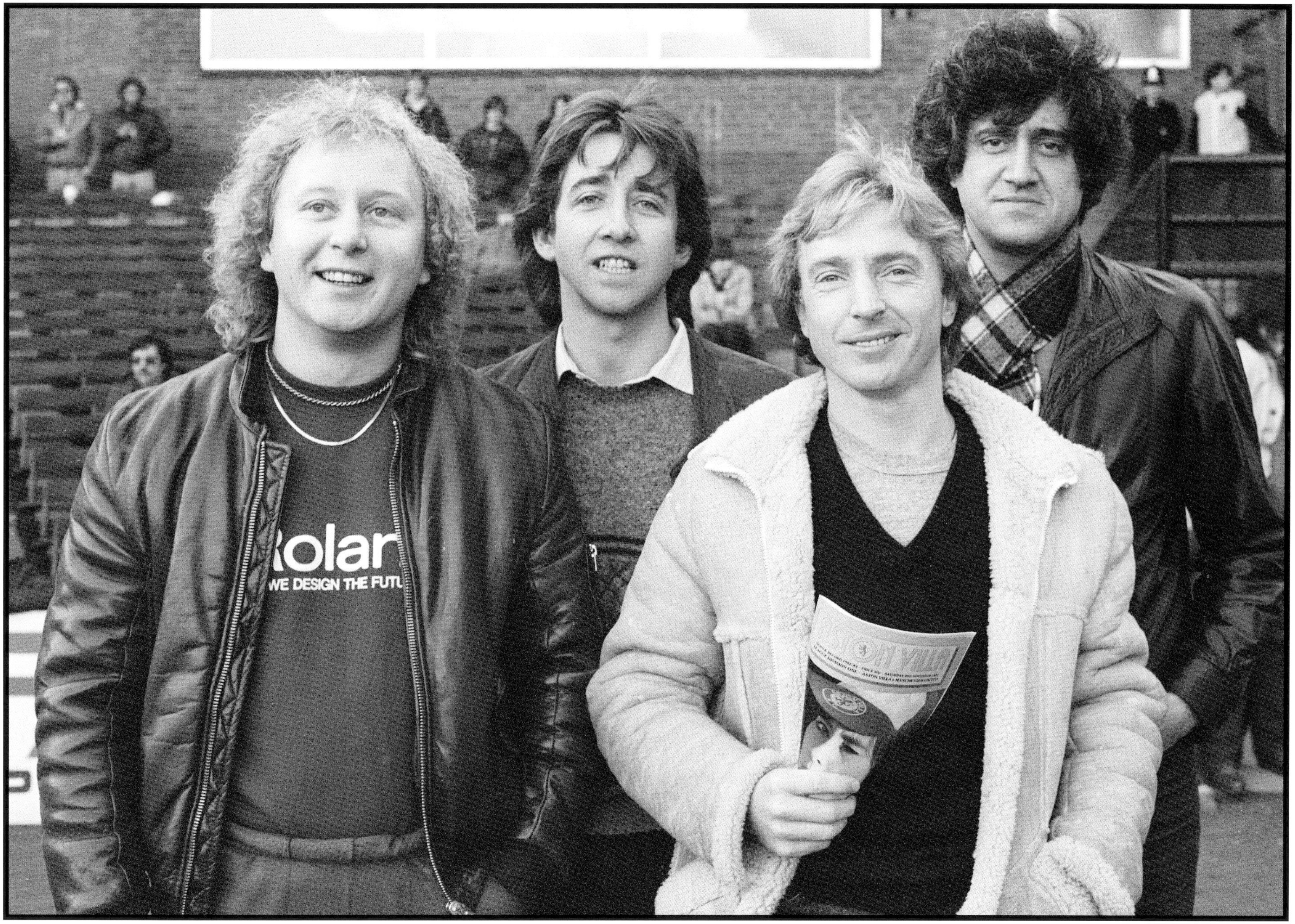
WE DESIGN THE FUTU

no game today

The sign says it all, even if such notification isn't required these days of electronic communication.

It was a different matter in the late 70s, when news of a postponement took take some time to filter its way on to radio and television, and I had more than one wasted journey to Villa Park.

This was early December, and the pitch had been rendered unplayable by heavy frost – another thing of the past now we have undersell heating.

When I got home, my wife Annie told me Villa had phoned to say the match was off, but had just missed me. No mobile phones then, of course.

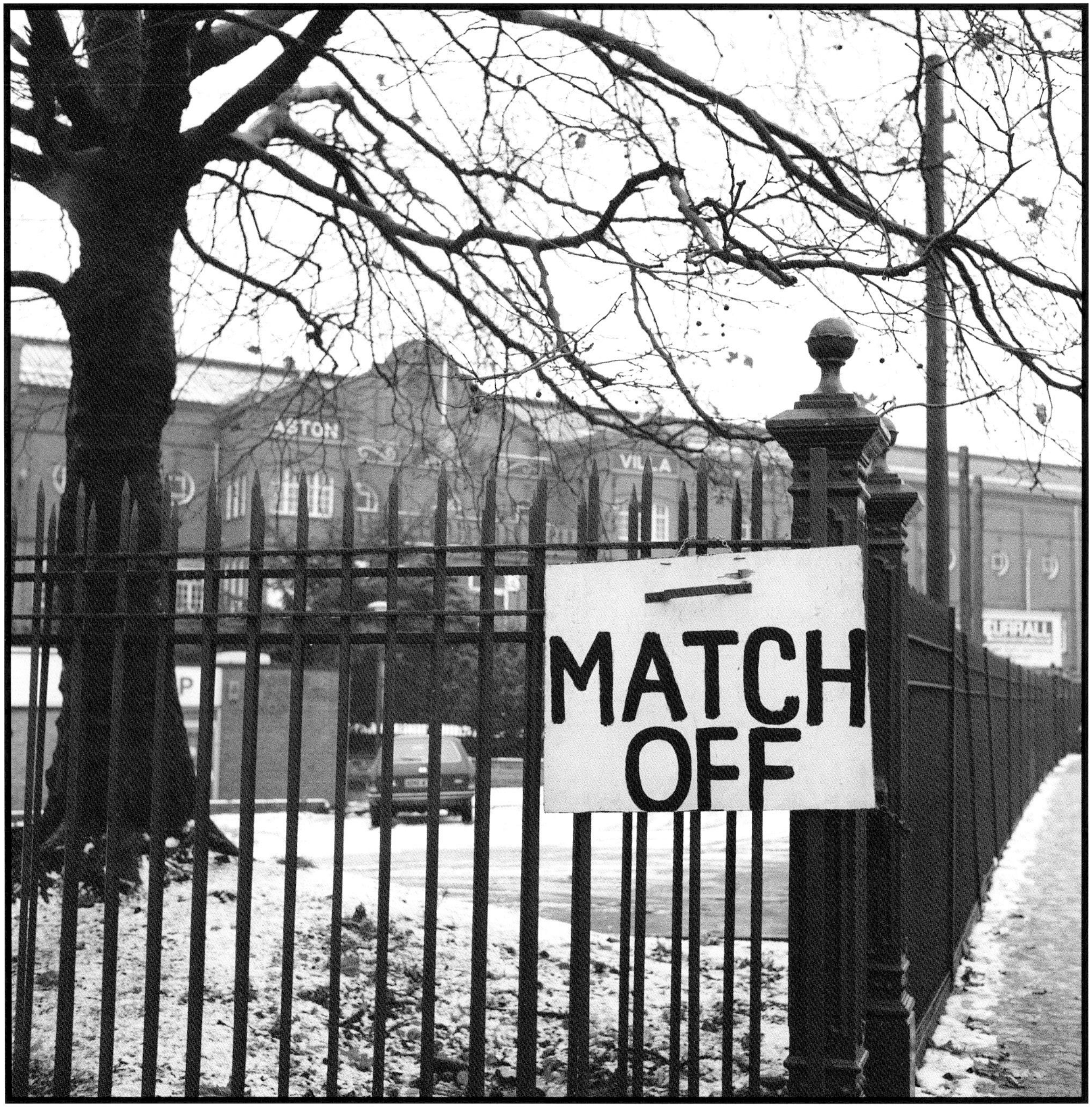

taylor made

As manager, Dick Taylor tried to get the best out of Villa's players between 1964 and 1967. As a sports outfitter, he subsequently ensured that they looked their best.

In the days before kit supply and sponsorship became such big business, Dick was the club's official supplier from his shop in Witton Road.

Apart from being a thriving business, Dick's store was also a meeting place for Villa players and other people from the club.

It was Dick, of course, who instigated Graham Taylor's appointment as manager in 1987. Although they are not related, Dick knows Graham's father Tom and became aware that the Watford boss would not be averse to a change of job....

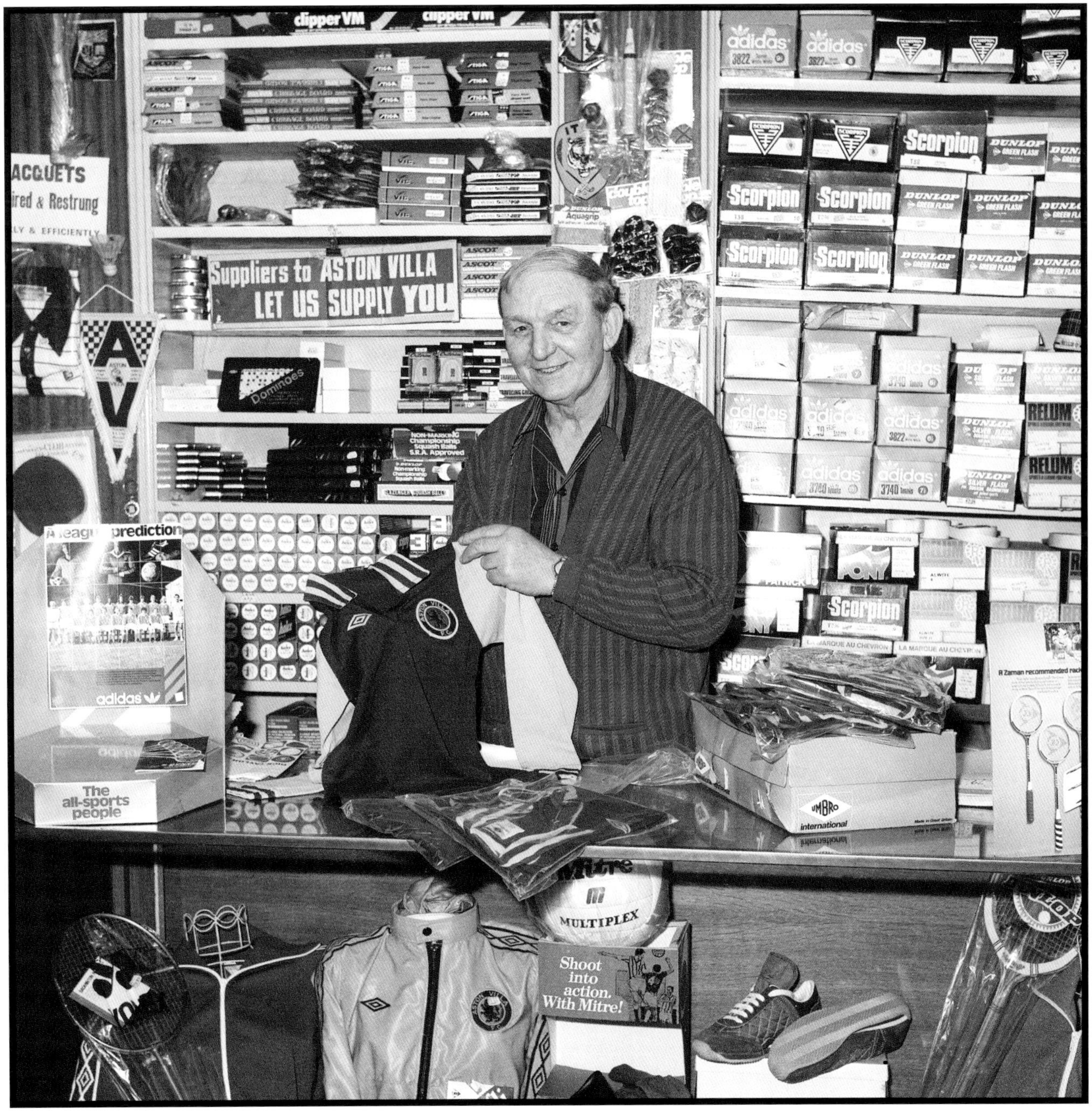

corner of the net

Nigel Spink obviously wasn't too busy during this practice match at Bodymoor. He certainly had time to turn and smile through the net for the camera.

Nigel seemed to be around for an eternity before he broke into the first team, but what an impact he made when he did so!

He had played only one senior match when he went on to replace the injured Jimmy Rimmer in the 1982 European Cup final, but became the hero of the hour in Rotterdam with some magnificent saves to deny Bayern Munich.

That was just reward for a goalkeeper who had been extremely patient after joining Villa from Chelmsford in January, 1977.

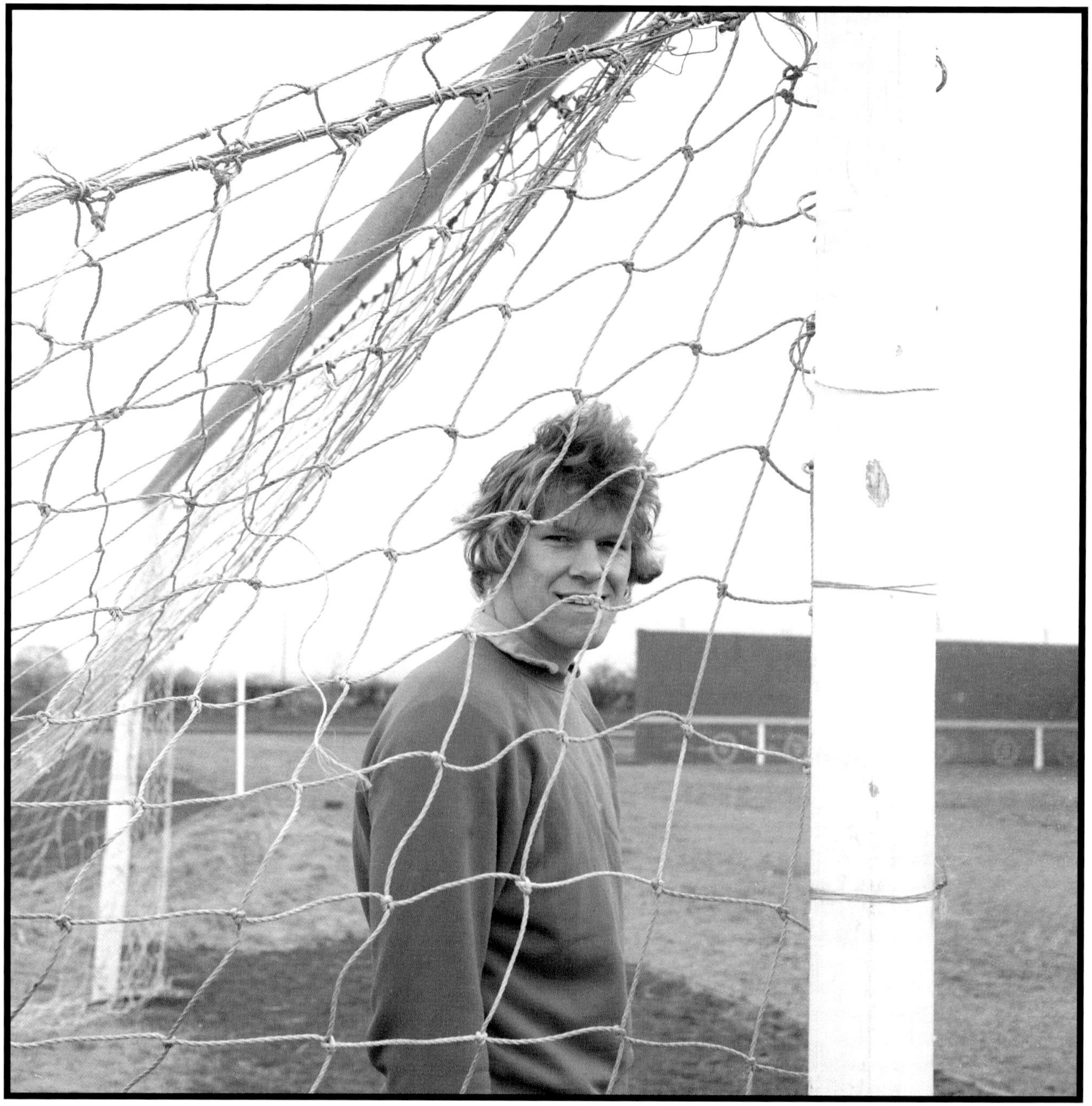

a dog's life

When he wasn't cutting a dominant figure at the heart of Villa's defence, Allan Evans had something of a reputation as a breeder of dogs.

When his faithful St Bernard, Hanna, gave birth to pedigree puppies, Allan offered two of them for sale at £150 each. This picture was taken after training at Bodymoor when they were seven weeks old.

The thing I really like about this one is the way Hanna is looking so affectionately at Allan. Perfectly understandable, of course – he's a real gentleman.

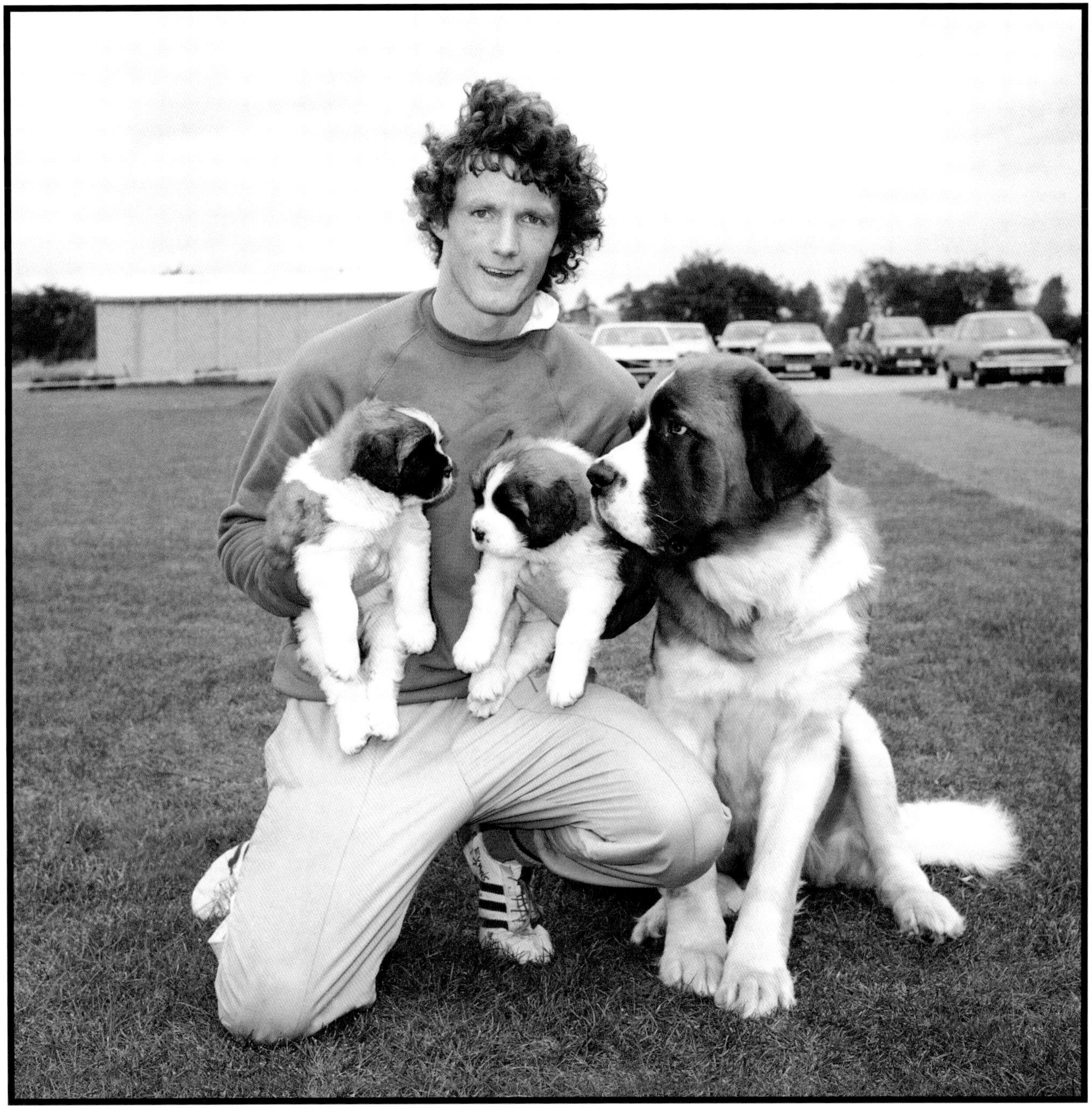

dressing down

This group of youth team players were in laid-back mood when I captured them in the Bodymoor Heath dressing rooms after a training session.

You may spot goalkeeper Mark Kendall and midfielder Robert Hopkins in the centre of the picture, although I'm not sure about the others.

I was frequently asked by young players to take their photo, either for proud parents or possibly for their local newspaper if they came from other parts of the country.

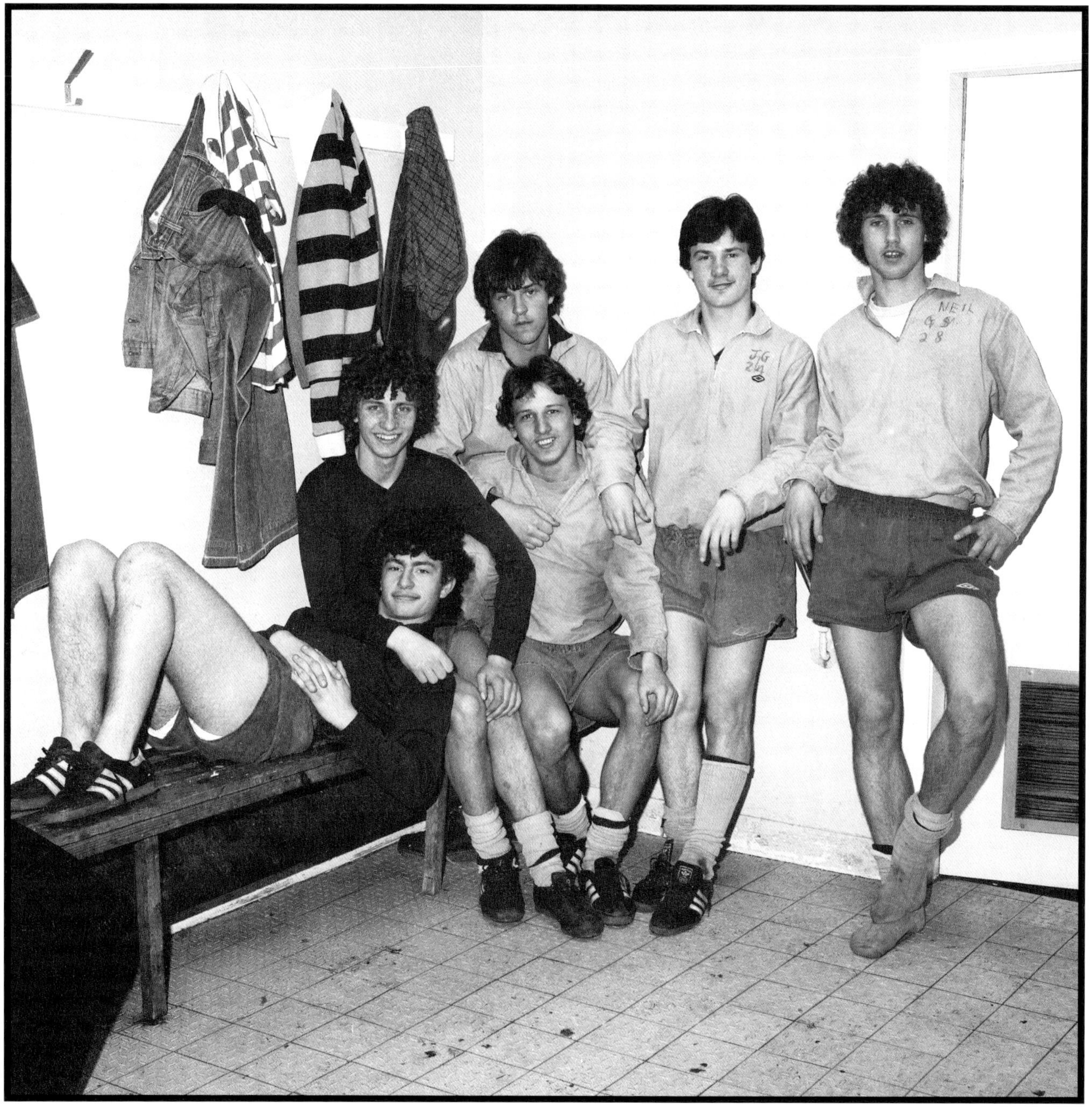

in the corner

Photographers are always looking for a different angle, so I decided to experiment with a picture directly behind a corner kick.

It probably wouldn't have been possible to get this close during a first team match, but I was rather pleased with the result as the ball left the kicker's foot and hurtled towards the goalmouth during a reserve game at Villa Park. It looks like an inswinger to me.

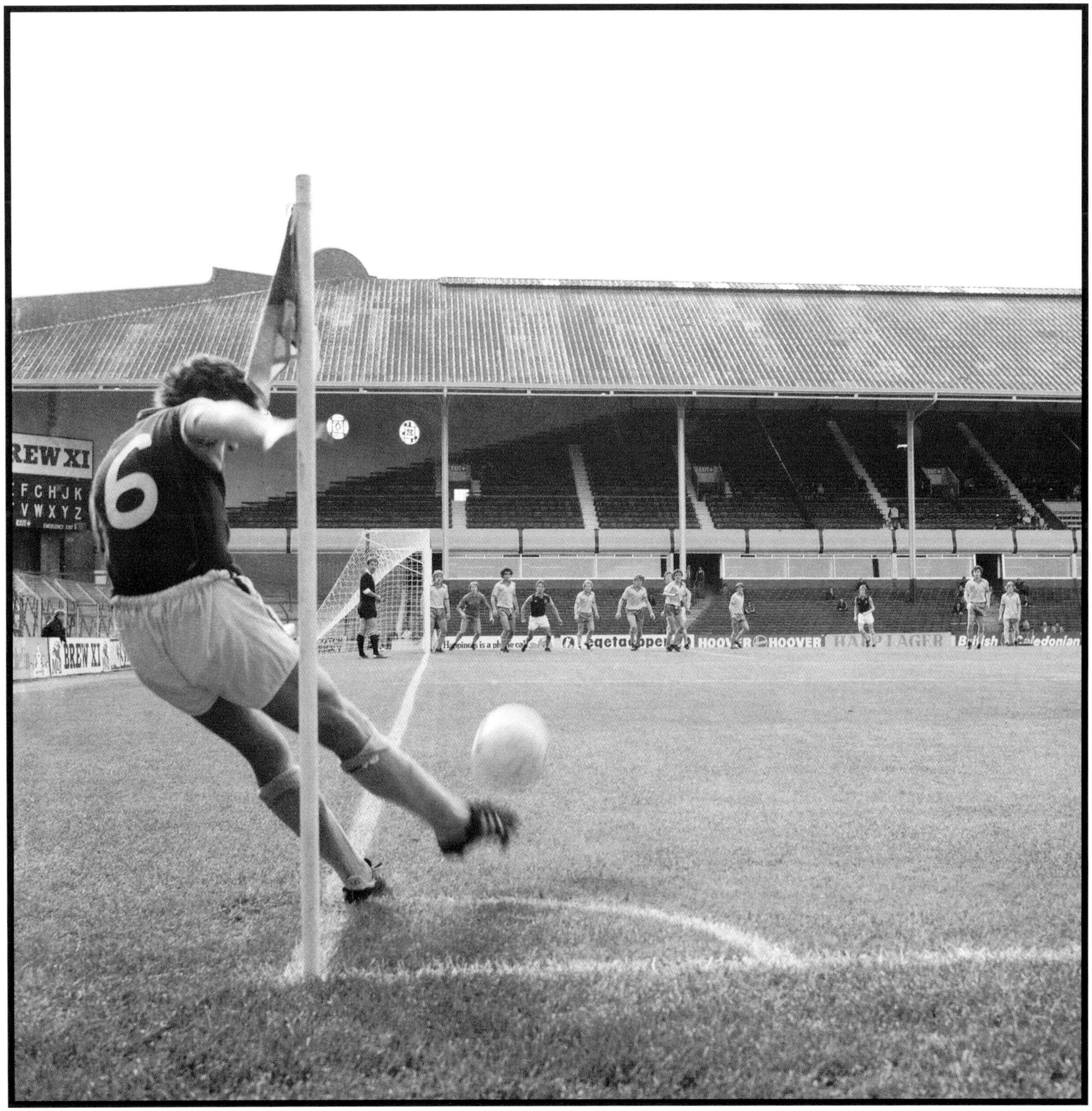

shaw thing

Players who score a hat-trick are traditionally presented with the match ball, but Gary Shaw found himself with three after his treble against Bristol City at Ashton Gate in December, 1979.

Gary had established himself as a first team regular that season and had already knocked in a couple of goals, but his hat-trick in the West Country was obviously something special.

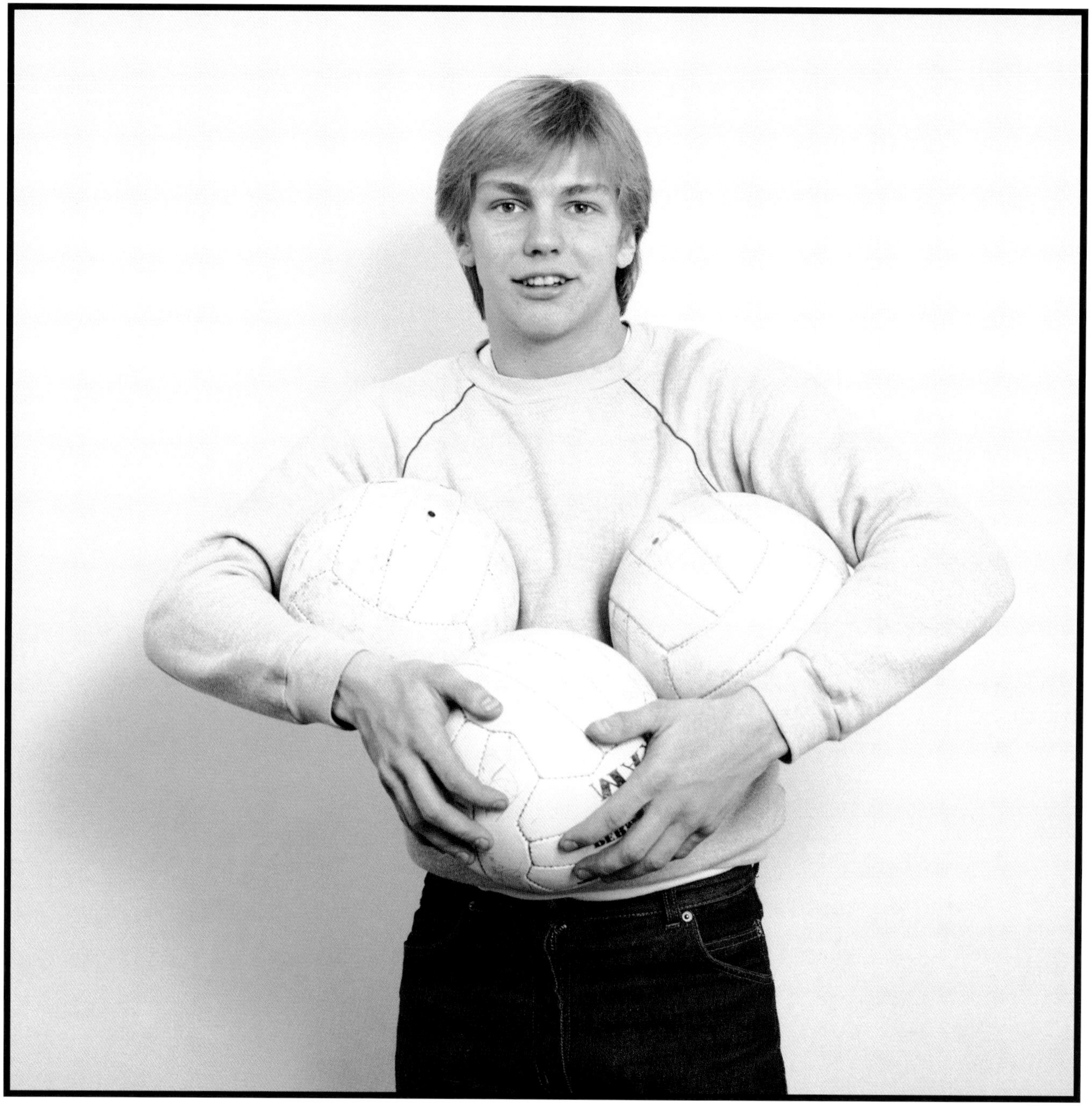

father and son

Terry Donovan was never a regular first team player during his time with Villa, but he came close to creating a piece of club history.

Standing in for the injured Gary Shaw, Terry scored twice in the 5-0 victory over Icelandic club Valur in the first round of the European Cup, and then squandered a glorious opportunity which would have given him Villa's only hat-trick in the competition.

I photographed Terry in the studio I used to have at home, along with his father Don, who had played for Everton.

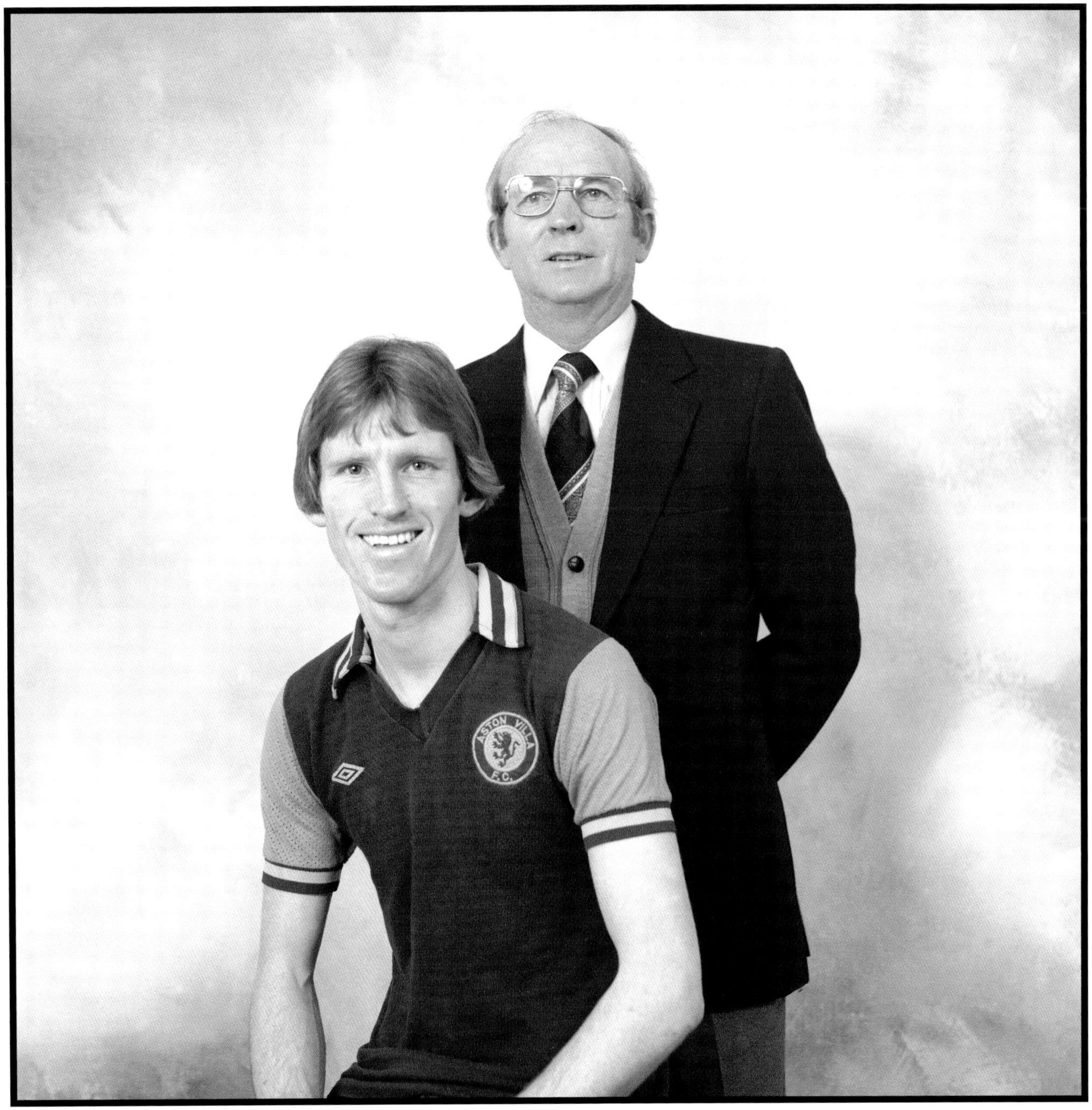

glamour and clamour

This started out as a good idea, but turned into a bit of a headache. The attractive girl displaying her bedroom wall of Villa memorabilia appeared in the programme in a feature carrying the headline 'Is Beverley Villa's No1 female fan?'

No doubt 18-year-old telephonist Beverley Clarke was an avid fan – she was a regular on the Holte End – but that article prompted a flood of complaints from other ladies who had been following the club for considerably longer.

One indignant supporter even phoned in to say she had been watching Villa before Beverley's mother was born, so you could see how much uproar it caused.

Still, it was nice to have a touch of glamour in the matchday publication.

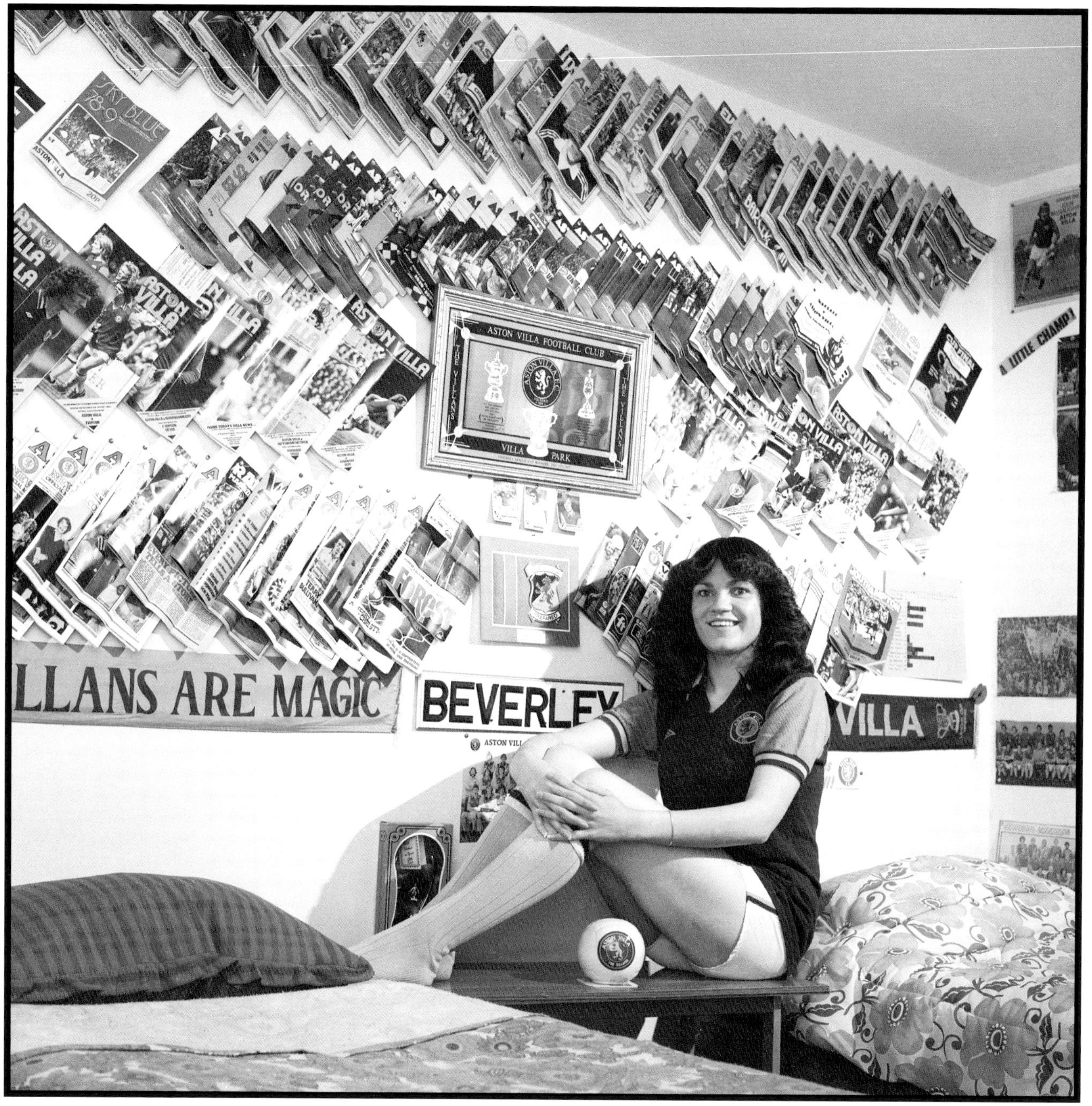

scoreboard veterans

Jack Watts is an institution at Villa Park, having followed the club for more than 70 years and served them in various capacities.

In the days of the old scoreboard, Jack and his friend Sam were responsible for slotting in the numbers which informed supporters, every 15 minutes, of the latest scores from other games around the country.

Before the advent of local radio, no information was available until the end of BBC's Grandstand or the Sports Report radio programme, so you used to find Albion and Blues supporters coming along to Villa matches, just to see how their own teams were getting on!

When the board was demolished, I asked Jack for numbers four and six, because 46 is my house number.

Every club needs someone like Jack, who still conducts tours of Villa Park at the age of 84.

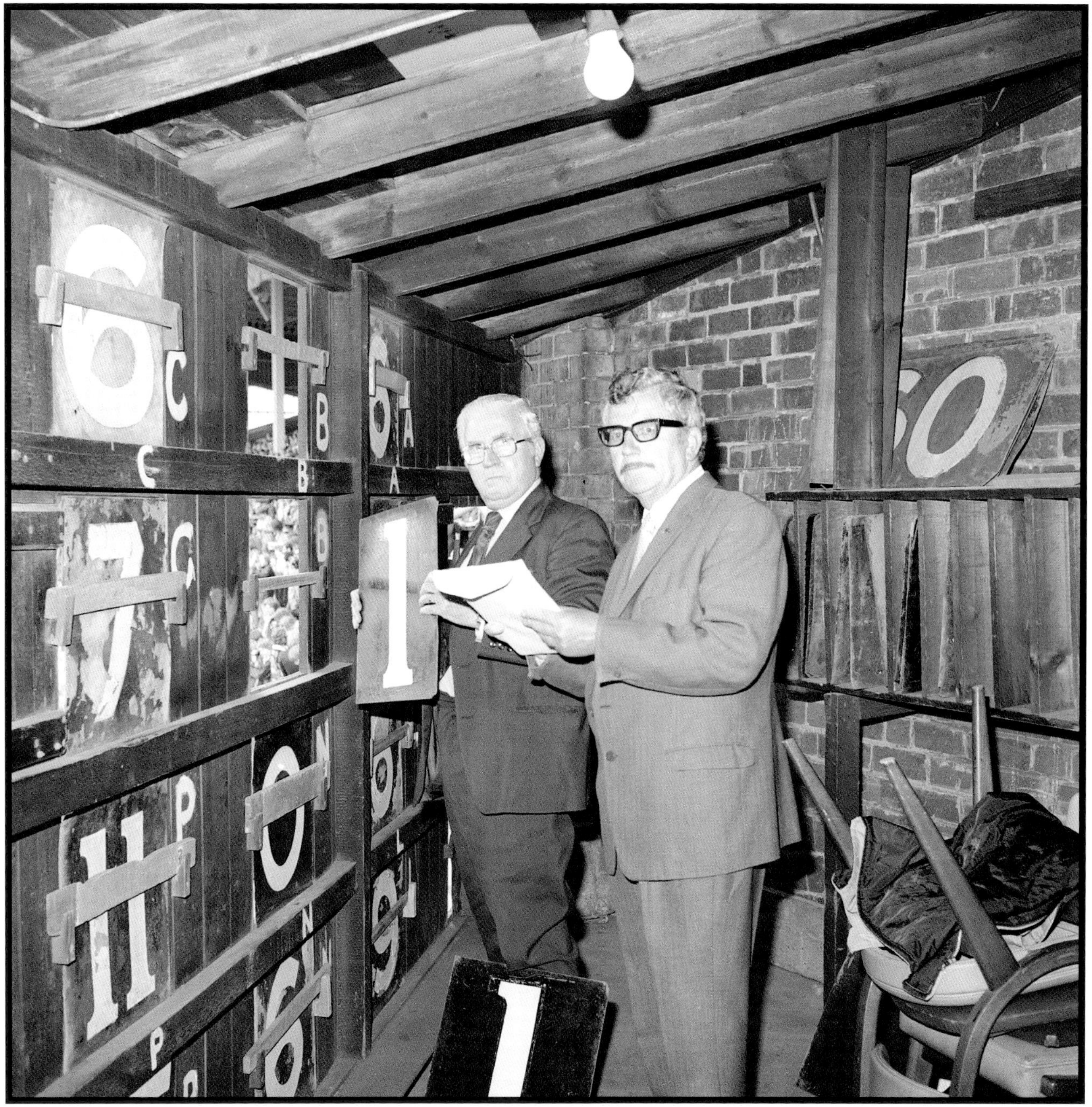

man of steel

Nicky Steele was a Villa man through and through, and for several years he was the matchday presenter at Villa Park.

Even when he was working in the studio at BRMB Radio, he couldn't resist showing his true colours. His death in 2001 at the age of 53 robbed us of a true friend of the club. He is sadly missed.

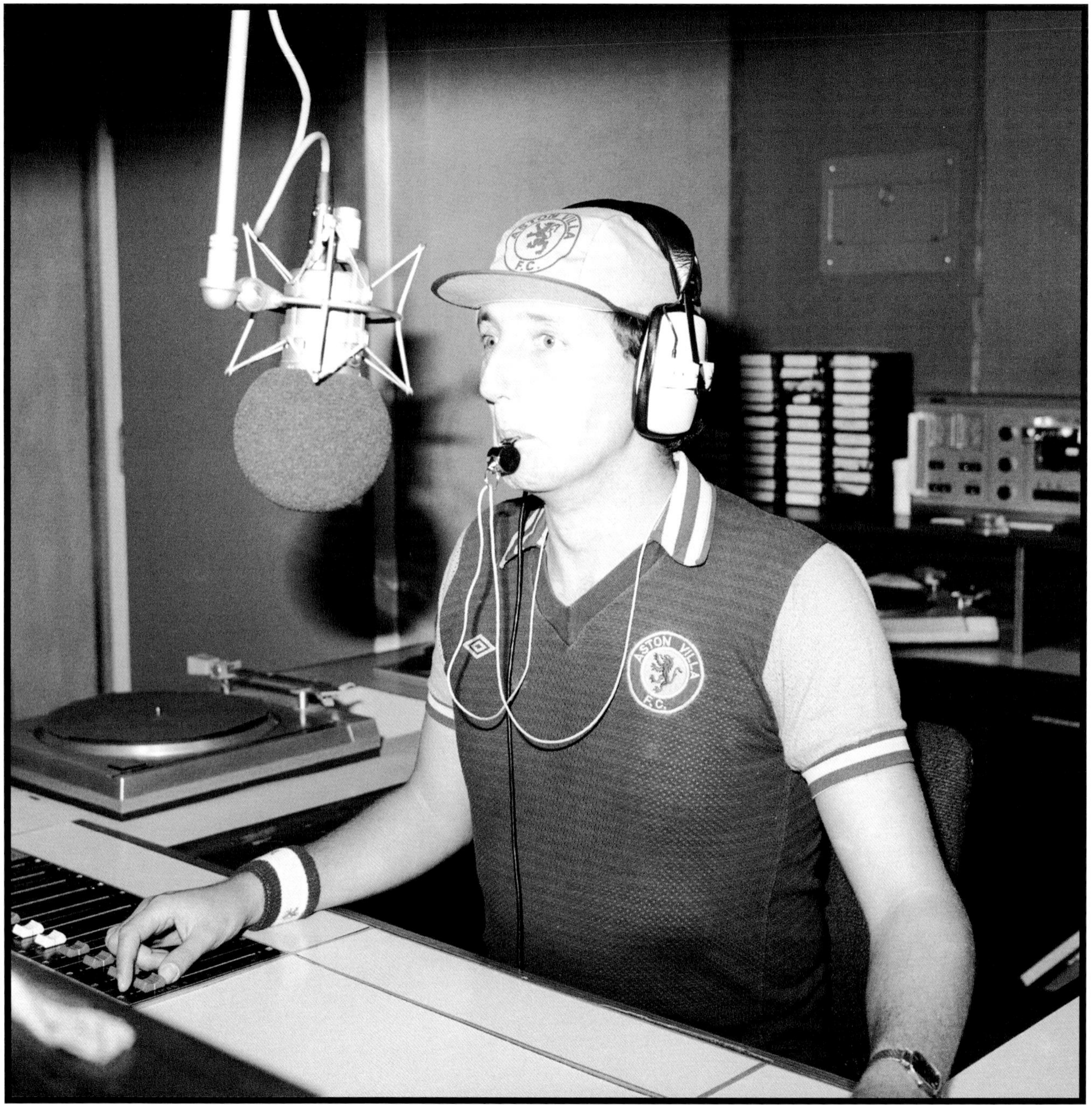

time to move

There's nothing like a touch of nostalgia, but sometimes things inevitably have to move on.

Many people mourned the passing of Villa's former offices in 1981-82, although those who worked there couldn't wait to vacate a building which was literally falling down around them, even before the bulldozers moved in.

There had once been a charm about the place, but not by the time this picture was taken and the staff had moved to more luxurious accommodation in the North Stand.

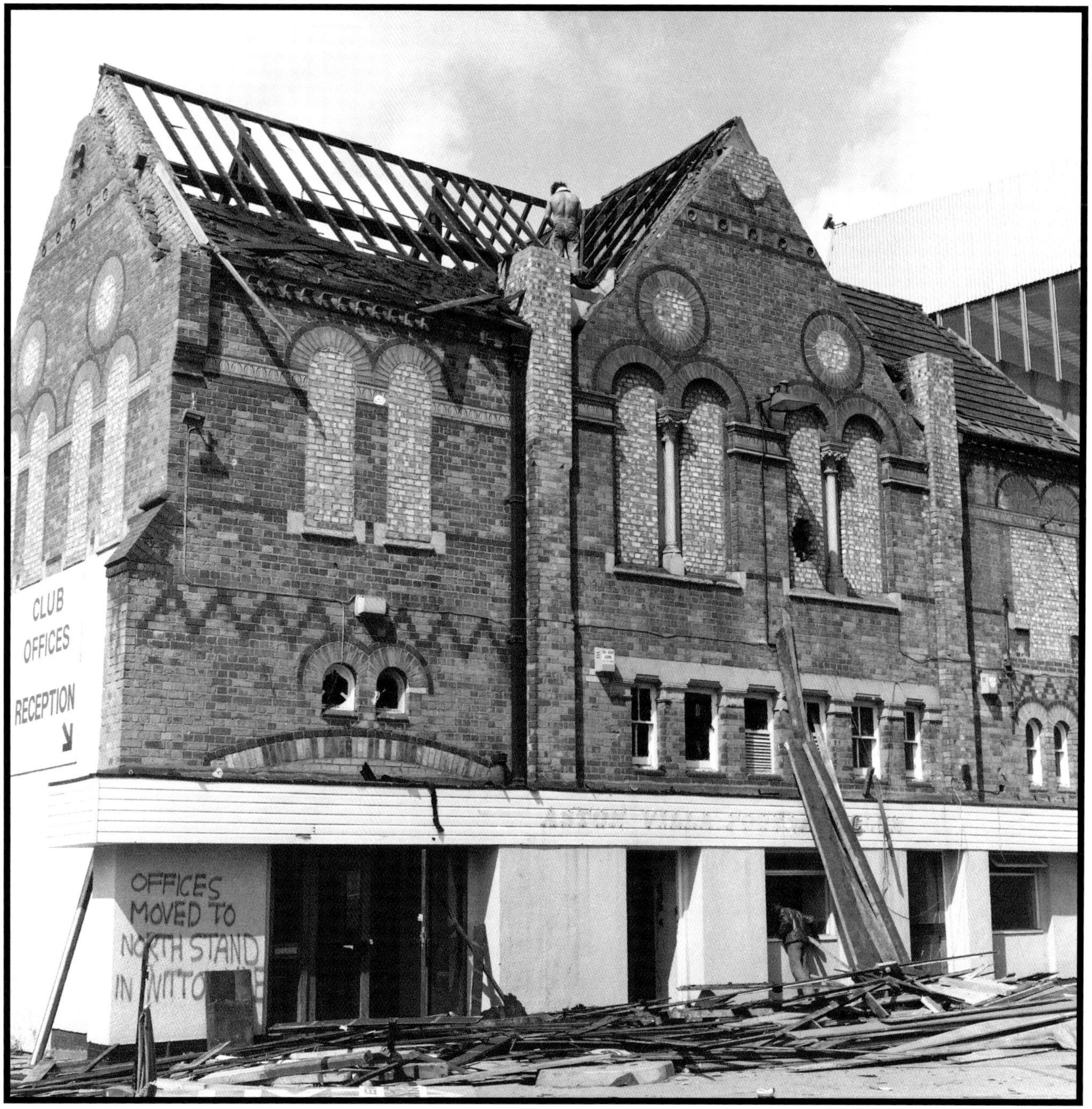

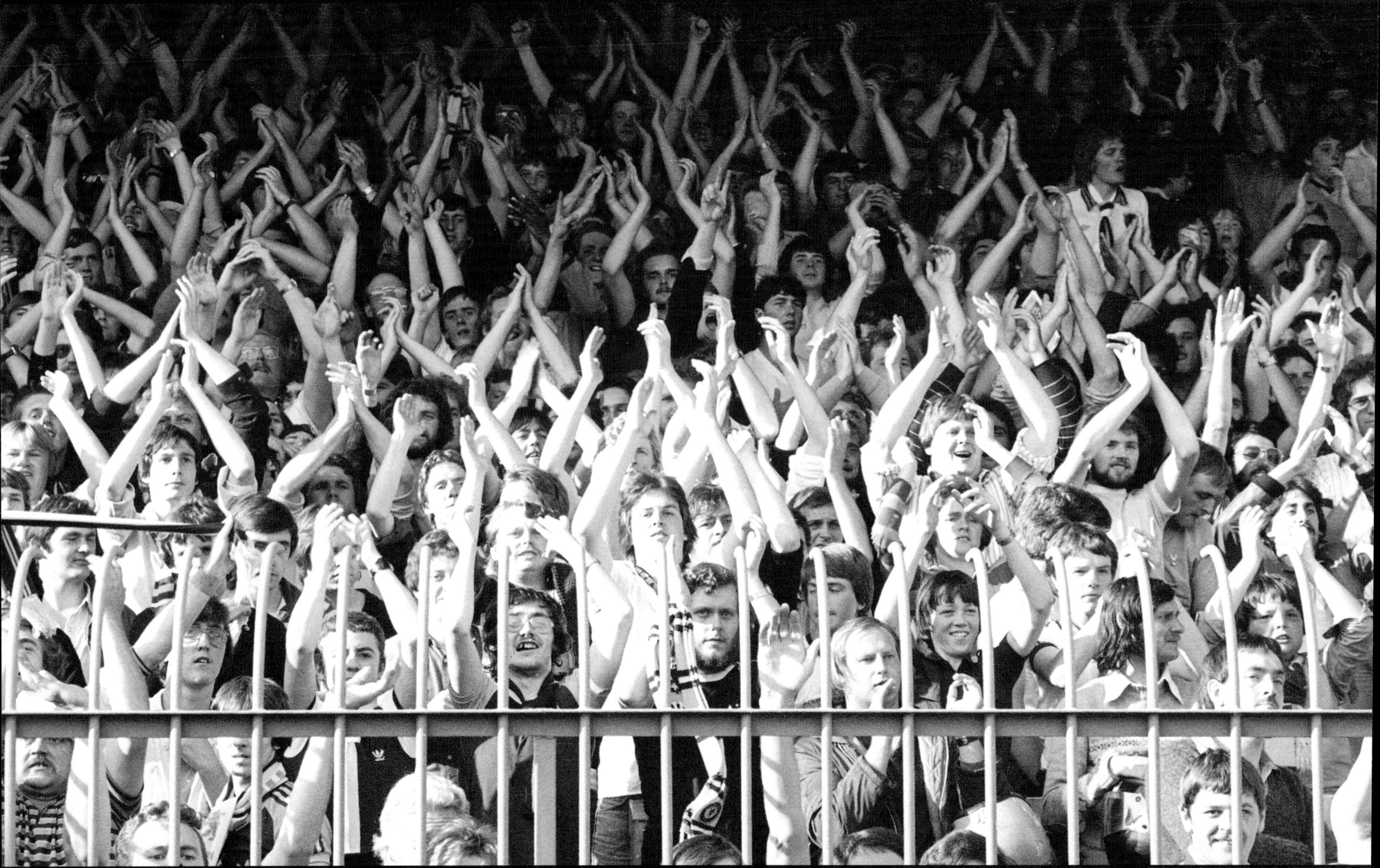

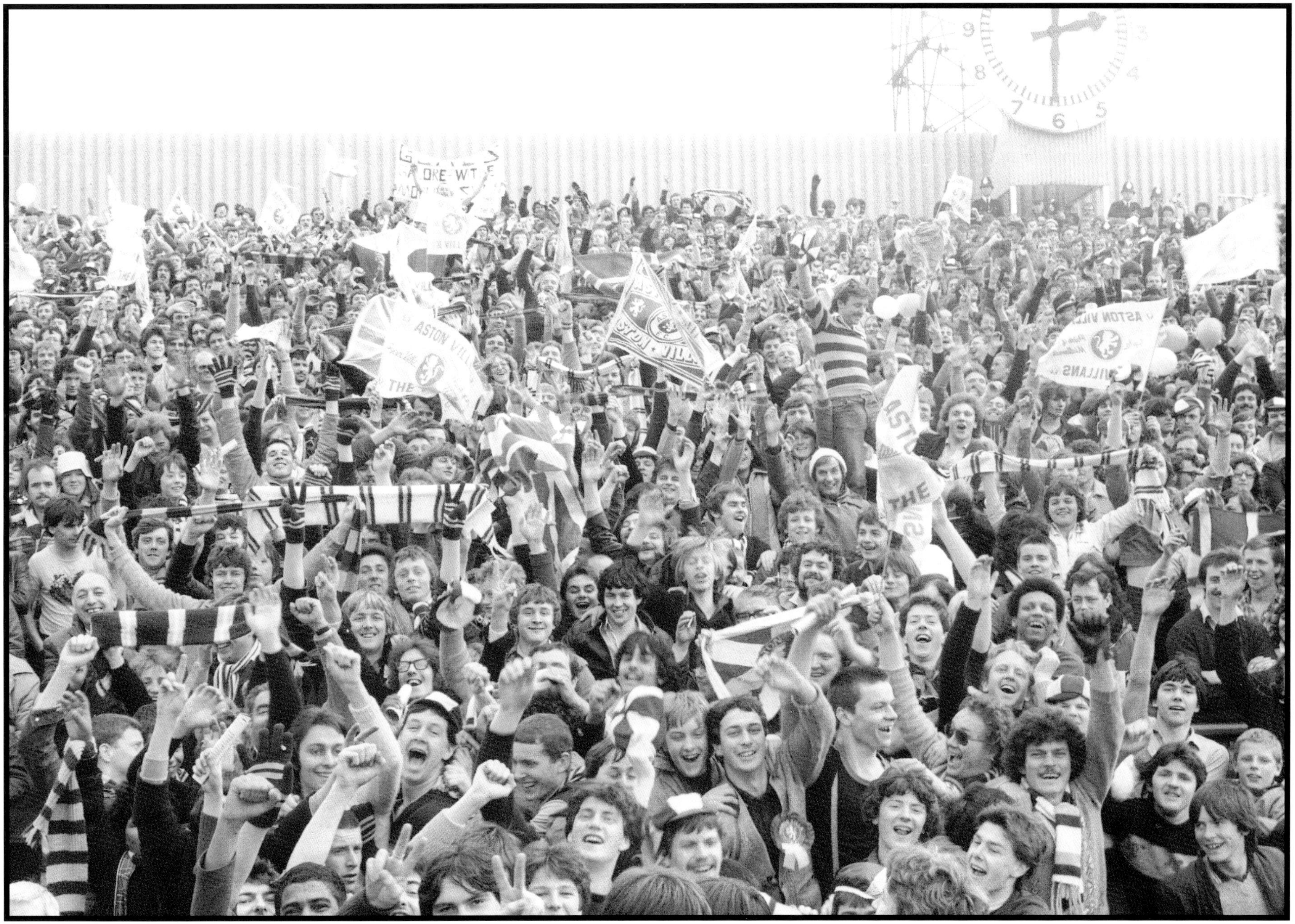

hands up

No-one ever conducts a football crowd, yet they always seem to know instinctively when to burst into song or deliver a fervent chant in support of their favourite team.

Even so, actions speak louder than words, and these Holte Enders are in perfect unison as they salute their claret and blue heroes.

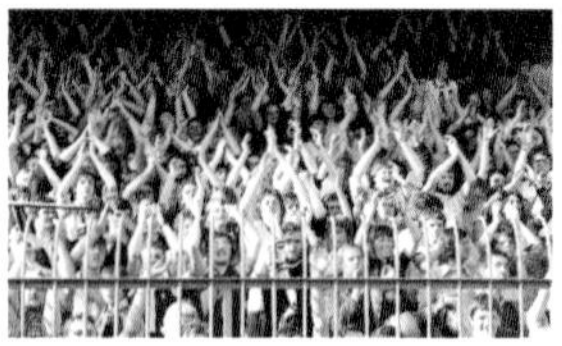

countdown to glory

If Arsenal's Clock End was filling up nicely at 2.30pm, it was heaving by kick-off time on Saturday 2nd May, 1981. The reason was simple enough. Villa were on the verge of becoming League Champions for the first time in 71 years and everyone connected with the claret and blue cause wanted to be at Highbury.

We lost 2-0, of course, but Ipswich Town's defeat by Middlesbrough meant the title was ours after all those years.

Ron Saunders told me that if Villa won, I should take as many pictures as possible. I would have done anyway, but he wanted them for a book he was having published.

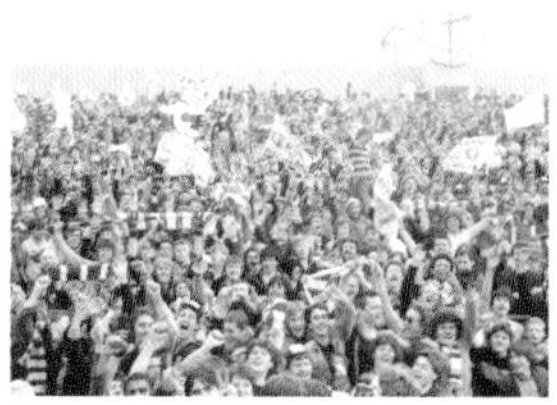

on top of the world

Villa's players became accustomed to open-top bus rides in the early 1980s, celebrating both their League Championship and European Cup triumphs in the time-honoured manner.

But Irishman Eamonn Deacy (second right) clearly wanted a seat nearer the front when the team paraded the Championship trophy through the streets of Birmingham in 1981.

Also featured in this happy gathering are Gordon Cowans, Mike Pejic, Kenny Swain, Gary Williams, Colin Gibson, David Geddis, Tony Morley and Des Bremner.

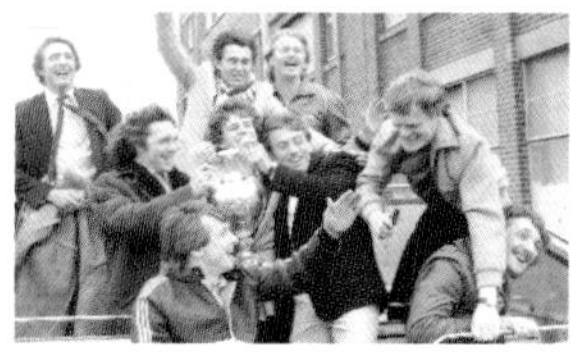

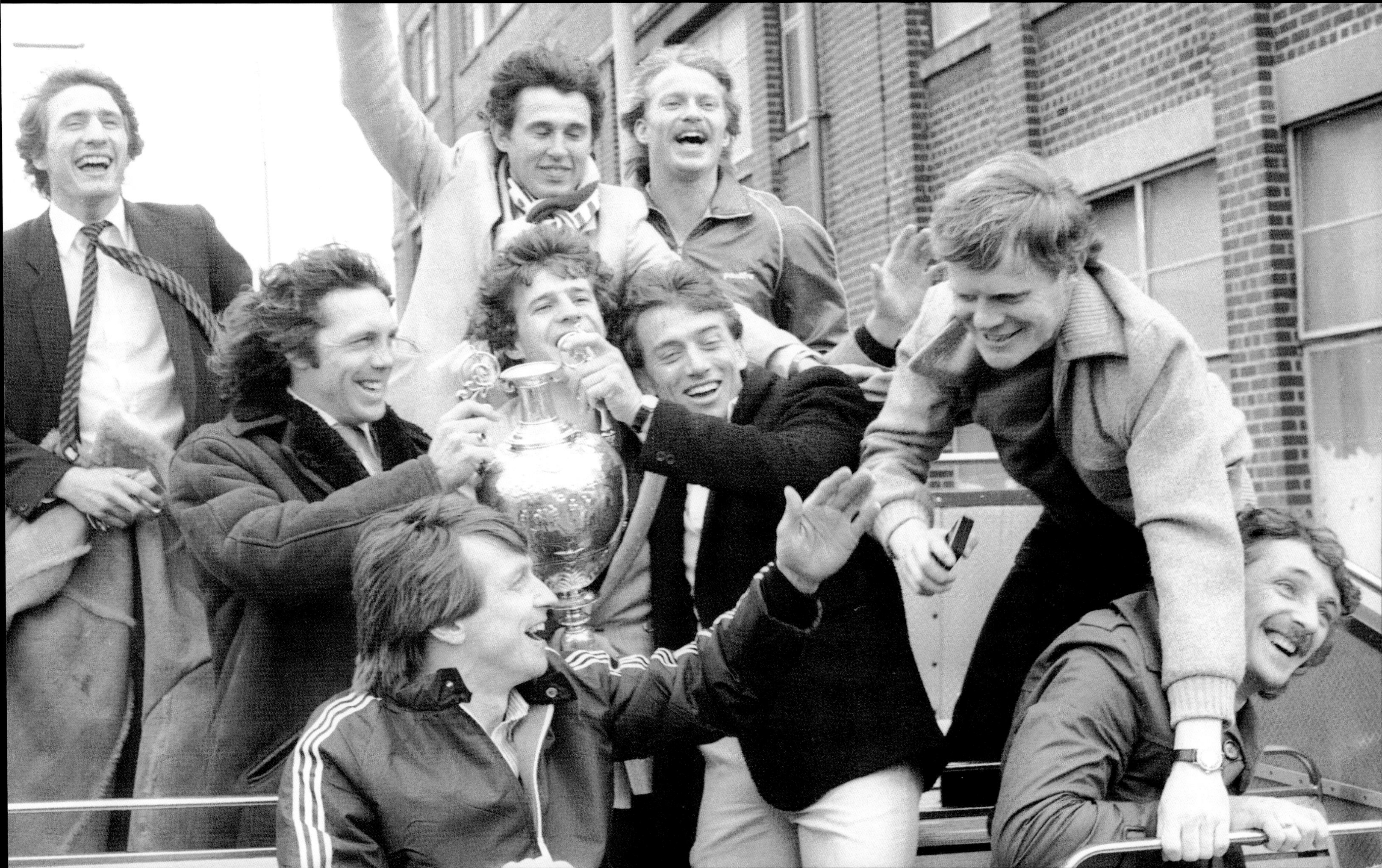

gangway, please

Ron Saunders, followed by secretary Steve Stride and goalkeeper Jimmy Rimmer, leads the Champions on to the open-top bus for the celebrations which followed the 1981 title triumph.

The team left from the Aston Villa Leisure Centre and enjoyed a tour of the city before attending a civic reception at Birmingham Council House.

Even if the rest of the football world didn't give Villa the credit they deserved for their success, the people of Birmingham certainly turned out in force.

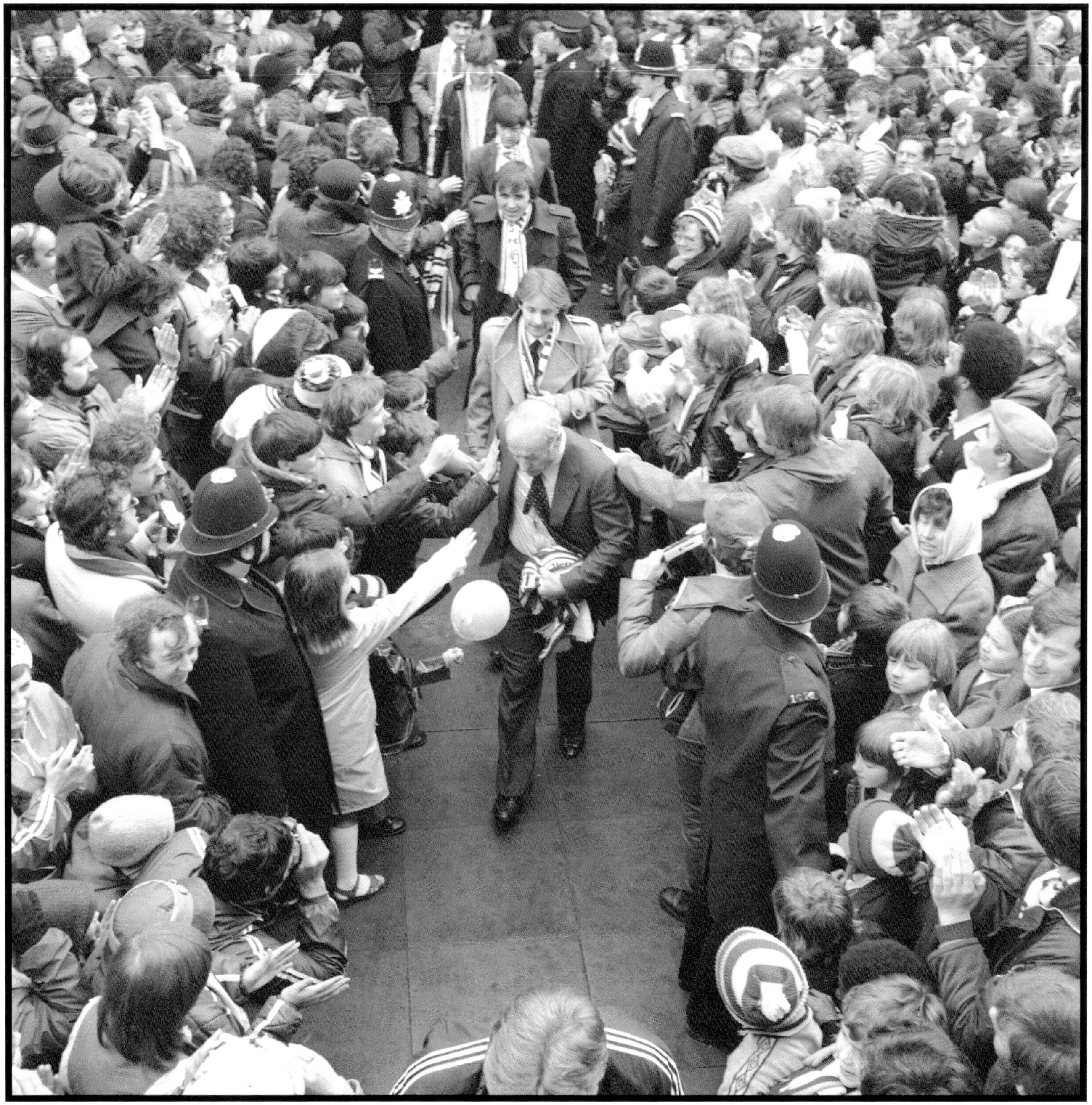

journey's end

The mass of people, both along the bus route and in Victoria Square, was a sight to behold.

This was just as the squad were arriving in front of the Council House, ready to appear in front of thousands of supporters who had turned out for the occasion.

When the players appeared on the balcony, Peter Withe grabbed the microphone and took over the proceedings.

To complete a memorable day, the trophy was presented by the Football Association's Jack Wiseman, who just happened to be chairman of Birmingham City!

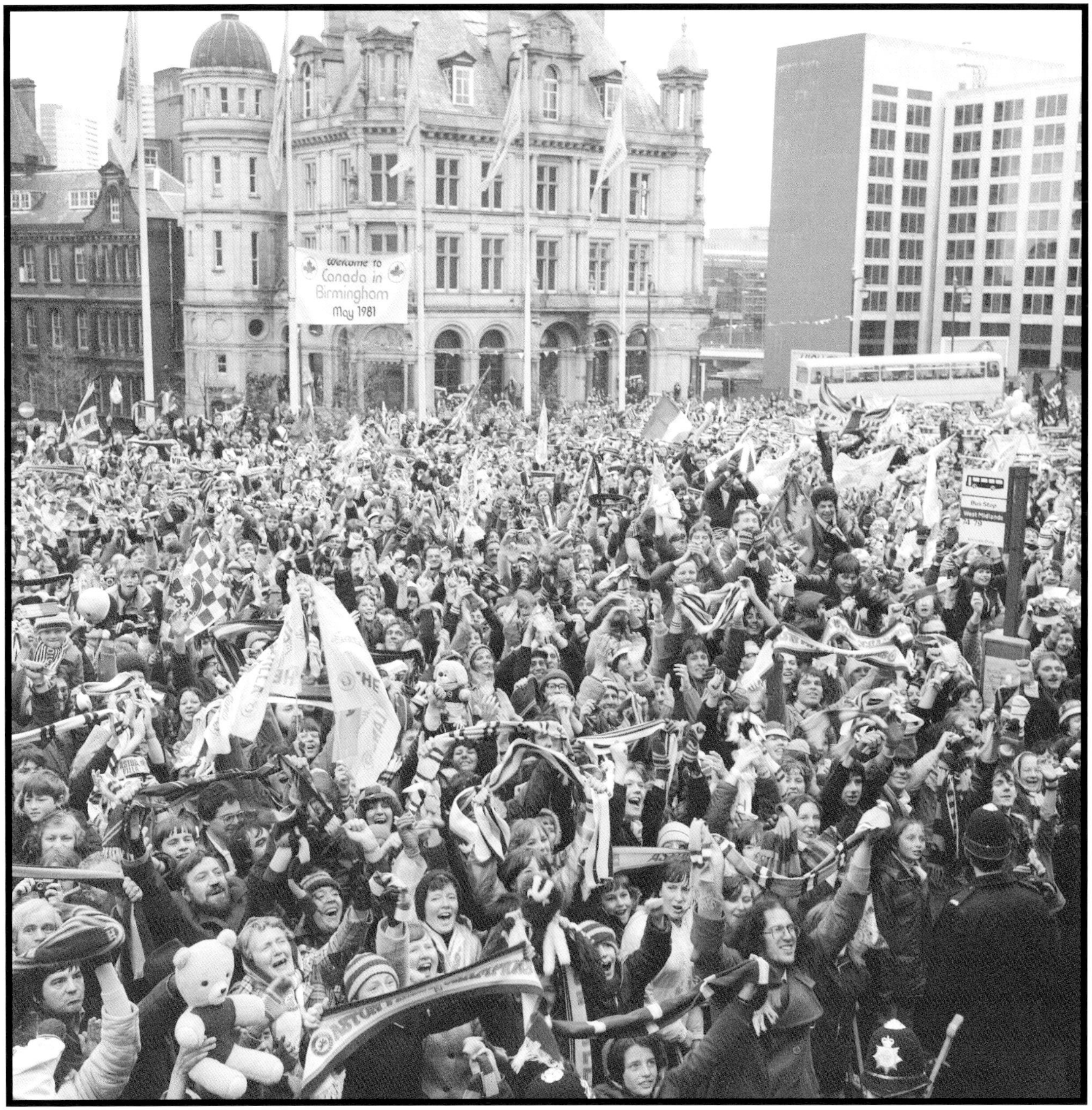

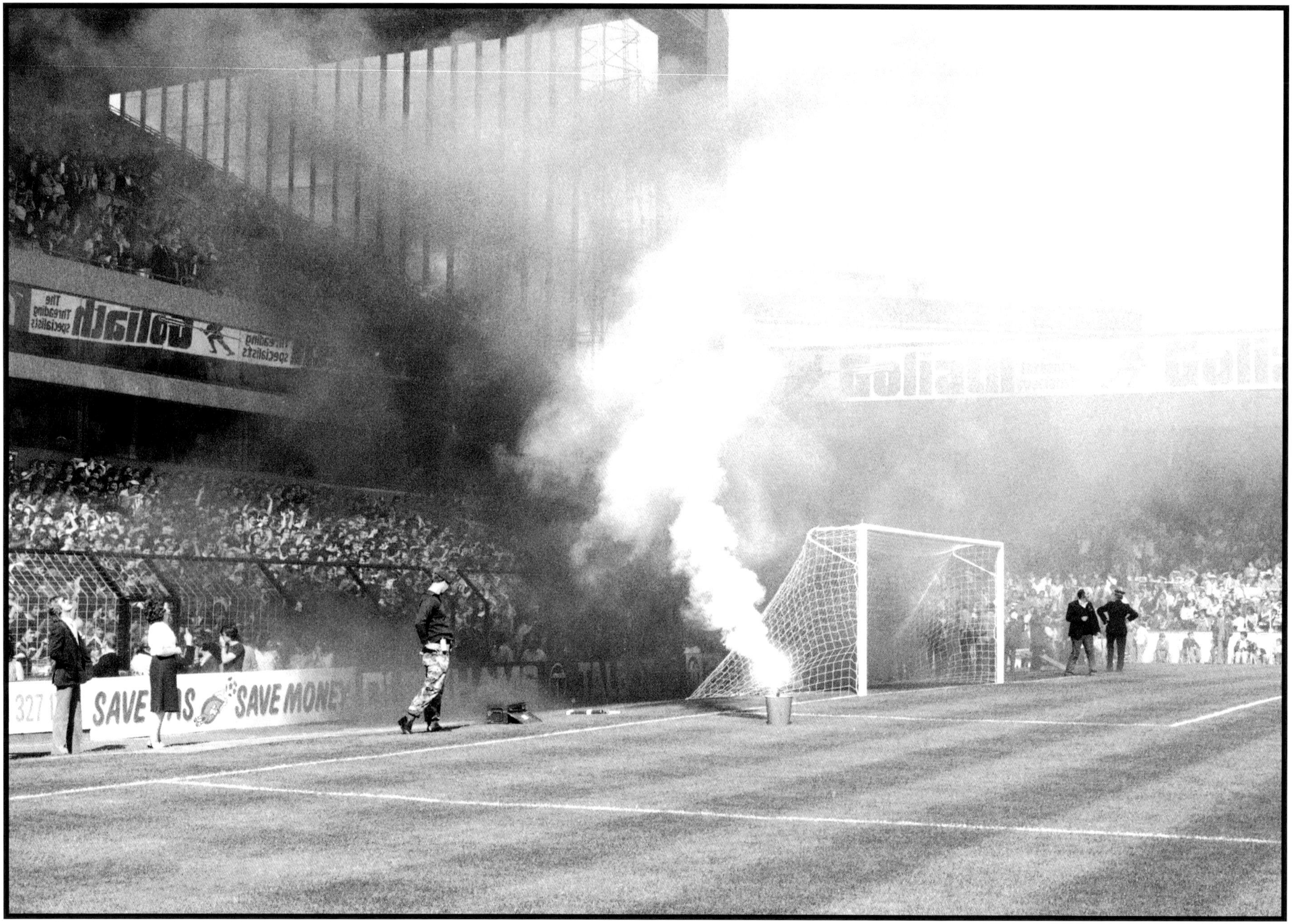
SAVE MONEY

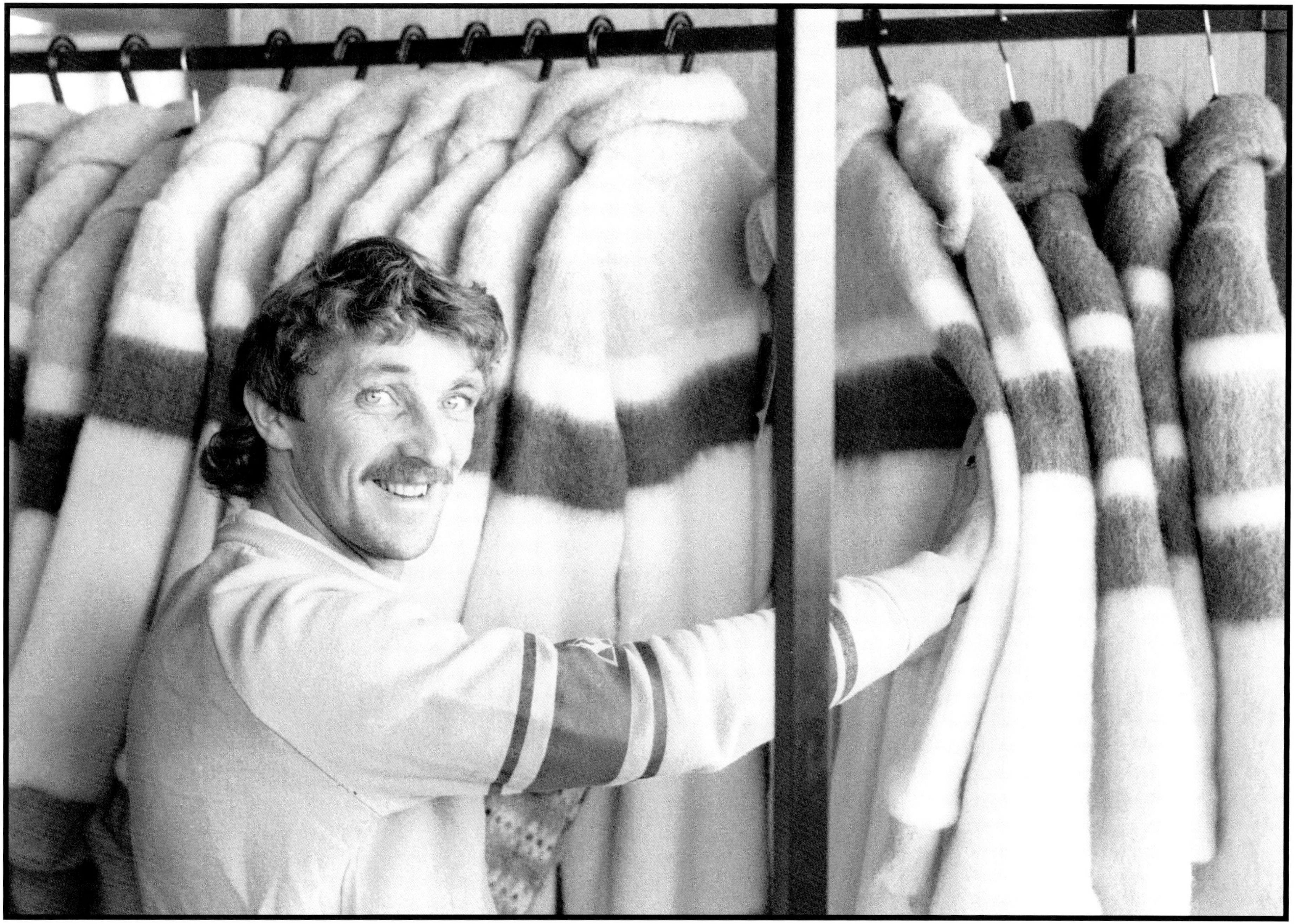

flare-up

It's almost like a scene from a match in Spain or Italy as a flare sends smoke billowing into the skies above the North Stand.

It was there for a very good reason, though. A demonstration parachute jump was taking place before a match against Manchester United and the flare provided a marker.

The ploy made a lot of sense, particularly when you consider the terrible injuries suffered by Nigel Rogoff when he landed on the old Trinity Road stand in December, 1998 and crashed on to the cinder track.

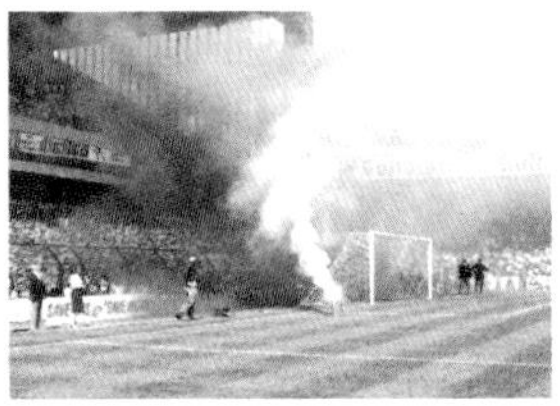

icelandic shopper

While Villa were in Iceland in September, 1981 for their first round European Cup-tie against Valur, Des Bremner learned he had become a father.

His wife Pat had given birth to a baby son, so the Scottish midfielder headed down to the hotel boutique in search of presents. He didn't find anything suitable, but soon discovered a rack of coats which were ideal for keeping out the cold of Reykjavik.

Like everything else in Iceland, though, they were very expensive, so he decided to settle for his tracksuit top!

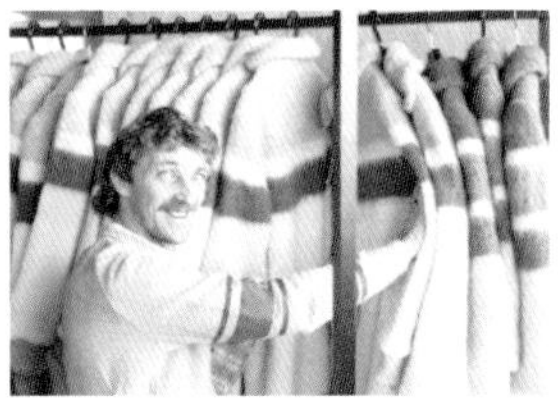

easy rider

Peter Withe was the match-winner in the European Cup Final, but I reckon he got almost as big a kick from getting astride this police bike following the civic celebrations.

The team coach was escorted by police outriders on its journey back from the Council House, and when we arrived back at Villa Park, Peter couldn't resist the opportunity of revving up one of the bikes.

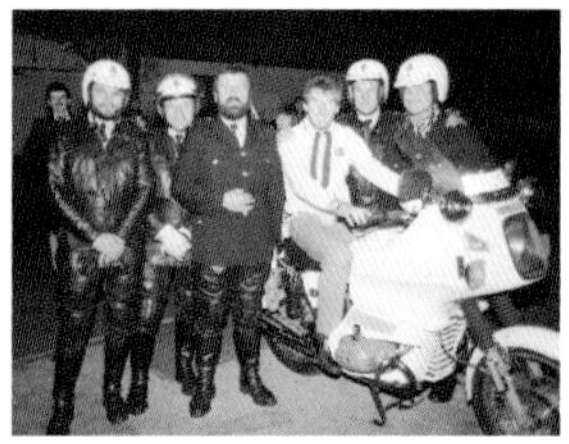

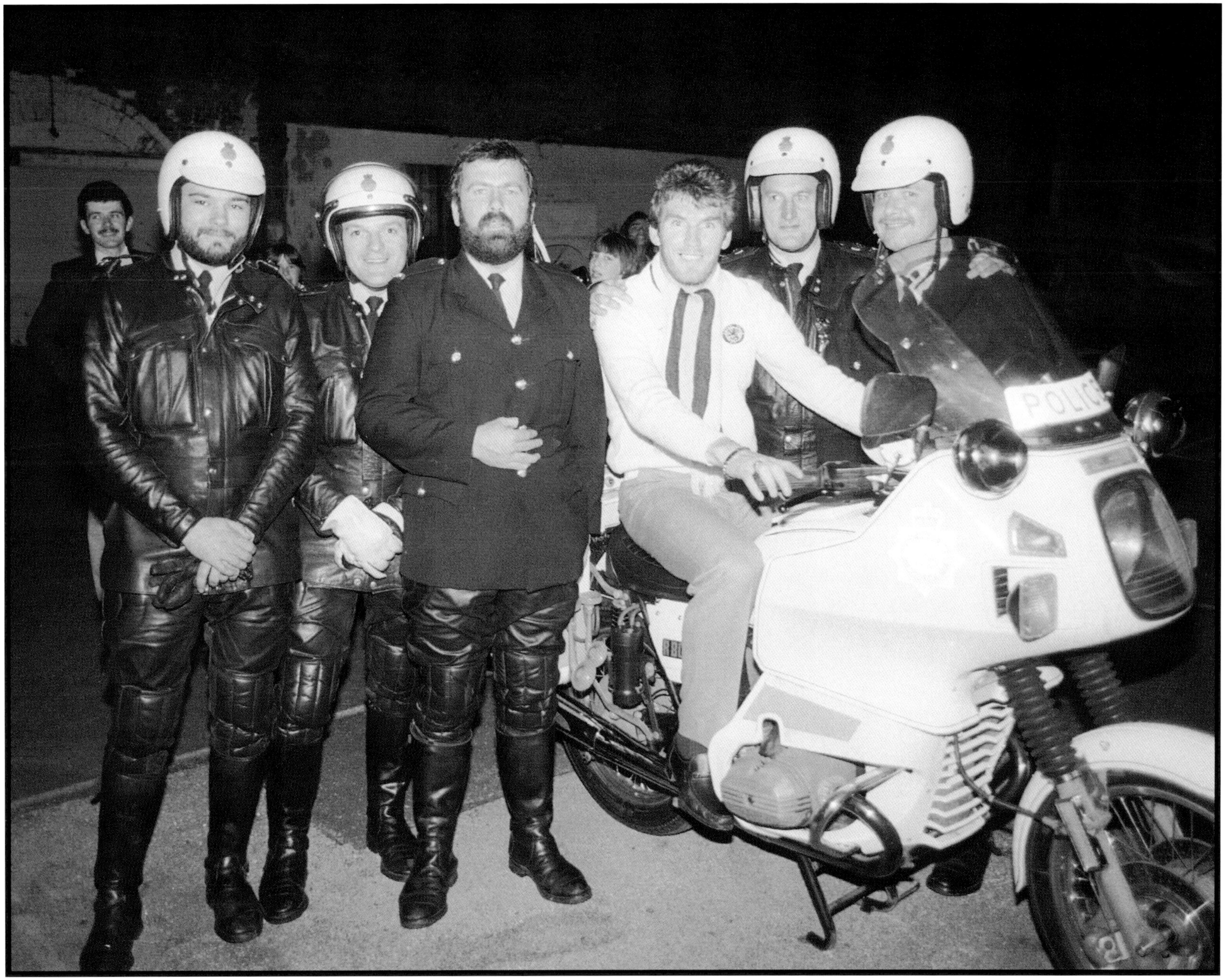
POLICE

embraceable you

Gordon Cowans (number 10) and Tony Morley can't hide their delight after Gordon had scored against Sunderland on the opening day on the 1982-83 season, but the afternoon ended in bitter disappointment for Villa.

The Wearsiders showed absolutely no regard to the fact they were facing the European Cup holders, and headed home with a 3-1 victory. Spoilsports!

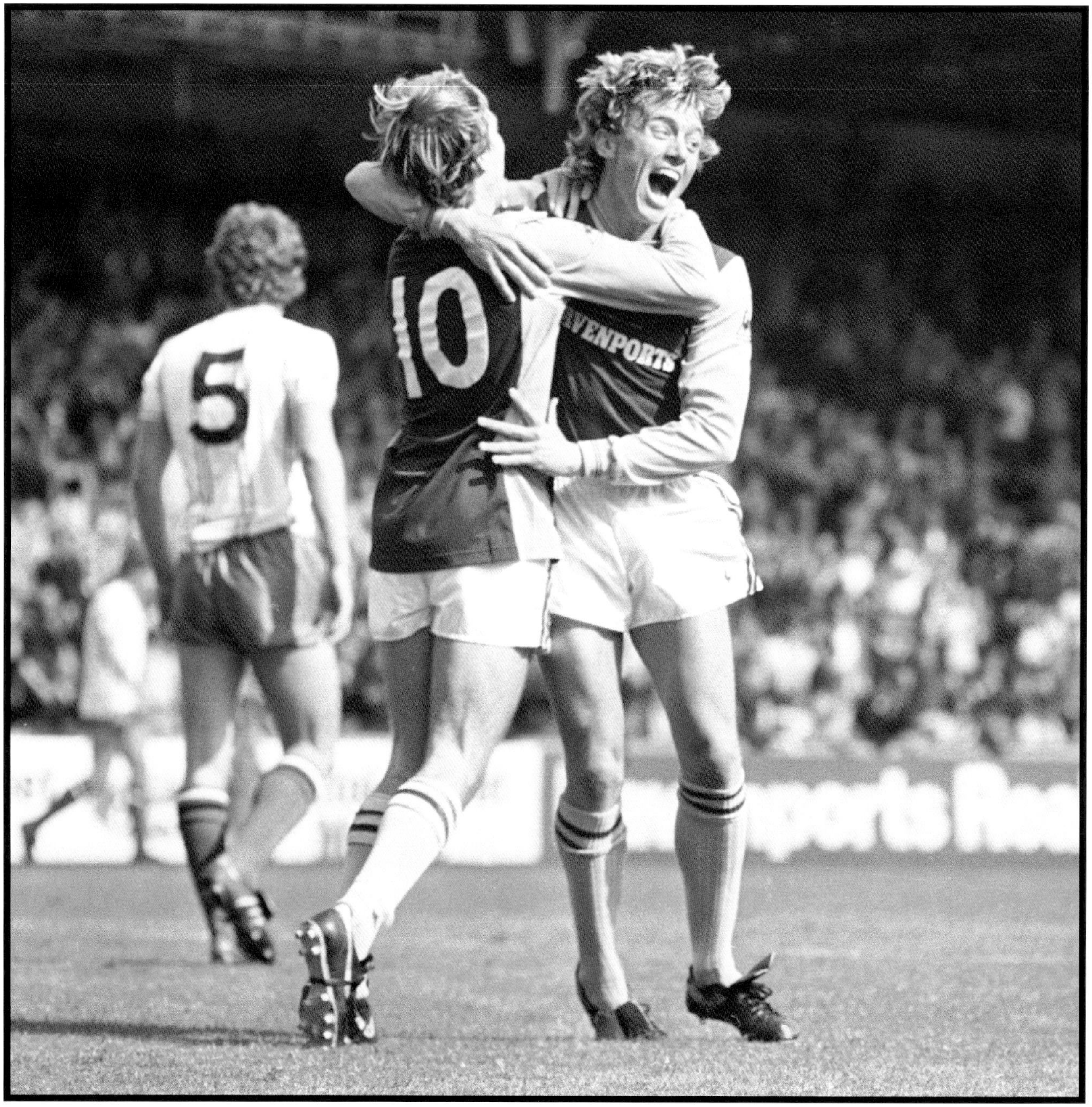

the streaker

Here's Erika Roe as you may not have seen her... wearing clothes! The divine Miss Roe, of course, achieved infamy by 'streaking' across the pitch during a rugby international at Twickenham, but she looked just as good in Villa kit when the club launched their first shirt sponsorship deal with Birmingham brewers Davenports in 1982.

Erika was big news at the time, in the wake of her nude dash at Twickers, so it made perfect sense to invite her along for the sponsorship launch.

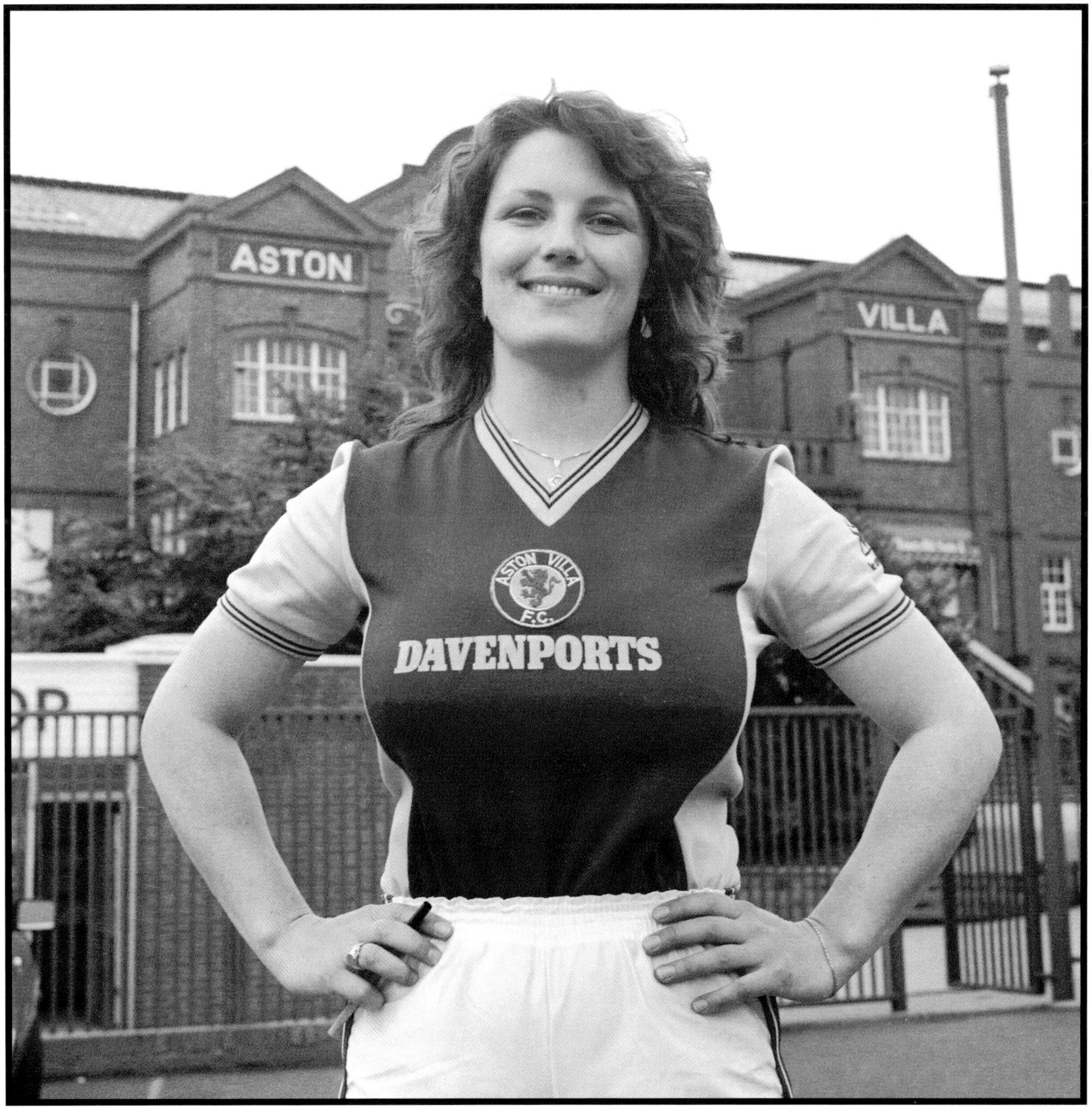

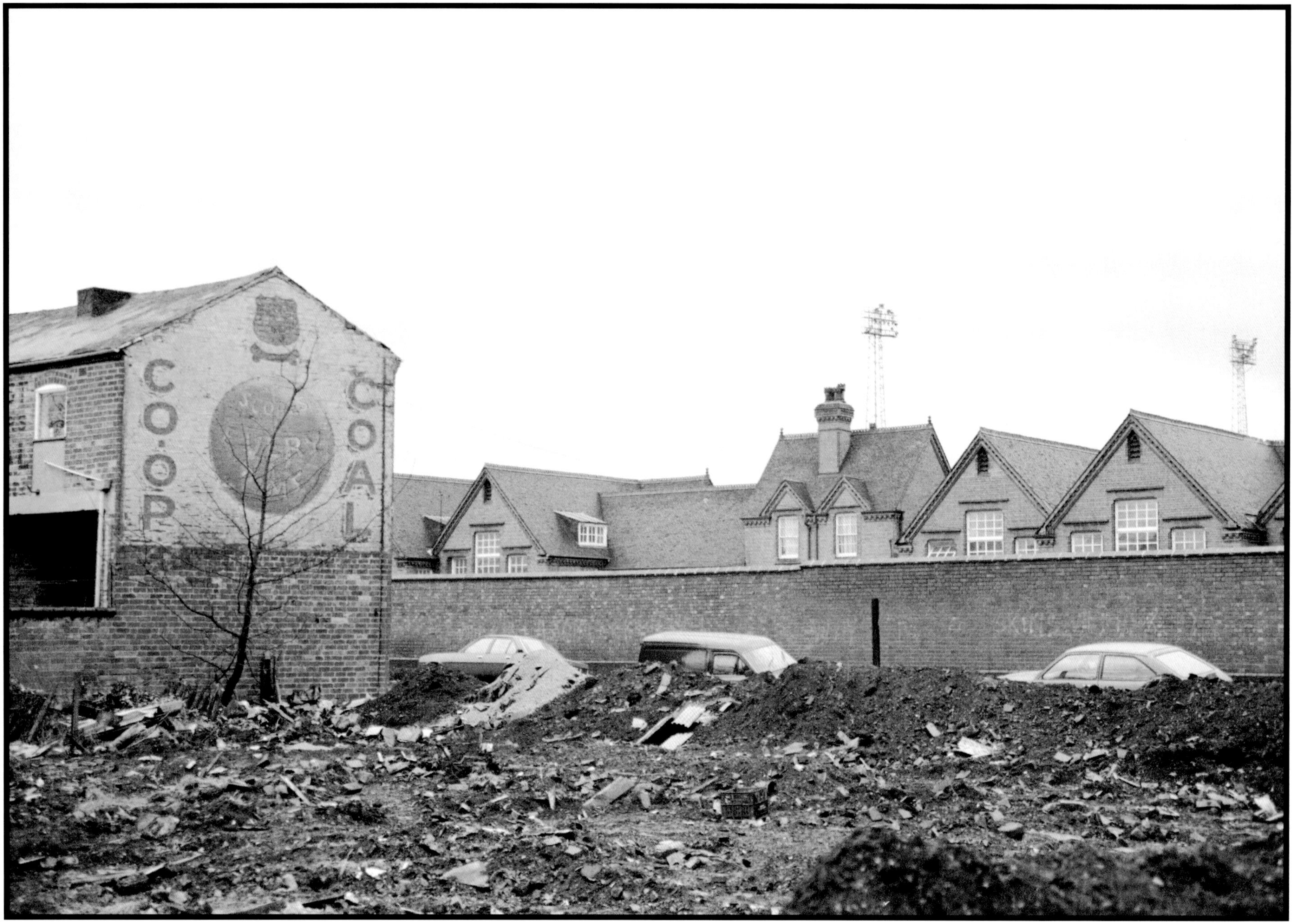
CO-OP
COAL

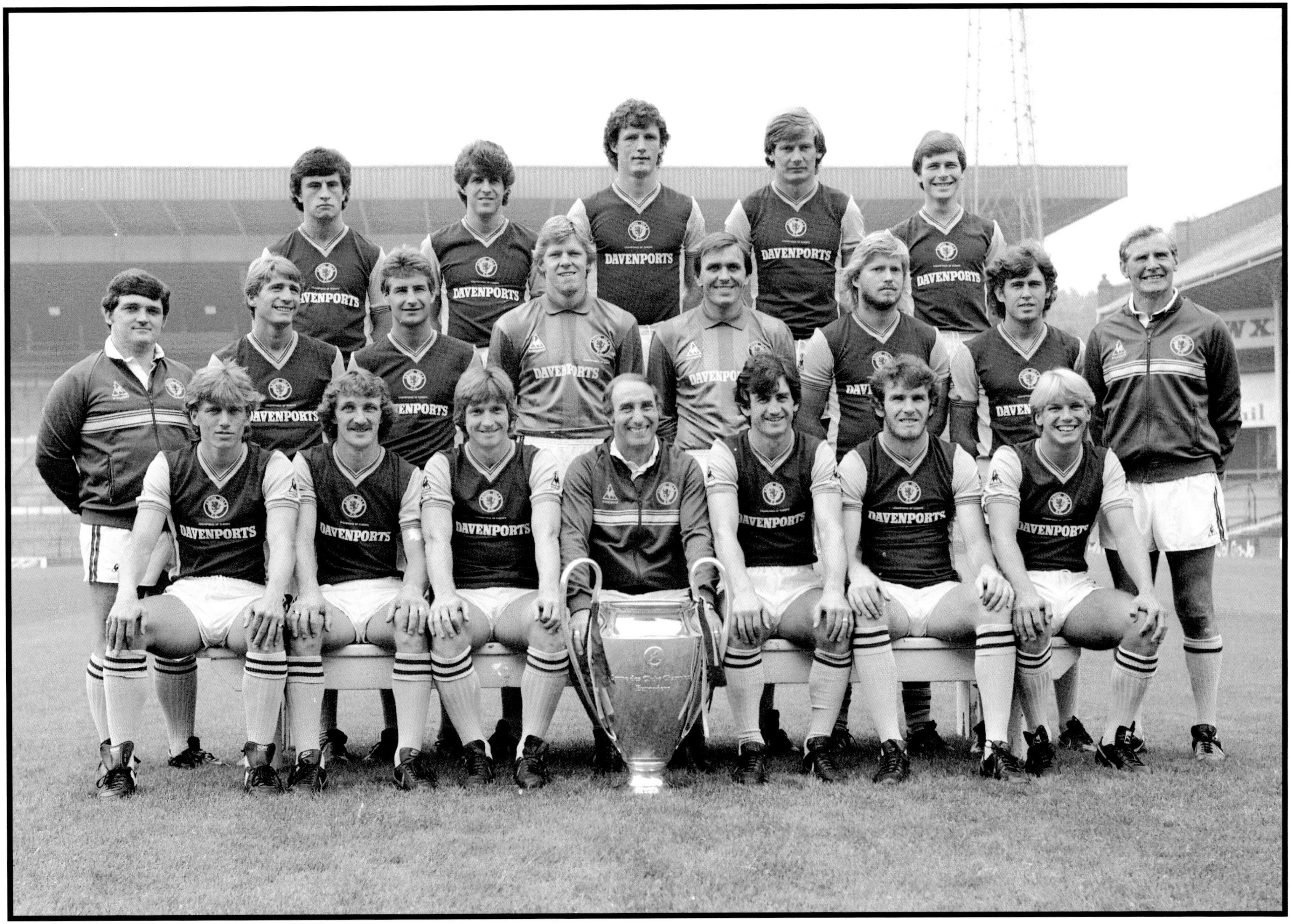
DAVENPORTS

house warming

It's amazing what can come to light when demolition is in progress. When houses in Village Road were demolished in 1981, an advertisement for Co-op Coal was revealed on a gable end – together with a Villa badge which had also been painted on the wall.

The large circle in the centre is a picture of a football, carrying the logo: 'Scores Every Time.' We never established when the advert first appeared, but it was clearly one of the first commercial links between a football club and a local company.

The land where the houses have been demolished is now a grassed play area which belongs to the Yew Tree Community School across the road. In the background are the old Holte End floodlights.

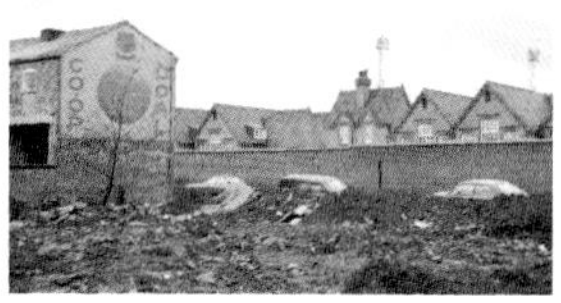

champions of europe

This book isn't about team groups, but would not have been complete without an historic picture of the 16-man squad who triumphed in Rotterdam in May, 1982, when they beat Bayern Munich 1-0 in the European Cup Final.

Back row: Mark Jones, Colin Gibson, Allan Evans, Ken McNaught, Pat Heard. Middle row: Jim Williams (physio), Gordon Cowans, Andy Blair, Nigel Spink, Jimmy Rimmer, David Geddis, Gary Williams, Roy McLaren (assistant manager). Front: Tony Morley, Des Bremner, Kenny Swain, Tony Barton (manager), Dennis Mortimer, Peter Withe, Gary Shaw.

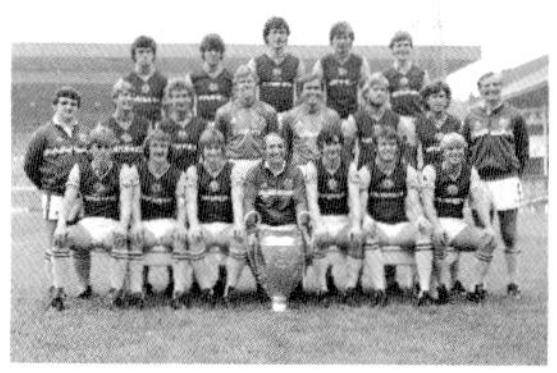

press test

It was quite an experience when Villa played Dynamo Kiev in the European Cup in March, 1982, and the basic conditions in Simferopol – the town where the match was played – have been well chronicled down the years.

But the Russians did, at least, provide a working area for the English press lads to file their match reports back to their respective newspapers – albeit in a corridor under the main stand.

Dave Horridge of the Daily Mirror and John Wragg of the Daily Express are in the foreground, but where's the man from the Birmingham Evening Mail?

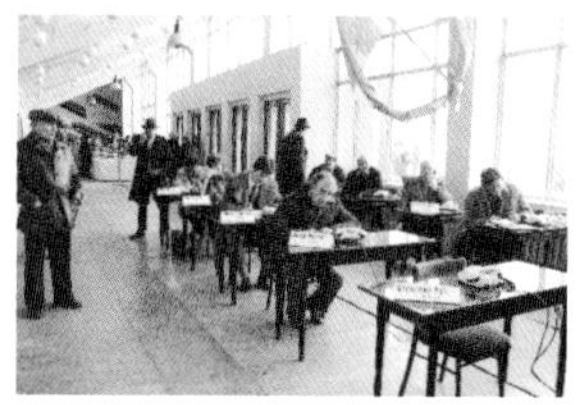

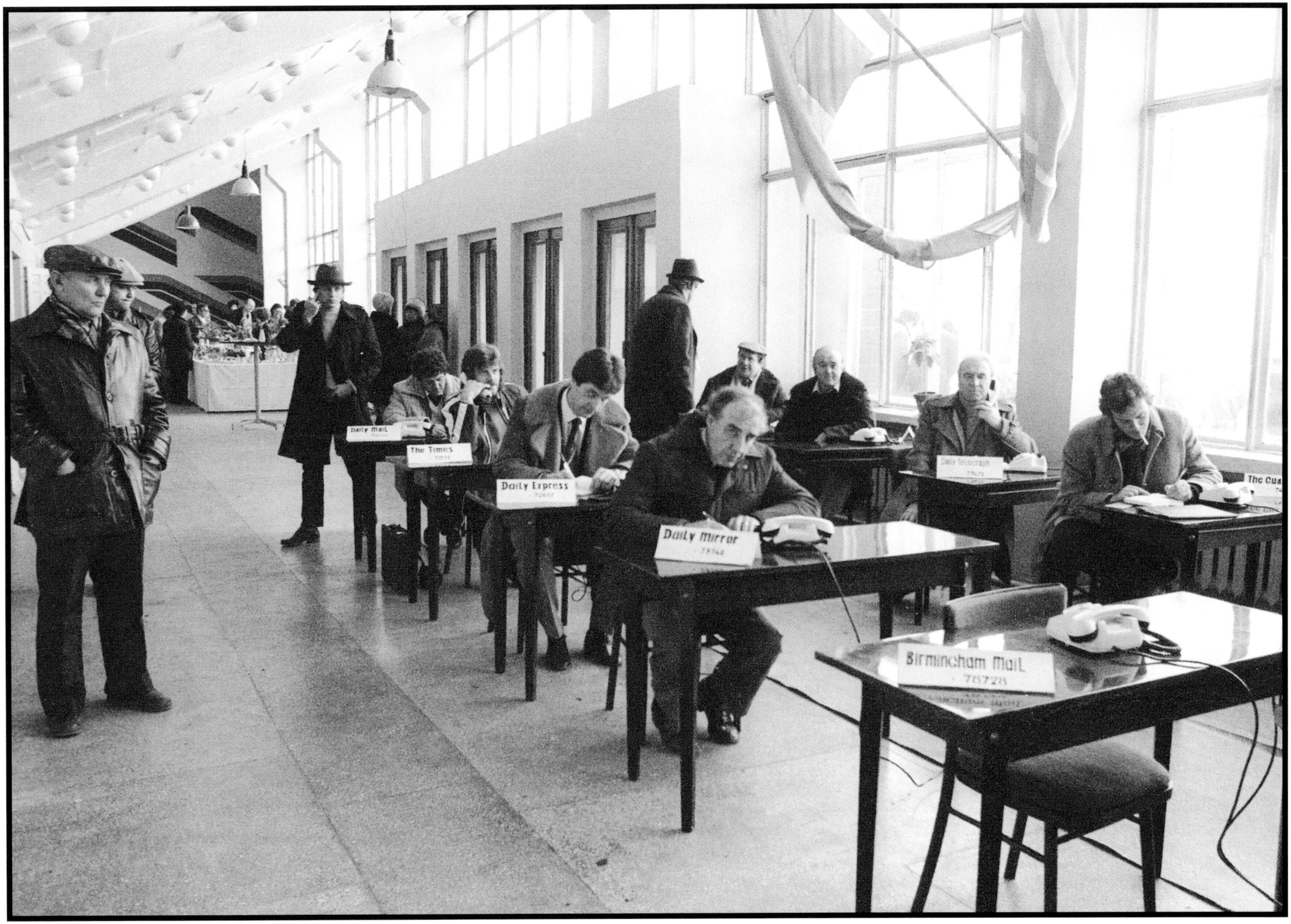
Daily Mail
The Times
Daily Express
Daily Mirror
Birmingham Mail
78728

in the net

Bill Shorthouse brought a wealth of experience to his role as reserve team coach, even if he always ended up doing menial tasks.

During his playing days, Bill had played alongside Billy Wright in the great Wolves teams of the 1950s, but his easy-going nature invariably led to Villa's youngsters taking advantage of him.

After training sessions at Bodymoor Heath, he would tell the players to gather up the loose balls, but usually found himself doing the job. Perhaps he should have been stricter with the lads, but he was a smashing guy.

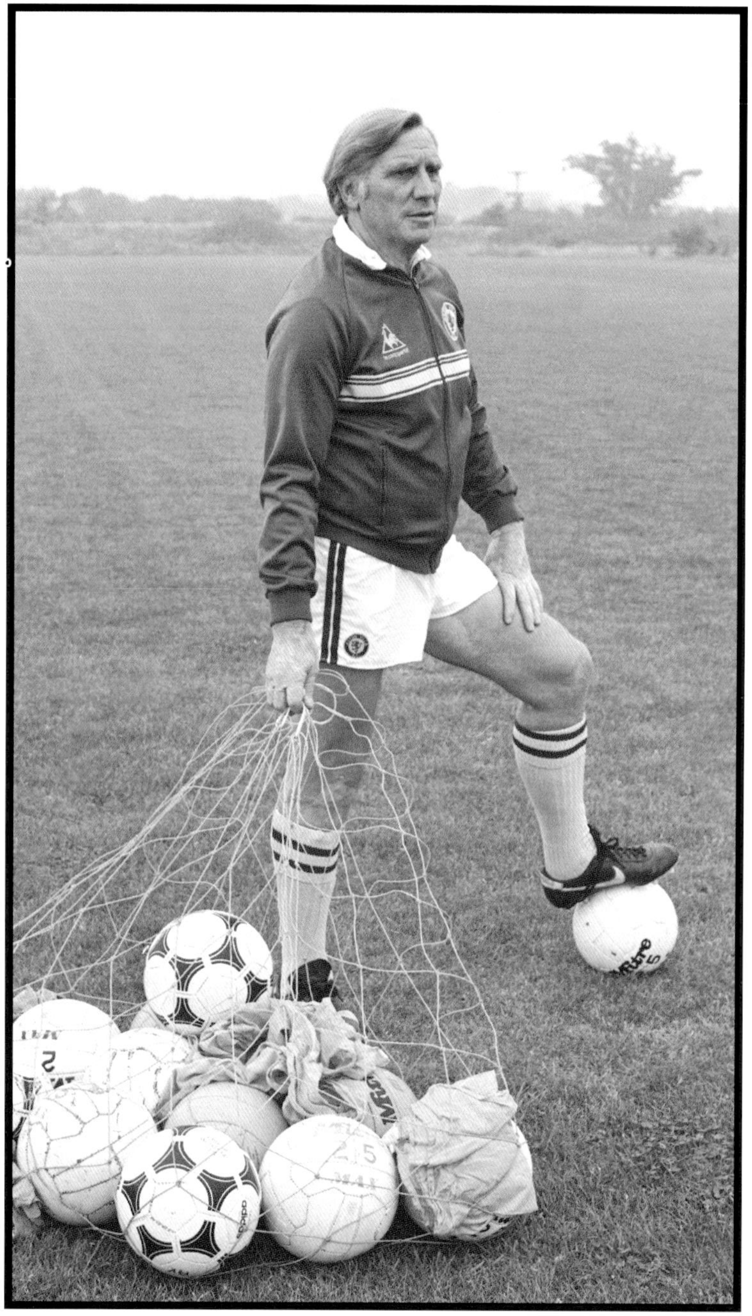

matchday angels

The volunteers of the St John Ambulance were not necessarily football supporters, and these three ladies were deep in conversation when I snapped them on standby for duty.

The St John people used to occupy a room in the old Witton Lane Stand, but they were provided with better facilities after the North Stand was erected.

The match couldn't have been very good that day, or I wouldn't have turned round and taken this picture.

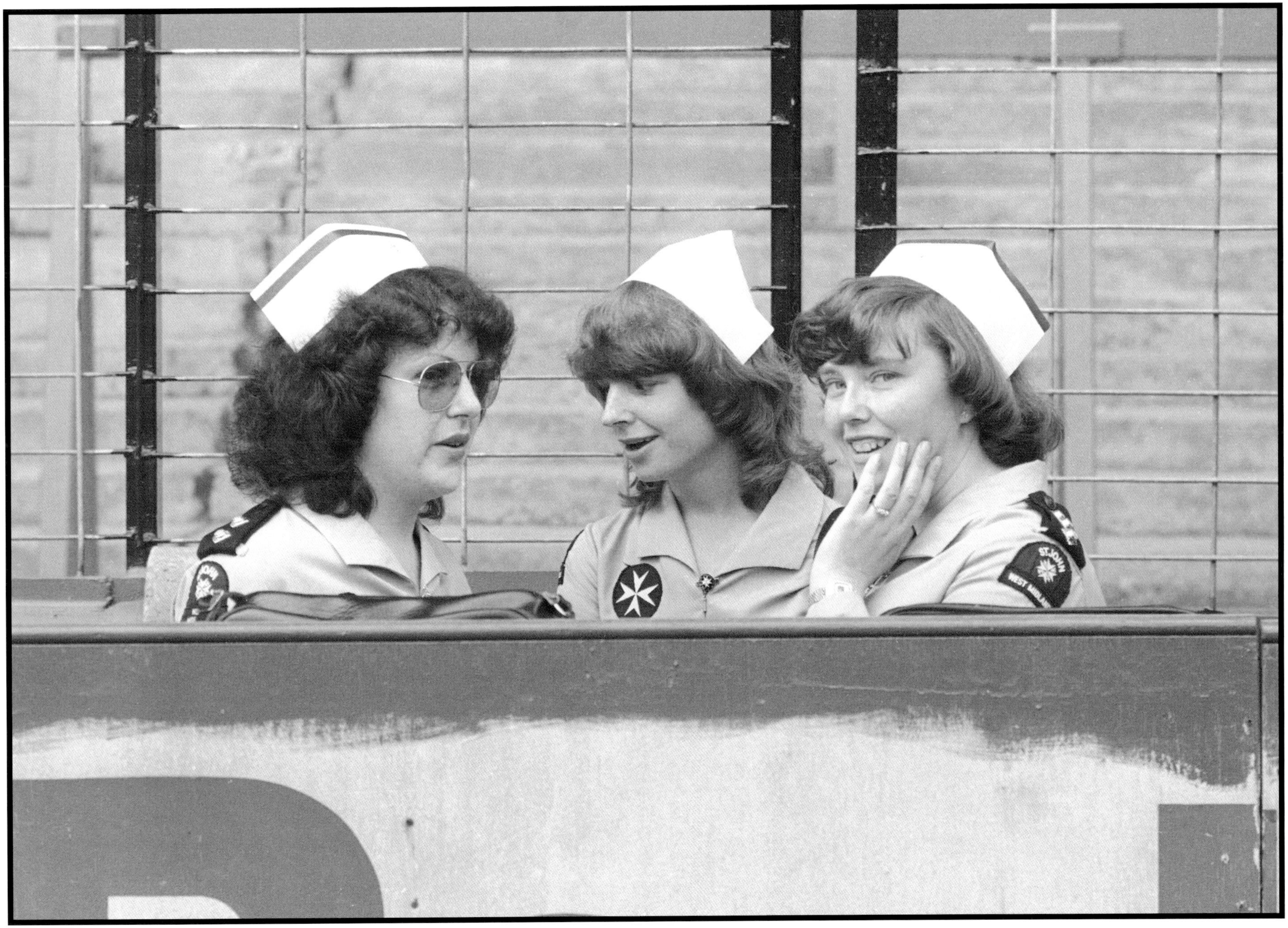

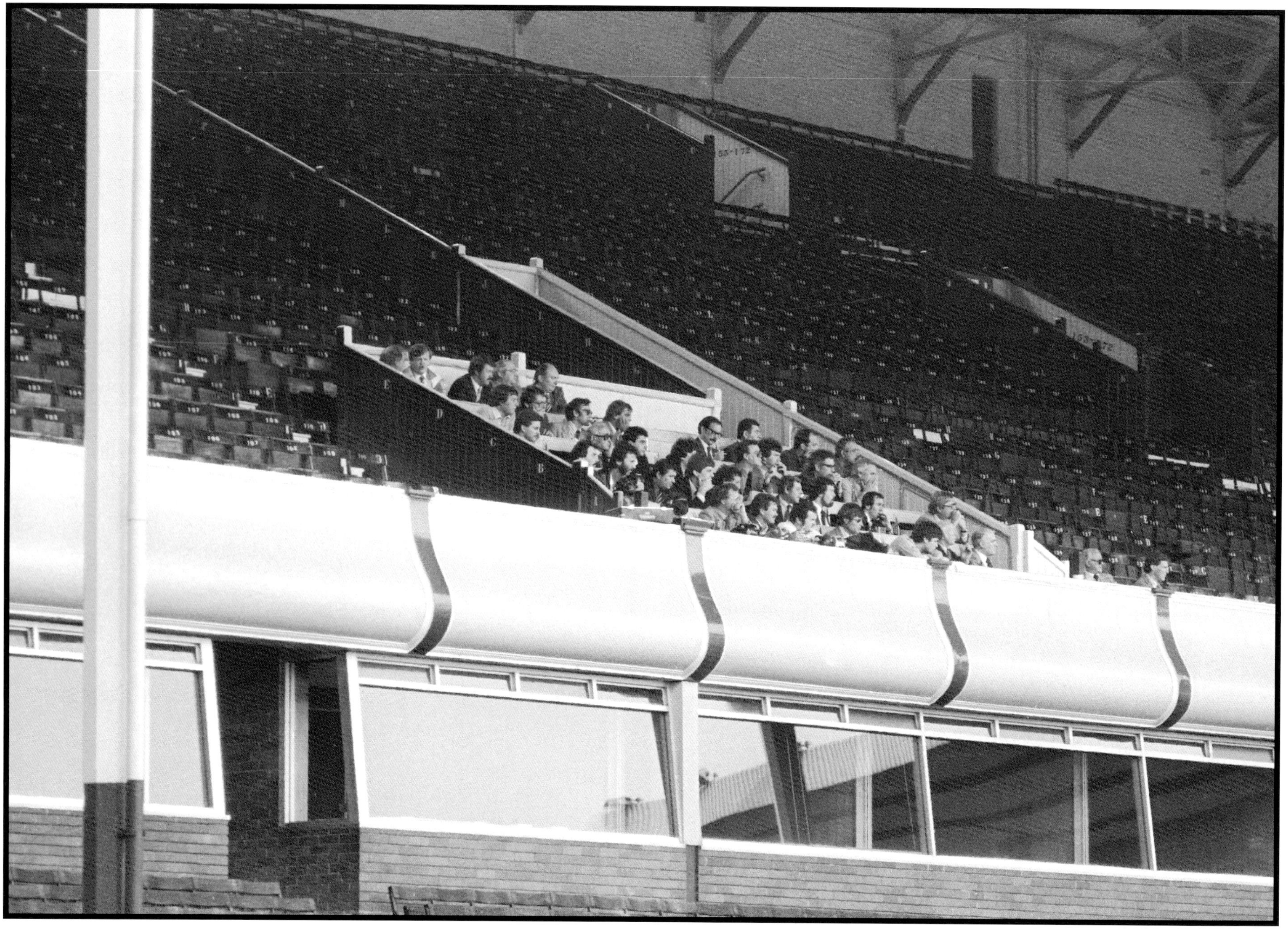

house empty

The 'sold out' signs have been posted at Villa Park on numerous occasions down the years, but we witnessed a rare phenomenon on the afternoon of 15th September, 1982.

Villa were unfairly punished for crowd trouble in Brussels during the previous season's European Cup semi-final against Anderlecht by having to play their next European tie behind closed doors.

When Besiktas came to town, the turnstiles were locked, and the only people allowed in the ground were reporters and security officers. The 'official attendance' was listed as 167, although none of the spectators paid admission money.

There was a surreal atmosphere in the round that day. I'll never forget Tony Morley throwing his arms in the air after scoring – only to be greeted by a deathly silence.

tony barton

The burden of being a football manager can be pretty heavy, even when you are successful.

Tony Barton led Villa to their finest hour when they won the European Cup in 1982, and they successfully overcame the first hurdle the following season, beating Turkish club Besiktas 3-1 on aggregate.

Tony, though, is hardly full of the joys of spring as he chats on the telephone at the stadium after the goalless second leg in Istanbul.

Tony was a lovely guy and his untimely death in 1993 was a blow to everyone who knew him. It was good to see his widow Rose at the Tribute Dinner held in honour of the Villa's European champions at Birmingham's Metropole Hotel in May, 2002.

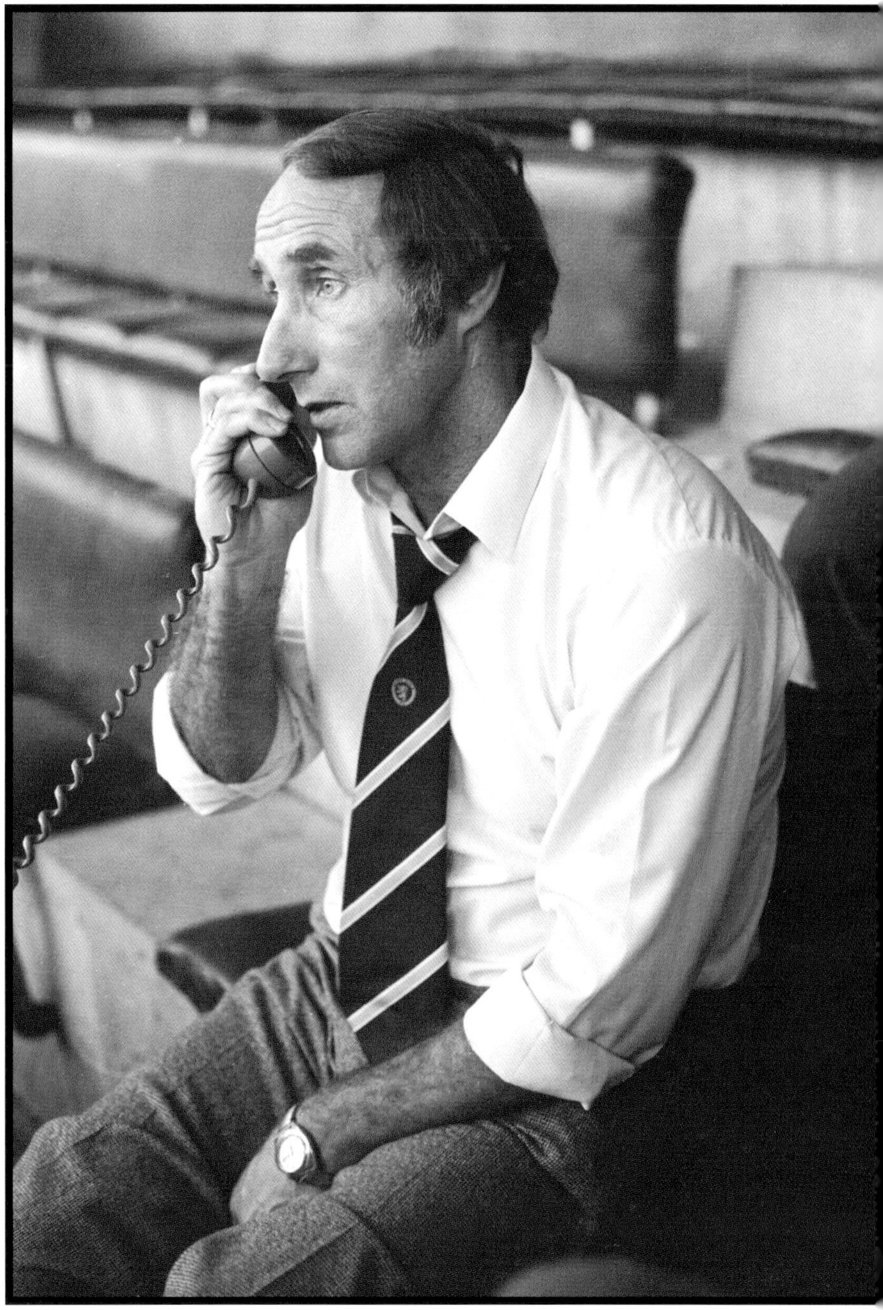

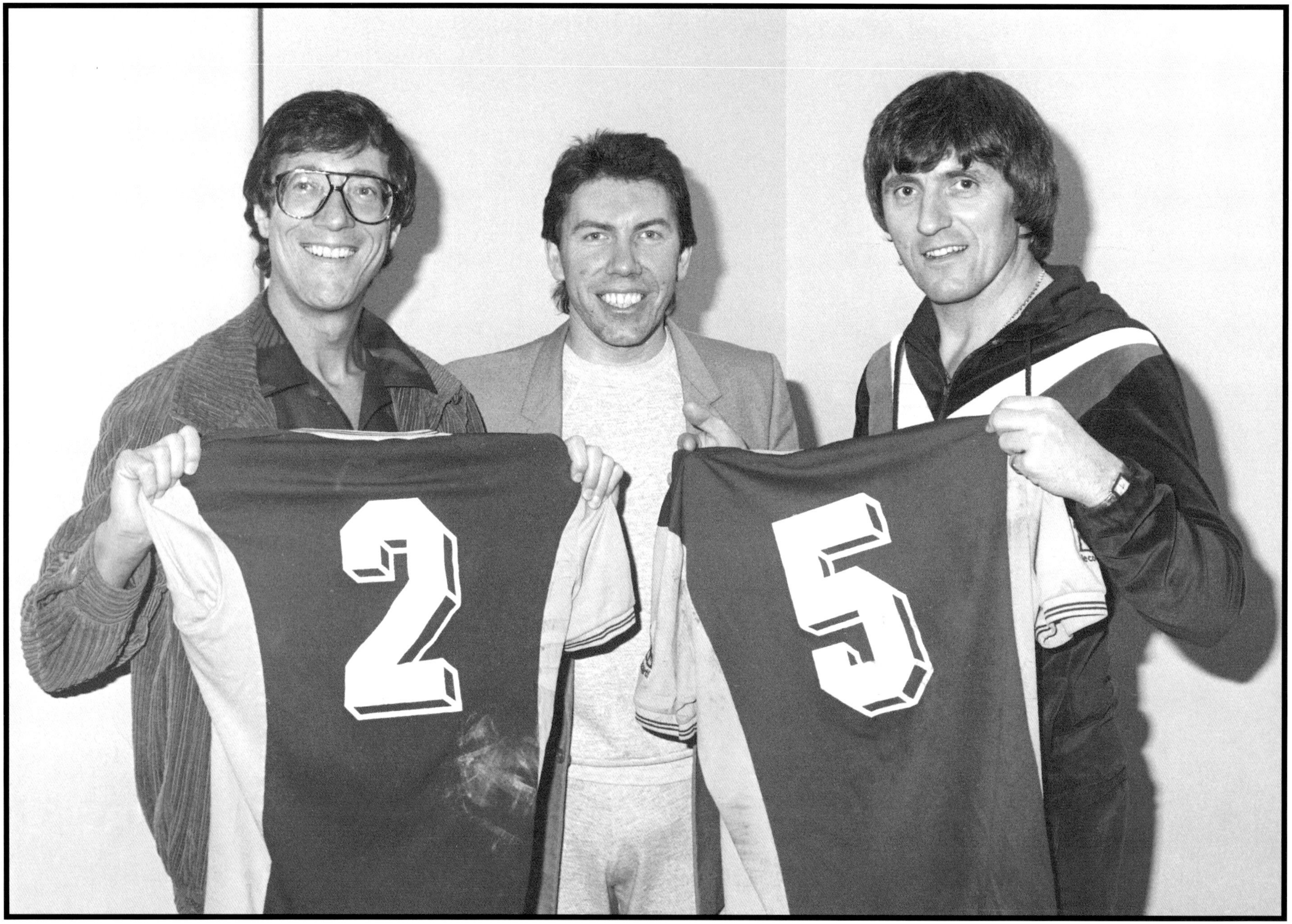
2
5

silver shadows

The Shadows had been together for a quarter of a century when they came to Villa Park as guests in 1982, so it seemed appropriate to mark the achievement with a couple of football shirts.

Out came number two and number five, with original group members Hank Marvin (left) and Bruce Welch only too happy to display their 25th anniversary.

the cup that cheers

By their very nature, annual meetings can be tedious affairs, but 1982 was a notable exception – thanks to a special visitor. The European Cup was on display that night, and most people at the Villa Leisure Centre couldn't wait for the business to end so they could get their hands on it.

The looks on the faces of these fans say it all – there was almost a feeling of disbelief among the Villa faithful. Some of them probably still can't believe it actually happened.

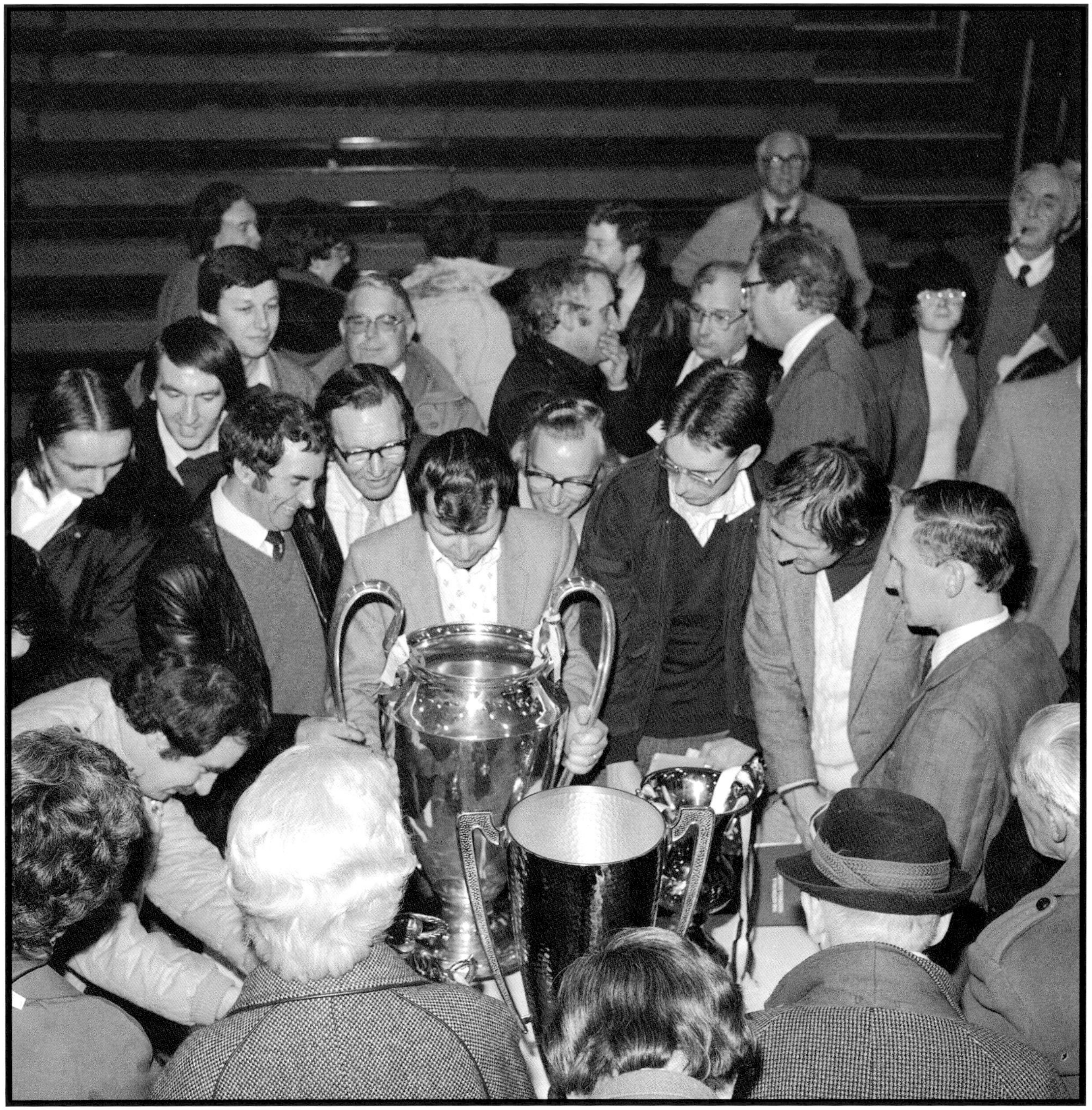

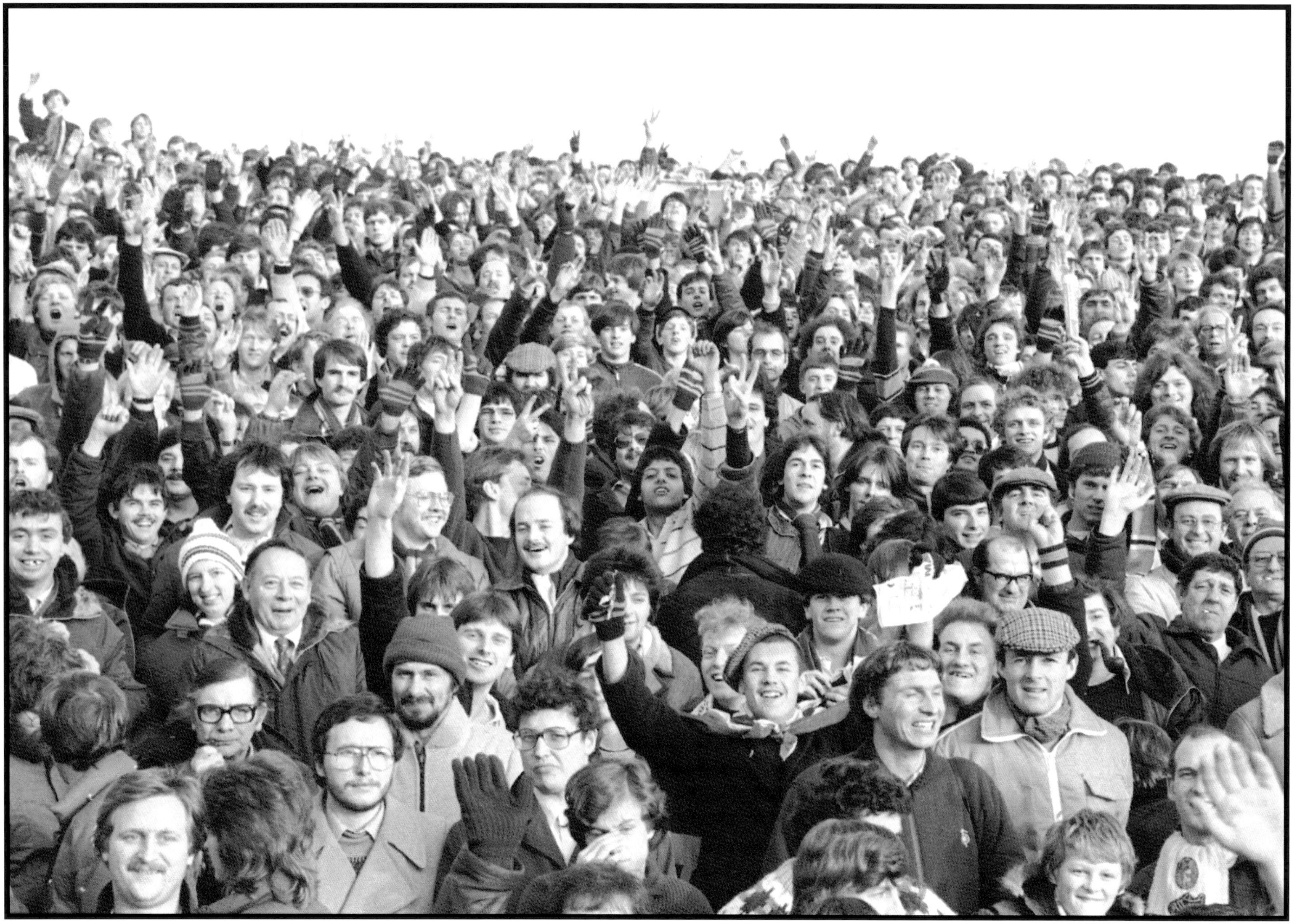

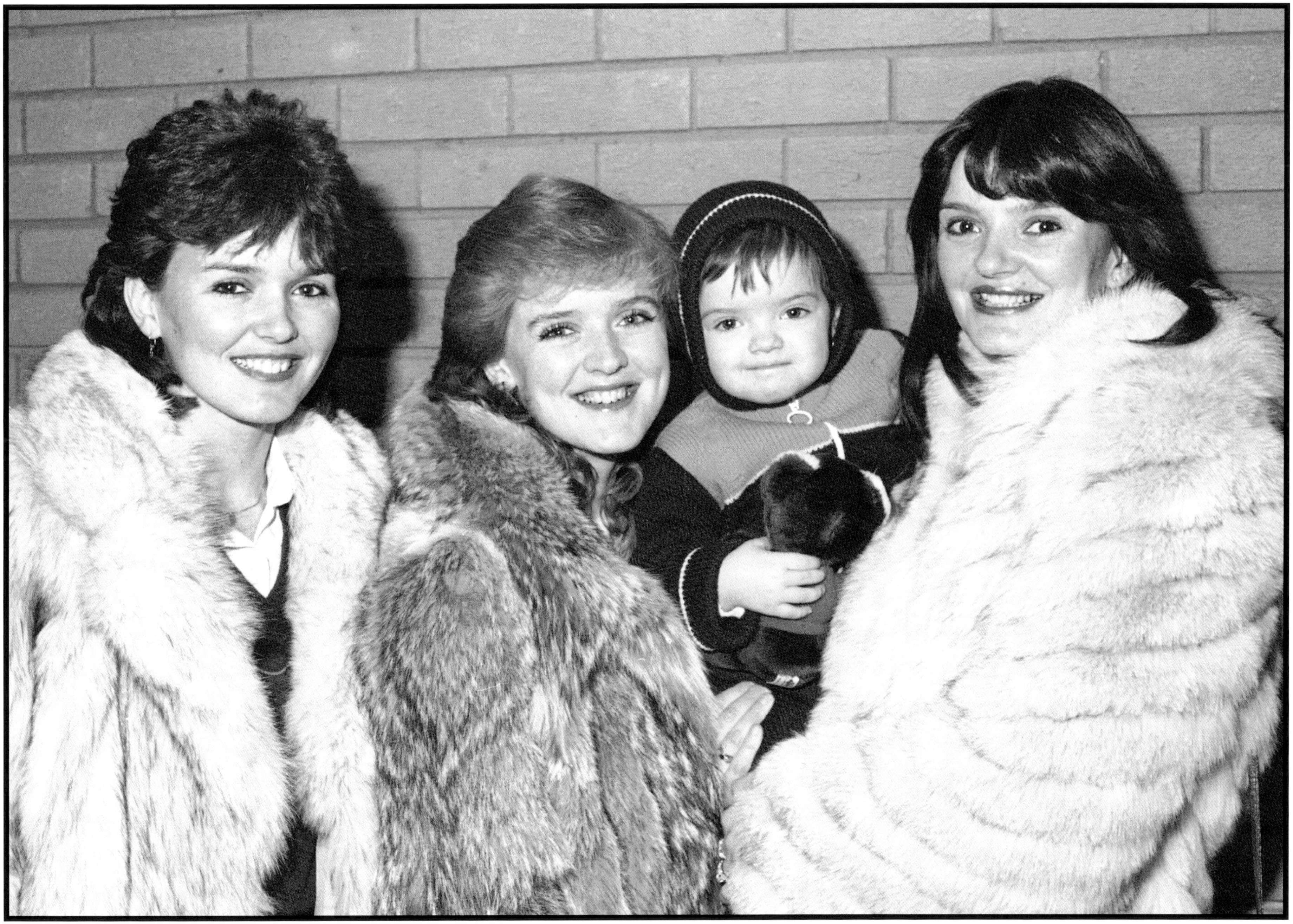

county ground

Here's a scene which will never be repeated – Villa's fans on the terraces at Northampton Town before a third round FA Cup tie in January, 1983.

Northampton have since left the County Ground, which is now used exclusively for county cricket, and moved to a modern stadium at Sixfields.

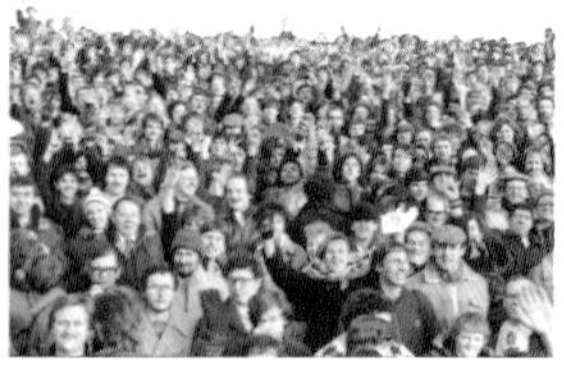

nolan sisters

This one made its way into the Nolans' fan club magazine after their secretary spotted it in the Villa News & Record.

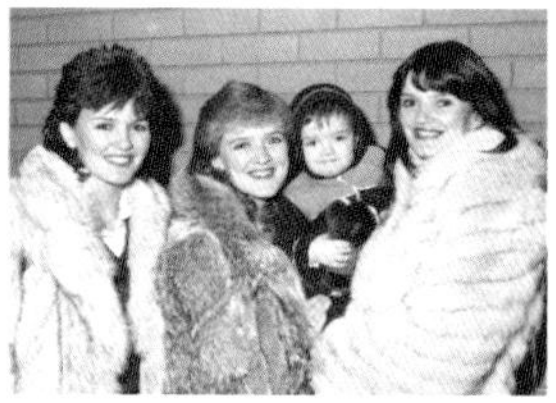

santa snapper

It's Christmas,1982, and photographer Bernard Gallagher decides to get in the spirit of things by wearing a Santa Claus outfit for the home match against Liverpool on 18th December. That's Yours Truly just behind Bernard, while Gerry Armes is the snapper wearing the cap.

Bernard took a fair bit of stick that day from Liverpool supporters who suggested he'd only dressed up to get in for nothing!

To his credit, Bernard kept the suit on for the second half, when we sat at the Holte End, but he didn't have any presents in his sack for Villa. We lost 4-2.

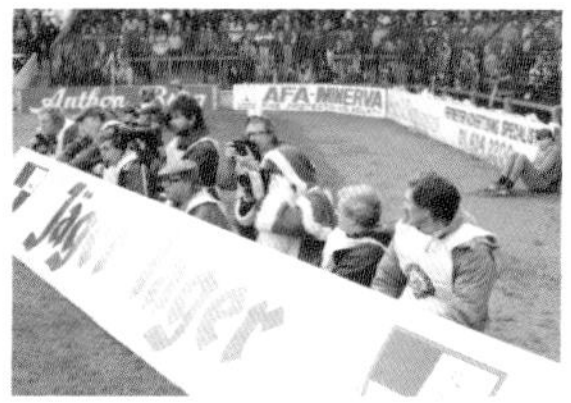

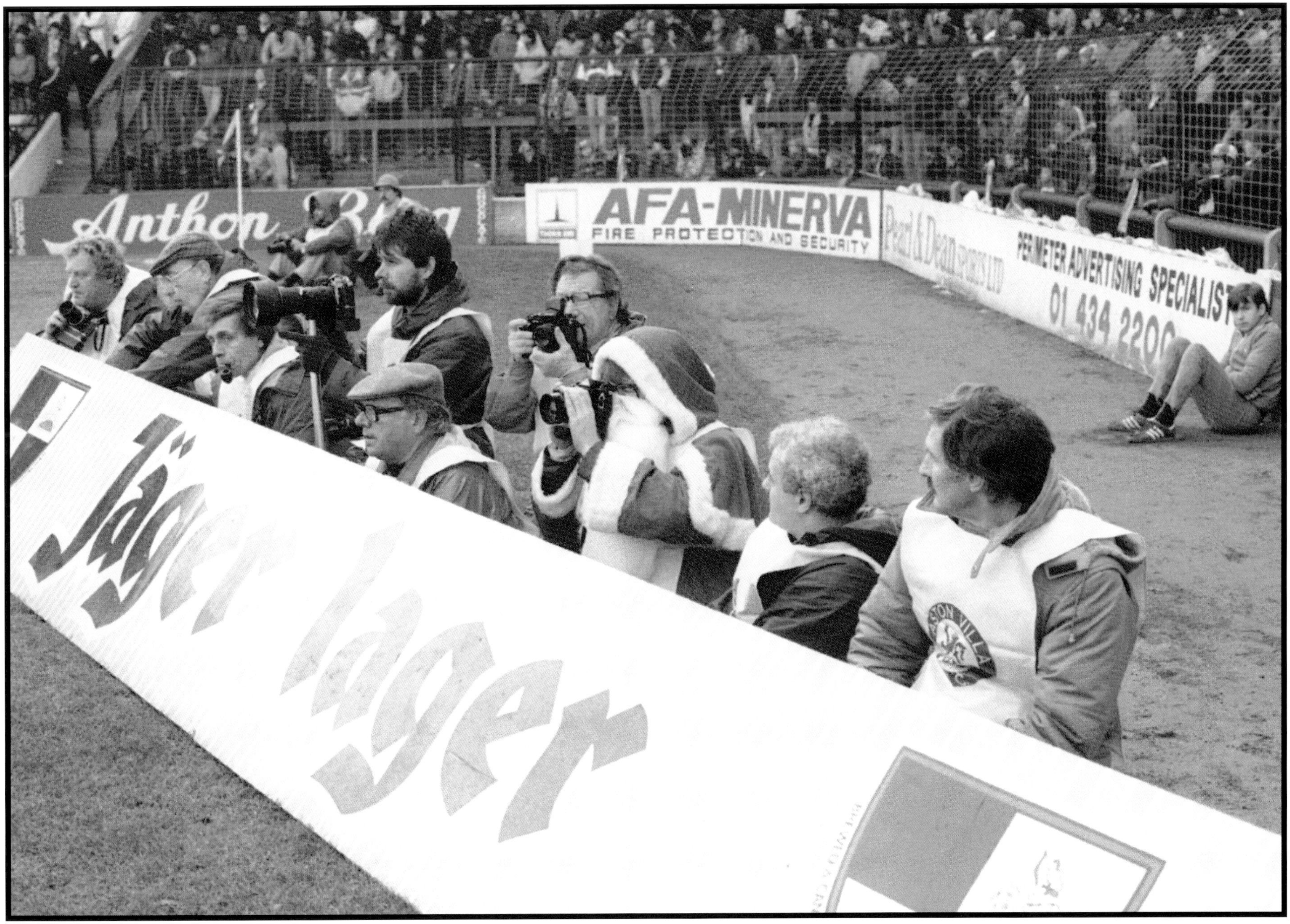
AFA-MINERVA
FIRE PROTECTION AND SECURITY
Pearl & Dean SPORTS LTD
PERIMETER ADVERTISING SPECIALIST
Jäger lager

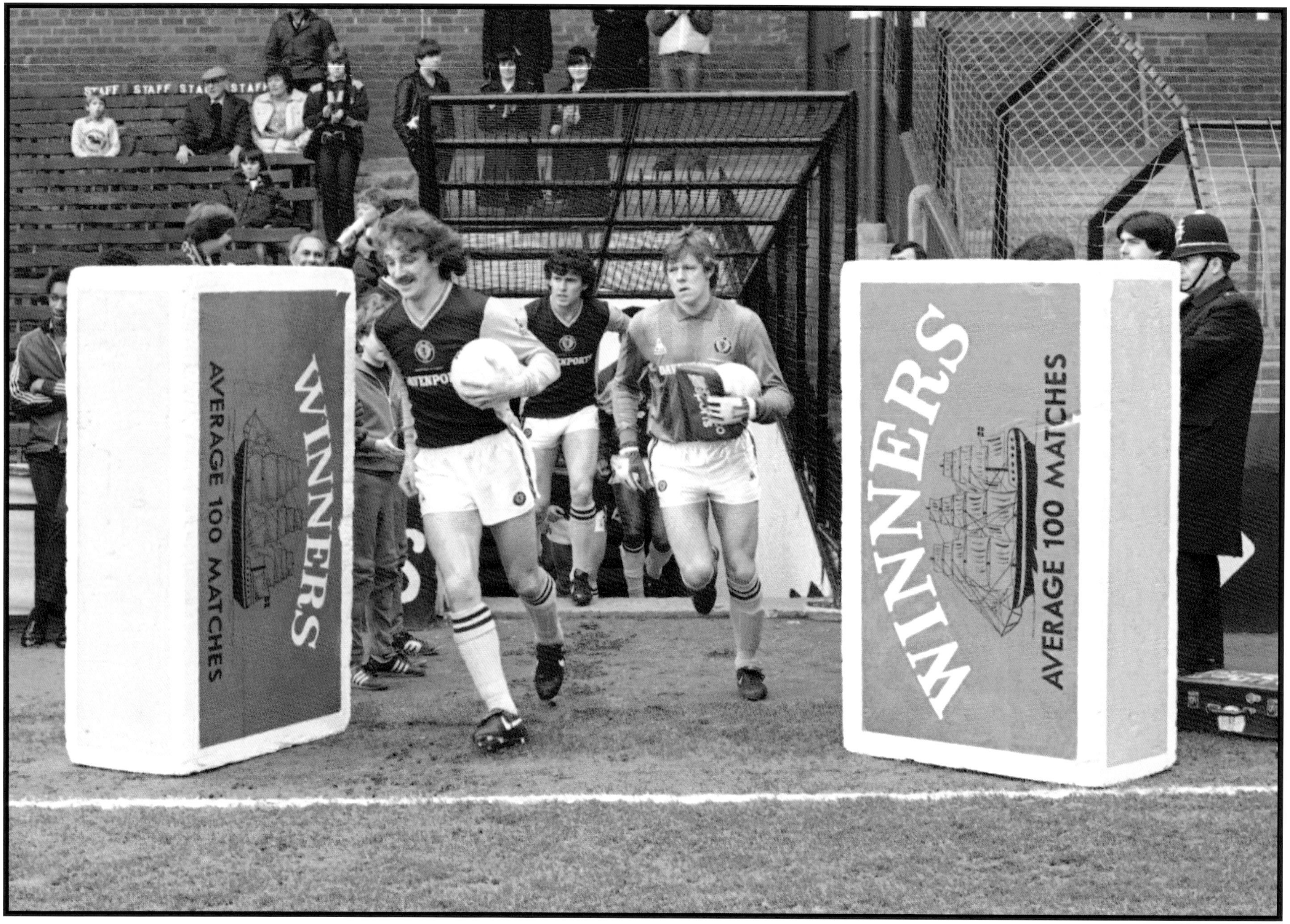
WINNERS
AVERAGE 100 MATCHES
WINNERS
AVERAGE 100 MATCHES

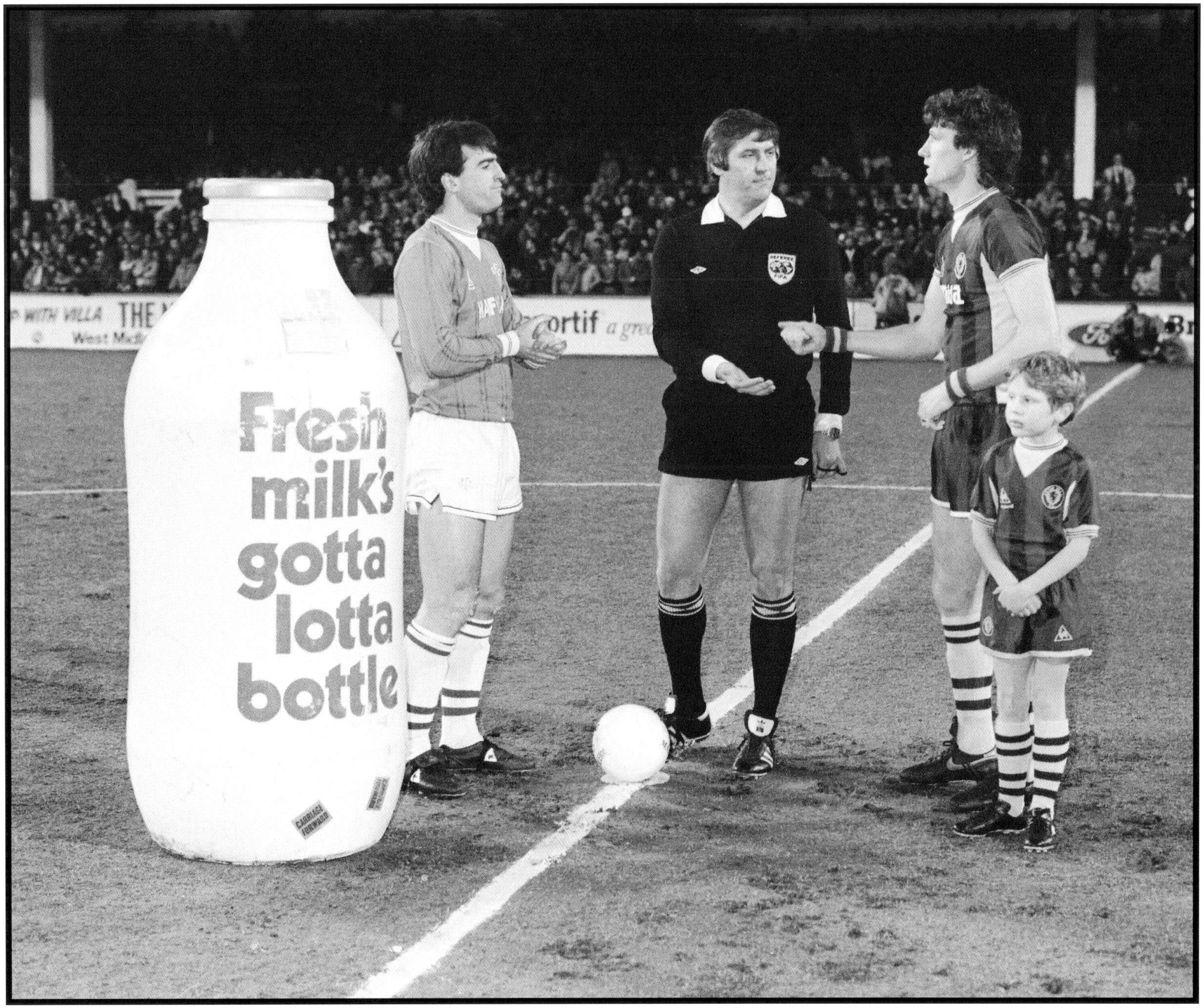
Fresh
milk's
gotta
lotta
bottle

pitch promo

Sponsorship has become increasingly important in football, both for clubs and competitions.

The Big Match, for instance, took on a whole new meaning when Villa struck a deal with Winners matches, anyone buying a box of matches being allowed concessions on ticket prices. As part of the deal, a couple of huge matchboxes were situated at the mouth of the tunnel.

Product placement also featured strongly when the League Cup was known as the Milk Cup, hence the huge plastic milk bottle which stands almost as tall as Everton skipper Kevin Ratcliffe. By the time this picture was taken, the base of the bottle had been weighted – after it had blown all over the pitch before a previous tie!

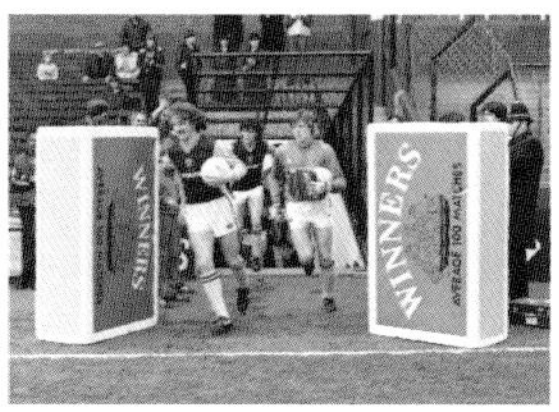

watching shirts

There's an old saying that diehard football fans will turn up just to look at 11 shirts of their favourite team. It actually happened at Villa Park in August, 1988 when Graham Taylor organised an Open Day ahead of the club's first season back in the top flight.

Supporters were able to look around the ground, and the dressing room was understandably a big attraction, as you can see from the faces of this particular group.

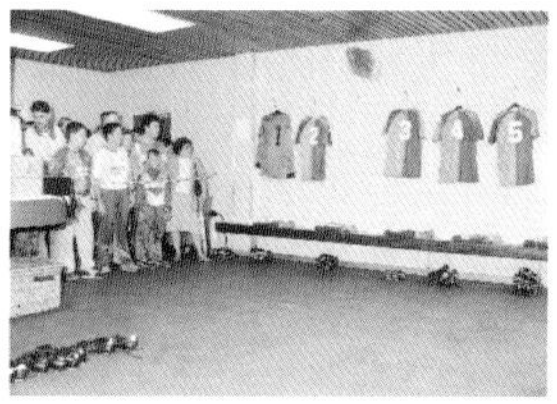

simon says

Spectators are normally told to keep off the pitch, but it was the only place to be when rock concerts were staged at Villa Park.

Duran Duran certainly drew the crowds when they performed on stage in front of the North Stand in July, 1983, thousands of fans clamouring for a view of lead singer Simon Le Bon and his chums.

The best view of all, though, was afforded to photographers, who can be seen immediately beneath the stage, looking for the best pictures of these pop idols.

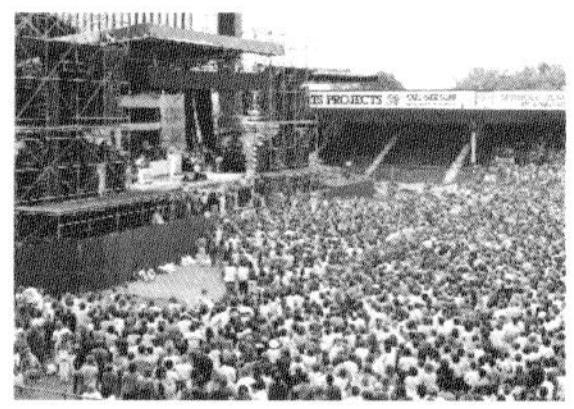

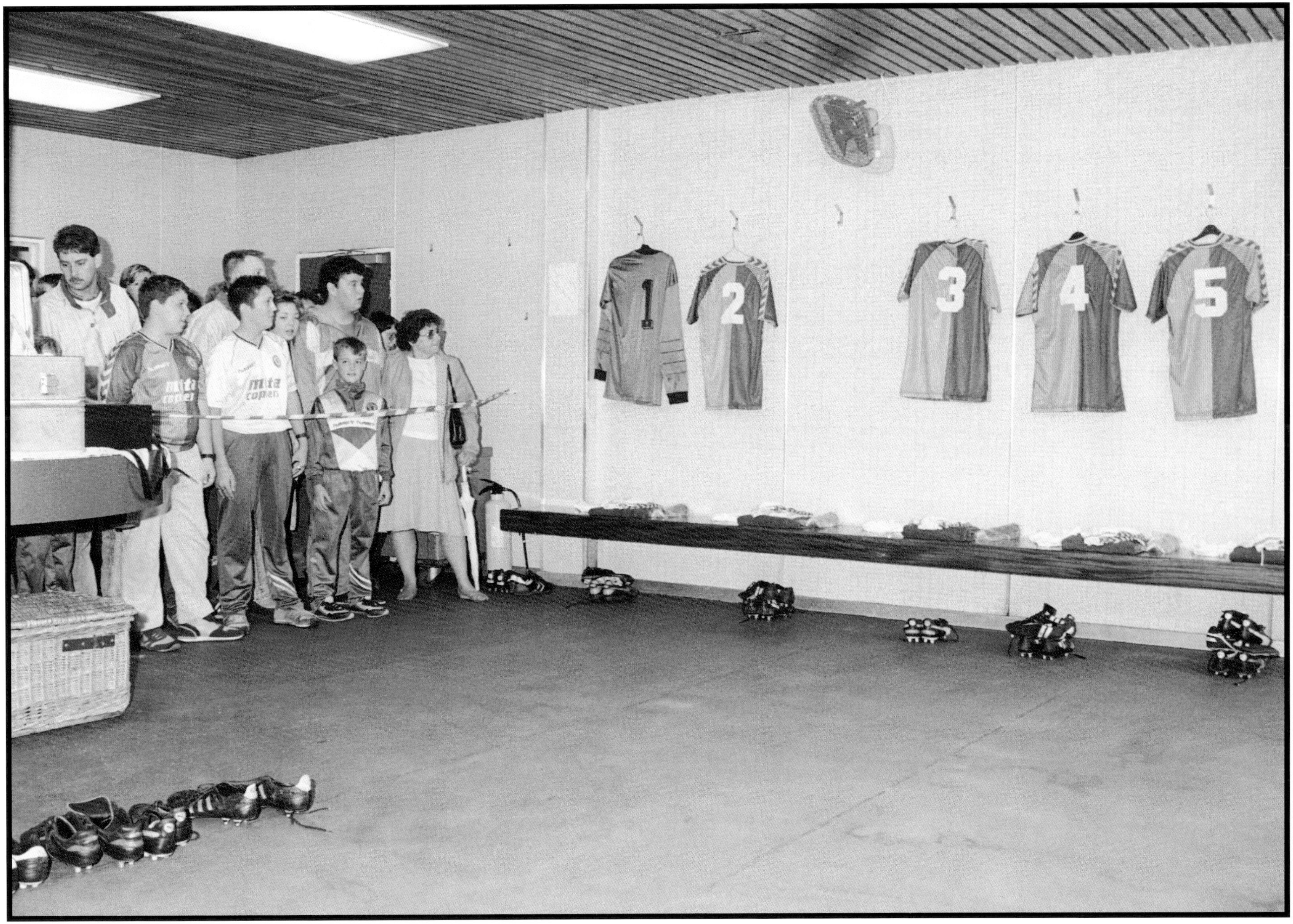

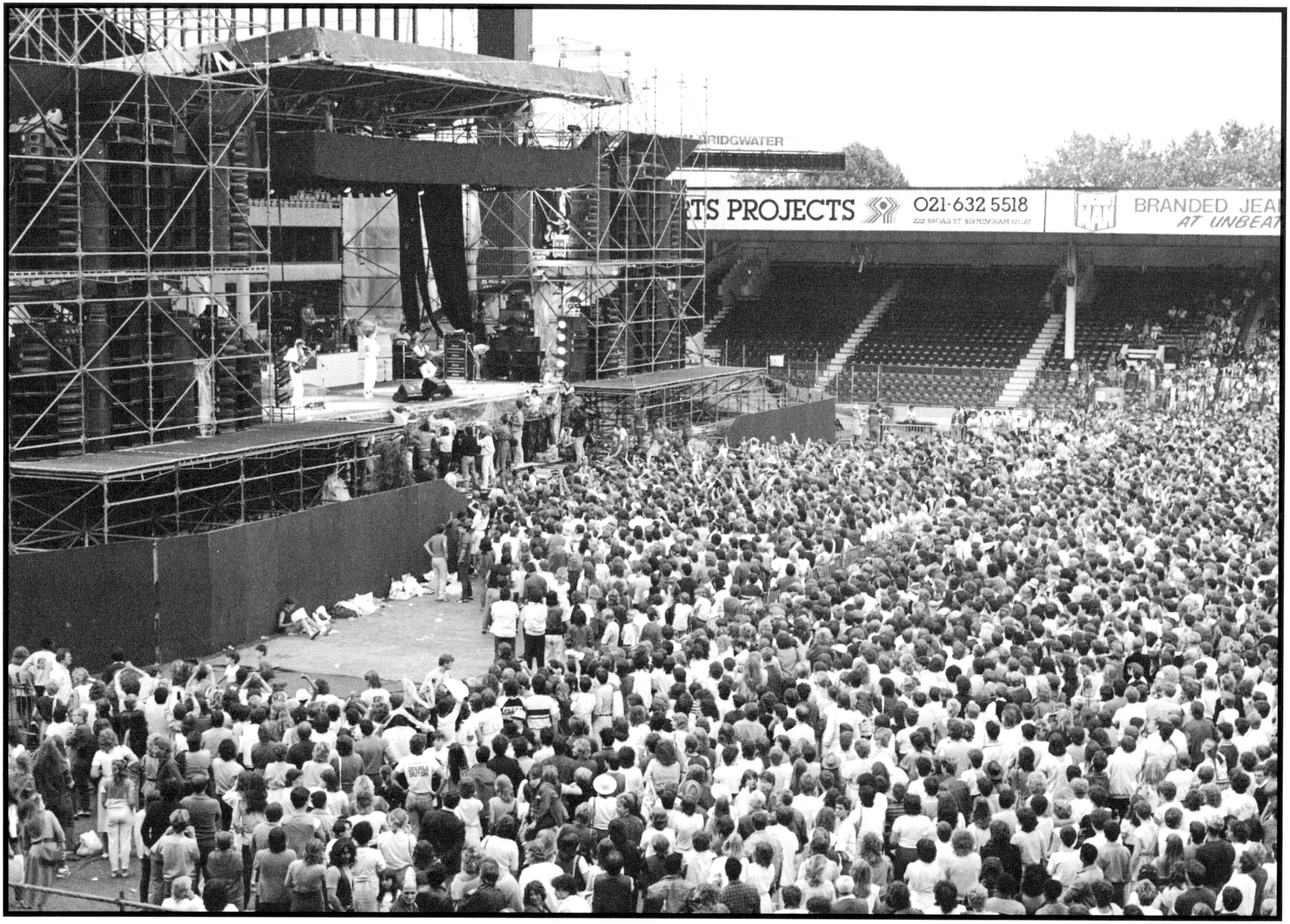
RIDGWATER
TS PROJECTS
021-632 5518
BRANDED JEA
AT UNBEAT

call to armes

Apart from being a fine photographer, Gerry Armes was also a colourful character on the Midland football scene, and was never timid when it came to giving his opinion.

Gerry is now retired, but he was a good companion to the other 'snappers', always willing to pass on his vast experience and share in a joke at the side of the pitch. I recently spoke to a press photographer, who admitted he was bored with his job. We were never bored when Gerry was around.

He was certainly in jovial mood when he found himself on the other side of the lens for this picture, which shows him sharing a laugh with Miss Aston Villa. And who can blame him?

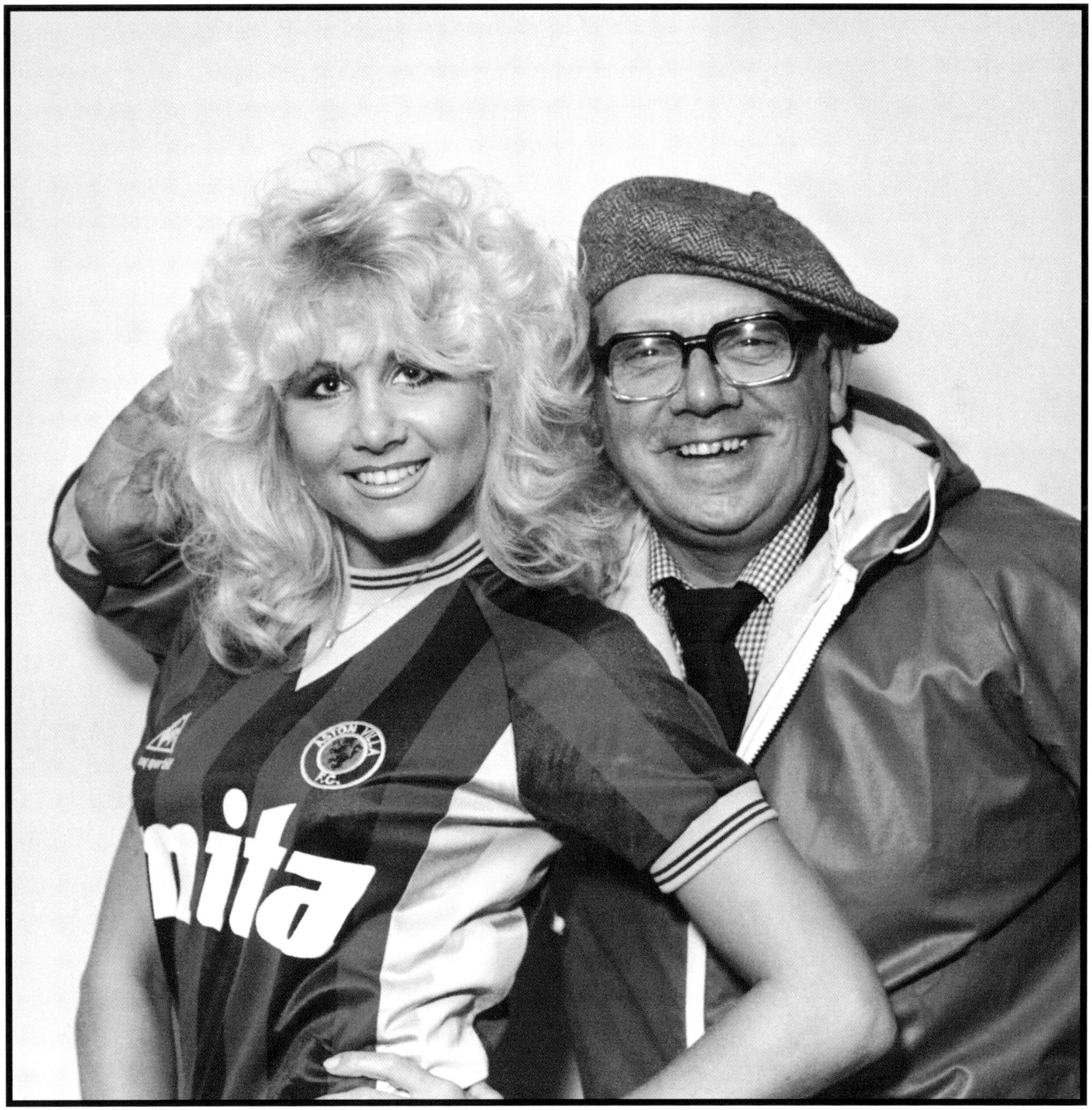

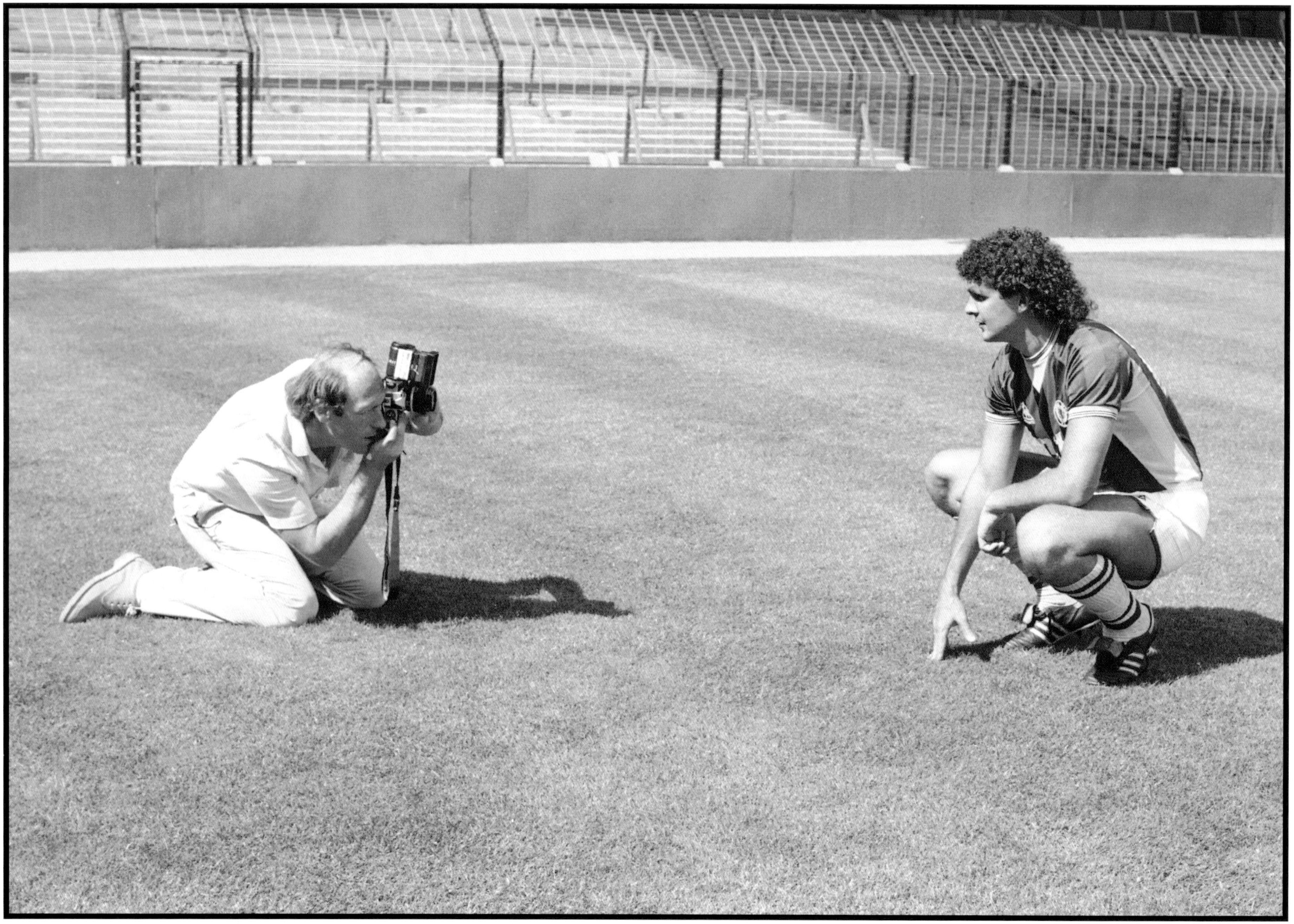

brought to his knees

It was Villa's annual photo-call in July 1984, and the snapper was taking a picture of centre-half Steve Foster, who had joined us from Brighton towards the end of the previous season. Foster wasn't with us long before moving on to Luton Town, but he liked a bet. He once gave me £30 to put on a horse, which was a tidy sum in those days. When I placed the bet, everyone in the betting shop gathered around, thinking I knew something they didn't – but the horse finished nowhere.

billy graham

it was quite an event when Billy Graham brought his religious roadshow to Villa Park in 1985.
Photographers were allowed 10 minutes to snap away before being required to leave at a given signal. As I moved away, thousands of people were heading in the opposite direction to be saved. The attendance that night was the ground's highest of the 1984-85 season.

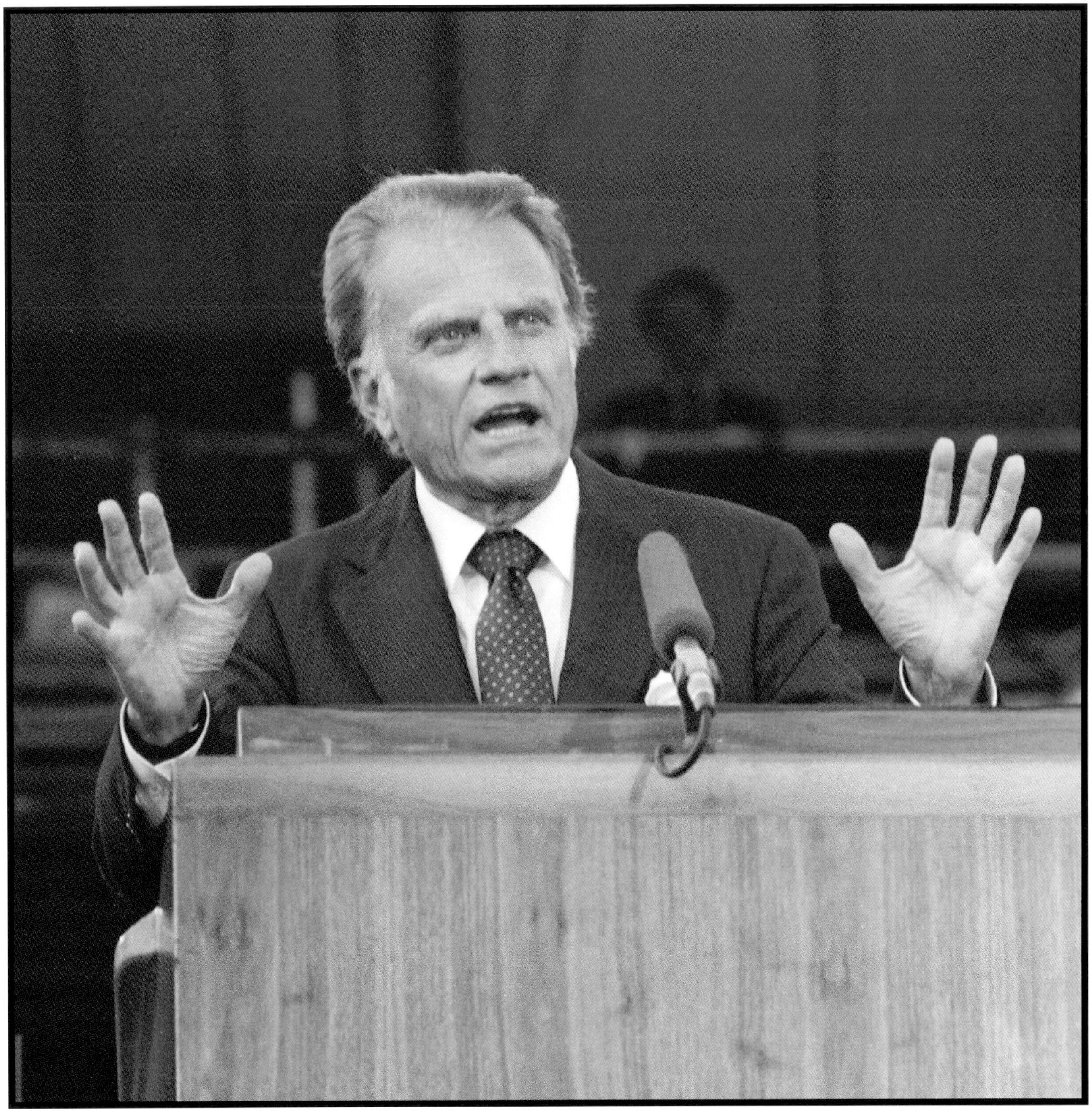

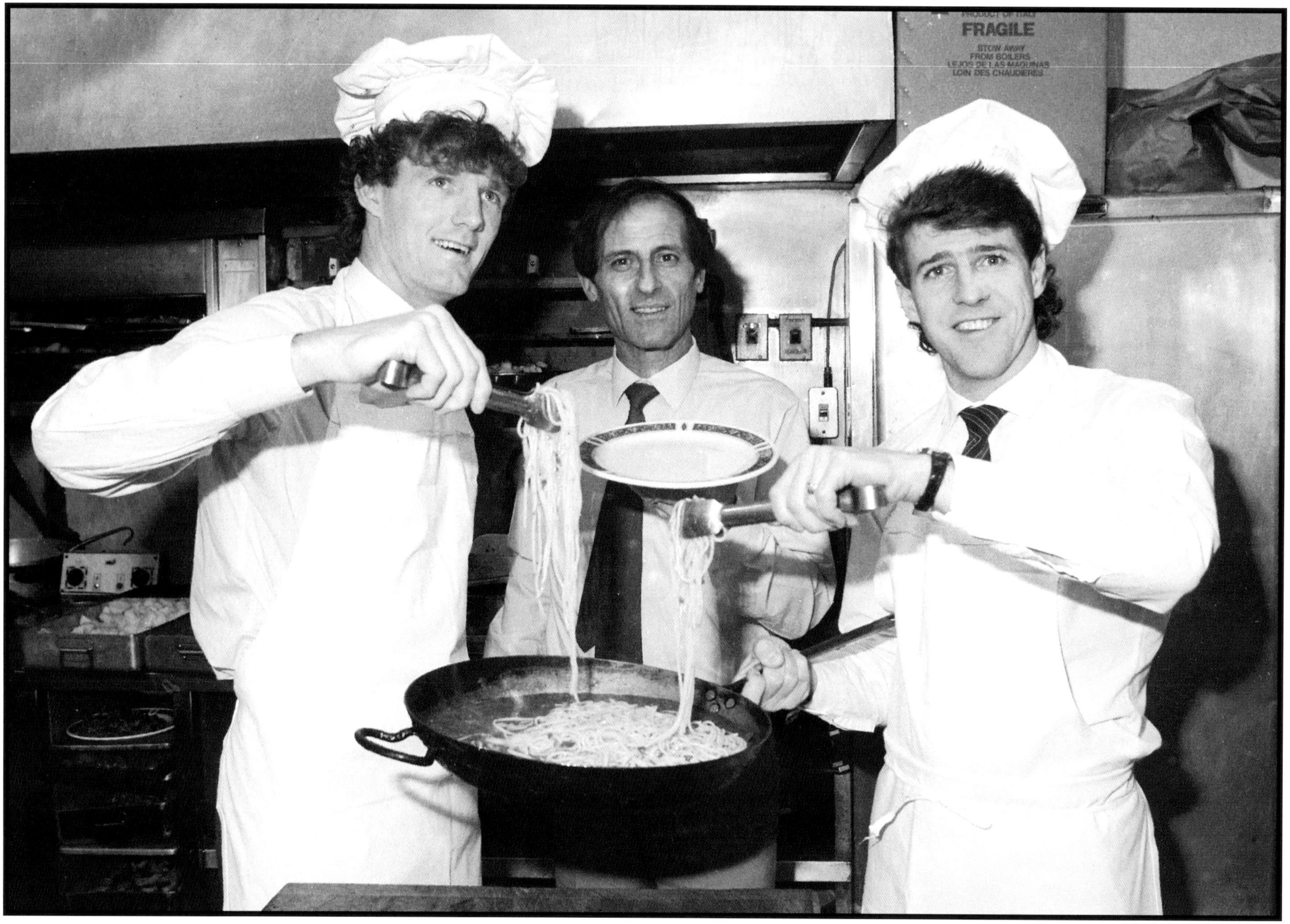
FRAGILE
STOW AWAY
FROM BOILERS
LEJOS DE LAS MAQUINAS
LOIN DES CHAUDIERES

little italy

La Galleria in Birmingham has always been a popular restaurant with Villa folk, but Allan Evans and Colin Gibson had to earn their supper. They are pictured preparing a spaghetti dish, under the watchful eye of proprietor Marcello Manca.

Marcello is a keen Villa supporter, and I enjoyed his company when we travelled to the 1996 League Cup Final together. He even provided a breakfast at his restaurant before the coach set off for Wembley.

little wonder

Quite apart from being one of the finest players in Villa's history, Brian Little also served the club in various other capacities.

He was youth team coach for a spell and also worked in the club shop, returning in 1994 to succeed Ron Atkinson as manager. Brian is seen here enjoying a cuppa at Bodymoor Heath during his time as youth coach. He also sold second half cars at one stage, and I bought a vehicle from him.

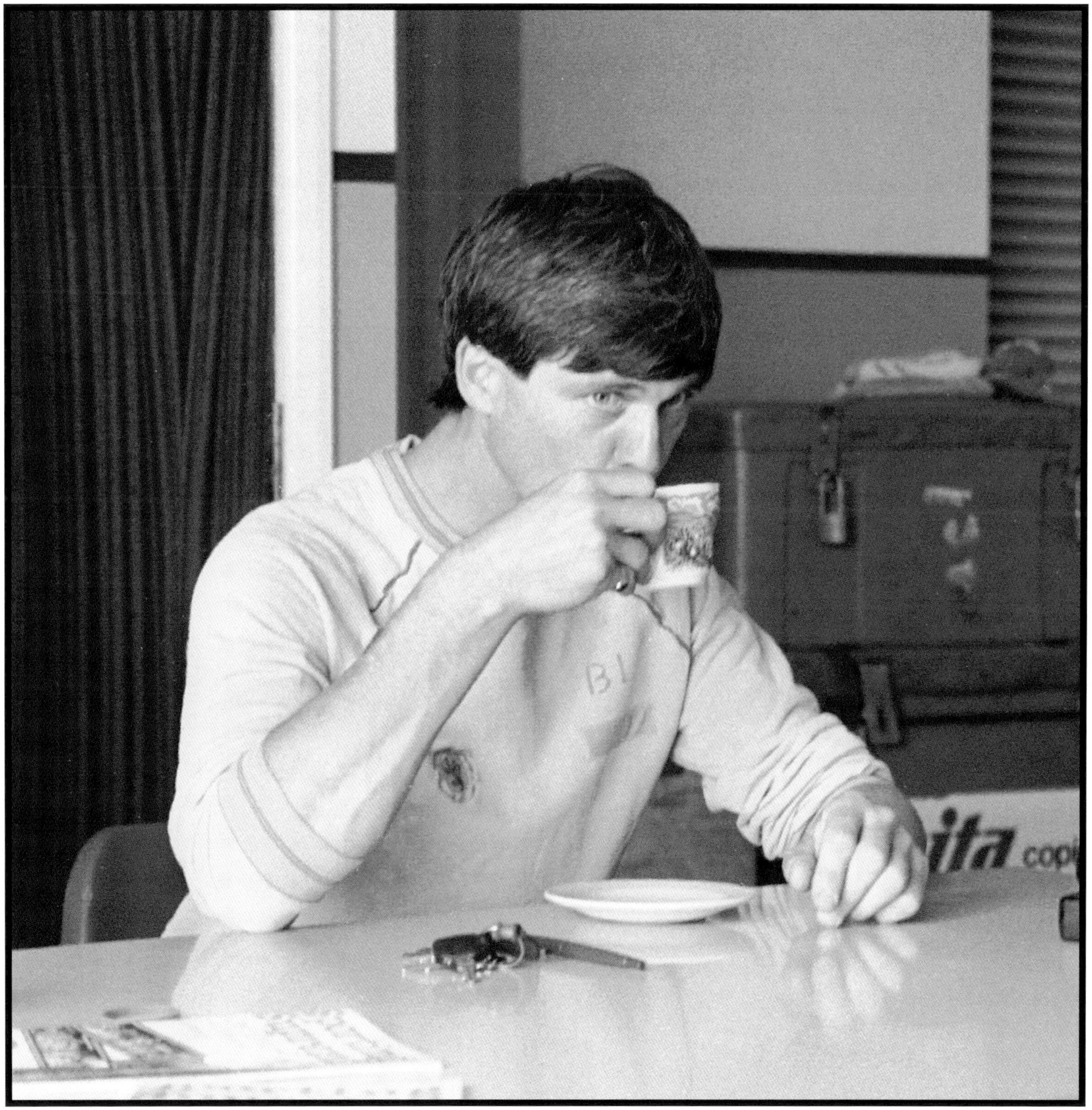

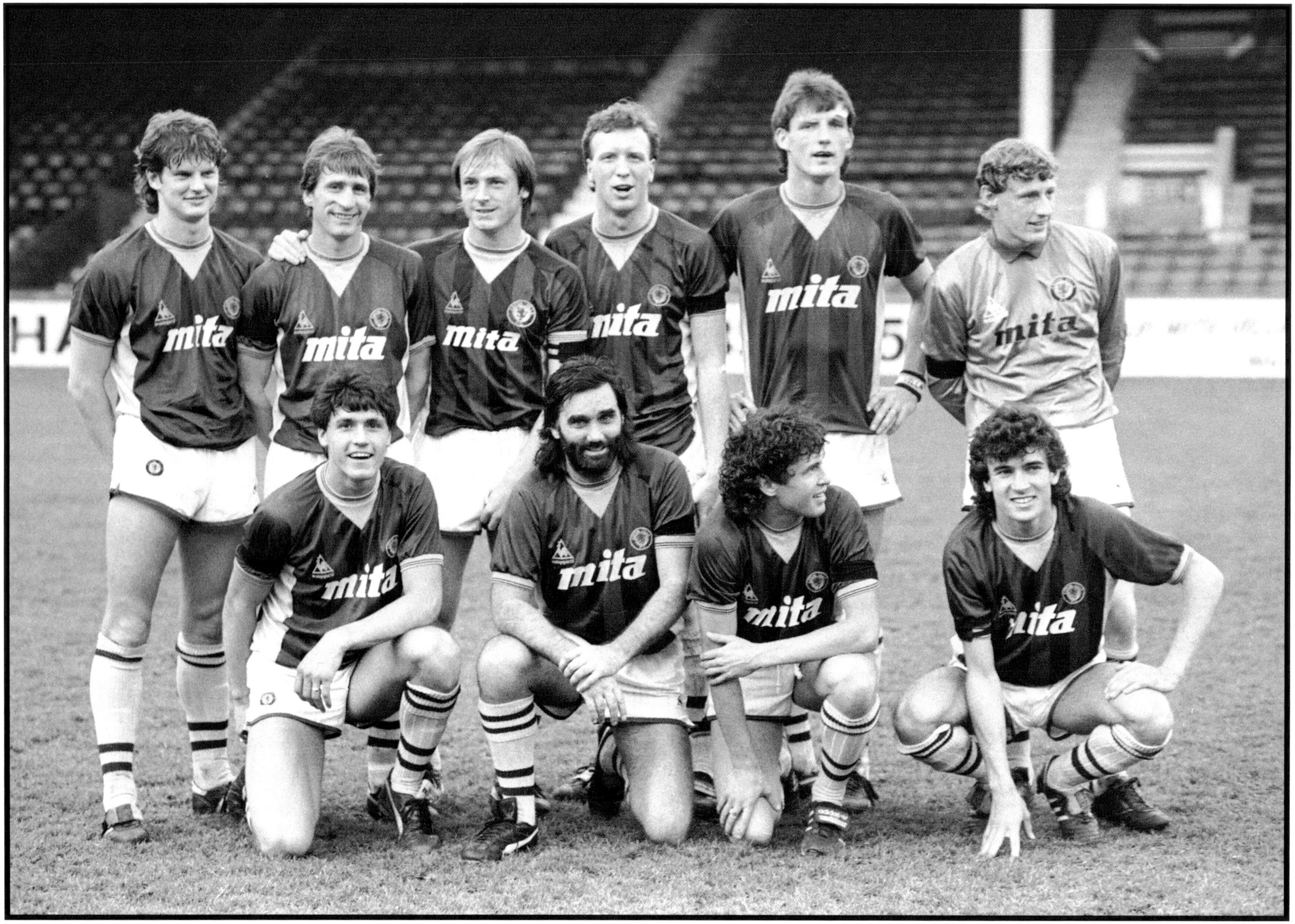
mita
mita
mita
mita
mita
mita
mita
mita
mita
mita

villa's best

In the wake of the horrific Bradford City fire in 1985, Villa hosted a charity match against the Midland All-Stars to raise funds for victims of the Valley Parade tragedy – with a very special guest.

George Best, one of the greatest players to ever grace a football pitch, donned a claret and blue shirt for the occasion. Joining George in this line-up are: Ray Walker, Gordon Cowans, Steve McMahon, Brendan Ormsby, Allan Evans, Kevin Poole, Paul Rideout, Best, Gary Williams, Tony Dorigo.

collectors corner

Just imagine the conversation:
'We collect stickers and put them in an album, granddad.' 'Yes, lad, in my day we used to call them cigarette cards!'

Football memorabilia has remained popular down the years, and the Panini stickers of the late 80s and early 90s were a huge success with young supporters.

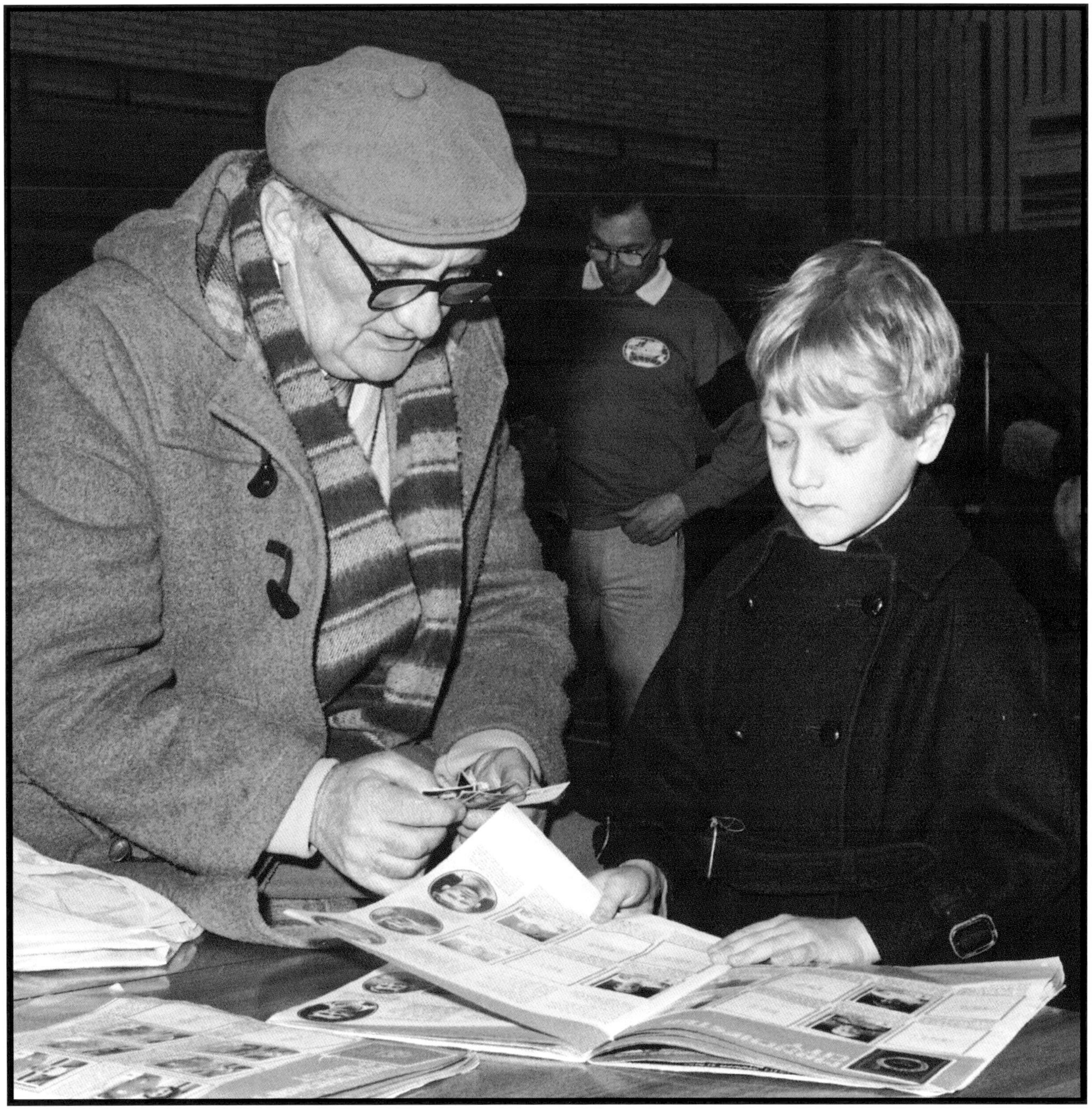

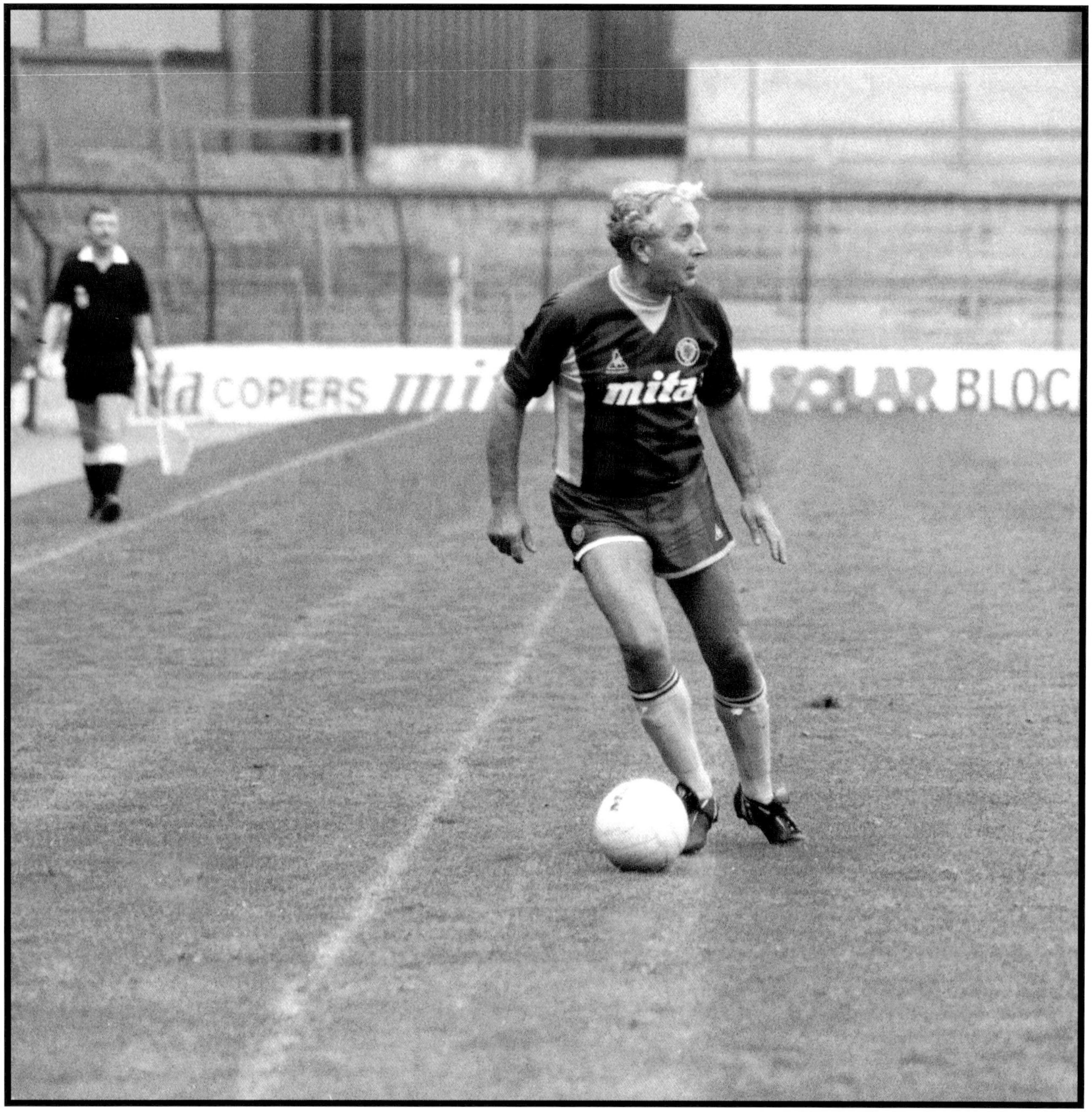

wing wizardry

He may be the club chairman, but Doug Ellis is essentially a frustrated footballer. He certainly looked the part when he played in a charity match at Villa Park, displaying good close control as he ventured down the right wing while eyeing up where to deliver his pass. He once joined in a penalty competition which was taking part at Villa Park, and despite wearing a suit and overcoat, he planted his kick right in the corner of the net.

airtime

The sight of former players in the press box, as radio commentators or summarisers, is fairly common these days. But Brendan Ormsby did it years ago – while he was still a Villa player. George Gavin acted as a touchline reporter for BRMB at one match, and Brendan – who was presumably injured at the time – decided to try his hand at radio commentar. I've no idea how good he was, but it made a nice picture.

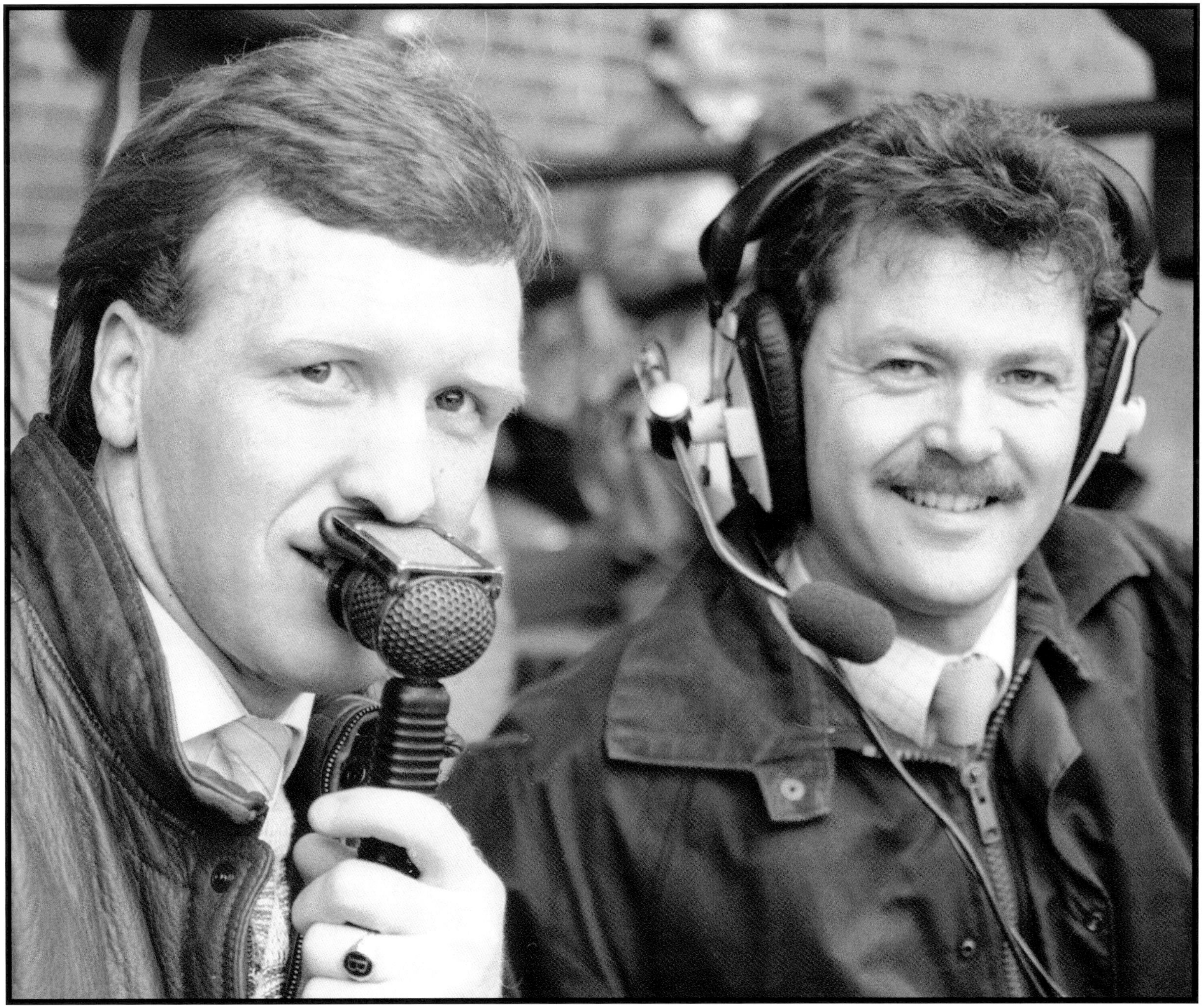

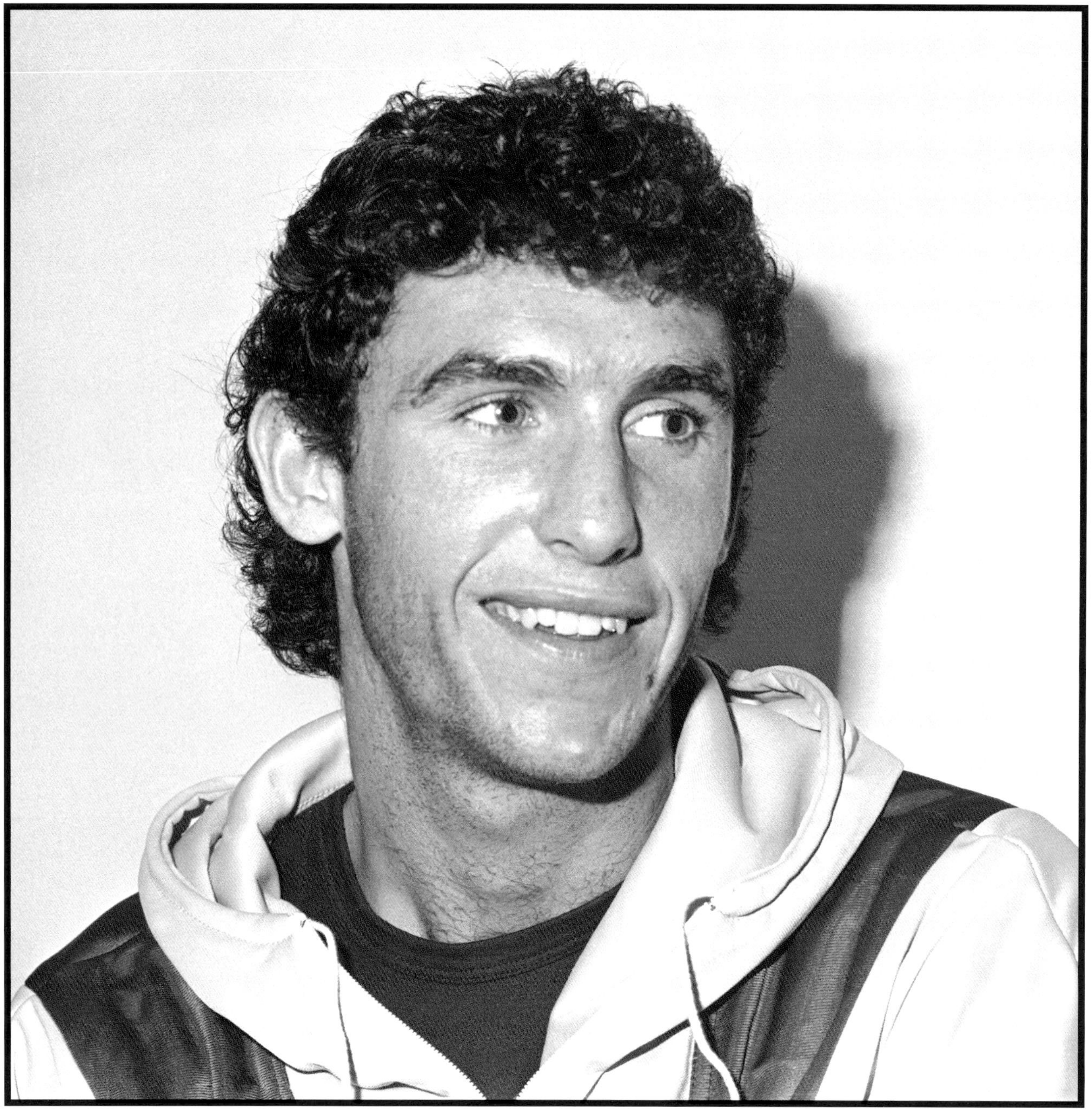

classy keown

Martin Keown was a hell of a player. Most Villa folk didn't know much about the young defender when Graham Turner signed him from Arsenal in the summer of 1986, and his signing coincided with relegation the following season. But he helped Villa back to the top flight at the first attempt and subsequently developed into one of the classiest defenders in the country. It was a pity when he left to join Everton in 1989.

playing for villa

Every big club have a celebrity supporter, and Villa are no different. Nigel Kennedy's devotion to the club came to light when he was emerging as a virtuoso violinist, and he never failed to mention the fact whenever he appeared on television.That prompted the club registrar, Bert Sisk, to suggest that he be invited along to the ground – and he was delighted to say he had played at Villa Park! At one stage, Kennedy used to turn up to games in a Jaguar which was sprayed in claret and blue graffiti.

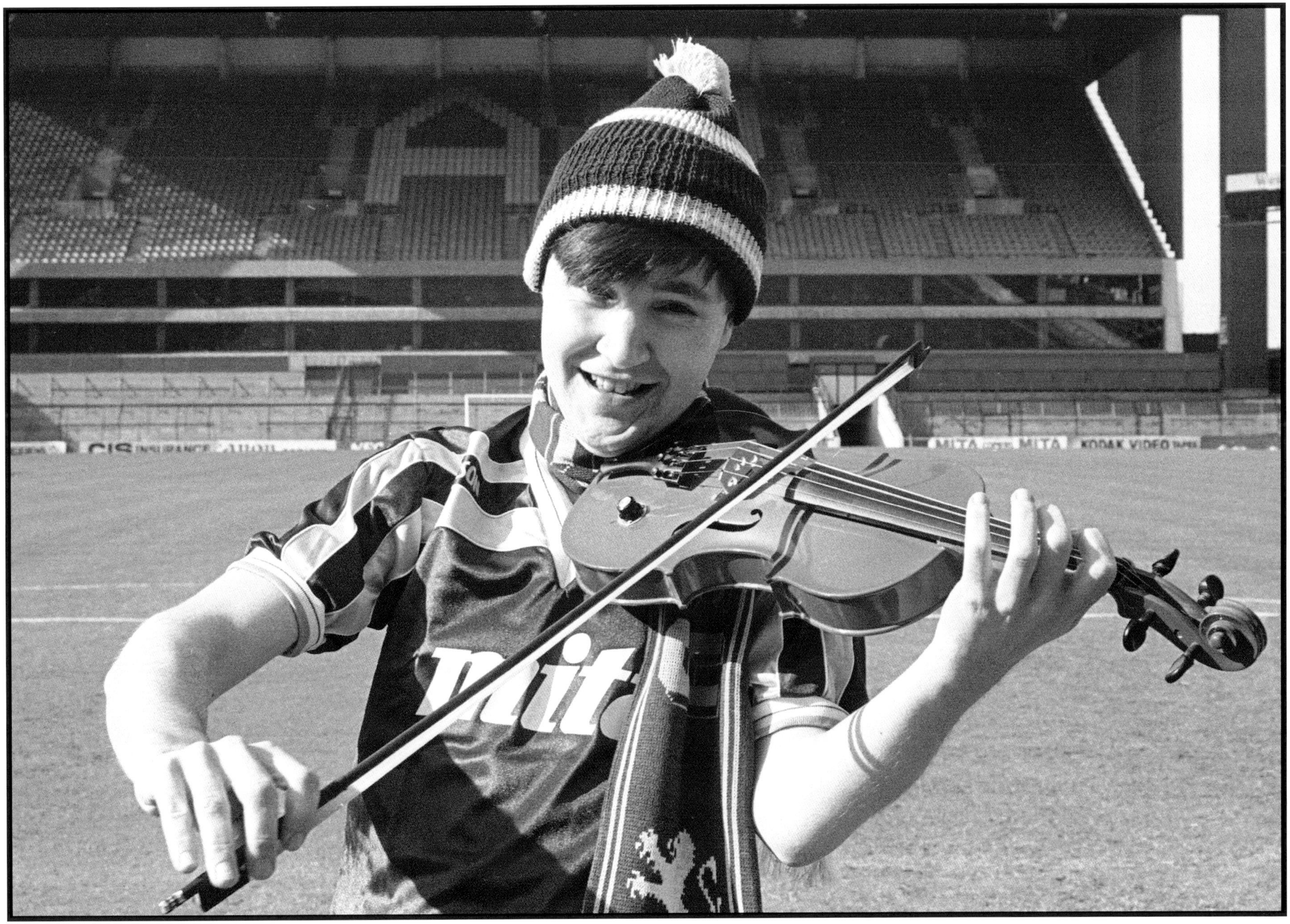
MITA
MITA
KODAK VIDEO
mit

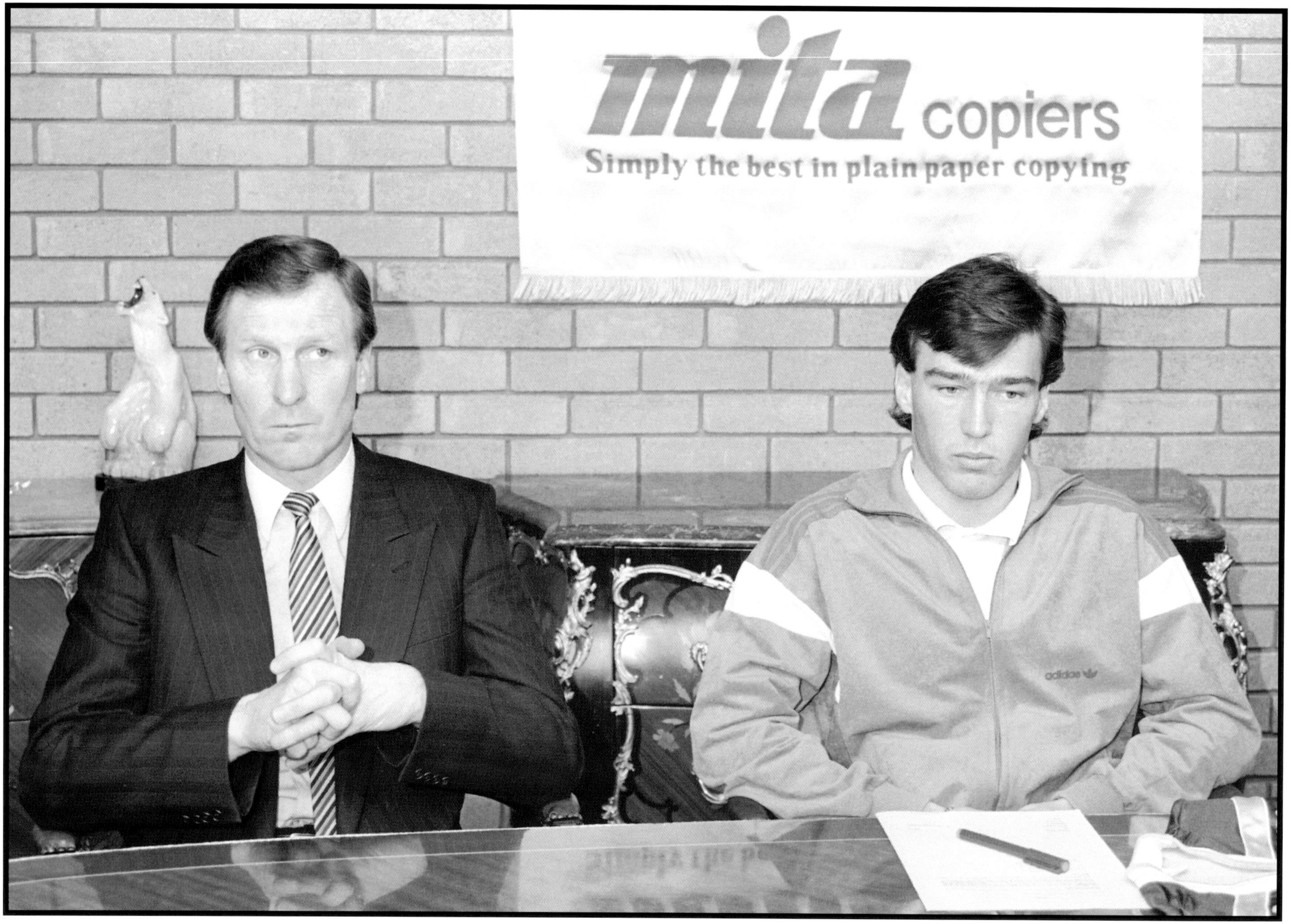
mita copiers
Simply the best in plain paper copying

down, down

Billy McNeill made his only Villa signing when he bought striker Warren Aspinall from Everton in February, 1987, but neither man looks convinced about the wisdom of the deal. Their apprehension was justified, too. Aspinall scored only three goals before the end of the season, and that wasn't nearly enough to stave off relegation.

brian tiler

A lot of former players regard Villa Park as their spiritual home, even after they have moved to new pastures. Brian Tiler, who was Tommy Docherty's first signing, made 127 appearances for the club between 1968 and 1973, and couldn't resist the temptation of having a peek inside the dressing room when he returned a few years later. Sadly, Brian was killed in a car accident in which Harry Redknapp was also involved, during Italia '90. He was already planning his trip to the 1994 USA World Cup Finals at the time of his death.

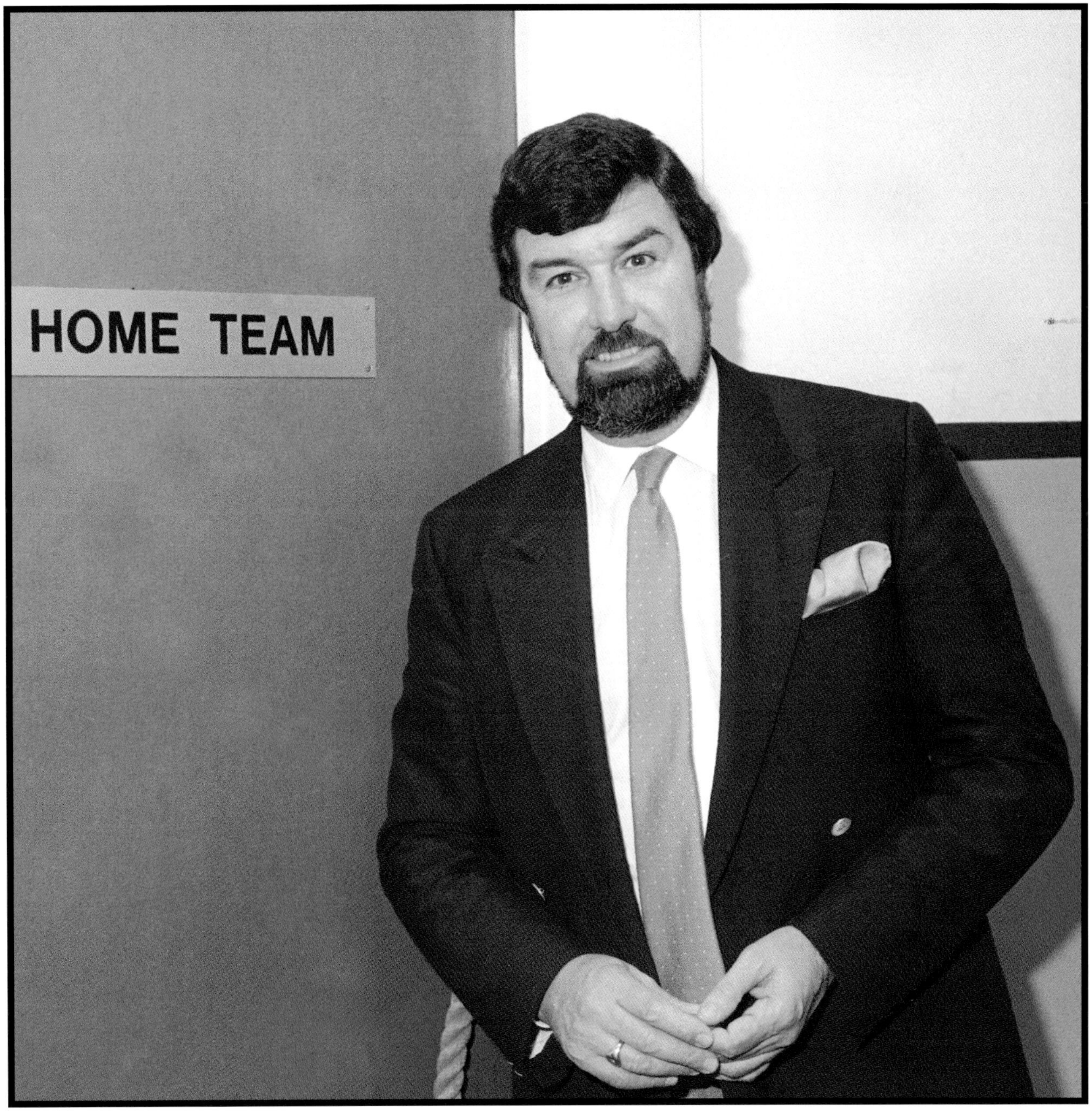

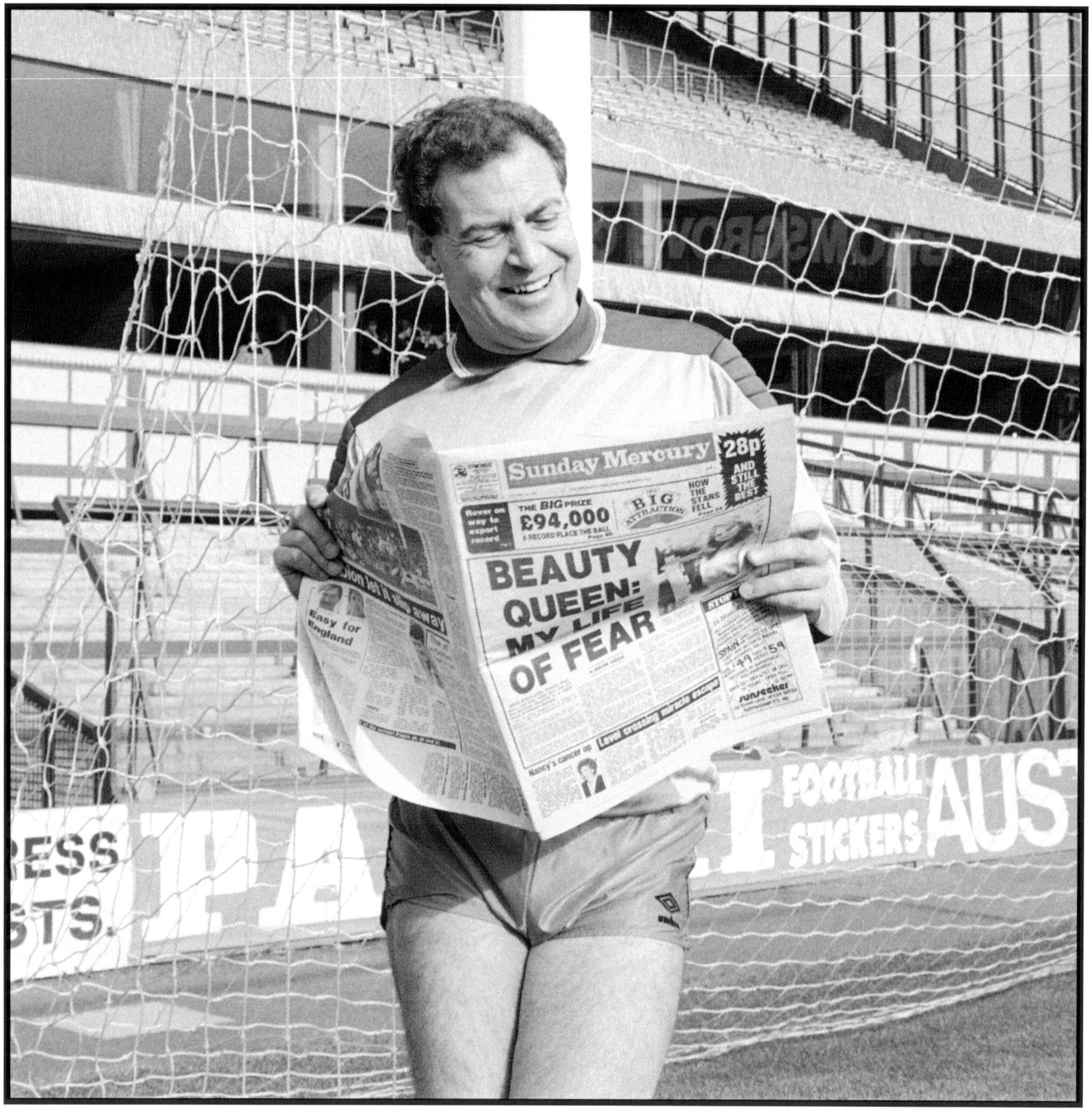

keep me posted

'The goalkeeper didn't have a shot to save...' No doubt you've read that phrase in match reports, and it was very much the case when Villa's Community Services manager Dave Ismay took part in a Sunday morning match at Villa Park.

Dave played in goal, but had so little to do that he took time out to read the Sunday Mercury.

If I remember correctly, it was an East Enders match.

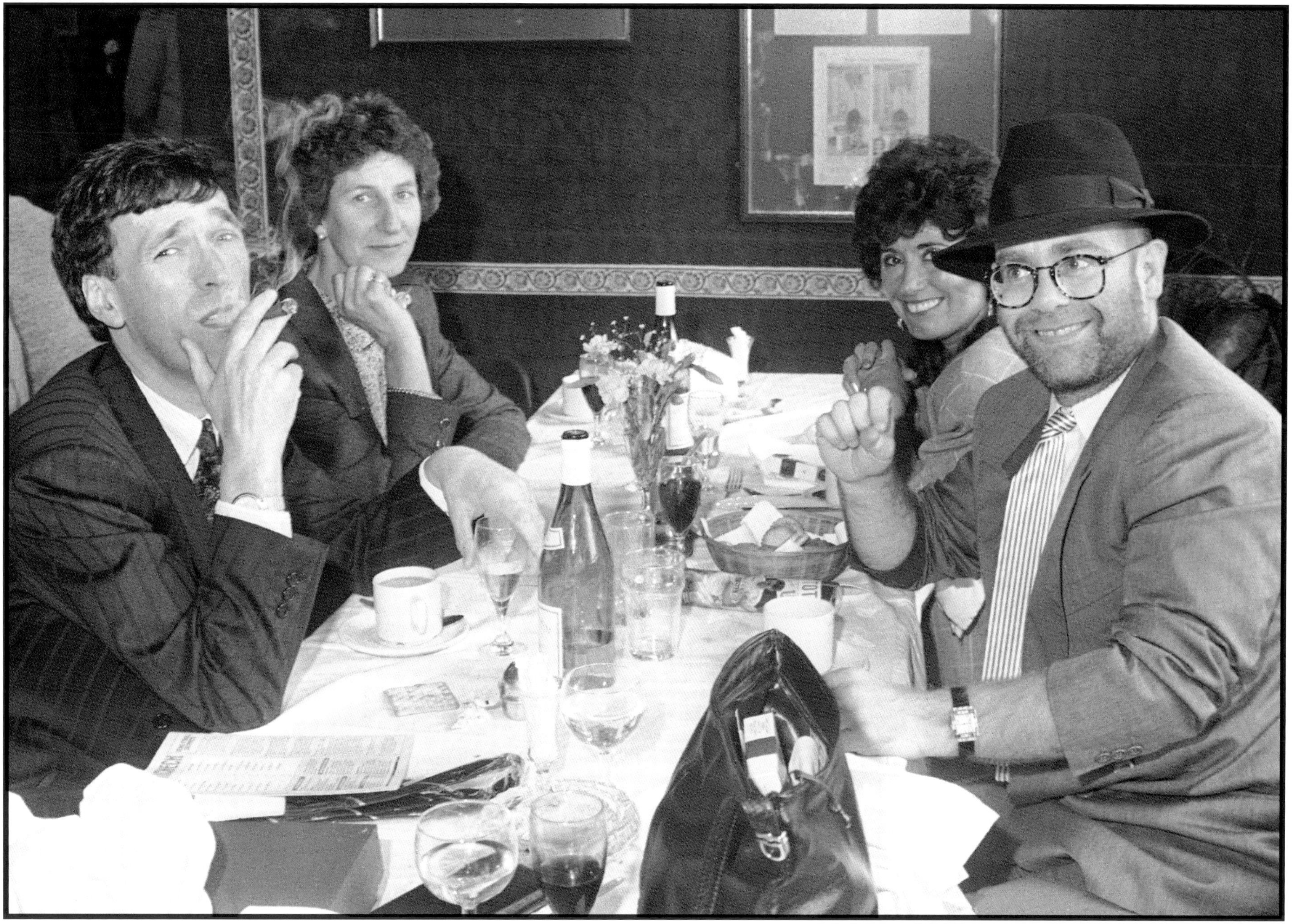

elton's sad song

Not long before Graham Taylor became Villa manager for the first time, he was at Villa Park with Watford for the 1987 FA Cup semi-final against Spurs. On the day, though, there was far more media focus on Watford's rock star chairman Elton John.

Press photographers had to settle for a long-range picture taken from the touchline, but I was able to catch up with Elton while he was enjoying his lunch with Mervyn Winwood, who had just become a director of the Vicarage Road club. Rock fans may remember 'Muff' Winwood better as the bass player in 60s band, The Spencer Davis Group.

Watford were hoping their cup success would Keep On Running, but they ended up only with Sad Songs. Spurs won 4-1.

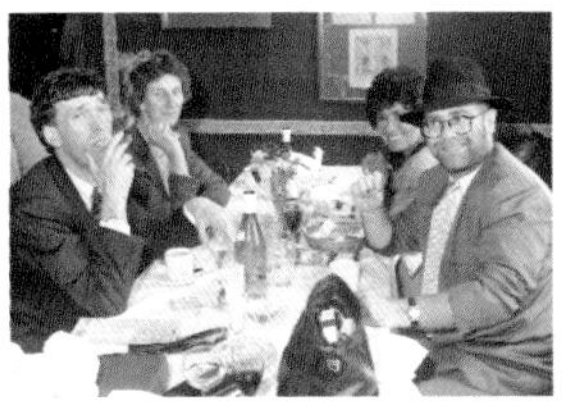

up where we belong

Striker Garry Thompson is hoisted on to the shoulders of jubilant supporters, who had just learned that Villa had won promotion to the First Division after just one season in the lower grade.

The odds were stacked heavily against Graham Taylor's side when they travelled to Swindon on the final day of the 1987-88 campaign, particularly as they only drew 0-0.

But defeats for their rivals Middlesbrough and Bradford City on the same afternoon meant Villa were promoted automatically, pipping Boro to second place by virtue of having scored more goals. It was 10 minutes or more before the Boro and Bradford results filtered through, and it seemed like an eternity – but it was worth the wait.

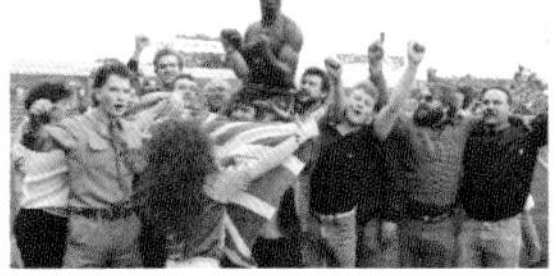

the long and short

Pictures of players on the day they sign for a new club are ten a penny, but this shot tells the other side of the story.

Towering striker Ian Ormondroyd and winger Nigel Callaghan are posing patiently after signing from Bradford City and Derby County respectively, while press photographers jockey for position in a bid to get the best picture for their various publications.

This duo were the most expensive players in Villa's history when they arrived in January, 1989, Ormondroyd costing a club record £650,000. How things have changed!

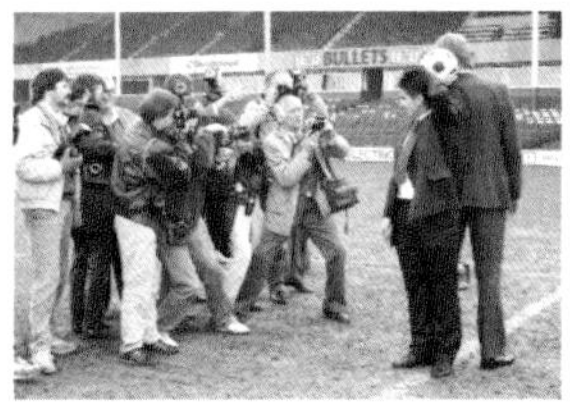

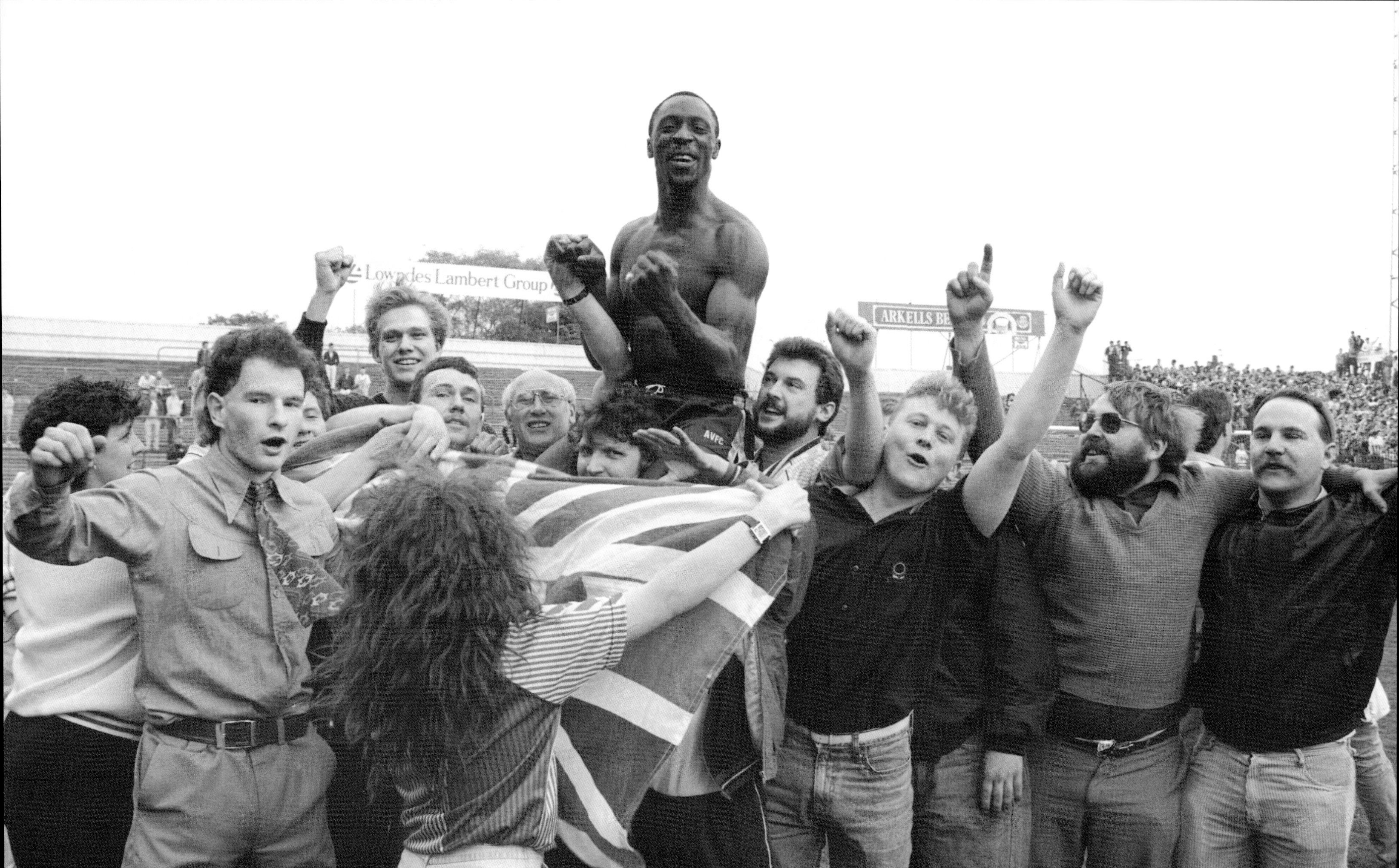
Lowndes Lambert Group
ARKELLS BE
AVFC

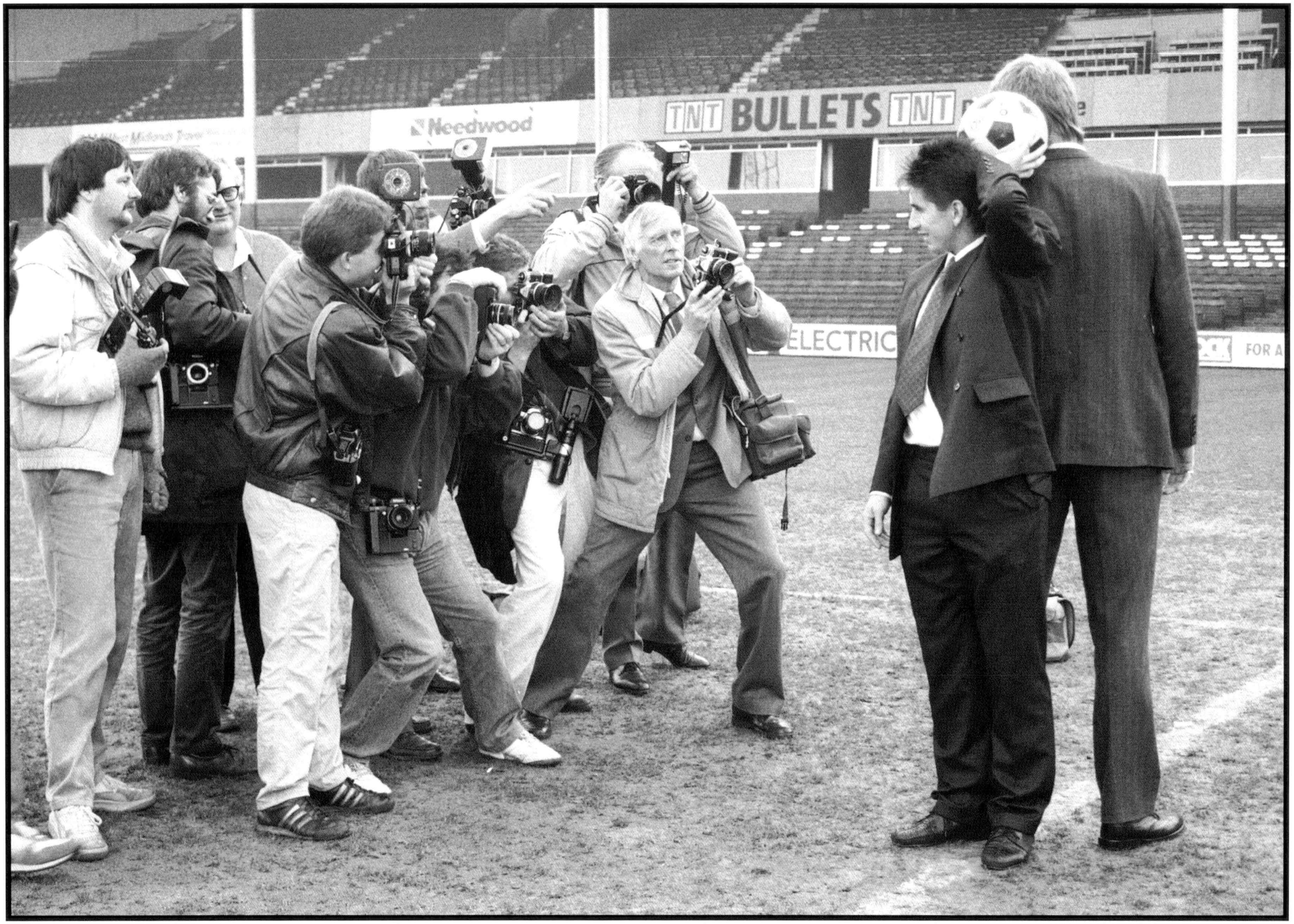
Needwood
TNT BULLETS TNT
ELECTRIC

macca magic

Alan McInally was a Villa player for only a couple of seasons, but he undoubtedly made his mark before heading off to join German giants Bayern Munich in 1989.

His £1.1million move was the result of a prolific campaign in which his 14 goals helped Villa to stay in the top flight.

Two of those goals came in an early season 2-2 draw against West Ham at Upton Park, and the popular Scot's delight is clearly evident as he celebrates one of them with Andy Gray.

McInally, of course, has since carved out a career for himself in TV, where his personality shines through just as it did on the pitch.

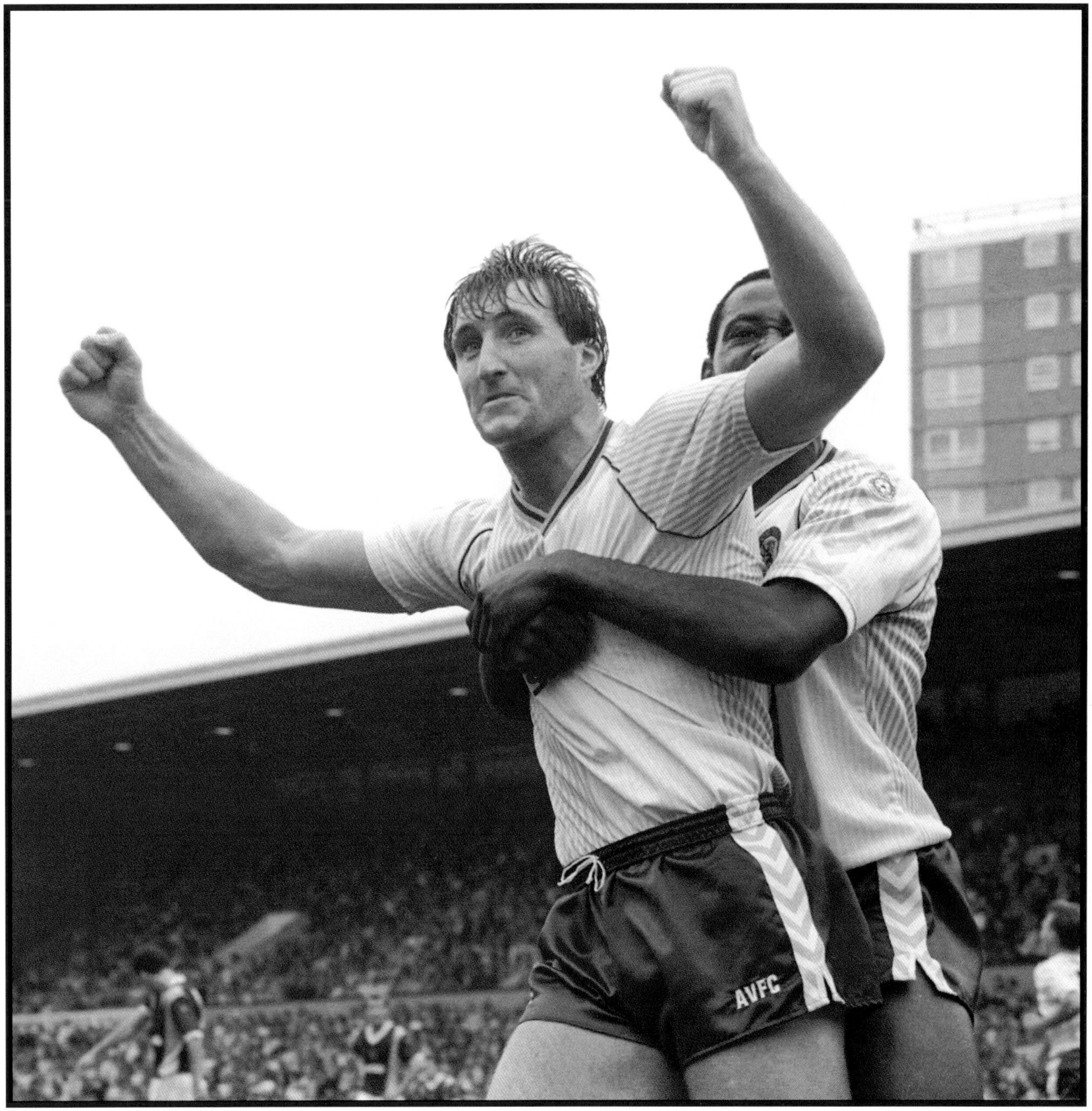

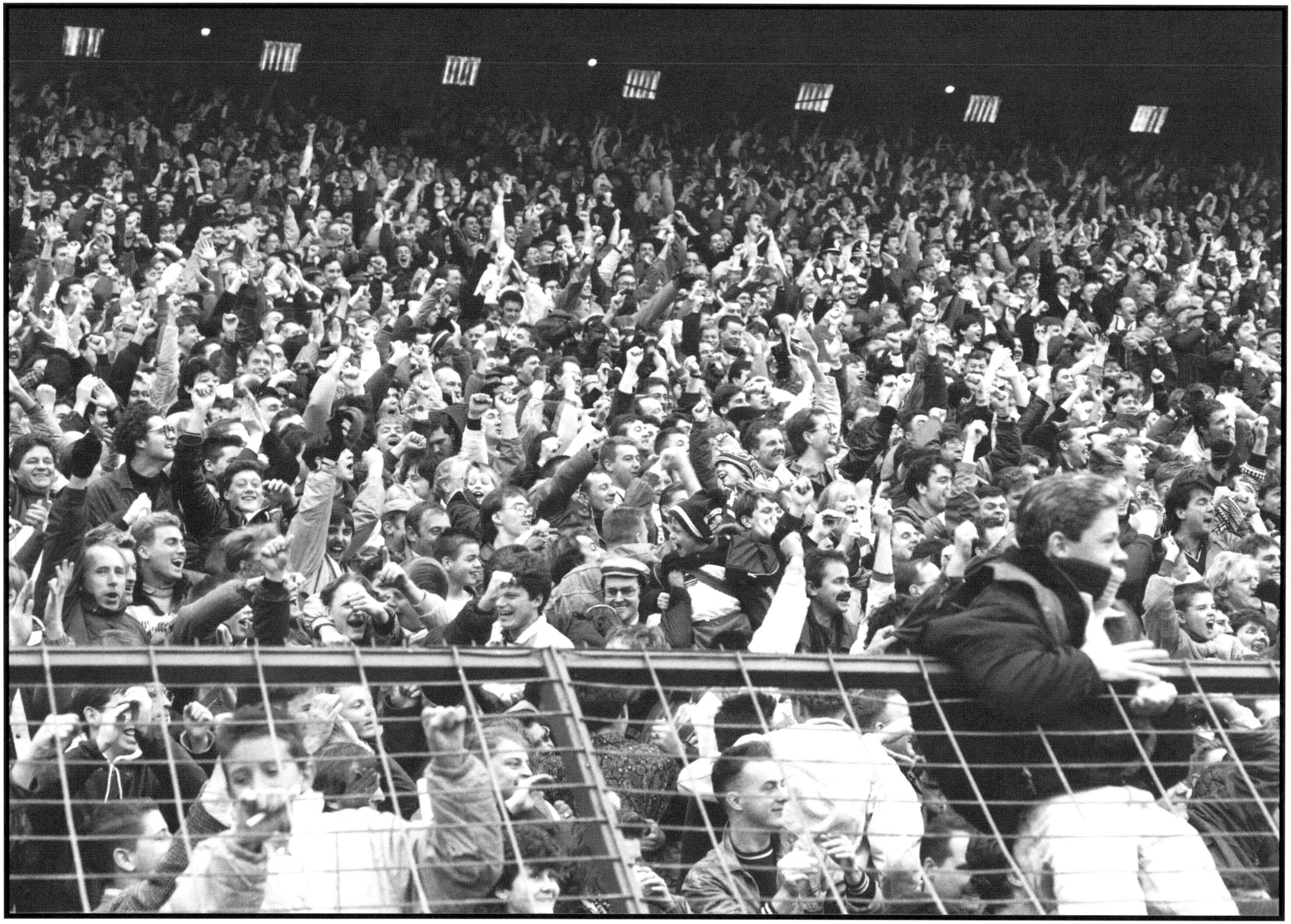

terrace fervour

The 1989-90 season was hugely successful for Villa, Graham Taylor's men finishing runners up to Liverpool in the old First Division and reaching the quarter-finals of the FA Cup. The success on the pitch was mirrored by fervour on the terraces, which is illustrated in this crowd shot at the Holte End.

czech mates

Which player signed for Villa and scored for Villa – but never actually played for the club? The answer is Ivo Stas, who signed from Banik Ostrava in 1990, shortly after scoring an own goal against Villa when the clubs met in the UEFA Cup. Ivo was plagued by injury almost from the moment he arrived and although he played a couple of pre-season friendlies, he never pulled on a Villa shirt for a competitive match. This was the day he signed, facing the press at Bodymoor Heath along with his fellow countryman Jo Venglos, Villa's manager at the time, and assistant manager John Ward.

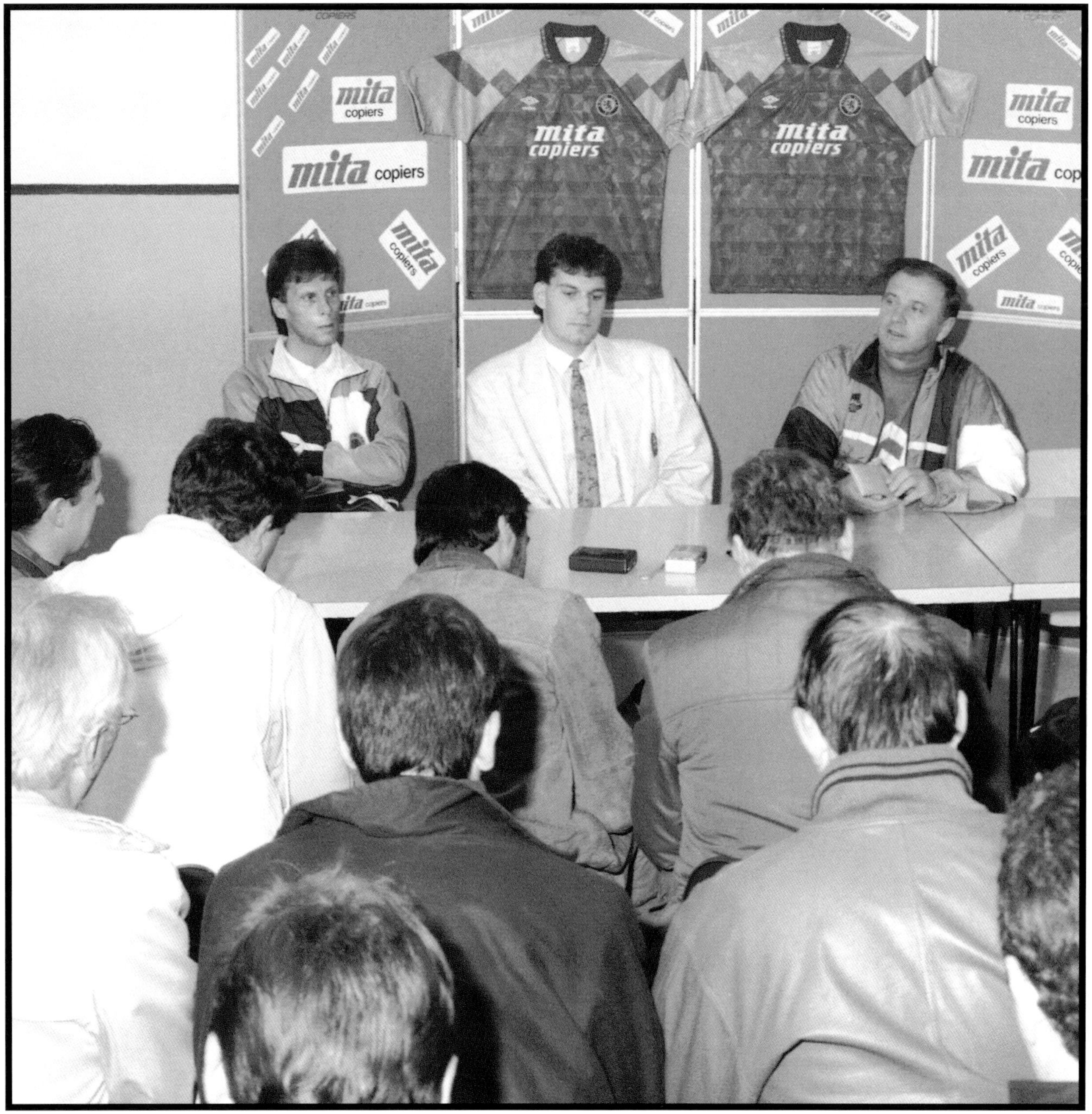

uncle eric

His name was Eric Houghton, but for countless people he was Mr Aston Villa.

Eric served the club as a player for many years, and was manager when they last won the FA Cup in 1957. And even when his days in an active role were over, he was a superb ambassador for the club, right up to his death in 1996, just short of his 86th birthday.

He always had a tale to tell about Villa, and I learned a lot about the club through talking to him. I'm also privileged to have been present when Eric played his last match for Villa, a reserve game against Huddersfield Town in 1946.

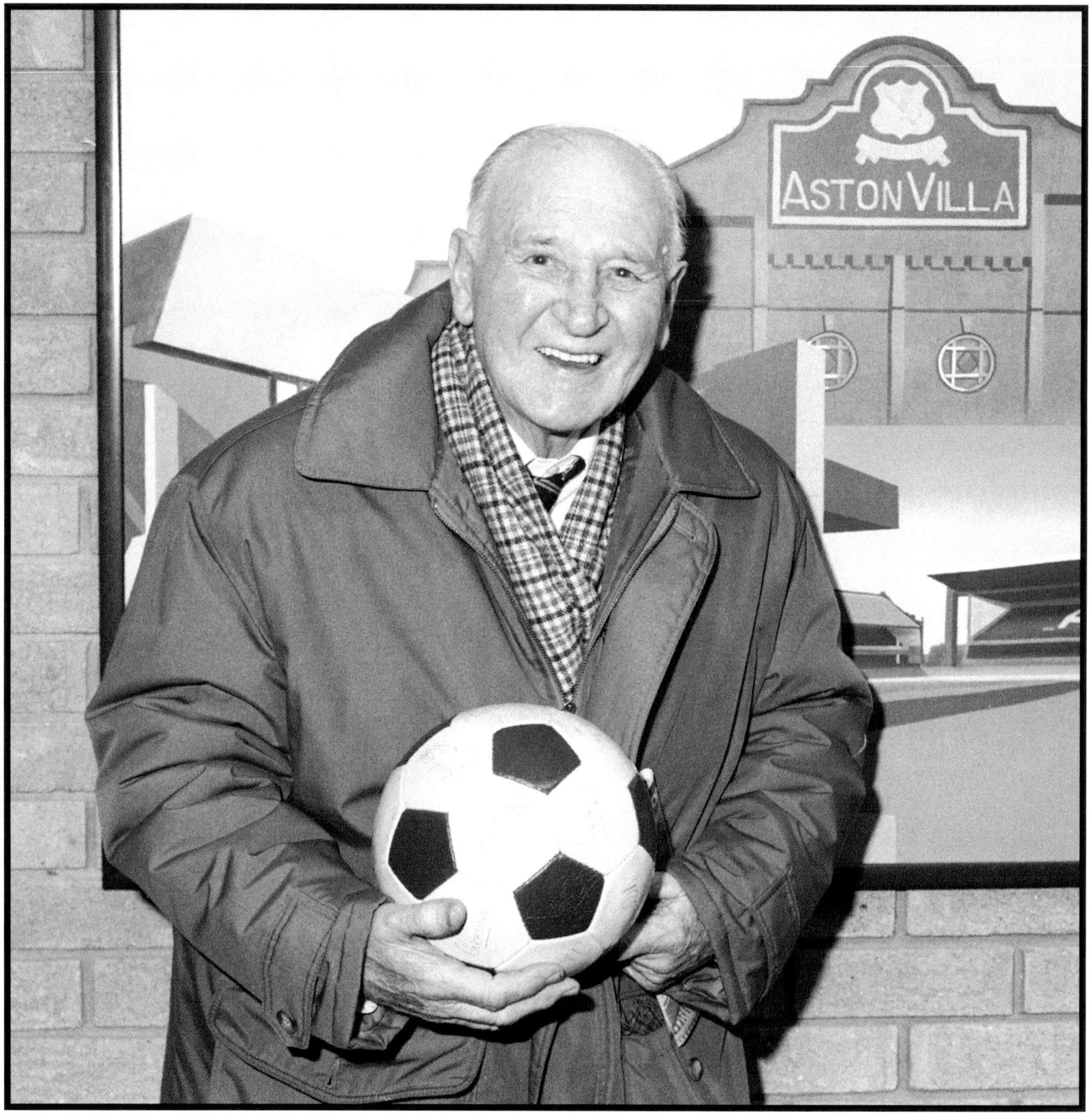

take that!

Chatting away to someone I hadn't previously met before a home match one week, I enquired: 'First time at Villa Park, young man?'

'No,' he replied. 'I was here when they played Port Vale.'
'Oh, yes, fourth round of the FA Cup. We won 5-0.'
'No,' he corrected, 'Actually, it was 6-0.'

Robbie Williams may be a mega name in the pop world, but he also takes his football very seriously. I didn't realise who he was at the time, but Steve Stride introduced us properly before having this picture taken with Robbie and Mark Owen, his partner from Take That!

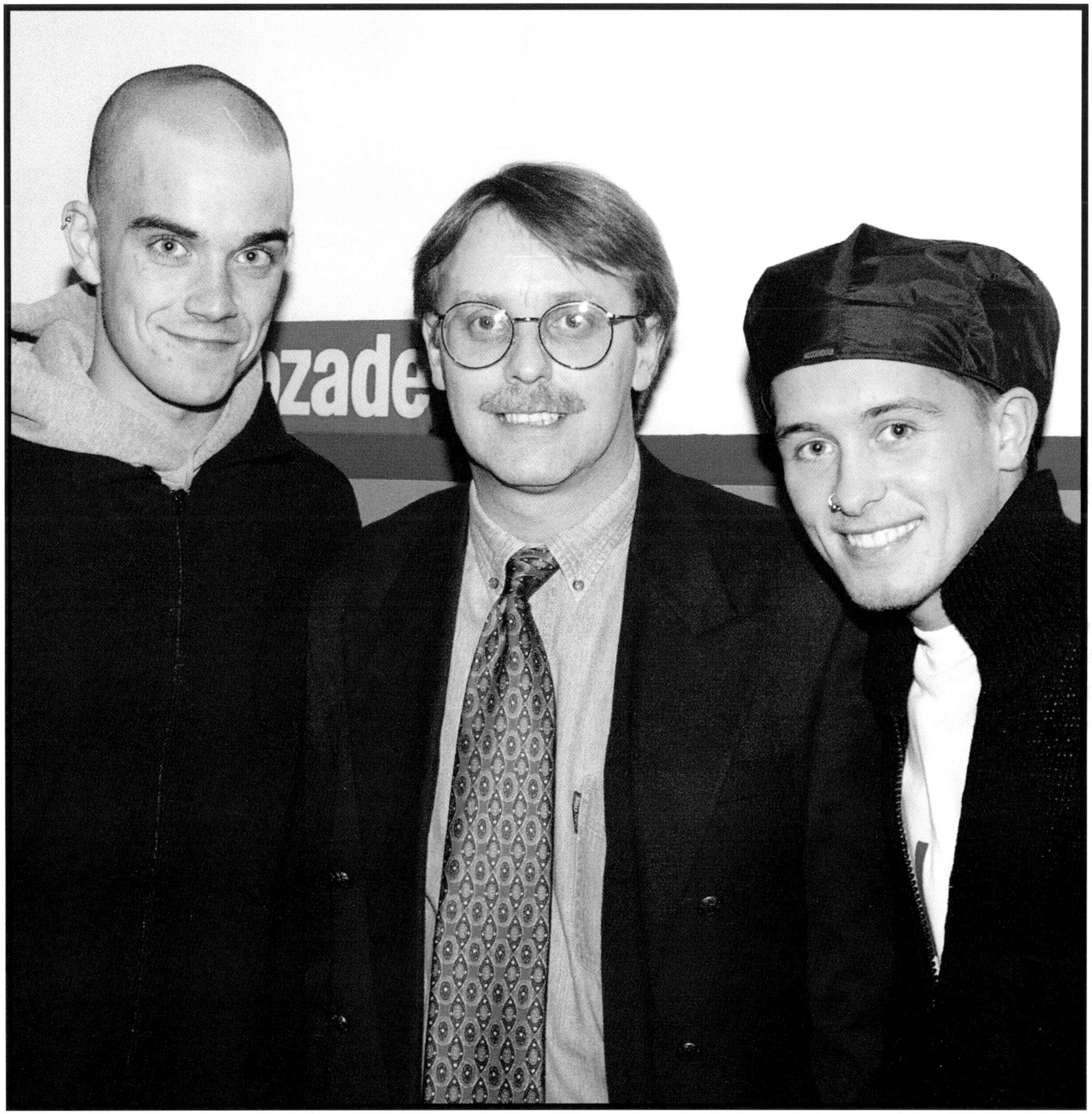

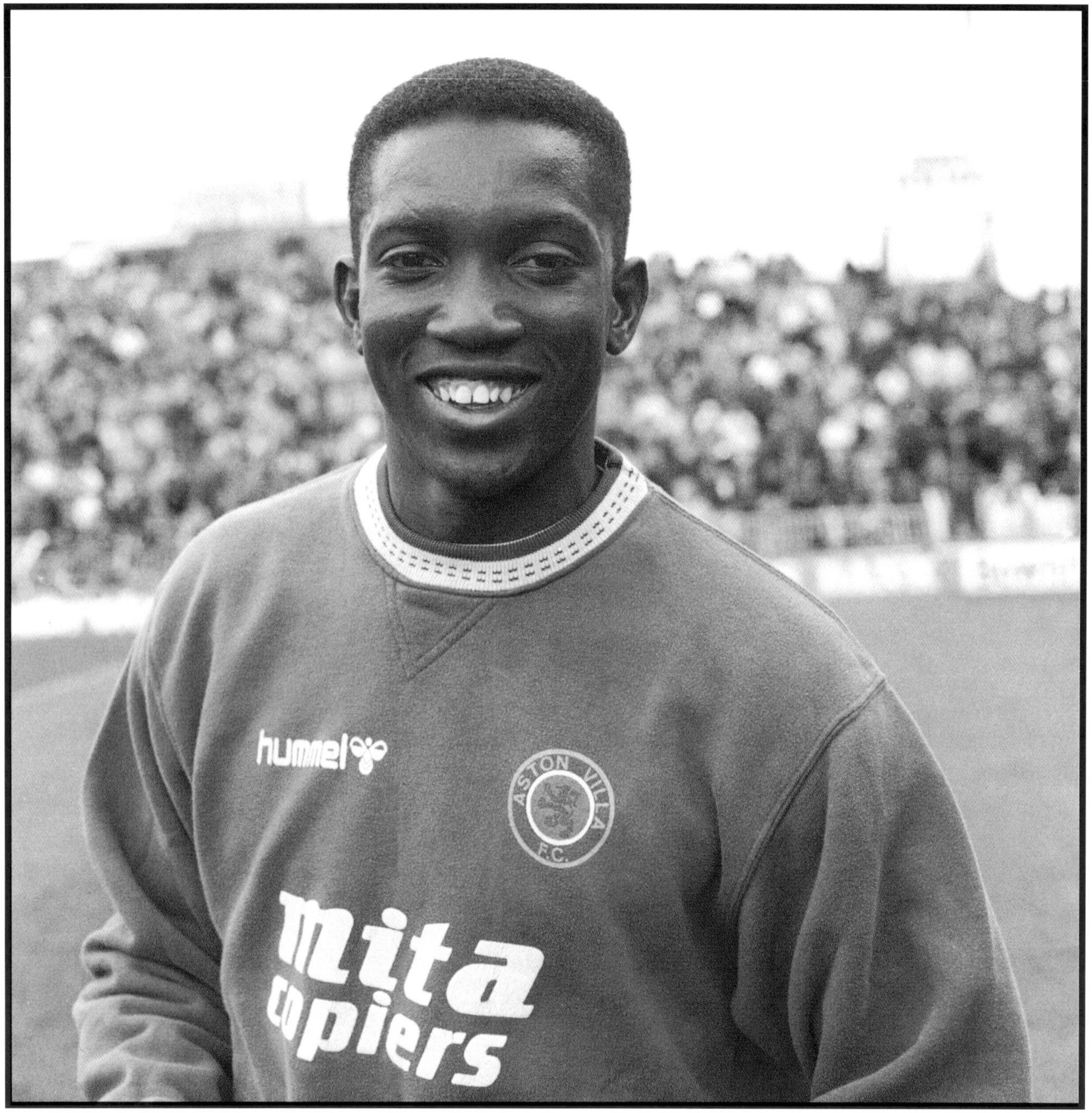

calypso kid

This unmistakable grin lit up Villa Park for the best part of nine years before Dwight Yorke's transfer to Manchester United netted the club a record incoming fee of £12million in 1998.

The Calypso Kid was a wonderful player, oozing Caribbean flamboyance as well as a deadly eye for goal, although Holte Enders hadn't seen him in action when this picture was taken.

There's a small piece of history here – it was at Selhurst Park on 24th March, 1989, the day Dwight made his first team debut as a substitute in a 1-0 defeat by Crystal Palace.

Dwight had a sweet tooth, and was forever dipping his hand into my coat pocket to see if I had any wine gums. It was a big blow when he left, but you could understand why – he won the treble with United the following season.

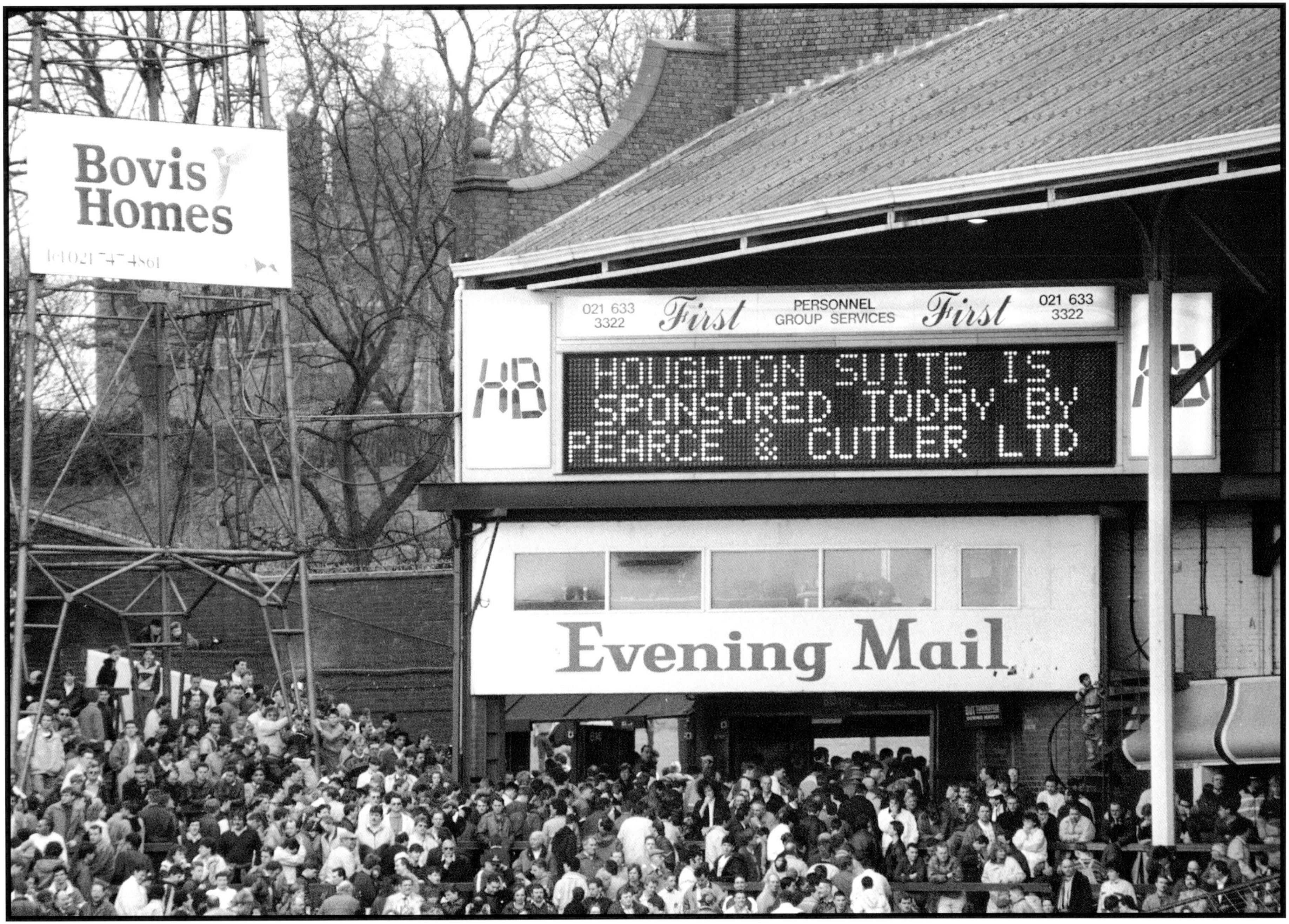
Bovis Homes
021 633 3322
First
PERSONNEL GROUP SERVICES
First
021 633 3322
HB
HOUGHTON SUITE IS
SPONSORED TODAY BY
PEARCE & CUTLER LTD
Evening Mail

names in lights

Companies involved in matchday sponsorship were featured on Villa's electronic scoreboard – and I had to take a picture of every one, so that the sponsors concerned could be sent a souvenir of the occasion.

The big problem was that you never knew if there were going to be three names on the board, or 23, so I bought a second-hand camera solely for the purpose, knowing there was always a full roll of film available.

To ensure that none of the sponsors were overlooked, a message used to flash up after the last one, saying: 'That's all, Terry.'

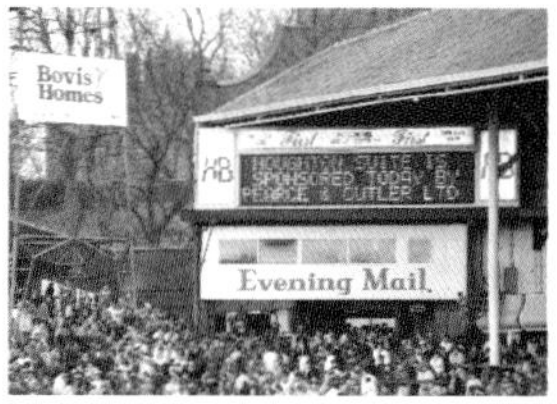

sign here...

Irishman Paul McGrath and Dane Kent Nielsen, two of the best defenders to pull on Villa shirts, signed their contracts on the same day in the summer of 1989, having arrived from Manchester United and Brondby respectively.

The pens they used were subsequently offered an prizes in a competition run by the Birmingham Evening Mail.

Macca was, in my view, the best defender Villa have ever had, and few players, before or since, have possessed his incredible sense of anticipation. Kent was also pretty special and I was delighted when he went on to win a European Championship medal with Denmark in 1992.

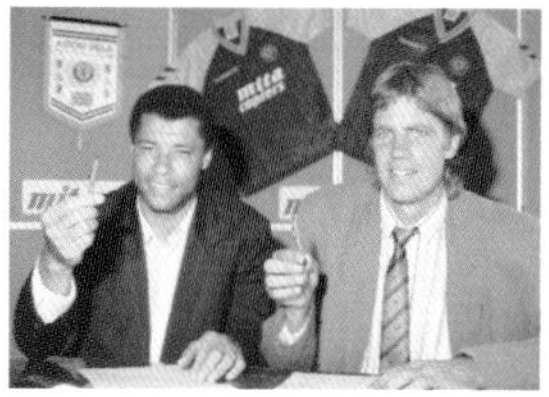

sky's the limit

The advent of Sky TV brought a whole new meaning to live coverage of football, with each match becoming a show in its own right.

It also resulted in the return to Villa Park of former Holte End favourite Andy Gray, who was beginning to forge a new career in the broadcasting world.

Andy was surprised to see me when I opened the door to the TV studio situated between the North Stand and the Trinity Road stand, but still managed a smile for the camera. Elton Welsby, unfortunately, was rather less impressed at being interrupted....

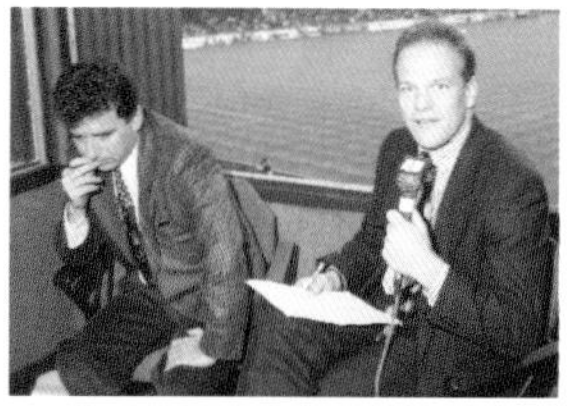

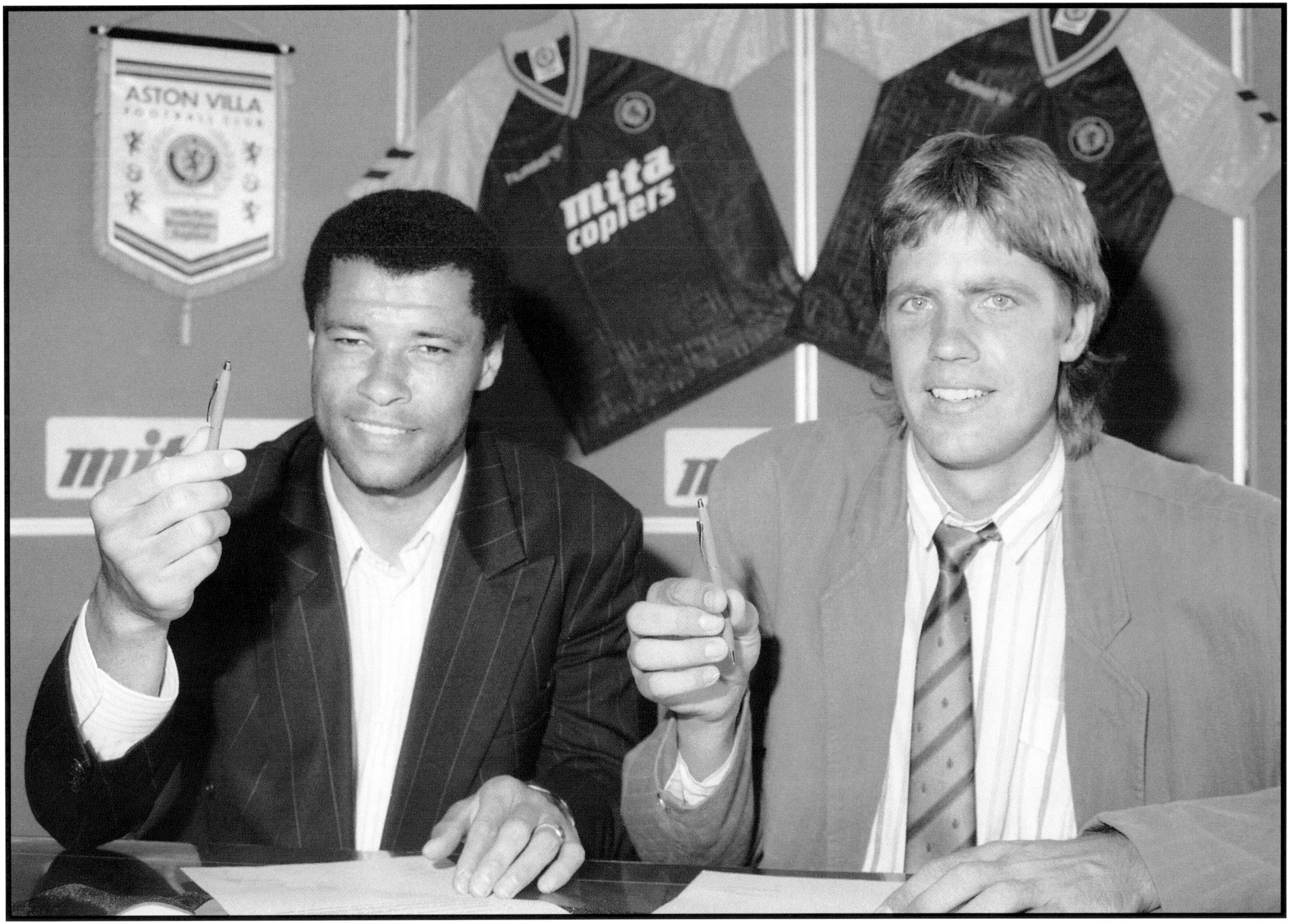
ASTON VILLA
mita
copiers

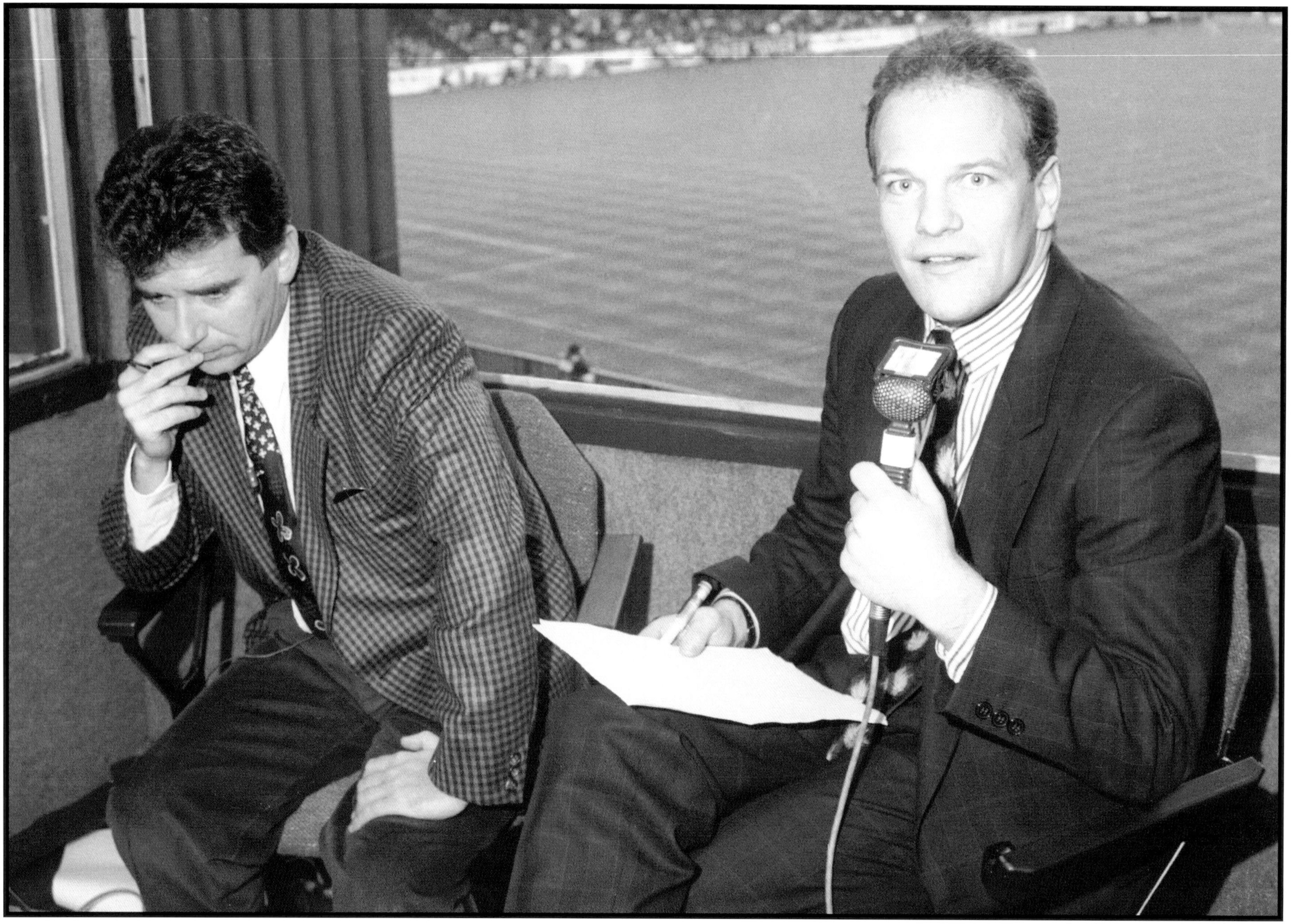

stage fright

The idea of being a mascot is always appealing to wide-eyed young fans, but coping with the situation is not quite so easy.

Older kids usually savour the moment, but sometimes the occasion is simply too much for toddlers as they run from the tunnel to be greeted by a huge roar from the crowd.

This youngster clearly wasn't too happy, but Graham Taylor came to the rescue by picking him up and giving him a hug, with a linesman also helping to console him.

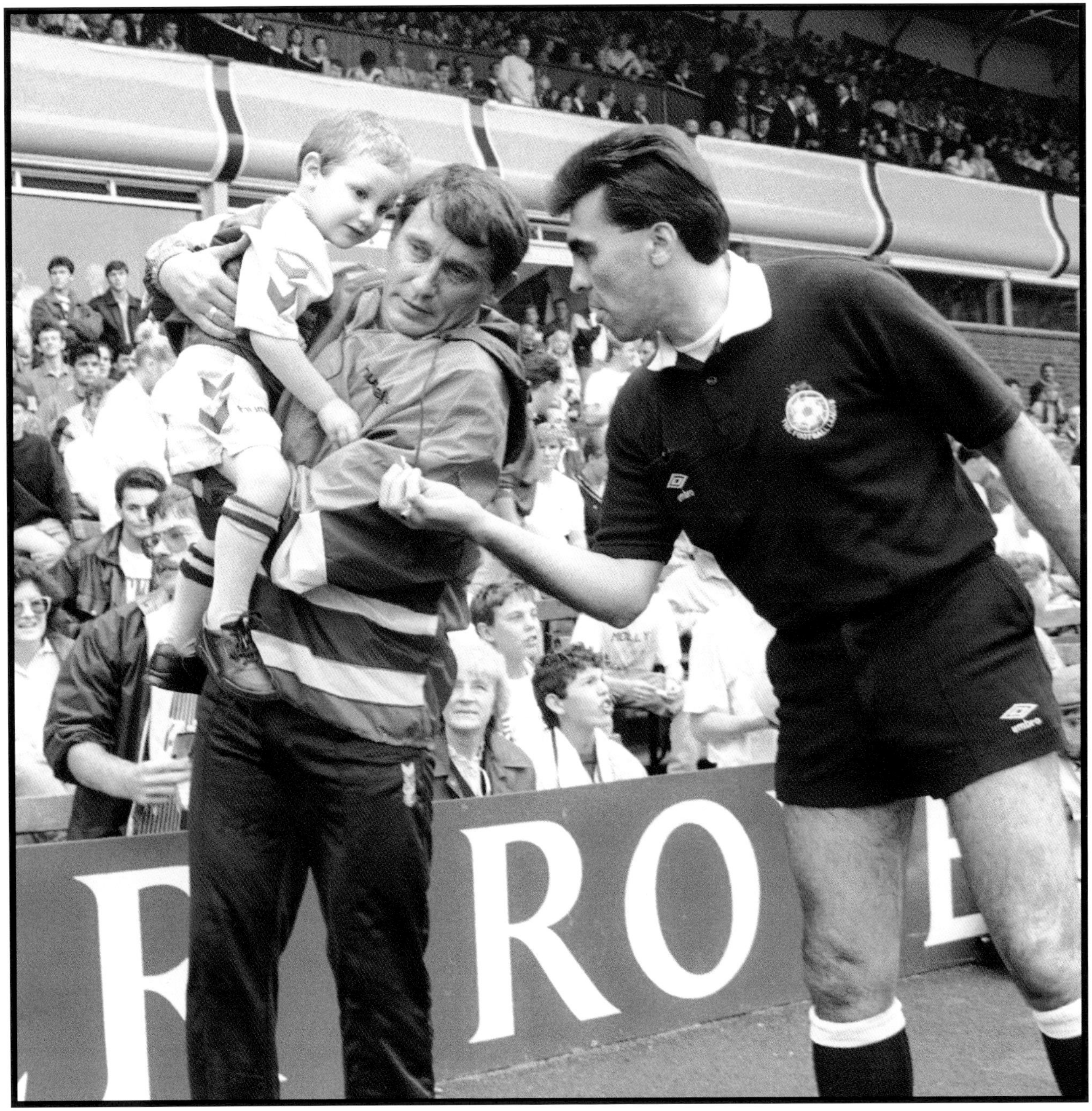

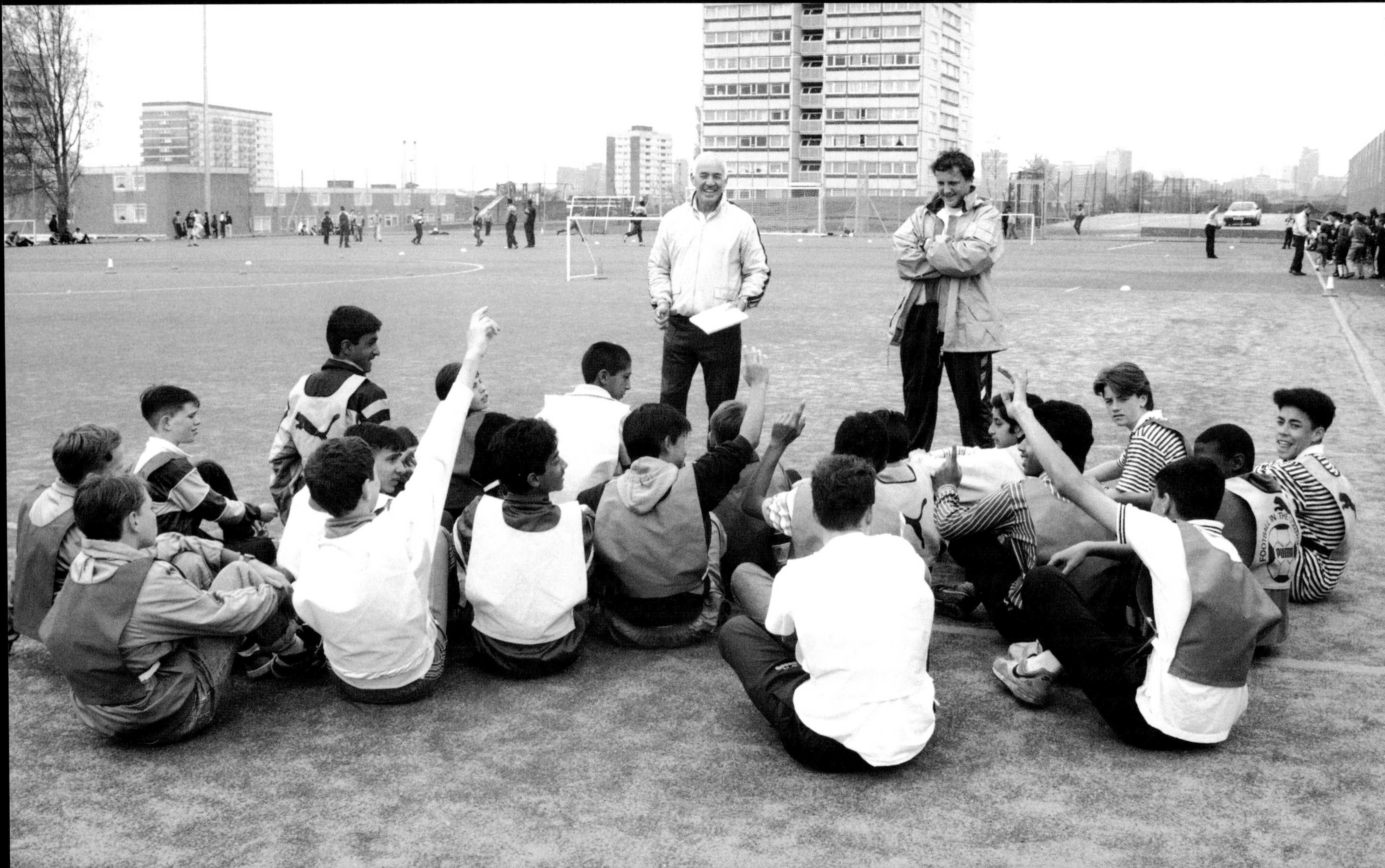

learning for fun

Modern day football isn't just about what happens on the pitch for 90 minutes. Clubs have become increasingly aware of the need to promote their image beyond the confines of their home grounds, and Villa's Football in the Community project has been a huge success.

Former skipper Ron Wylie, who has been instrumental in taking the club into the local community, is pictured addressing youngsters during a coaching session at Lozells.

bosom pals

Graham Taylor received a rapturous ovation when he was appointed Villa manager for the second time, but it wasn't the first occasion on which he had received a warm welcome.

He came back on one occasion and was greeted by Marion Stringer, who was chairman Doug Ellis's PA and has since become company secretary.

'We're bosom friends,' said Graham, as this picture clearly illustrates.

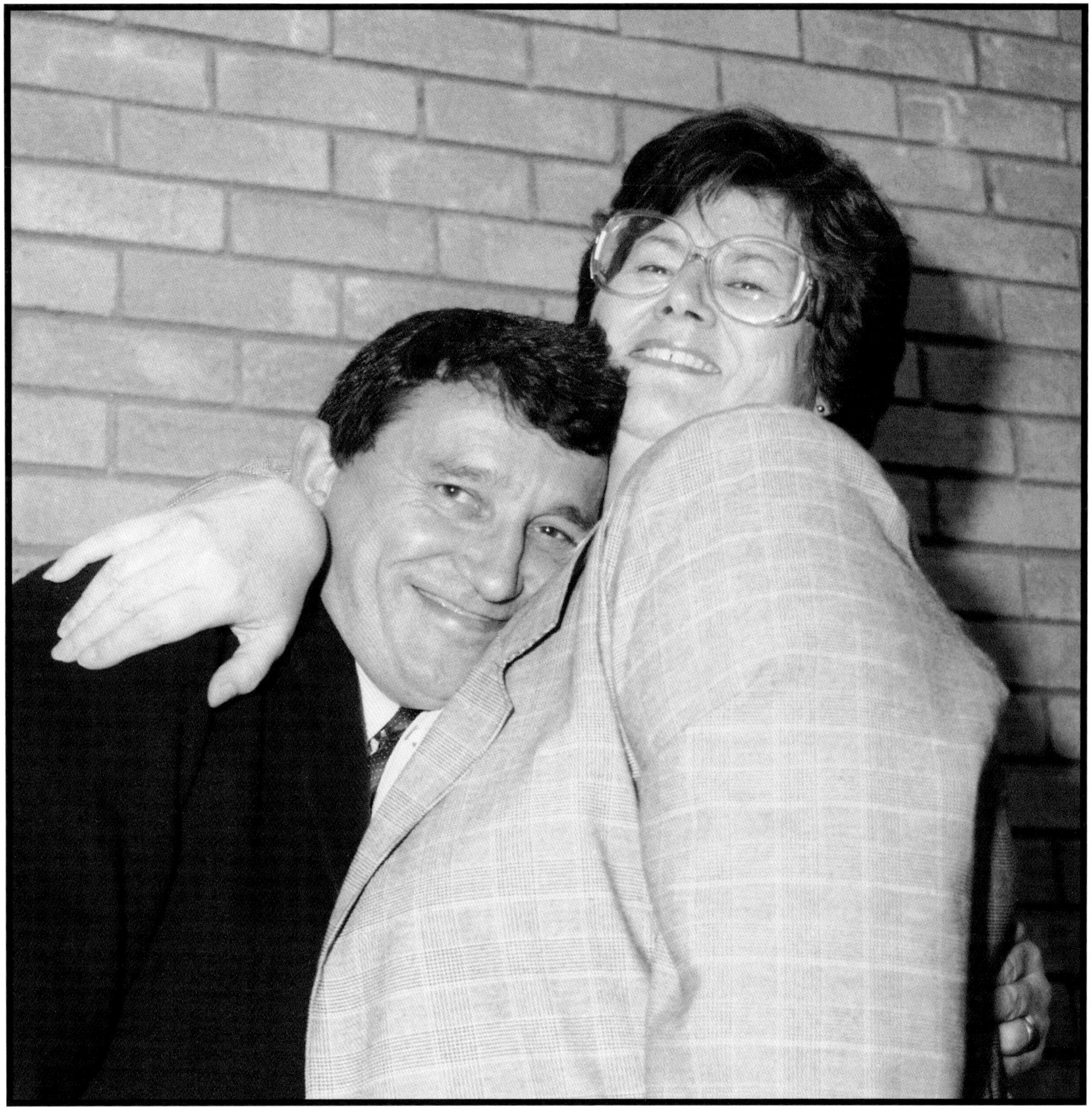

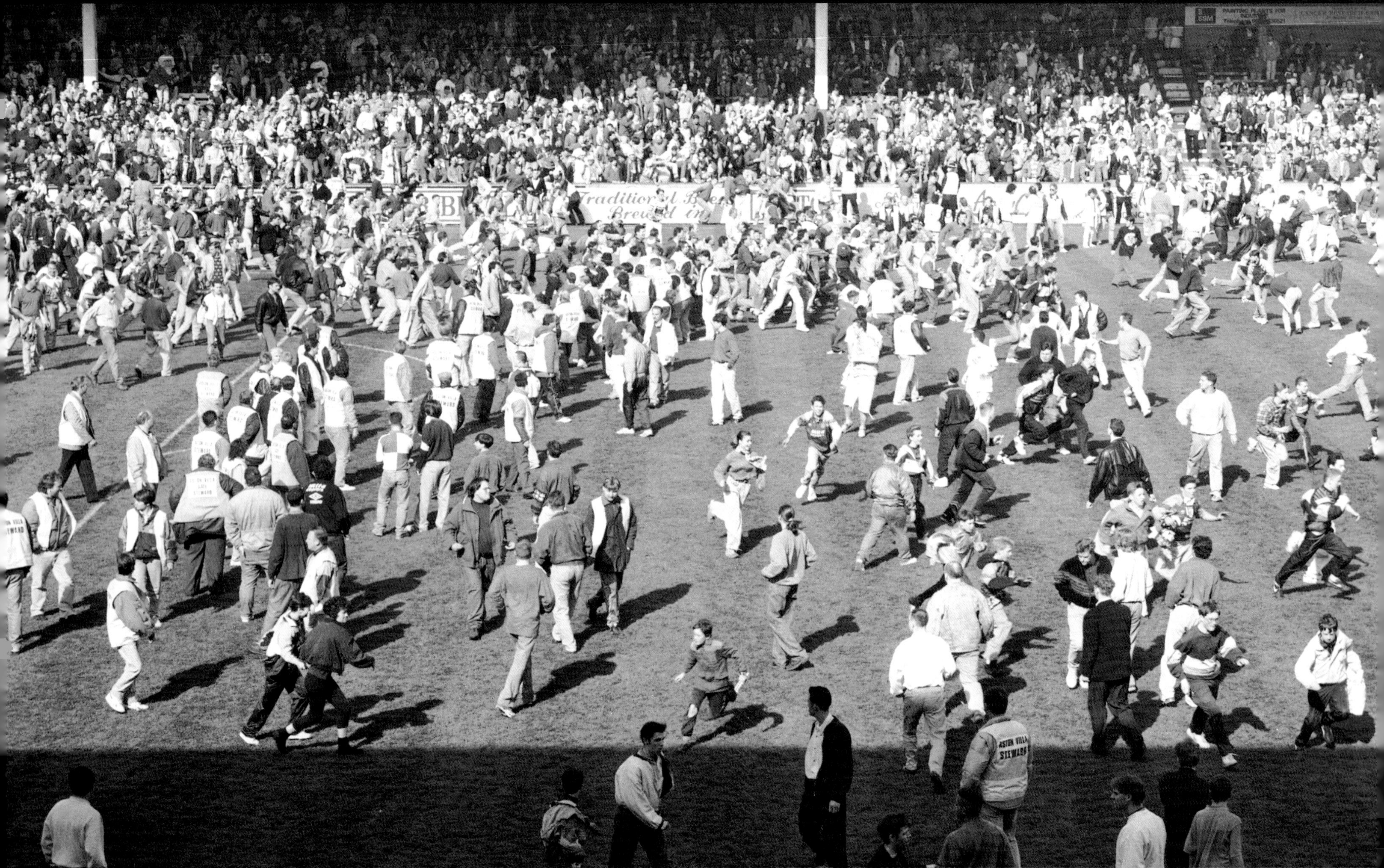
ASTON VILLA
STEWARD

breaking the bar

Apart from the infamous 'friendly' against Glasgow Rangers in 1976, there has never been a great deal of crowd trouble at Villa Park, but the final day of the 1990-91 campaign brought some unsavoury scenes in front of the North Stand.

After the 2-2 draw against Chelsea, a group of visiting supporters ran on to the pitch and broke the crossbar.

That piece of wanton destruction was a sad end to Jo Venglos' only season in English football.

up the villa!

The beauty of a zoom lens is that you can capture people in a natural state. If I'd tried to snap this youngster as close range, he would have been self-conscious, but as it is, he's a picture of concentration as he watches Villa from the Holte End during the 1992-93 campaign.

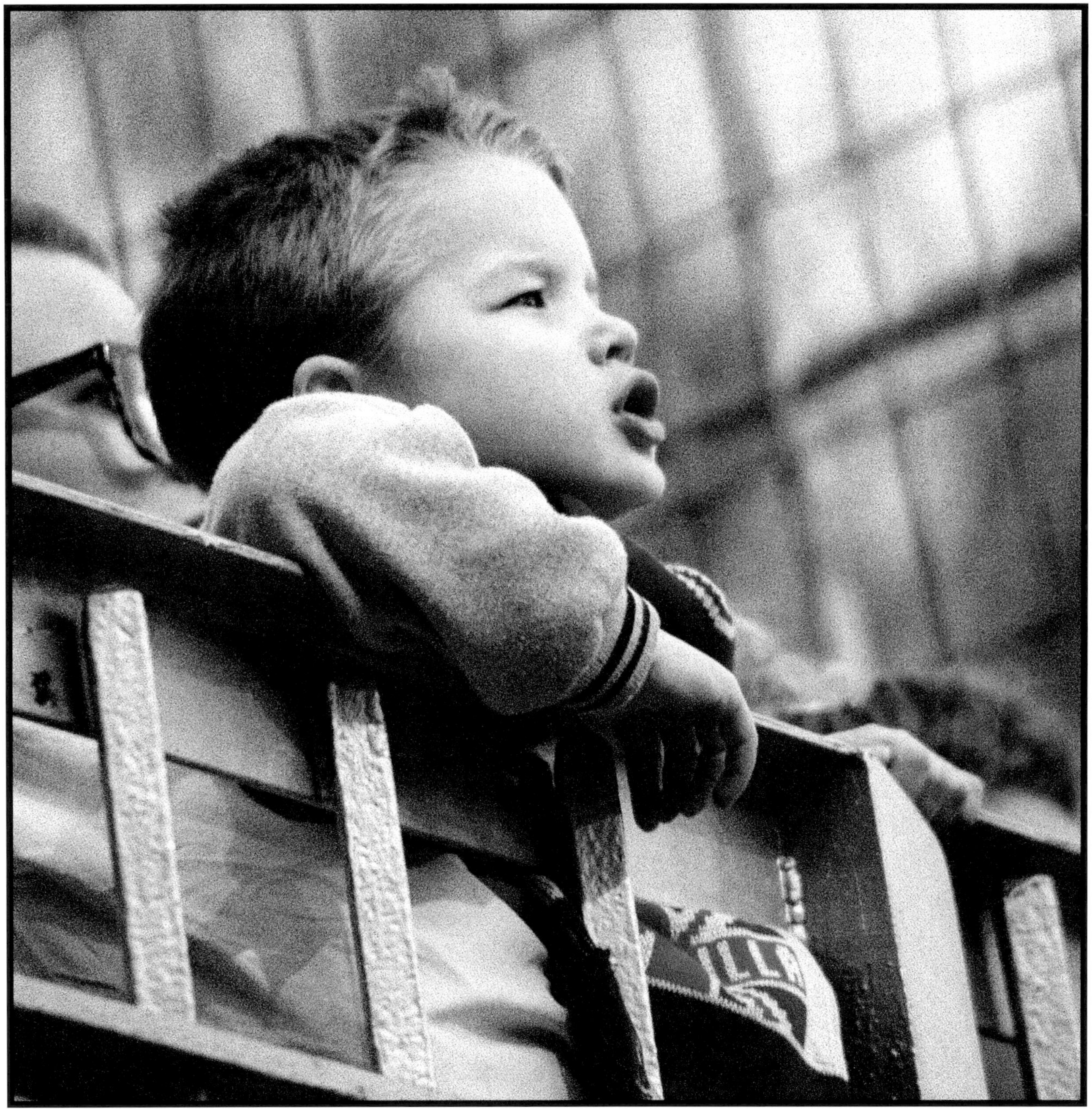

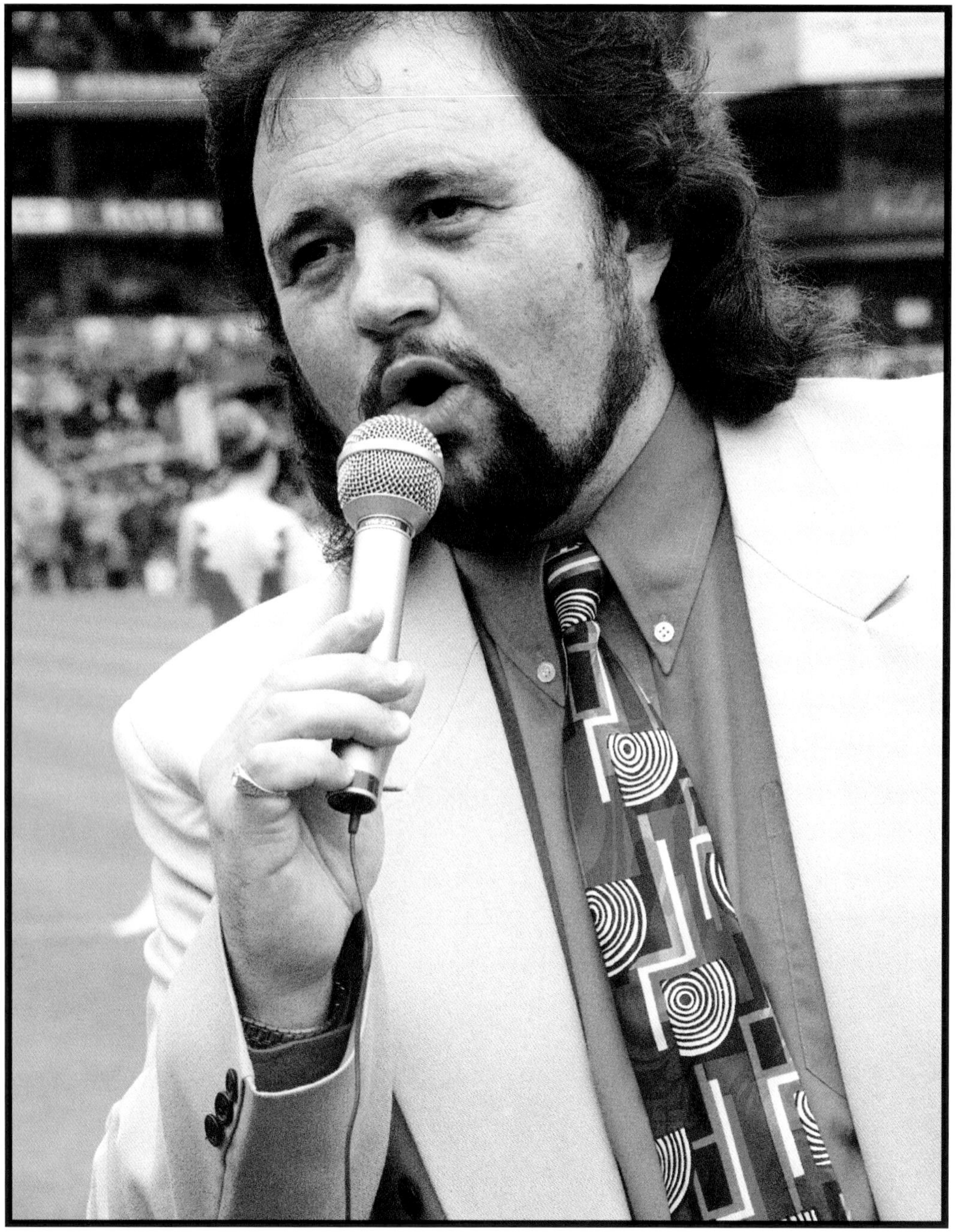

chancing it

It was a sentimental occasion when the Holte End existed for the last time as a terrace in May, 1994, although the event almost turned sour.

Before the final home match, singer Dave Chance encouraged supporters to join in with what he imagined would be a moving rendition of 'You'll Never Walk Alone', but was met with a largely muted response.

There was more noise from the other end of the ground, in fact, and no wonder – Villa were playing Liverpool that day.

At least the day ended on a high note. Dwight Yorke scored twice at the Holte End in the second half and Villa won 2-1.

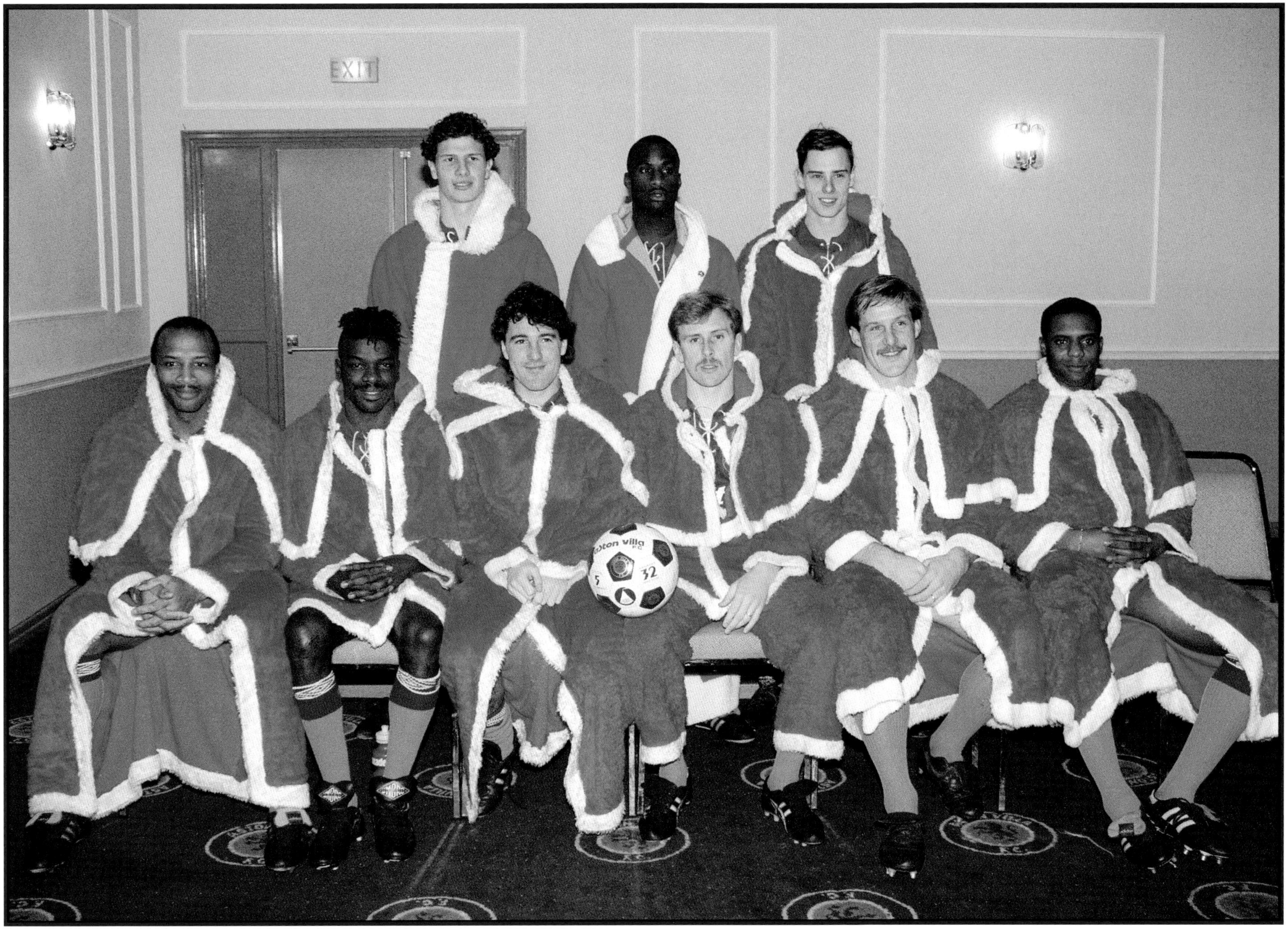
EXIT

santa villa

Christmas 1992 saw a group of players dressing up as Father Christmas for a publicity shot, but they would all have struggled as the real Santa – they wouldn't go outside because it was too cold!

Instead, this picture was taken in one of the suites in the North Stand. I wonder if they all came down the chimney together.

Back row: Neil Cox, Bryan Small, Dave Farrell. Front: Cyrille Regis, Tony Daley, Dean Saunders, Kevin Richardson, Shaun Teale, Dalian Atkinson.

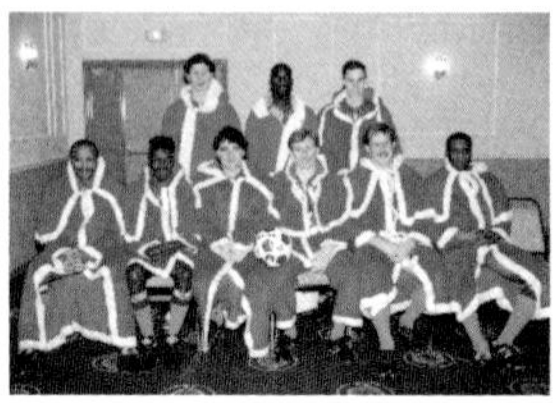

cold cheer

Even in these days of all-seater stadiums, watching Premiership football can be uncomfortable if the elements are unfavourable.

Wrapping up warm, with hats and scarves, is essential, and these two youngsters were well prepared for the business of cheering on their team on a miserable day during the 1993-94 season.

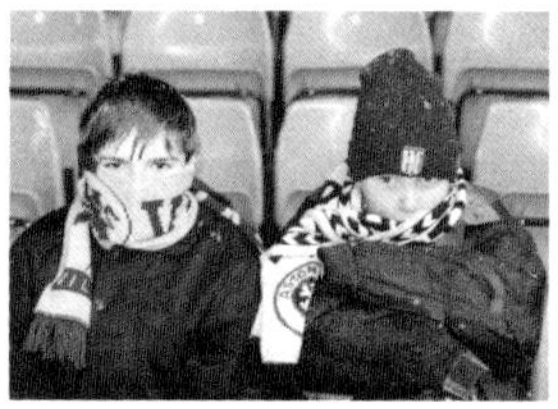

heaven in hell

It was a case of into the unknown when Villa were paired with Turkish club Trabzonspor in the 1993-94 UEFA Cup.

No one knew a great deal about Trabzon, situated on the Black Sea, but when word came back that is was 'sheer hell', the English press jumped at the chance of sensational headlines.

The locals did their best to live up to their reputation, but in reality it was one of the most enjoyable trips on which I've been.

Trabzon was a lovely fishing port and the people could not have been more friendly. One lady came up to is in the town, asked if we were from Birmingham, and said: 'Welcome to my country.'

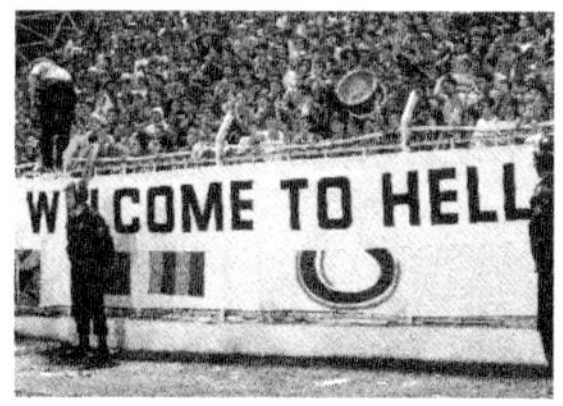

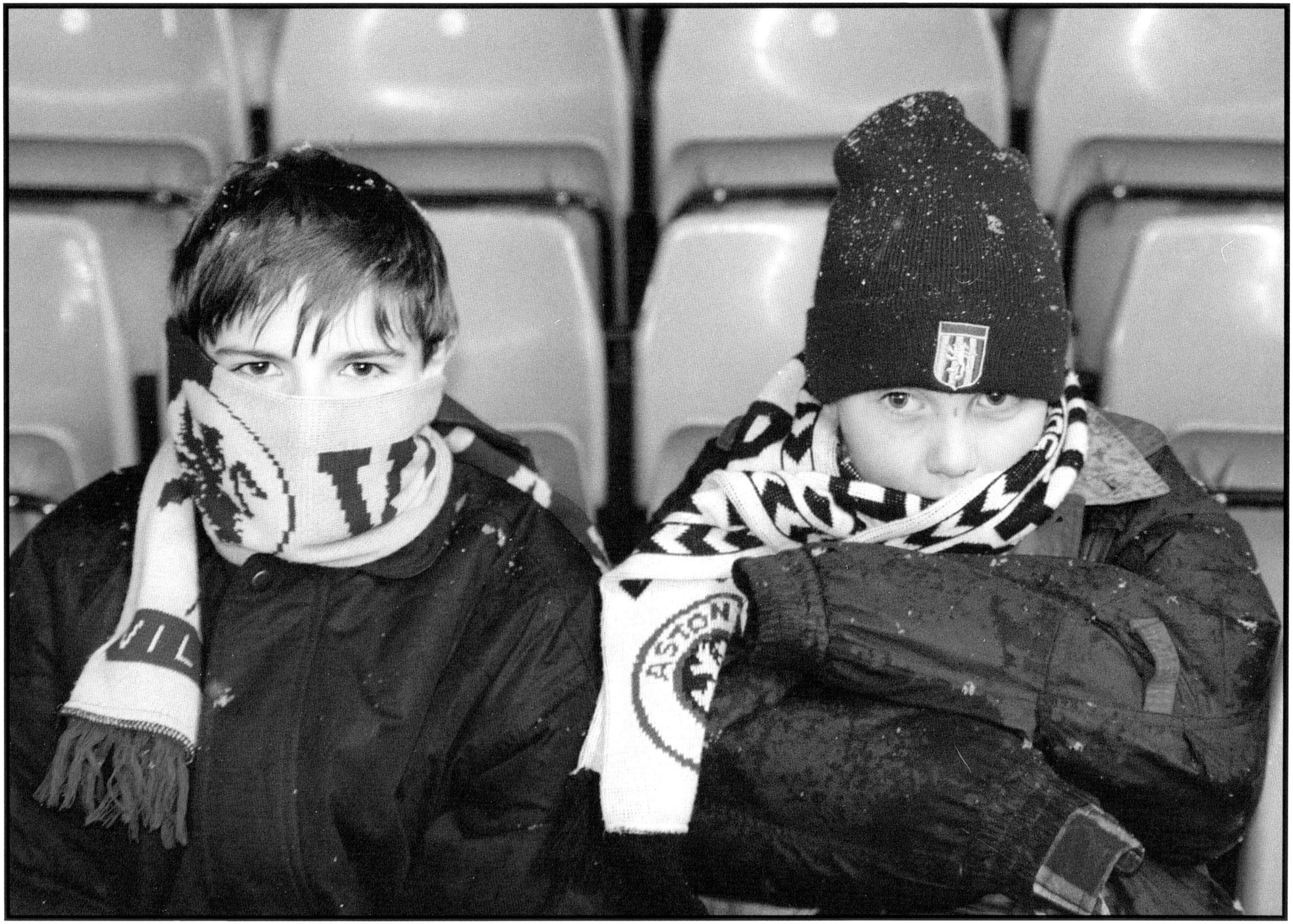
ASTON

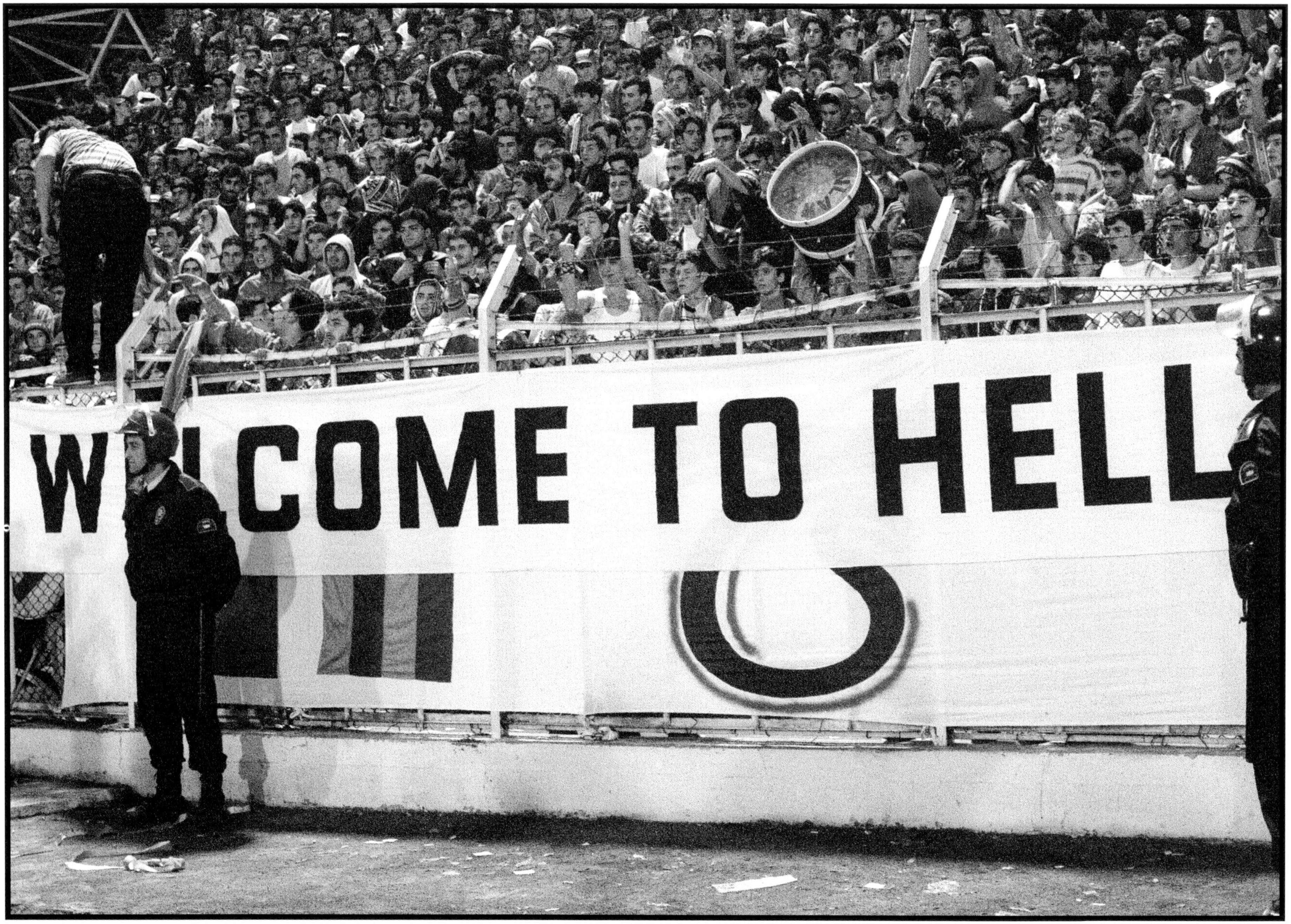
WELCOME TO HELL

prepared

Villa's new Trinity Road stand may boast large, state-of-the-art dressing rooms, but nothing will ever replace the aura which surrounded the tunnel in the old stand.

From the dressing rooms, the players made their way down a flight of steps before emerging from the narrow passageway to the sight of Villa Park in all its glory.

Trinidad and Tobago striker Dwight Yorke always liked to be the last player on to the pitch, and he is followed down the steps here by manager Brian Little – with the club's motto reminding them of the duties which lie ahead.

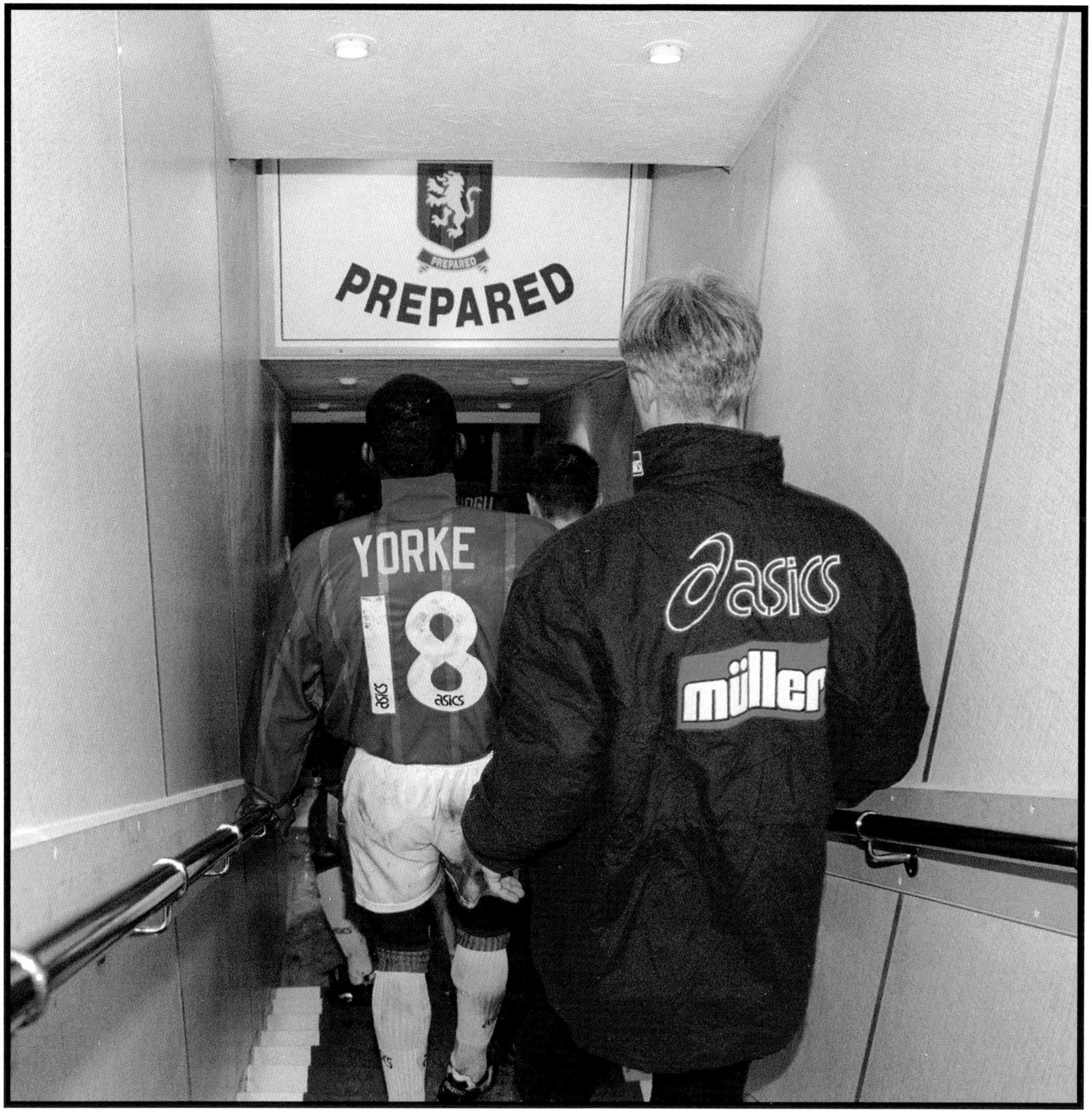

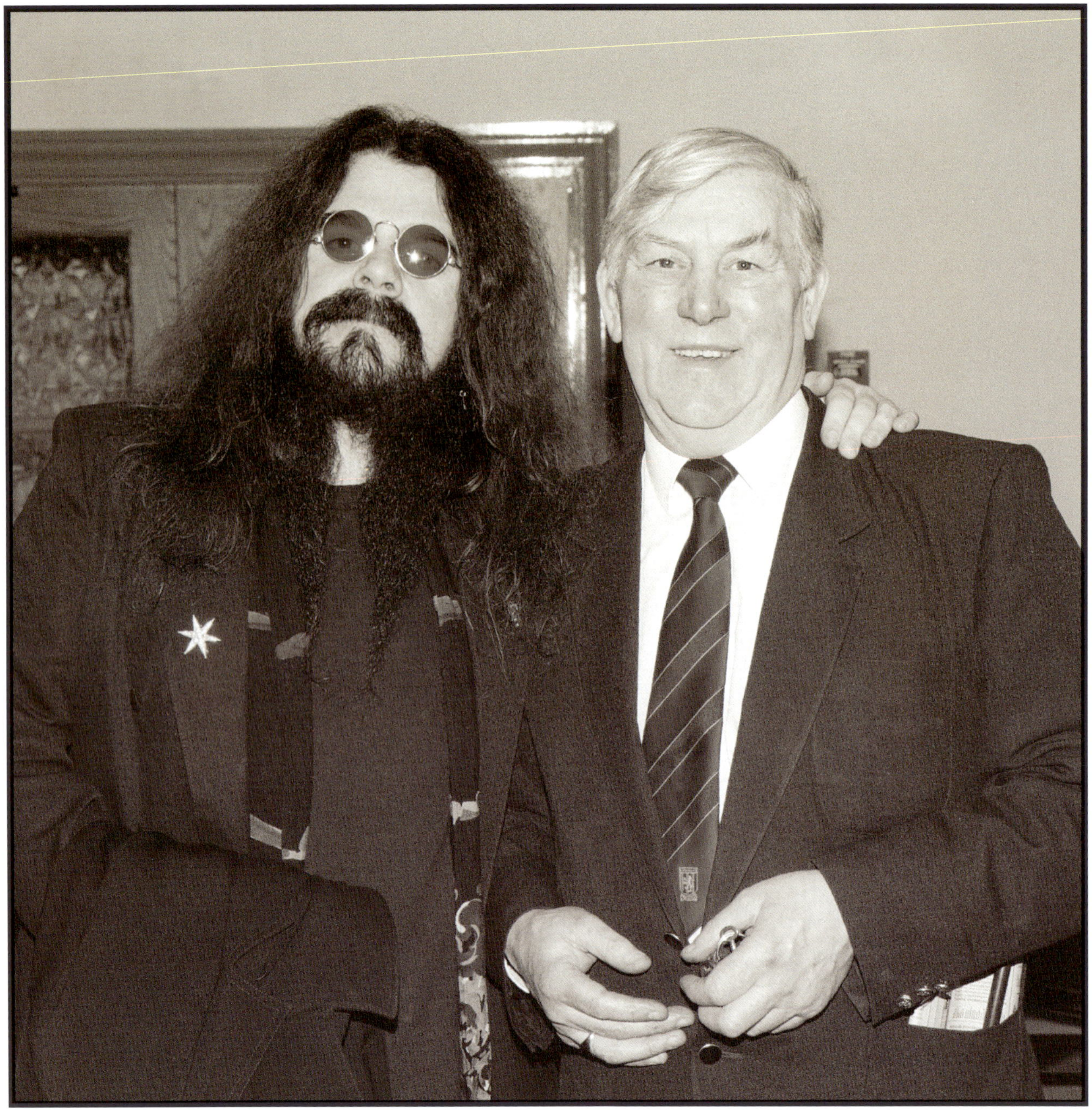

the wizard

Former Stadium Manager Ted Small is probably more of a Mantovani fan, but he was delighted to meet Brummie star Roy Wood, lead singer with the group Wizard. Ted did a great job for Villa, saving the club thousands of pounds by undertaking building projects and using his own workforce rather than putting the job out to other companies.

player managers

Warren Barton tackled Dean Saunders when Villa played Wimbledon, and it dawned on me that they had the same surnames as two former Villa managers. That seemed like a good idea for a picture – until an even better one came along. Never mind Wimbledon, our squad at the time included three players who shared their names with Villa bosses. For Ray Houghton read Eric, for Dean Saunders read Ron and for Dalian Atkinson read Big Ron, who was, in fact, the man who signed his namesake.

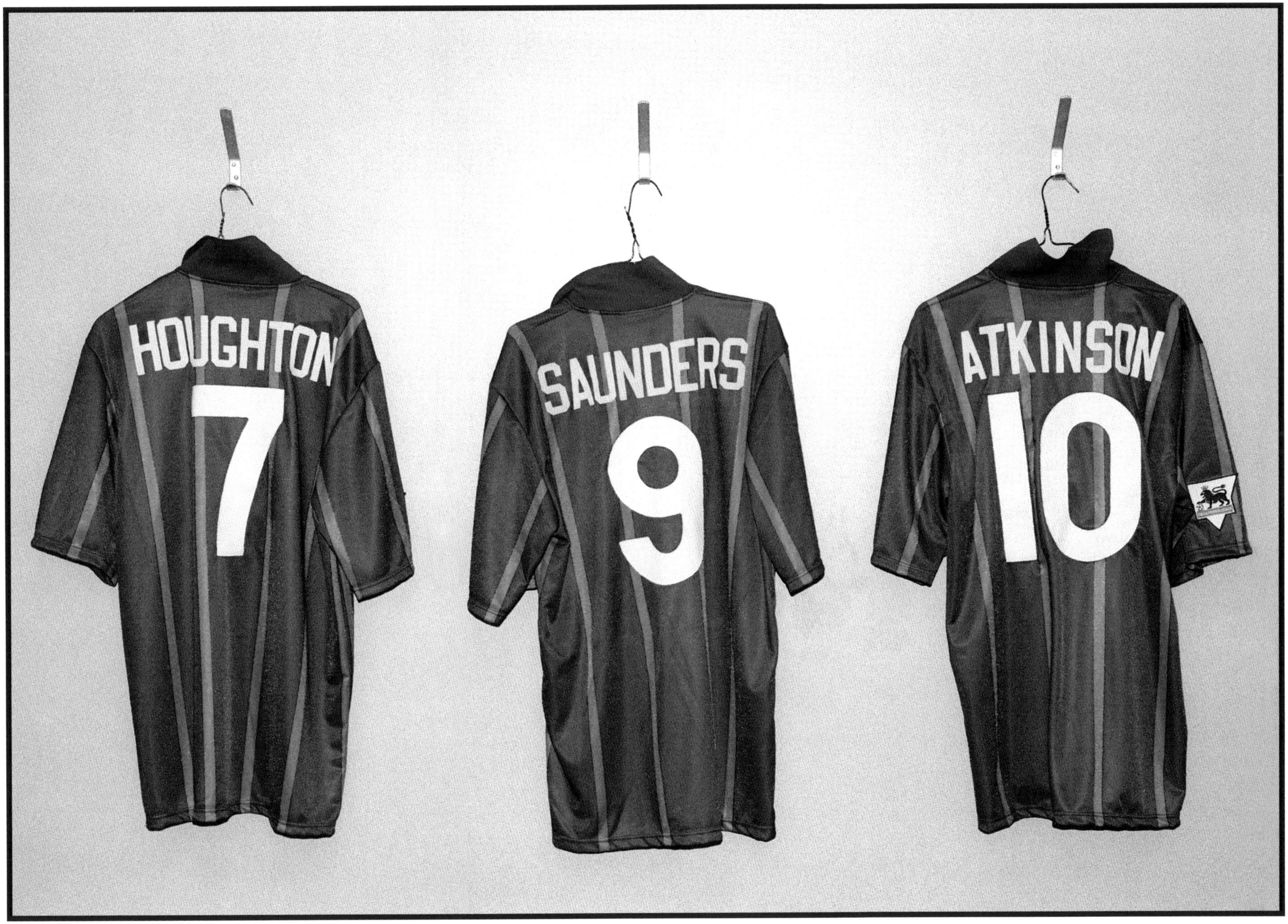
HOUGHTON
7
SAUNDERS
9
ATKINSON
10

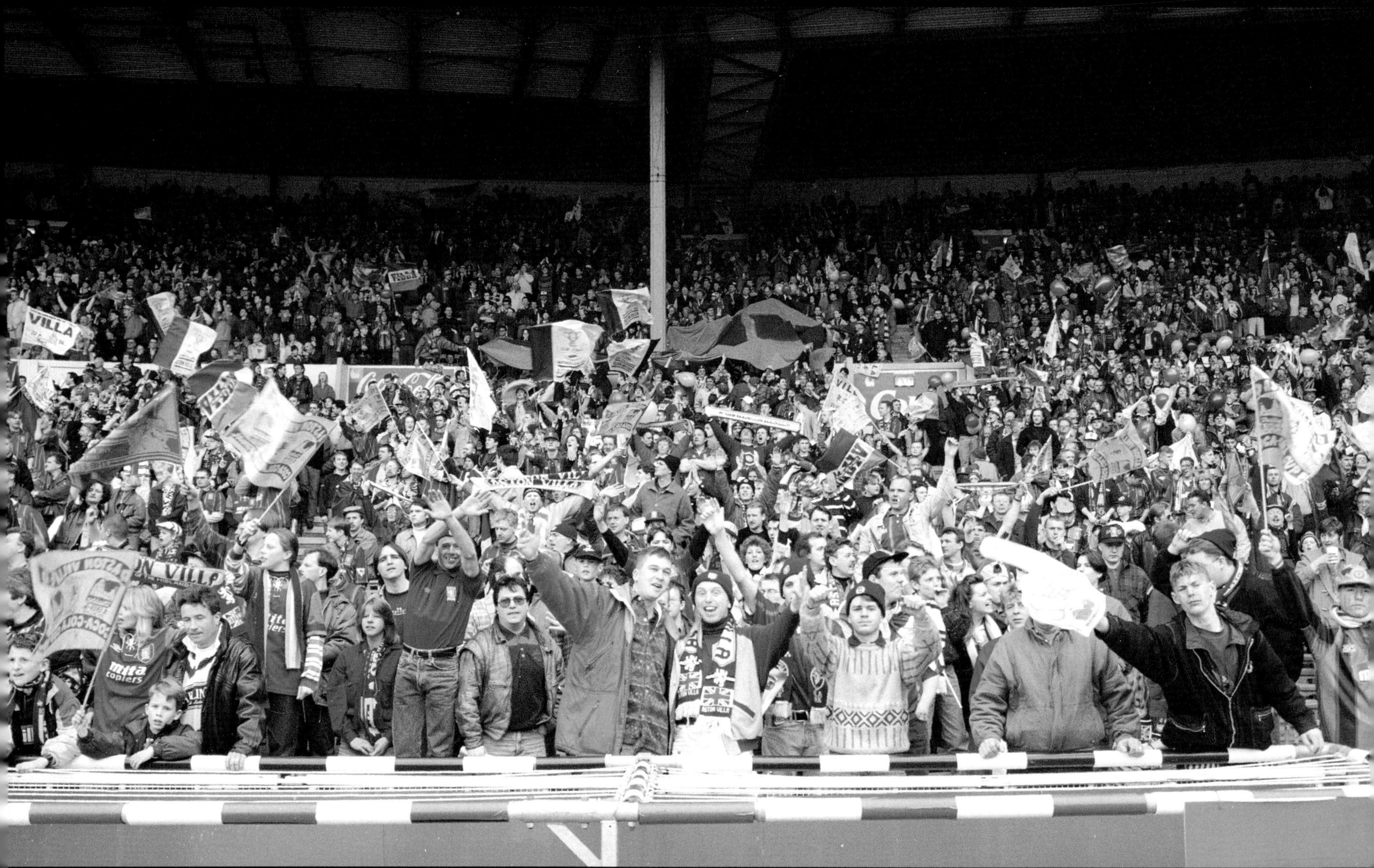
VILLA
ASTON VILLA
mita copiers

towers of strength

Villa supporters gather in the shadow of one of Wembley's famous twin towers before the 1994 Coca-Cola Cup Final against Manchester United – with a lion finding his way into the happy gathering.

The fans created a wonderful atmosphere that day, putting United's following very much in the shade with their tremendous vocal backing – and it was a similar story on the pitch. Villa's performance in a 3-1 victory was among the best I've seen.

United went on to win the double that season, but Villa ensured it would be another five years before they managed a treble!

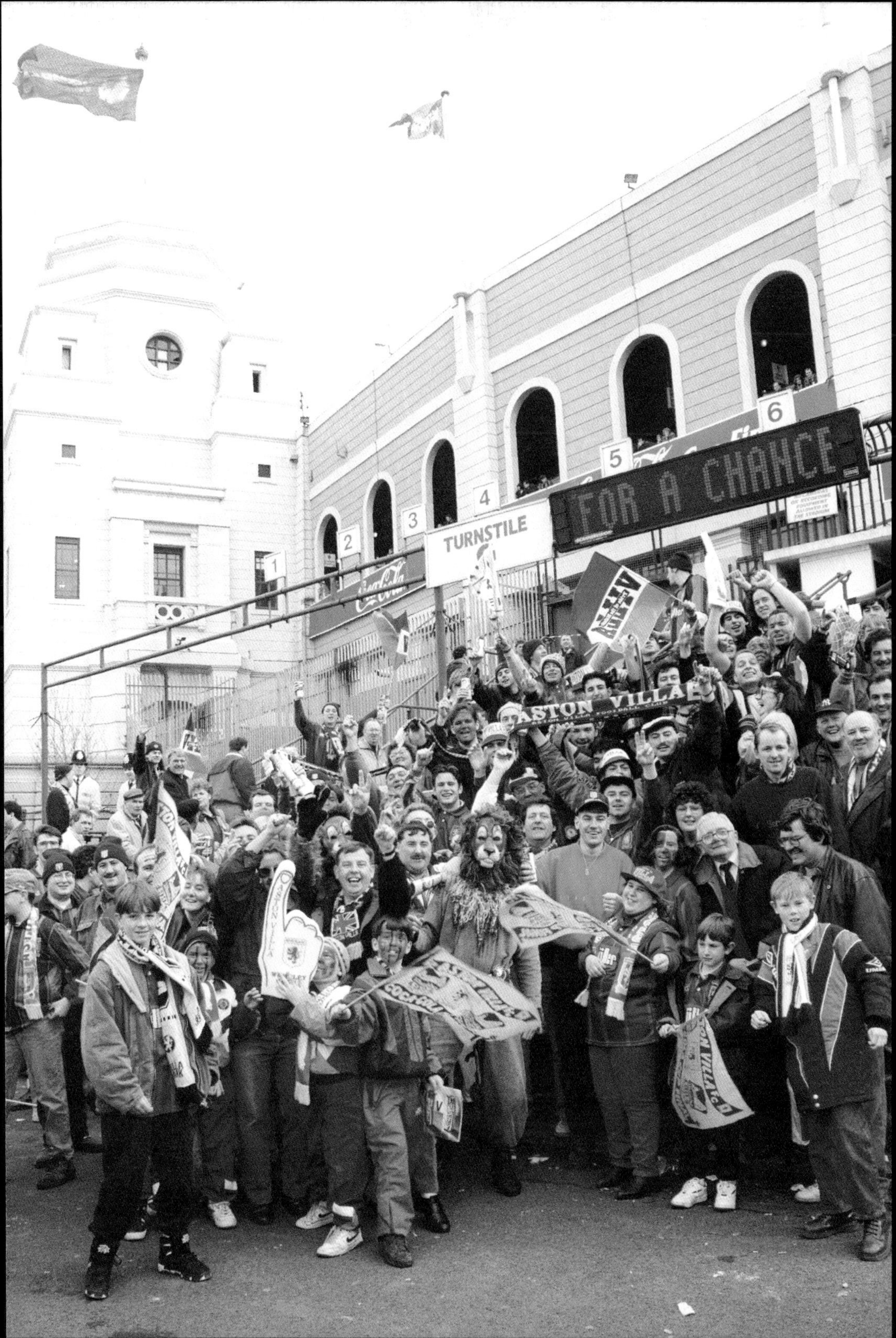

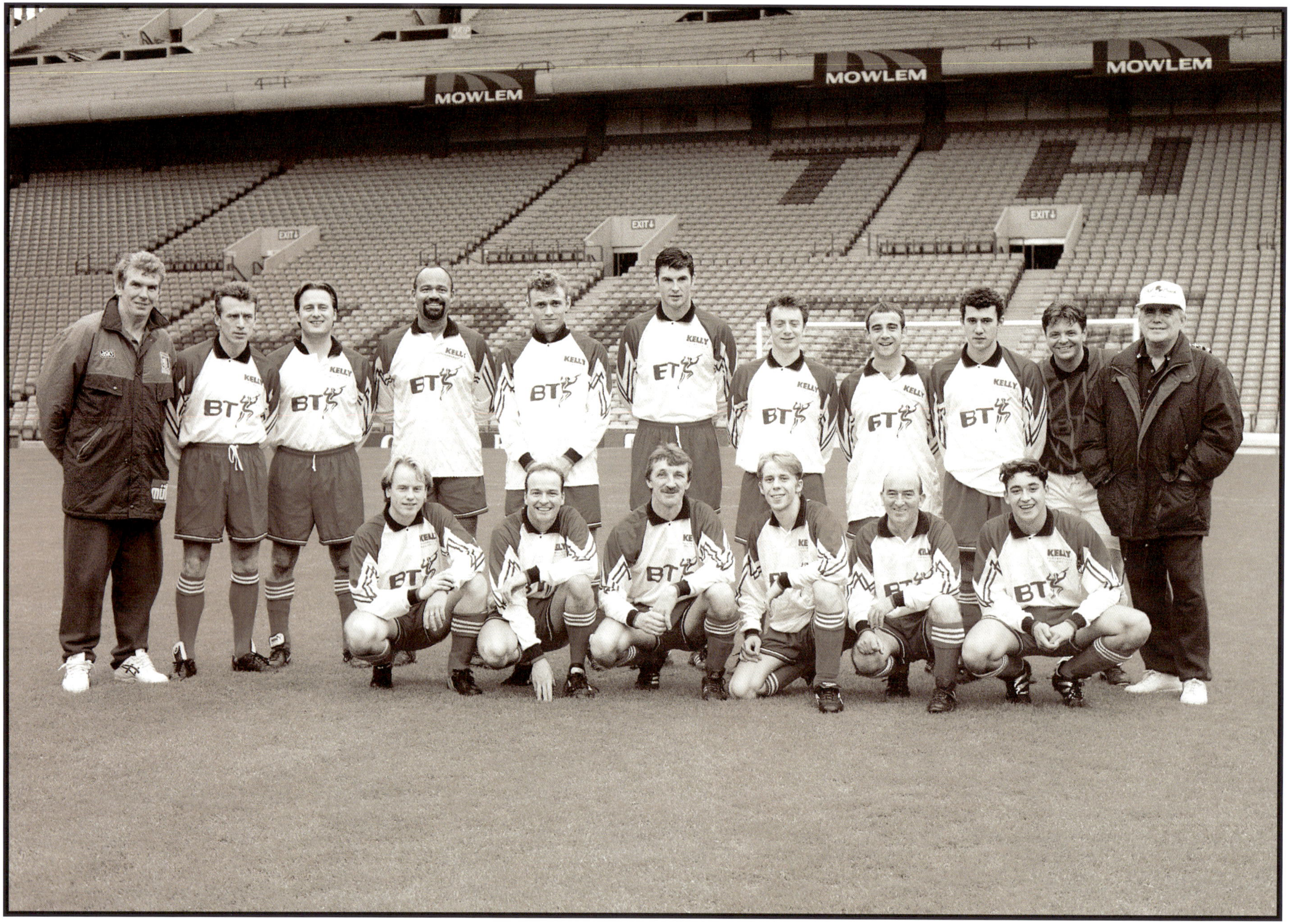
MOWLEM
MOWLEM
MOWLEM

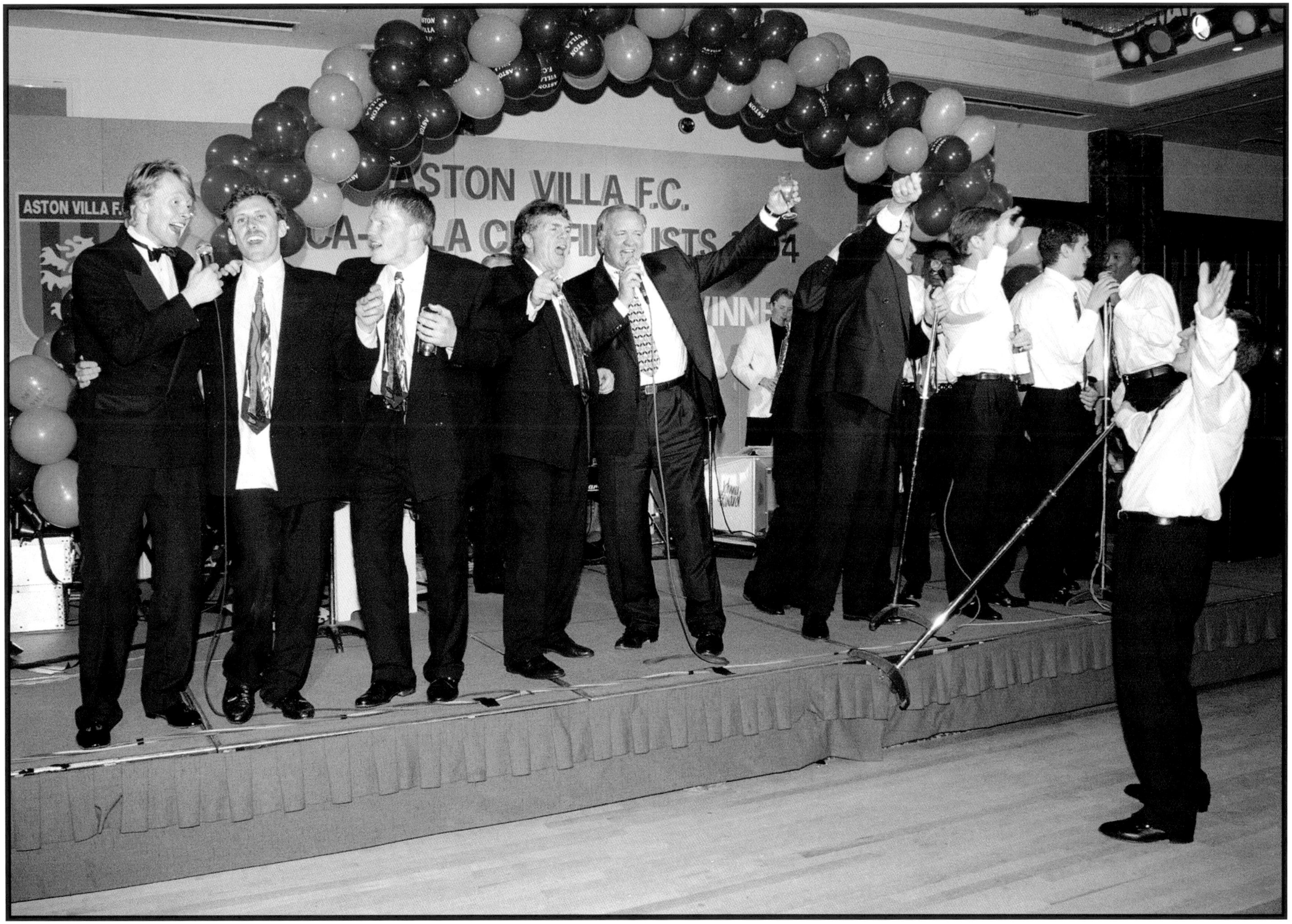
ASTON VILLA F.C.

soap stars

Various cast members from Coronation Street and Brookside also fancy themselves as footballers, and a BT-sponsored match at Villa Park one Sunday morning enabled them to exhibit their skills in one of the game's finest arenas.

To be fair, they had a little assistance from two former Villa stars. Peter Withe (far left) assumed the role of manager for the occasion, while Des Bremner (front row, third left) was in the line-up.

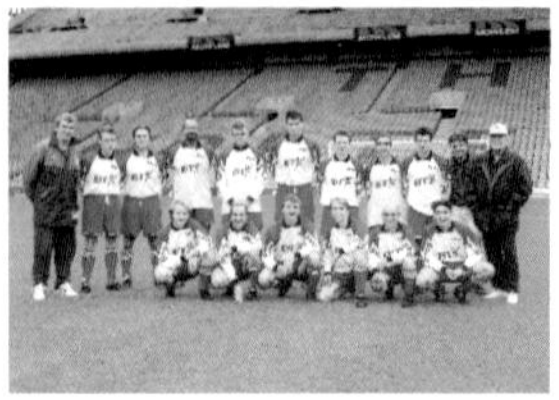

spreading the news

A post-match banquet had been organised, regardless of the outcome against Manchester United, but Villa's victory turned the proceedings at the London's Royal Lancaster Hotel into a real claret and blue party.

At one stage, manager Ron Atkinson and comedian Stan Boardman joined the band for a rendition of New York, New York, and were quickly joined by Kevin Richardson, Graham Fenton, Nigel Spink, Shaun Teale, Neil Cox and Earl Barrett.

Andy Townsend and Tony Daley are also in there somewhere, while Ray Houghton has taken it upon himself to act as conductor.

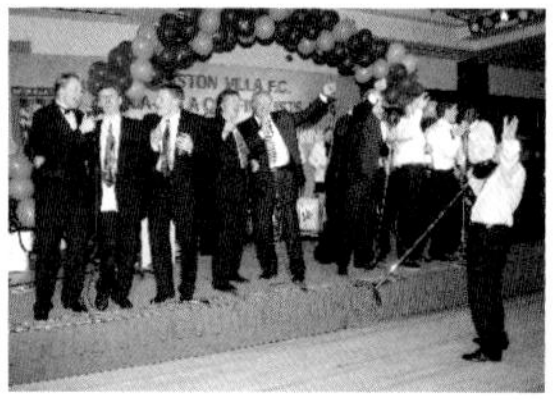

beauty parade

The Player of the Year Awards night always featured the club's own beauty contest. Miss Aston Villa was crowned annually, and the 1994 title went to Julie Gillan from Leamington Spa.

Julie (back row, second left) is pictured with the seven other finalists at Birmingham's Grand Hotel. They all look like winners to me.

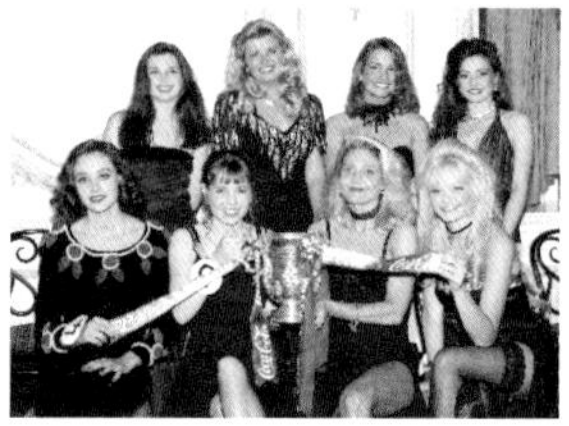

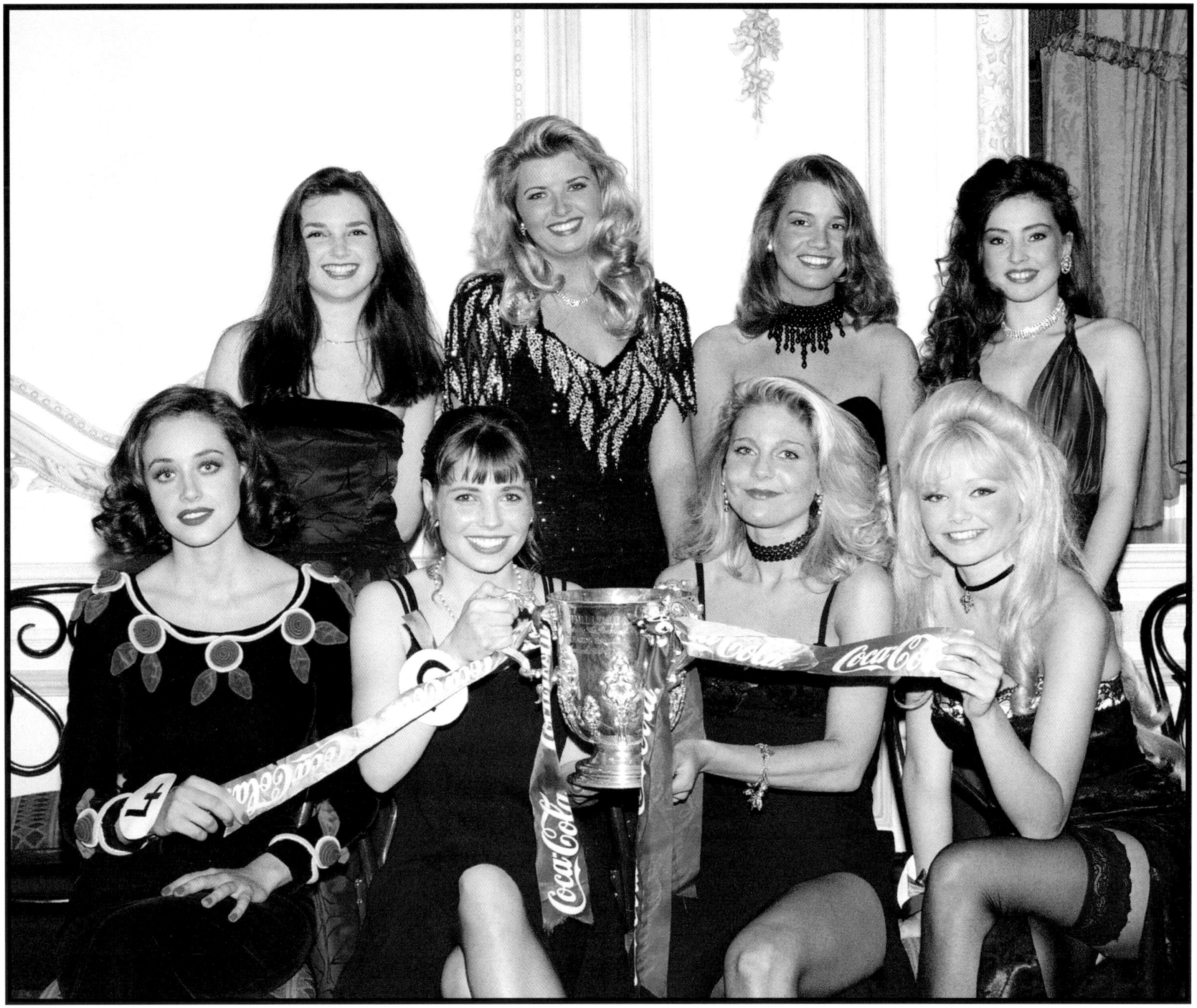
Coca-Cola

and finally...

Terry Weir's photographs adorn the pages of this book, but it seemed only fitting to sign off with a picture of the man himself.

And what better image than Terry holding aloft a trophy? Villa had just won the 1975 League Cup Final, beating Norwich City at Wembley, and when the club held their annual presentation night, the snapper snapped up the silverware.

Hopefully, this collection of Terry's work will become an equally prized possession.

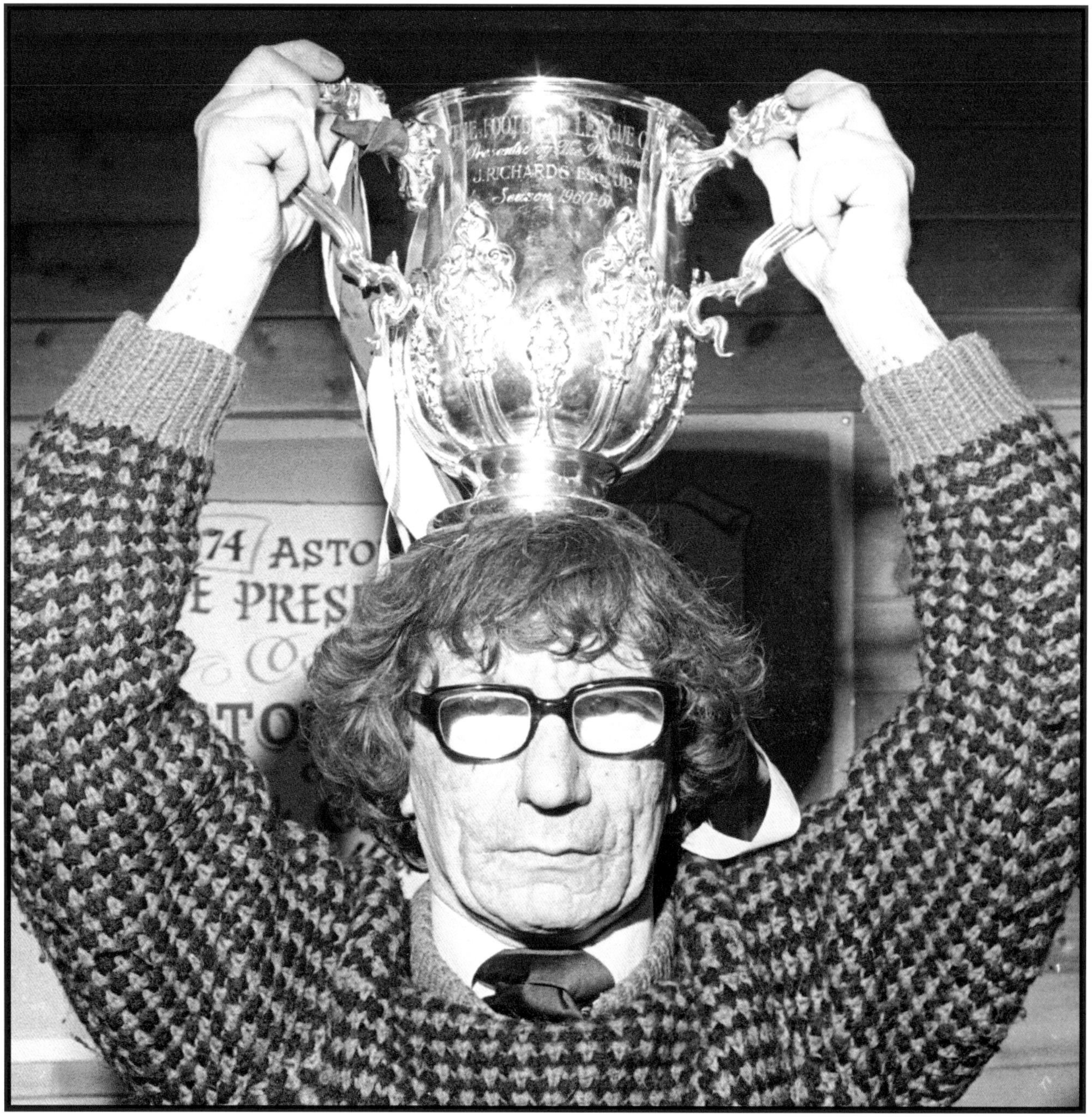

subscribers

001 John Kartz
002 Warren H. McDivitt
003 Graham John Coates
004 David Hodges (Southam)
005 Stephen & James Coldicott
006 Philip Gray
007 Ken Baldwin
008 David T. Barlow
009 Daniel Anthony Rose
010 Andrew Willis
011 Stephen J. Evans
012 C. J. Whitaker
013 Roger Wooldridge
014 Pauline Knibb
015 Ken Taylor
016 Bill Marron
017 The Sutton Family
018 Andrew Gee
019 Sue & Mick Tilt
020 Phil Reading
021 Andrew Michael Brown
022 Ben Halford (Grandson)
023 Matthew Idoine
024 Neil Strevens
025 Matthew Lingard
026 Craig Gutteridge
027 Gerry Coniff
028 Mary Smith
029 Damian Barrow
030 David Graham Lane
031 Andrew Stuart Lane
032 'Captain & Daz' Slater
033 Ann & Jim Drew
034 Keith Potter (Castle Vale)
035 Martin Greenslade
036 The Foster Family
037 John A. Gould 1934
038 Richard Thacker
039 Malcolm Taylor
040 Andreas Foecker
041 Roger Henney
042 Matthew Hales
043 Anthony Woolley
044 Stuart Crowe
045 Peter J. Ross (Belbroughton)
046 Adrian Thorne (Horsham)
047 Paul Dockerill
048 Dr. Len Liebling
049 Mervyn King
050 Graham Arthan
051 Thomas Sheldon
052 Christopher J. Turner
053 Barry Haggitt
054 Peter Harris
055 The Berwick Family
056 John Moore
057 Rev. Leo Osborn
058 Richard Houghton
059 Andrew Collins
060 Stephen Tovey
061 David Yeomans
062 Michael Knight (Malvern)
063 Adrian Price (Malvern)
064 James Price (Malvern)
065 Tony Dunn
066 Keith Hawkes
067 John Desaulles
068 Mike Jeffries
069 Paul Withers
070 Alan Phipps

071 John Ward
072 Ian Paul Sanders
073 Mr & Mrs Byrne
074 Peter Robert Hunter
075 Dirk Unschuld
076 Roger Houghton
077 F. Moland
078 Paul Marshman
079 Gregory Upton
080 Chris Dight
081 Hayden C. Wakeling
082 William Annison (Holte End)
083 Wendy Jordan (Staffordshire)
084 Jim McDonald
085 The Eagle Family
086 Roger Birch
087 Jake Shilvock
088 Martin James Cowley
089 Stuart Paul
090 Jonathan Cunniffe
091 Brian C. Seadon
092 Laurence Flounders
093 Jim Wainwright
094 Nicholas Tuite
095 John Gallivan
096 John (Villa) Power
097 Tim Murphy
098 Chris Newby
099 Geoffrey Wright
100 Mark Pearce
101 Thomas Johansson
102 Ken Noon
103 Stephen Brady
104 The Fairfield Family
105 Georgia Payne
106 Sam The Villa Fan
107 Mr B. J. & J. P. Hughes
108 Mark Haywood
109 Vince Kiely
110 Mark Hickin
111 Anthony Lines
112 Richard Moore
113 Alan B. Chambers
114 Cameron Emms
115 Rob & Mike Painting
116 Bill Rangeley
117 Paul A. Jones
118 Keith Hince
119 Ian & Scott Purvey
120 Peter Hannon
121 K. Booth
122 Mark Napier (Stafford)
123 Lloyd Ball
124 The Toney Family
125 D. J. Owen
126 The Connolly Family
127 Michael Rose
128 Kevin Mcgovern
129 Ray Oakes
130 Peter Leydon
131 Bob Curry
132 Phillip Windridge
133 Paul Williams
134 Mark Lench
135 Dean Parker
136 Andy Beck
137 Dennis James
138 Miss Alison Grosvenor
139 Roy N. Foster
140 Matthew Ross
141 Jonathan Jones
142 Gray Mullen

143	Kevan Shephard	167	Jodie Horton	191	Ray Tolley
144	Campbell Wiseman	168	John Mellor	192	The Palmer Family (Ravenshead)
145	Nick McGrail	169	The Coxall Family	193	W. A. Harvey
146	Robert Bishop	170	Andy Bates	194	Robert Edwards
147	Steve Whyte	171	Arthur Owen Morris	195	Harris Villans (Bridgnorth)
148	The Lea's of Sutton Coldfield	172	John Buckley	196	Lars Nilsson
149	Roger Davis	173	David Moon	197	D. S. Willetts
150	Wayne D. Adams	174	G. S. Clarke	198	Jon Farrelly
151	In Memory Of Brian Renshaw	175	The Shanahan Family	199	Louis Joe Worth
152	Matthew Ellis	176	Robert Prichard-Jones	200	Clive James Moss
153	J. V. Whitby	177	Joseph Henry Cook	201	Sharon Anson (Blackburn)
154	David Willetts	178	The Hodgkinsons	202	Nigel 'The Villan' Horton
155	S. A. Chambers	179	The Martin Family (Wakefield)	203	Brian Hugh Richards
156	Ben 'Villan' Smith	180	Jake Aston Foxall	204	Christopher Charles Long
157	Kirk Hensby	181	Bob James	205	Keith Stubbs
158	Jim Stelfox	182	Clive Simkins	206	Peter Avery
159	Steve	183	Steve Todd	207	Michael Tabberner
160	Mick Kenna	184	Joan Taylor	208	Alan Robinson
161	Alex Perkins	185	Mark H. Russell	209	Mr J. J. Howard
162	Wendy E. Roberts	186	Nicholas Tassell	210	The Edwards Family
163	Philip Flint	187	Jack Halling	211	Richard Moreton
164	The Forman Family	188	Martyn Kelly	212	Vera Ellen Ragsdale
165	George & Dorothy Meacham	189	Gareth C. Jones (Bristol)	213	Stephen A. Lines
166	Carol Maguire	190	Mervyn Morris	214	Alexander Allen

215 Peter Brett
216 Stephen Hill
217 Nick Walker
218 Martin Beaver
219 Allan Mills
220 John Collins
221 Terry F. Chorley
222 Brendan Casey
223 David J. Warren
224 Eddie Mills (Weoley Castle)
225 Barry Geddis
226 Joshua Dugdale
227 Brian E. Tustain
228 Alan F. Jasper
229 Colin Brown
230 Scott Mackenzie
231 Alex Ashford
232 Michael P. McTiernan
233 Oliver Trouth
234 Simon Kerr-Edwards
235 Paul Williams
236 Michael Thompson
237 Vaughan Ellis
238 Clive Simkins
239 Nigel S. Shaw
240 Adrian Paul Rogers
241 John Holder
242 Jason Norbury
243 Derek Moreton
244 R. O. Evans
245 Mark Brown
246 David Weir
247 Leslie James Stanley
248 Graham Jackson
249 Stuart Caldwell
250 The Harris Family
251 Andrew Colyer
252 Keith & Raymond Baker
253 Anne Edwards
254 Bernard Gallagher
255 Neil Gallagher
256 Wayne O'Neill
257 Geoff Nokes
258 Steve Knott
259 Robin Peck
260 Paul Mcgowan
261 Kevin Ethan Aidan Fox
262 Colin & Sally Burgess
263 Lynn Wain
264 The Boundys
265 Ryan Mellor
266 Gareth Owen
267 The Lee Family
268 Lee Jackson
269 Denis Box
270 Jack Hughes
271 Jeff Careless
272 Stephen Evans
273 Andrew Webb
274 Paul K. Newell
275 Steve Chapman
276 Peter Lawrence
277 Carl Bourne
278 Andy Lamb
279 Desmond John Nevin
280 Richard Smith
281 David Evans
282 Philip Blunt
283 Paul & Imogen Best
284 Nick Becerra
285 The Hobbs Family
286 The Santy Family

287 Glynn C. Miller
288 Phil Cashmore
289 Rory O'Donnell
290 Andy Campkin (Aylesbury)
291 Neil Pearson
292 Jack Bullivant
293 Alan Nigel White
294 Garth Tilt
295 John S. Davies
296 Paul Davies
297 Ray Geary
298 Andy Woodhull (Worcester)
299 Alexander Garraty
300 Ian David Parkes
301 Phil O'Connor
302 Stephen Bishop
303 Wayne Tandy
304 Kenneth J. Marrio
305 Paul Michael Tregellas
306 Mark Mcdonagh
307 Roy Vickers
308 The Diggory Family
309 Dave Collett
310 Steve Richards
311 David John Edward Clayton
312 Robert Carson
313 John Slim
314 Nicholas De Jong
315 John Willcox
316 Tony Friel
317 Stephen Sturman
318 Brian Richards
319 Robert Gough
320 Ian Hooper
321 Albert Ball
322 David Thursfield
323 Andrew Taylor
324 Geoffrey Horton
325 Fred Vassallo
326 Mike Davis
327 Shawn Morris (Hereford)
328 Harley Caswell
329 Ed Thomas
330 Keith Kirkpatrick
331 Anthony Robert Shill
332 Martin Maguire
333 Arthur Edwards
334 Ian Edwards
335 Andrew Edwards
336 Steven Edwards
337 Steve Duffy
338 Andrew 'Noel' Turner
339 John D. Palfreyman
340 David Tilley
341 Des Brennan
342 The Devaney Family
343 Cliff Teale
344 George Barker
345 Christopher E. Smith
346 Kay Flint
347 Roger Halfpenny
348 Arthur Bent
349 Alston Taylor
350 Robert Basil Price
351 Brendan Casey
352 Edward Forde
353 Patrick McDonagh
354 Steve Johnson
355 Duncan Webb
356 David & Pam Bridgewater
357 Sgt Ted Alsop's Family
358 Thomas Edward Palfreyman

359 Colin Winfield

360 Stephen I. Willis (Leominster)

361 Ralph Willis (Middlesbrough)

362 Alan Ash

363 The Keeling Family

364 Derrick Spinks

365 Simon Cleaver

366 Alan Robinson

367 Raymond Brookes